TOP

VAULT GUIDE TO THE TOP
FINANCIAL
SERVICES
EMPLOYERS

2009 EDITION

FINANCIAL
SERVICES

The media's watching Vault!
Here's a sampling of our coverage.

"For those hoping to climb the ladder of success, [Vault's] insights are priceless."
— *Money magazine*

"The best place on the web to prepare for a job search."
— *Fortune*

"[Vault guides] make for excellent starting points for job hunters and should be purchased by academic libraries for their career sections [and] university career centers."
— *Library Journal*

"The granddaddy of worker sites."
— *US News and World Report*

"A killer app."
— *The New York Times*

One of Forbes' 33 "Favorite Sites"
— *Forbes*

"To get the unvarnished scoop, check out Vault."
— *SmartMoney Magazine*

"Vault has a wealth of information about major employers and job-searching strategies as well as comments from workers about their experiences at specific companies."
— *The Washington Post*

"A key reference for those who want to know what it takes to get hired by a law firm and what to expect once they get there."
— *New York Law Journal*

"Vault [provides] the skinny on working conditions at all kinds of companies from current and former employees."
— *USA Today*

VAULT GUIDE TO THE TOP
FINANCIAL SERVICES
EMPLOYERS

2009 EDITION

DEREK LOOSVELT
and the staff of vault

Library of Congress CIP Data is available.

ISBN 13 : 978-1-58131-569-1

ISBN 10 : 1-58131-569-4

Printed in the United States of America

ACKNOWLEDGMENTS

We are extremely grateful to Vault's entire staff for all their help in the editorial, production and marketing processes. Vault also would like to acknowledge the support of our investors, clients, employees, family and friends. Thank you!

Table of Contents

APPENDIX   377

Visit the Vault Finance Career Channel at **www.vault.com/finance** — with
insider firm profiles, message boards, the Vault Finance Job Board and more.

VAULT CAREER LIBRARY   xi

INTRODUCTION

A Guide to this Guide

All of our profiles follow the same basic format. Here's a guide to each entry.

Firm facts

• **Departments:** The firm's major divisions.

• **The Stats:** Basic information about the firm, usually information that's available to the general public. This includes the firm's leadership (generally, the person responsible for day-to-day operations, though it can include the chairman and relevant department heads), employer type (e.g., public, private, or subisdiary), ticker symbol and exchange (if public), 2007 revenue and net income (usually only for public companies; we do have some estimates from third-party sources for private companies and in some cases, the firm has confirmed that information), number of employees and number of offices.

• **Key Competitors:** The firm's main business rivals. Size, business lines, geography and reputation are taken into account when evaluating rivals.

• **Uppers and Downers**: The best and worst things, respectively, about working at the firm. Uppers and downers are taken from the opinions of insiders based on our surveys and interviews.

• **Employment Contact:** The person (or people) that the firm identifies as its contact(s) for submitting resumes or employment inquiries. We've supplied as much information as possible, including names, titles, mailing addresses, phone or fax numbers, e-mail addresses and web sites. Because companies process resumes differently, the amount of information may vary. For example, some firms ask that all employment-related inquiries be sent to a central processing office, while other firms mandate that all job applications be submitted through the company web site.

The profiles

Most profiles are divided into three sections: The Scoop, Getting Hired and Our Survey Says; (some profiles have only Scoop and Getting Hired sections).

• **The Scoop**: The company's history, a description of the business, recent clients or deals and other significant developments.

Visit the Vault Finance Career Channel at **www.vault.com/finance** – with insider firm profiles, message boards, the Vault Finance Job Board and more.

VAULT CAREER LIBRARY

3

• **Getting Hired:** An overview of the company's hiring process, including a description of campus recruiting procedures, the number of interviews, questions asked and other tips on getting hired.

• **Our Survey Says:** Quotes from surveys and interviews done with employees or recent employees at the company. Includes information on culture, pay, hours, training, diversity, offices, dress code and other important company insights.

Industry Overviews

State of the Industry: Financial Services

Like a bazaar that offers something to satisfy every customer's potential needs, the financial services industry presents a little bit of everything to prospective clientele. But while the trade is a vast one, its subdivisions are specialized to meet individuals' fiscal needs. Many of these specialized financial categories are covered in this guide.

The firms we chose to profile as the top financial services firms primarily operate in one of the following categories: credit cards, insurance, mortgages, auto financing, ratings, financial data services or diversified financials. (Noticeably missing categories include accounting, investment banking, commercial banking and investment management—all of which are covered in other Vault guides.)

Although the evolution of the financial services business has been a long and storied one, its development and expansion continues well into this century. What follows is a brief overview of the financial services fields covered in this guide.

Credit Card Services

Looming large

Issuing credit cards is one of the most common ways in which financial services firms provide credit to individuals. Via the credit card, firms provide individuals with the funds required to purchase goods and services, and in return, individuals repay the full balance at a later date, or make payments on an installment basis. Via the debit card, people avoid debt by withdrawing the purchase amount from their bank accounts and transferring it to the seller. Though you're most likely familiar with how credit and debit cards work, you might not be familiar with just how large the industry is. According to Reuters, as of 2007, there were more than 640 million credit cards in circulation in the U.S. And according to CreditCards.com, Visa had a 46 percent U.S. market share based on credit card receivables outstanding in 2007, followed by MasterCard with 36 percent, American Express with 12 percent and Discover with 6 percent. On a global scale, Visa accounted for 65 percent of the market, MasterCard had a 30 percent

Visit the Vault Finance Career Channel at **www.vault.com/finance** – with insider firm profiles, message boards, the Vault Finance Job Board and more.

VAULT CAREER LIBRARY

5

share, followed by American Express and Japan-based JCB card (both of which had unknown shares).

A bumpy ride

In the first quarter of 2008, Visa and MasterCard spent $860,000 and $720,000 apiece in order to attempt to combat proposed federal regulations, which would shield consumers from high interest rates and let merchants who take credit cards negotiate their transaction fees. The proposed legislation, called the "Credit Card Fair Fee Act of 2008," as spearheaded by the Federal Reserve, the Office of Thrift and Supervision, and the National Credit Union Administration.

Potential legislation against Visa and MasterCard was only the tip of the iceberg of credit card companies' difficulties in 2008. MasterCard posted a $746 million loss for the second quarter of the year, due in no small part to the $1.8 billion the company ended up paying American Express in a settlement stemming from a 2004 lawsuit contending that MasterCard— along with competitor Visa—had barred some financial companies from distributing cards through American Express. In the third quarter of 2008, MasterCard will make its first $150 million payment to American Express—a practice that will continue for 12 quarters. Meanwhile, Visa, in its settlement, is paying American Express a total of $2.25 billion.

Consumer credit purgatory

Credit card companies were hardly the only ones to feel the pinch of the credit crunch. Consumers worldwide felt the breakdown of the subprime market in many ways, and those in the U.S. took the brunt of the fallout. In late 2007, International Monetary Fund Director Rodrigo Rato predicted the U.S. would be the hardest hit throughout 2008. Sadly, his predictions seemed to be fulfilled quickly—by June 2008, The Guardian reported on the trend of more and more middle-class citizens being forced to live in their cars due to the foreclosures brought on by the subprime crisis. And that wasn't the end of the market backlash. In July 2008, the Senior Loan Officer Opinion Survey on Bank Lending Practice reported that 65 percent of U.S. banks admitted to stiffening their overall lending practices over the course of the year as a result of the credit crisis, a 30 percent jump versus its April 2008 report.

Heavy metal

The credit card traces its roots back to 1914 when Western Union began doling out metal cards, called "metal money," which gave preferred customers interest-free, deferred-payment privileges. Ten years later, General Petroleum Corporation issued the first metal money for gasoline and automotive services, and by the late 1930s, department stores, communication companies, travel and delivery companies had all began to introduce such cards. Then, companies issued the cards, processed the transactions and collected the debts from the customer. The popularity of these cards grew until the beginning of World War II, when "Regulation W" restricted the use of cards, and as a result, stalled their growth.

After the war, though, cards were back on track. Modes of travel were more advanced and more accessible, and more people were beginning to buy expensive modern conveniences such as kitchen appliances and washing machines. As a result, the credit card boomed in popularity, as consumers could pay for these things on credit that otherwise they couldn't afford to buy with cash.

Charge-it

In 1951, New York's Franklin National Bank created a credit system called Charge-It, which was very similar to the modern credit card. Charge-It allowed consumers to make purchases at local retail establishments, with the retailer obtaining authorization from the bank and then closing the sale. At a later date, the bank would reimburse the retailer and then collect the debt from the consumer. Acting upon the success of Franklin's Charge-It, other banks soon began introducing similar cards. Banks found that cardholders liked the convenience and credit line that cards offered, and retailers discovered that credit card customers usually spent more than if they had to pay with cash. Additionally, retailers found that handling bank-issued cards was less costly than maintaining their credit card programs.

The association and the Master

Bank of America masterminded credit card innovations in the 1960s with the introduction of the bank card association. In 1965, Bank of America began issuing licensing agreements that allowed other banks to issue BankAmericards. To compete with the BankAmericard, four banks from California formed the Western States Bankcard Association and introduced the MasterCharge. By 1969, most credit cards had been converted to either

Visit the Vault Finance Career Channel at www.vault.com/finance — with insider firm profiles, message boards, the Vault Finance Job Board and more.

VAULT CAREER LIBRARY

7

the MasterCharge (which changed its name to MasterCard in 1979) or the BankAmericard (which was renamed Visa in 1977).

Cutting the cost of transaction processing and decreasing credit card fraud were the next innovations introduced to the industry. Electronic authorizations, beginning in the early 1970s, allowed merchants to approve transactions 24 hours a day. By the end of the decade, magnetic strips on the back of credit cards allowed retailers to swipe the customer's credit card through a dial-up terminal, which accessed the issuing bank cardholder's information. This process gave authorizations and processed settlement agreements in a matter of minutes. In the 1980s, the ATM (Automatic Teller Machine) began to surface, giving cardholders 24-hour access to cash.

The debut of the debit, the climb of the cobrand

The 1990s saw the debit card rise in popularity. The debit card grew from accounting for 274 million transactions in 1990 to 8.15 billion transactions in 2002. (According to the Packaged Facts report "Debit Cards in the U.S.," there were 28 million debit card transactions in the U.S. in 2007, worth a total of $1.4 trillion.) The 1990s also witnessed the surge of cobranded and affinity cards, which match up a credit card company with a retailer to offer discounts for using the card (think Citibank's AAdvantage cards and American Express' Mileage Rewards program). Although cobranded cards took a dip in the late 1990s—according to some industry experts, this was because issuers had exhausted the most lucrative partners—they returned in full force during the early part of the new millennium. In 2003 alone, MBNA—called "The King of the Plastic Frontier" by BusinessWeek—struck some 400 new deals with various companies such as Merrill Lynch, Royal Caribbean and Air Canada. Additionally, it renewed deals with another 1,400 organizations, including the National Football League and the University of Michigan. In 2004, MBNA signed agreements with numerous other companies and organizations such as A.G. Edwards & Sons, the Massachusetts Institute of Technology, Arsenal Football Club (U.K.), Charles Schwab, and Starwood Hotels and Resorts. (In 2005, MBNA was acquired by Bank of America.)

And then there were four

In September 2003, a federal court upheld a lower court ruling that cost credit card powerhouses Visa and MasterCard a combined $3 billion. The court found Visa and MasterCard rules preventing the companies' member banks from also issuing American Express and Morgan Stanley's Discover cards to be illegal and harmful to competition. MasterCard was forced to pay $2 billion in damages and Visa paid $1 billion.

In October 2004, the U.S. Supreme Court decided not to hear Visa and MasterCard's appeal in the government's antitrust suit against them, effectively ending the two companies' rules that had prevented banks from issuing cards on rival networks. As a result, Amex and Discover became free to partner with the thousands of banks that issue Visa and MasterCard. This allows Amex and Discover to gain ground on the two credit powerhouses that, together, control at least 80 percent of the U.S. credit card purchase volume (as of July 2007), according to the National Retail Federation.

Re-Discovering the possibilities

In the midst of Morgan Stanley's great personnel exodus of March 2005, the firm announced plans to spin off its Discover credit card unit. Former Morgan Stanley CEO Philip Purcell reasoned that Discover "will be more properly valued as a stand-alone entity" than as a piece of Morgan Stanley. Soon after the announcement, analysts began estimating the Street value of the huge credit card unit. The range fell between $9 billion and $16 billion. Analysts also disagreed over whether or not the spin-off would maximize shareholder value.

However, new CEO John Mack's first big after taking over the reins in mid-2005 was to reverse course on the Discover business, which predecessor Purcell had talked of selling off. "Discover is not only a strong business, but also an attractive asset for Morgan Stanley," Mack said in a statement. "It is a unique, successful franchise with growth opportunities that gives Morgan Stanley a consistent stream of stable, high-quality earnings and substantial cash flow, diversifies the company's earnings and broadens our scale and capital base."

But despite the kind words, there was ultimately a change of heart for Morgan Stanley. Although Discover delivered record before-tax earnings of $16 billion in 2006, Morgan Stanley announced the same year that it planned to spin off Discover, which some analysts said would allow both businesses to grow more quickly. The deal was finally completed in June 2007, and though financial terms weren't disclosed, analysts estimated Discover's worth to be $13 billion at the time.

Visit the Vault Finance Career Channel at **www.vault.com/finance** — with insider firm profiles, message boards, the Vault Finance Job Board and more.

VAULT CAREER LIBRARY

9

As an autonomous firm, Discover is now led by CEO David W. Nelms, and as of August 2008, its stock was trading at $15.52 a share. Net income for the second quarter 2008 was $234.15 million, up from $209.24 million in the second quarter 2007. Being its own entity has hardly exempted Discover from dealing with a few roadblocks. In August 2008, a lawsuit from Discover asserting a conspiracy between MasterCard and Visa was deemed limited in reach by a judge who also rejected allegations from Discover that MasterCard was excluding Discover from distributing debit cards.

The big buy

In June 2005, BofA announced its acquisition of credit card behemoth MBNA in a 35 billion deal, following closely on the heels of its $49 billion purchase of FleetBoston Financial in 2003. The MBNA purchase made Bank of America one of the largest card issuers in the U.S., with $143 billion in managed outstanding balances and 40 million active accounts. Bank of America added more than 20 million new customer accounts as well as affinity relationships with more than 5,000 partner organizations and financial institutions. It achieved overall expense efficiencies of $850 million after-tax, fully realized in 2007, and a restructuring charge of $1.25 billion after-tax. Cost reductions came from a range of sources, including layoffs. (In unrelated cuts, the bank announced plans to slash 7,500 jobs in its mortgage, home-equity and insurance groups in summer 2008).

In November 2006, BofA announced that it had agreed to acquire US Trust, the wealth management subsidiary of Charles Schwab Corporation. The $3.3 billion acquisition, completed in July 2007, helped BofA strengthen its capabilities in serving high net worth clients and increase its assets under management.

The big IPOs

At the end of August 2005, MasterCard, which became a private share corporation in 2002, announced plans to become a publicly-traded company. On May 25, 2006, MasterCard finally went public, and began trading on the New York Stock Exchange (NYSE) under the ticker 'MA.' "Listing on the NYSE marks a major milestone for MasterCard and reinforces our commitment to continued growth and building value for our customers and stockholders," Robert Selander, the company's president and chief executive officer, told the Associated Press. The market had expected the issue to open in the $40 to $43 range, but MasterCard was at $39 after a series of setbacks delayed the process. But by most accounts, the IPO has been a huge success. As of August 2008, the stock had zoomed to over $234 per share, thanks in part to solid growth rates. During the second quarter 2008, 951 million MasterCard cards were issued, up 11 percent. MasterCard's worldwide purchase volume went up 12.8 percent to $655 billion, while transactions processed went up 13.6 percent to 5.2 billion.

MasterCard wasn't the only piece of plastic that's dazzled IPO investors. On March 19, 2008, Visa set a record for stateside IPOs when it raised $17.9 billion in its initial public offering. (The deal got even bigger when Visa's underwriters decided to exercise their option to buy 40.6 million more shares at $44 each for about $1.8 billion.) The firm's shares were initially valued at $44 per share—higher than the expected $37 to $42 range—and increased 35 percent to $59.50 almost immediately upon going public. At the end of the first day of trading, Visa's shares (which trade on the NYSE under the symbol 'V') closed at $56.50, a 28.4 percent increase from its opening price. As of September 2008, Visa's stock was still going strong, trading for around $74 a share.

The road, however, has been rocky as MasterCard and Visa have recently weathered some storms. In November 2007, MasterCard and Visa announced that they would be paying American Express $1.8 billion and $2.25 billion, respectively, in a settlement stemming from a 2004 lawsuit contending that the companies had barred some financial companies from distributing cards through American Express.

No contact credit

"Contactless" cards and finger-swiping systems are the latest advances in the world of plastic purchasing. According to CreditCards.com, by mid-2007, banks had issued about 27 million debit and credit cards that could be scanned via a radar-like beam, rather than having to be run through a machine. The popularity of contactless credit and debit cards—which can be used at numerous retailers such as McDonald's, 7-Eleven and CVS—is only expected to skyrocket. According to market research firm Packaged Facts, there will be approximately 109 million cards in circulation by 2011. Other than not having to run the cards through a machine, another benefit is that no signature is required for purchases less than $25.

Another no-contact credit payment system is now in place: the pay-by-finger system, in which individuals' fingers are scanned and linked to their payment information. All you have to do is press your finger (its print) against a device, enter some personal information, such as your phone

Visit the Vault Finance Career Channel at www.vault.com/finance — with insider firm profiles, message boards, the Vault Finance Job Board and more.

VAULT CAREER LIBRARY   11

number on a keypad and your payment is made; fingerprints are linked up with credit or debit cards. The system is already in place at hundreds of U.S. supermarkets such as Albertsons and Piggly Wiggly.

A worrying trend

There's been a number of reports detailing the disturbing trend of cash-strapped homeowners declining to pay their mortgages as the U.S. economy has continued to tank. Maybe because of this trend—or in spite of it—American Express and Visa began a rewards program that allows customers to pay their monthly mortgage or rent with a credit card. Although the companies said that customers have the potential to earn exponentially more bonus points than they had before, some analysts pointed out that the main concern with such a program is that credit card owners who are already in debt will only continue to fall deeper into credit issues. And those debt issues already run deep with Americans to begin with. A Sallie Mae/Gallup poll released in August 2008 revealed that parents of college students who borrowed on credit cards put an average of more than $5,800 on their cards while students put about $2,500 on their plastic. Besides big-ticket items like education, other accouterments of wealth are also frequently put on Americans' credit cards without a second thought—swimming pools and car payments are no longer a rarity to charge.

But is it preferable to put college payments on a credit card rather than luxury items that would otherwise be out of reach? It may be, according to some credit card companies. CompuScore, which markets Visa cards, came under fire from the Federal Trade Commission in August 2008 for profiling cardholders' transactions, reducing the credit limits of customers who used their cards at marriage counselors, tire shops, billiard halls and pawn shops. The FTC hasn't called the company's actions illegal, but it did allege that the company wasn't upfront about its actions. Either way, it may pay for consumers to watch where they use their cards.

Insurance

Risky business

The insurance industry combines to form a multi-trillion-dollar market dealing in risk. In exchange for a premium, insurers promise to compensate, monetarily or otherwise, individuals and businesses for future losses, thus taking on the risk of personal injury, death, damage to property, unexpected financial disaster, and just about any other misfortune that could occur.

The industry is often divided into categories such as life/health and property/casualty. Life insurance dominates the mix, making up about 60 percent of all premiums. The bigger categories can be subdivided into smaller groups; property insurance, for instance, may cover homeowner's, renter's, auto and boat policies, while health insurance is made up of subsets including disability and long-term care.

But these days, you can find insurance for just about anything, including weddings and bar mitzvahs, policies for the chance of weather ruining a vacation and policies for pets (a market that grew 342 percent from 1998 to 2002, had sales of $160 million in 2005 and exploded to $195 million by 2007, according to the industry publication Small Business Trends). Even insurance companies themselves can be insured against extraordinary losses—by companies specializing in reinsurance.

Although insurance isn't the sexiest business around, celebrity policies always get a lot of press. While rumors that Jennifer Lopez had insured her famous asset for $1 billion proved to be unfounded, other such policies do indeed exist. In fact, the phrase "million dollar legs" comes from Betty Grable's policy for that amount (a similar policy is held by TV's Mary Hart); other notable contemporary policies include Bruce Springsteen's voice, reportedly covered at around $6 million.

The world's top five

Though the U.S. is well ahead of the rest of the world in terms of insurance coverage, insurance is a truly global business. The industry is the biggest in the world, raking in more than $4 trillion in revenue annually, according SocialFunds, an investment news site. Ranked by sales, the top five insurance companies are Germany's Allianz, the Netherlands' ING, New York-based American International Group (AIG), France's AXA and Japan's Nippon Life Insurance Company. Other leading U.S. insurers include State Farm, MetLife, Allstate, Prudential, Aetna and Travelers.

Consolidation is the name of the game—Hoovers reports that the top 10 property/casualty insurers account for nearly half of all premiums written. Perhaps the most notable example of the mergers and acquisitions mania in the industry was the $82 billion merger in 1998 between Citicorp and the Travelers Group, which created Citigroup (now known as Citi). Some insurance companies have also begun to reconfigure themselves from

Visit the Vault Finance Career Channel at **www.vault.com/finance** — with
insider firm profiles, message boards, the Vault Finance Job Board and more.

VAULT CAREER LIBRARY   **13**

mutual insurers, or those owned by policyholders (e.g., State Farm), to stock insurers, or those held by shareholders (e.g., Allstate). This process, known as "demutualization," promises to raise even more capital for insurance companies to indulge in more acquisitions.

The last 25 years have seen a shift in the industry away from life insurance toward annuity products, focusing on managing investment risk rather than the (inevitable) risk of mortality. With increasing deregulation in the U.S. and Japan, these insurers are moving ever closer to competition with financial services firms. Indeed, the business of the insurance industry doesn't end with insurance. The world's top insurance companies have broadened their array of financial services to include investment management, annuities, securities, mutual funds, health care management, employee benefits and administration, real estate brokerage and even consumer banking. The move towards financial services followed the 1999 repeal of the Glass-Steagall Act, which barred insurance companies, banks and brokerages from entering each other's industries, and the Gramm Leach-Bliley Act of 1999, which further defined permissible acts for financial holding companies. Now insurance companies are free to partner with commercial banks, securities firms and other financial entities.

At the speed of the Internet

Like many other industries, the insurance market has been transformed in recent years by the Internet. Traditionally, insurance products have been distributed by independent agents (business people paid on commission) or by exclusive agents (paid employees). But insurers who sell over the Web reap the benefits of lower sales costs and customer service expenses, along with a more expedient way of getting information to consumers, which is transforming traditional methods by cutting costs and increasing the amount of information available to consumers. Celent Communications estimates that the online insurance market takes in over $200 billion in sales each year. Of course, an automated approach to doing business means fewer sales people are needed—Celent reported that insurance giant Cigna, for instance, eliminated 2,000 jobs in 2002 because of increased efficiencies.

With more IT comes a greater need for IT security—Celent estimates that U.S. insurers spend about 2.5 to 3 percent of premium on security. Aside from the threat of viruses, hackers and the like, regulations have made security a top priority—the Health Information Portability and Accountability Act (HIPAA), for instance, which went into effect in 2003, sets strict standards for the privacy and security of the patient information transferred between health insurers and providers.

Recovering from September 11

The September 11 terrorist attacks sent shockwaves through the industry. Not only did they constitute perhaps the largest insured loss in U.S. history—with estimates ranging between $40 billion and $50 billion in claims for loss of life and property, injuries and workers' compensation—but they also caused insurers and re-insurers to take a hard look at how they would handle the risks associated with possible future terrorist acts. The Terrorism Risk Insurance Act, signed into law by President Bush in November 2002, aimed to deal with the nearly incalculable risk posed by this threat. Among other things, the law defines a terrorism-related event as one with a minimum of $5 million in damages. It provides for the sharing of risk between private insurers and the federal government over a three-year period, with each participating company responsible for paying a deductible before federal assistance is available. If losses are incurred above the insurer's deductible, the government is obliged to pay 90 percent. While the measure met with a considerable amount of grumbling from all parties involved, for the most part the industry acknowledged that the plan at least allows for the potential risk to insurers from terrorism-related disasters to be quantified.

Property insurance stalemate?

In parts of the U.S. such as California and Louisiana, which have dealt with rampant wildfires and Hurricane Katrina in recent years, another trend has arisen. More and more, property insurers are requiring homeowners to take precautions to protect their houses or confront the possibility of being dropped—a trend that has continued into 2008 with precautions from companies encouraging homeowners to guard against floods and winter freezing.

Some insurance companies in California are requiring homeowners to replace their roofs with fire-resistant ones, and other companies in hurricane-prone coastal areas are requiring policyholders to install storm-resistant shutters. Still, since the requirements are following three years of record profits for the property insurance industry, the Associated Press reported in June 2007 that many homeowners are up at arms about the potential cost. But the insurance industry isn't backing down on their requirements, and some companies have even decided to pull out of certain

Visit the Vault Finance Career Channel at www.vault.com/finance — with insider firm profiles, message boards, the Vault Finance Job Board and more.

VAULT CAREER LIBRARY   15

institutions—including 19 of the top 20 securities firms, 13 of the top 20 banks, and 11 of the top 20 life insurance companies—license its research for their investors and advisors.

DBRS, an international ratings agency, is headquartered in Toronto and gives ratings to borrowing entities. The company is split into corporate, financial institutions, public finance and structured finance divisions. The firm prides itself on being "the leading rating agency in Canada" as well as being the first rating agency to have a full-service web site for customers.

Suspect practices

Rating agencies have recently come under severe scrutiny for their ratings of mortgage-backed securities—specifically, whether or not these ratings helped contribute to the subprime mortgage crisis. In late 2007, the Securities and Exchange Commission (SEC) began an inquiry into whether appropriate procedures were followed for ratings companies like Moody's and S&P. The SEC has alleged that some ratings agencies gave unnaturally high rankings to mortgage-backed securities and some debt products.

The problems for the rating agencies didn't end with the SEC. In July 2008, Connecticut Attorney General Richard Blumenthal filed a lawsuit against Fitch, Moody's and S&P, alleging that the firms gave municipal bonds falsely low ratings and, consequently, caused customers to pay for unneeded bond insurance as well as elevated interest rates. Additionally, Blumenthal said the agencies ran afoul of the Connecticut Unfair Trade Practices Act by neglecting to mention "material facts that caused bond insurers in Connecticut to purchase bonds at higher interest rates."

Auto Financing

Revving up the payments?

Essentially the first on the scene, Ford Motor Credit was the forerunner when it came to auto financing. An indirect, wholly owned subsidiary of Ford Motor Company, Ford Motor Credit was incorporated in Delaware, in 1959, so that Ford dealers could provide competitive financing services to individuals and businesses interested in buying cars. The company's true origins, however, were about 40 years earlier, when founder Henry Ford sought to discourage excessive consumer borrowing by devising layaway plans in order to keep his $265 Model Ts rolling off the lot; this tactic sowed the seeds for Ford Motor Credit to later make ownership possible for customers unable or unwilling to meet the entire upfront cost of a car.

Other giants in the business include Chrysler Financial and GMAC, which have been making headlines lately. In May 2007, Cerberus Capital Management purchased 80 percent of Chrysler from DaimlerChrysler. (In late 2007, Daimler shareholders decided to drop the Chrysler after the sale to Cerberus, renaming the company "Daimler AG.") A few months later, Cerberus bought 51 percent of GMAC.

Chrysler and GMAC aren't the only big fish in the industry. GE Capital Auto Financial Services (the financing unit of General Electric) and Honda Financial Services are contenders as well, along with a plethora of banks' auto financing divisions, including HSBC Auto Finance, Wells Fargo Auto Financing and Capital One Auto Financing.

Lower resale values, longer leases

The auto financing business has existed for decades, but some recent developments have proven fairly tumultuous for the industry. In July 2008, Chase Auto Finance announced that it would stop financing Chrysler car and truck leases in the wake of leased vehicles having less value. Loans for retail vehicle sales will still take place, but Chrysler, Dodge and Jeep products won't get leases from Chase. Ford Motor, in the meantime, increased the prices on some of its vehicle leases due to the firm's lending unit experiencing heavy losses.

Additionally, The Wall Street Journal reported in June 2007 that loan financing plans for car owners have been extended longer and longer, due mostly to the rise of small monthly payments and arrangements that involve no money down. According to the Journal, this trend has resulted in consumers becoming blind to the full cost of a product, looking only at the monthly payments involved instead of the overall cost of the vehicle—often adding thousands of dollars to the overall cost.

USA Today reported on a similar trend in 2008, revealing that car loans now tend to average seven years or longer. Typically, consumers keep deciding to refinance the outstanding balance of their old car loan in order to lock in low monthly payments—but lengthen their loan term in the process. This trend has only seemed to worsen. In March 2008, the Cleveland Plain Dealer reported that Americans take an average of two years longer to pay off their car loans than consumers from 30 years ago. The newspaper,

Visit the Vault Finance Career Channel at www.vault.com/finance — with insider firm profiles, message boards, the Vault Finance Job Board and more.

VAULT CAREER LIBRARY   19

analyzing data from the Federal Reserve, reported that the average car loan stretches over five years—and many extend to seven years.

The Big Three are in big trouble

Many industry observers have speculated that life may get even tougher for the Big Three automakers, a group that has been through a rough ride recently. Some analysts are even speculating that General Motors, Ford and Chrysler may be headed for bankruptcy. Their latest results have not looked good, to say the least. GM reported a 2008 second quarter net loss of $15.5 billion, Ford endured a $8.7 billion loss for the same period and analysts believe that Chrysler (which doesn't report its financial results) doesn't have international sales to reinforce itself in tough times. Although the auto financial services companies won't be going out of business any time soon, they are increasingly seeking to get out of leasing. Chrysler Credit has been rumored to be on its way out of the business, while Ford Motor's credit unit and GMAC are stiffening their borrowing rules, the Financial Post reported in August 2008. Elevated borrowing expenses and write-downs on companies' lease portfolios have crippled the industry.

Mortgages

Before the crisis

Home mortgages were the turf of commercial banks at the outset of the century. But shortly after the Depression, the government created the Federal Housing Administration, which offered insured home loans. Fannie Mae, originally part of the FHA, was established in 1938 to help provide affordable homeownership. In 1968, it officially became a shareholder-financed company, but its mission remains the same. Similarly, Freddie Mac, founded in 1970, helps Americans finance homes and provides assistance in financing rental housing. Other major mortgage providers in the U.S. include Regions, Capital Home Loans and SunTrust. And on the Internet, online companies such as LendingTree connect potential homeowners with hundreds of lenders.

Enter the crisis

The subprime mortgage crisis that hit the U.S. in 2007 affected not only the lending industry but also sent aftershocks across a number of business sectors—with some analysts predicting that the financial disaster will ultimately lead the U.S. into a recession.

The crisis began when a number of subprime borrowers—consumers with low credit ratings paying interest rates above the prime rate—began to default on their home loans. As these lendees began to default in record numbers, subprime lenders began to go out of business. According to the Mortgage Lender Implode-o-Meter (a web site devoted entirely to tracking the collapse of the mortgage lending industry), between late 2006 and mid-2008, 277 major lending companies have folded.

The reverberations of the crisis have been felt everywhere, from domestic and international stock markets to government agencies.

Fannie and Freddie feel the heat

In July 2008, after losing billions in the previous year following a flood of homeowner defaults, Freddie Mac and Fannie Mae's stocks lost half their value—an event that some analysts said was worse for the financial markets than the collapse of Bear Stearns, the 85-year-old investment bank that crumbled as a result of the subprime crisis.

Following the stock nosedives, the U.S. Treasury finagled a few favors from Congress on behalf of the agencies: a temporary increase in a credit line for Fannie and Freddie, along with temporary authority to purchase equity in one or both of the mortgage companies. U.S. Treasury Secretary Henry Paulson was resolute that any plan to save the agencies does not benefit their shareholders.

But Paulson led a plan to save Freddie Mac and Fannie Mae nearly two weeks before their financial plight came to light, The Wall Street Journal reported in July 2008. In an attempt to help curtail the consequences of the housing crisis, Paulson assured the Fed and the Federal Reserve Bank of New York that any loans to Fannie or Freddie would serve only as an "interim step," not a permanent solution.

In August 2008, with its stock down 90 percent since the beginning of the year, Fannie Mae endured a few management changes as the firm's chief financial officer, chief business officer and chief risk officer all stepped down. (Fannie CFO Stephen Swad had only been with the firm for a year before a replacement stepped in.)

Visit the Vault Finance Career Channel at **www.vault.com/finance** — with insider firm profiles, message boards, the Vault Finance Job Board and more.

VAULT CAREER LIBRARY   **21**

Presidential hopefuls on the fate of Mae and Mac

In early September 2008, speaking about the agencies' fates, Democratic presidential nominee Barack Obama said in a news conference that if elected in November 2008, he first plans to decipher whether or not the companies are public or private. If the companies are determined to be public, he said "they have to get out of the profit-making business," but if they're private, the government won't "bail them out." Republican candidate John McCain, meanwhile, has pledged support for Fannie and Freddie. He has called them "vital to Americans' ability to own their own homes" and said that "we cannot allow them to fail."

Fannie and Freddie's new boss: Uncle Sam

On September 7, 2008, the U.S. government seized control of Fannie Mae and Freddie Mac in a drastic attempt to stop their ongoing losses. U.S. Treasury Secretary Henry Paulson said the government will take control of the firms and supplant each of the firm's CEOs with new heads. (After staying on for a transition stage, Fannie's current head Daniel H. Mudd will be replaced by former TIAA-CREF chairman Herbert M. Allison Jr., while Freddie's current head Richard F. Syron will be succeeded by Carlyle Group Senior Adviser David M. Moffett.) Additionally, the Treasury will obtain $1 billion in preferred shares for both Fannie and Freddie and will provide about $200 billion in funding. Paulson indicated that allowing either of the giants to fail would "cause great turmoil" for domestic and international financial markets. To this end, his predictions seemed accurate; stocks rallied after the takeover announcement was made.

As far as the big funding picture goes for the future, the Treasury will also restrict the size of each firm's mortgage portfolio to $850 billion. As of September 2008, Fannie had approximately $758 billion in mortgages and securities while Freddie had about $798 billion.

Financial Data Services

Big shots

The financial data services industry provides retirement and payroll services to screening services and credit monitoring. According to Fortune's 2008 Most Admired Companies in the U.S. list, the top five most admired firms in the financial data services sector are (in this order): Dun

& Bradstreet, Automatic Data Processing, MasterCard, DST Systems and Paychex. "Contenders" to these, according to Fortune, include First Data, Western Union, Alliance Data Systems, Fiserv and SunGard Data Systems. The firms made the list after receiving high rankings in factors such as innovation, people management, social responsibility, quality of management, financial soundness and quality of products and services.

Fortune also ranked top financial data services companies according to their profits. On that list, First Data came in as No.1, followed by Fiserv, SunGard Data Systems, Western Union, Fidelity National Information Services and MasterCard. An upswing in credit card transactions lifted First Data to its top ranking, and the August 2007 acquisition of electronic bill payment company CheckFree Corp. helped Fiserv secure the No. 2 ranking. Overall, Fortune ranked financial data services the 15th most profitable industry.

Visit the Vault Finance Career Channel at **www.vault.com/finance** — with insider firm profiles, message boards, the Vault Finance Job Board and more.

VAULT CAREER LIBRARY

23

TOP

EMPLOYER PROFILES

FINANCIAL SERVICES

Aflac (American Family Life Assurance Company)

1932 Wynnton Road
Columbus, GA 31999
Phone: (706) 323-3431
Fax: (706) 324-6330
www.aflac.com

DEPARTMENTS

Aflac Information Technology,
  Incorporated
Aflac International, Incorporated
Aflac Insurance Service Company,
  Ltd. (Japan)
Aflac Payment Service Company,
  Ltd. (Japan)
American Family Life Assurance
  Company of Columbus (Aflac)
Aflac Japan
Aflac U.S.
American Family Life Assurance
  Company of New York

THE STATS

Employer Type: Public Company
Ticker Symbol: AFL (NYSE)
Chairman & CEO: Daniel P. (Dan)
  Amos
President, CFO & Director: Kriss
  Cloninger III
Revenue: $15.39 billion (FYE 12/07)
Net Income: $1.63 billion
No. of Employees: 4,500

KEY COMPETITORS

MetLife
UnumProvident

UPPER

• "Product that is one I can believe in"

DOWNER

• "It's hard to become self-disciplined"

EMPLOYMENT CONTACT

See "careers" at www.aflac.com

THE SCOOP

The innovator

Founded in Columbus, Ga, in 1955 American Family Life Assurance Company (Aflac) began offering life, health and accident insurance. Today, the company focuses on the marketing and sale of supplemental health and life insurance policies, including short-term disability. In fact, Aflac is one of the largest supplemental insurance providers in the U.S., and is a dominant force in Japan. In 2008, Aflac was ranked No. 165 on the Fortune 500. *Fortune* has also named the company one of the Top 50 Employers for Women and Top 50 Companies for Minorities.

Goodbye Columbus

The Amos brothers opened their doors for business in November 1955 in a one-room office in downtown Columbus, Ga. As the brothers sought out untapped markets, they were inspired by premiums written especially for polio in the 1940s and 1950s. So, the Amos' chose to sell cancer insurance following their father's death from the disease. The company was one of the first to create cancer-expense policies in 1958, and after one year, Aflac had 6,426 policyholders and $388,000 in assets. By 1971, Aflac operated in 42 states. The 1980s found American sales lagging, but the Japanese market grew into the centerpiece of Aflac's revenue stream.

After building a multinational company on cancer insurance, John Amos succumbed to the disease in 1990. His nephew Dan Amos took the reins, and dubbed the company Aflac two years later. Amos explained the move was an attempt to promote the company's profile, taking into account so many other companies used the word "American."

FLEXibility

For individuals, Aflac U.S. offers a number, of voluntary benefit policies, including accident and disability, dental, life, vision, long-term care, short-term disability, and coverage for indemnity and hospital intensive care. The company also offers care plans, general medical expense plans, medical/sickness riders and a living benefit life plan. Aflac services include many programs for employers looking for coverage for their staff. The FLEX ONE plan allows employees to contribute pre-tax dollars towards qualified benefits, such as health insurance and child care, while the company's Single-

Point Billing option consolidates billing and financial requirements from multiple insurance carriers into a single overall benefits group.

Turning Japanese

John Amos first considered Japan as a prime market for Aflac's products after a trip to the 1970 World's Fair in Osaka. Noting that the country's national health care system neglected to protect its citizens from the enormous financial burden of cancer treatment, Amos spent the next four years seeking approval to enter into the Japanese market, finally getting licensing after convincing government officials that his policies did not compete with existing products. He also gained backing from prominent investors in the insurance and medical industries. In 1974, Aflac officially opened for business in Japan, only the second foreign company licensed to sell insurance policies there.

By 2004, Japan accounted for nearly 75 percent of the company's revenue. In the first nine months of 2007, total revenues rose by 4.1 percent to $11.4 billion, compared to $10.9 billion the year before. Aflac Japan reported increased sales results in the country, posting a 2.2 percent rise to $236 million in the third quarter.

The Japanese market has been beneficial to the company, as the firm insures one in four households in Japan. To be more competitive within the Japanese market, Aflac formed a marketing alliance with Dai-ichi Mutual Life, one of Japan's biggest life insurers. The company has sought to introduce new products. One example is the Japanese "living benefit," which includes lump sum payments for heart attacks and strokes.

Exclusive deal

Aflac execs must have been cheering in November 2007 when they landed an exclusive deal with the Japan Post Network Co. to distribute cancer insurance through the company's nationwide postal office network. The announcement of the news shot Aflac's shares up by more than 5 percent.

The Japan Post Network is one of four postal networks in the country, which privatized its mail services in 2005. Japan's postal offices also deal with bank deposits and sell insurance policies. The Aflac insurance will be sold beginning in 2008, starting at 300 Japan Post locations, and eventually expanding to all 24,000 locations.

Visit the Vault Finance Career Channel at **www.vault.com/finance** — with insider firm profiles, message boards, the Vault Finance Job Board and more.

VAULT CAREER LIBRARY   29

In the three-month period ending in September, Aflac's sales in Japan rose more than 2 percent, the first increase since 2005. Aflac executives likely saw this as a harbinger of good things, since the company relies on Japan for 75 percent of its revenue.

"We believe Japan Post's selection of Aflac reflects the quality of our newly introduced Cancer Forte product, the overall strength of the Aflac brand, a reputation for quality customer service and the support we provide to our sales force," Amos said in a company statement. "Although Japan Post has not yet established a specific time frame for sales to commence, we anticipate that sales should occur sometime in 2008."

Amos added that he expects Aflac's sales in Japan to increase by as much as 7 percent in 2008. According to Bloomberg, the Japan Post has $1.6 trillion in its cash pool, the largest of any private company.

Going first

In May 2008, Aflac became the first U.S. company to give shareholders a say in what Chairman and CEO Dan Amos and his top four executives earn. The shareholders had a chance to voice any concerns about the pay-per-performance salaries and bonuses of Aflac executives; 93 percent of the votes were cast in favor, with only 2.5 percent against Aflac's compensation practices, in a vote commonly referred to as "say-on-pay."

Aflac was the first American company to adopt such a resolution in February 2007, and according to USA Today, the say-on-pay option has not been popular with many other corporations. The newspaper does report that Aflac might have inspired Verizon, Motorola, Blockbuster, Ingersoll-Rand, and Clear Channel Communications, among others, to propose the option to their boards. None, however, had passed resolutions as of December 2007.

"We believe that our shareholders have embraced the expanded disclosure on executive compensation and it gives them the information they need to make an informed decision as they weigh pay versus performance," Amos said in a press release. "Aflac has a long history of generating strong returns for its shareholders and we remain committed to being transparent and responsive to our owners."

Aflac reports that since Amos took the reins as CEO in 1990, its total return to shareholders has increased by more than 3,800 percent, while the company's market value has grown from $1.2 billion to more than $30 billion, as of October 2007. In 2006, Amos received $5.2 million in salary, bonus and restricted stock, as well as $8.6 million in stock options. He is reportedly the second-highest-paid CEO in the U.S. insurance industry.

New digs, more jobs

In August 2007, Aflac completed the first phase of the largest office expansion that Georgia had ever seen. Execs hosted a ribbon-cutting ceremony for the new 95,000-square-foot facility in Columbus, attended by none other than the mayor himself.

The second phase, to be finished in 2009, will increase the facility to 165,000 square feet; the third phase will skyrocket the company's total office space in Columbus to more than 300,000 square feet.

"In addition to having a new state-of-the-art facility that will help streamline our operations, this project will support economic development throughout Columbus and the surrounding area with the creation of new jobs," Paul Amos II, Aflac U.S. president, said in a statement.

The company expects the expansion to allow for 2,000 new jobs in the next five to six years. The new $100 million facility will feature room for the company's customer service division, an auditorium for 500 people, 1,000 miles of walking trails, classrooms with high-tech equipment and many other amenities.

Duck walk of fame

In September 2005, the Aflac duck was added to Madison Avenue's Walk of Fame during an induction ceremony paying homage to America's most beloved advertising icons. The duck is one of the most successful corporate icons in memory, prompting an increase in brand recognition from 12 percent to over 90 percent, according to Aflac. The duck has been a generous performer over its career, sharing screen time with such luminaries as Melania Trump, Yogi Berra and Chevy Chase. The duck has also appeared in the film "Lemony Snicket's A Series of Unfortunate Events," and has been spoofed on the "Tonight Show with Jay Leno" and "Saturday Night Live."

And, for the seventh consecutive year, Aflac and Macy's partnered to sell the Aflac Holiday Duck. Sales from the plush toy have earned more than $1.6 million for pediatric cancer treatment and research centers across the country. Each year, the Aflac Holiday Duck is seasonally dressed and quacks his famous Aflac line when pressed.

Visit the Vault Finance Career Channel at www.vault.com/finance — with insider firm profiles, message boards, the Vault Finance Job Board and more.

VAULT CAREER LIBRARY   31

Just ducky

As a means of retaining personnel, Aflac offers corporate employees an array of benefits, including flextime and telecommuting, and the firm has the largest onsite childcare facility in the state of Georgia. There are also professional and personal development courses that help employees drive their career and personal life to the next level.

For the 10th consecutive year, Aflac was named to Fortune magazine's list of the 100 Best Companies to Work For in America in 2008. In June 2008, Black Enterprise magazine named Aflac to its 40 Best Companies for Diversity list for the fourth year in a row. Hispanic Trends magazine, meanwhile, named the company one of the best for supplier diversity in February 2008. In addition, for the second consecutive year, Ethisphere called Aflac one of the world's most ethical companies in June 2008. And in September 2008, InformationWeek 500 honored the insurer for its innovative business technology. On the philanthropic side, the Aflac Cancer Center and Blood Disorders Service of Children's Healthcare of Atlanta was named one of America's top five cancer hospitals for children by Child magazine for the second year in a row in 2007.

GETTING HIRED

Looking for passion

According to Aflac, the company is looking for applicants who are "truly passionate" about their work to join its team. The careers section of Aflac's web site offers information for sales positions and corporate employment. Sales positions are 100 percent commission-based. Those in the sales force manage their own time and schedule. New agents are encouraged to participate in specialized programs, including orientation, training and earning the proper certifications. For more information on becoming an independent sales agent, call Aflac at (800) 448-1771.

Corporate jobs are searchable on the Aflac web site and are separated into several job categories, including actuarial, aviation, administrative, facilities, government relations/legal, printing/press operations, communications, finance and accounting, human resources, management, information technology, sales support and administration, operations and project management. Interested candidates can post a resume on aflac.com and create a user profile. Potential corporate applicants can call Aflac at (800) 522-0011 if they have any specific questions. The company also recruits through career fairs and lists future events on its web site. The firm also offers internships, along with corporate housing. One insider says interning is a "great stepping stone to gain actual work experience for college-level individuals."

OUR SURVEY SAYS

Join the team

The firm has "great recognition for accomplishments" and there are a lot of "team efforts" where "everyone pitches in to bring success for the region." "Working for Aflac has been an awesome experience," raves one insider, adding that staffers are "highly valued as the driving force behind the success of the company." And the good feelings regarding corporate culture may just have something to do with the duck. One insider notes that "over the last 12 years, Aflac has gone through a major transition," adding that "the introduction of the advertising duck in 2000 has greatly increased our corporate recognition, and because of that, it has become easier to sell for Aflac."

One respondent calls the culture "very family-like, which is good and bad," adding that it's "really nice that people come together to do things for co-workers who have had death in the family or have a new baby." Management is also "very supportive" and "sincerely cares about my success," insiders say.

Depends on the day

For Aflac's corporate employees, the dress code is business casual. However, the firm's independent sales force does not have a dress code. One sales force insider calls the dress code "business casual to business attire, depending on the type of client seen" and another notes that "we dress day-to-day according to our activities for the day." (In fact, one insider reports that it's almost too casual, adding that "the agents and management in the office I work out of dress very casual all the time— the opposite of what I am used to.") For independent agents, hours are flexible, too, an insider reports, commenting that "we make our own hours around what the

Visit the Vault Finance Career Channel at www.vault.com/finance — with insider firm profiles, message boards, the Vault Finance Job Board and more.

VAULT CAREER LIBRARY   33

client's demands are." Another concedes, "Some areas, such as core business units, work a lot of overtime," and "the hours can be long in certain departments."

Training gets good feedback. One insider says the company offers "the best support and training available in the insurance industry." Training programs seem to have improved tremendously over the years. Another contact says, "The state and local training are also getting better and improving the retention of associates."

The "income potential is extreme," notes a source, who adds that "for sales associates, the income varies depending on the level of commitment." Be ready to hit the ground running. "Less committed associates make less money," adds the contact. And perks are pretty decent as well. "Aflac buys stock and gives it to us based on policies that are paid for more than twelve months," reports one insider. There are also "lots of trips and awards" offered by the company.

Get the skills

Diversity gets good marks from insiders. One says the firm "embraces diversity and offers many opportunities for advancement." Another adds that Aflac "targets a diverse group of cultures," and because the firm is "lacking in bilingual associates," there are "fantastic opportunities for candidates with these skills," and the firm notes it's "always" on the lookout for such candidates.

American International Group (AIG)

70 Pine Street
New York, NY 10270
Phone: (212) 770-7000
Fax: (212) 509-9705
www.aig.com

DEPARTMENTS

AIG American General Life
  Companies
AIG Annuity Insurance Company
AIG Star Life Insurance Co., Ltd.
AIG SunAmerica Life Assurance
  Company
Life Insurance & Retirement
Services

THE STATS

Employer Type: Public Company*
Ticker Symbol: AIG (NYSE)
CEO: Edward Liddy
Revenue: $110.06 billion (FYE 12/07)
Net Income: $6.2 billion
No. of Employees: 97,000

*In September 2008, the U.S. Federal Reserve and
Treasury Department seized control of AIG, taking
an approximate 80 percent stake in the firm.

KEY COMPETITORS

Allianz
AXA
Zurich Financial Services

UPPERS

- "Great place to learn"
- Good benefits

DOWNERS

- Diversity efforts could be better
- "The bar needs to be raised for hiring"

EMPLOYMENT CONTACT

See "careers" at www.aig.com

Visit the Vault Finance Career Channel at **www.vault.com/finance** — with
insider firm profiles, message boards, the Vault Finance Job Board and more.

VAULT CAREER LIBRARY　35

THE SCOOP

Uncle Sam takes control

On the night of September 17, 2008, the United States government seized control of the ailing American International Group (AIG), one of the world's largest insurance firms and second-largest life insurer in the U.S. Under the terms of the deal—one of the most radical in U.S. history, putting a private insurer into the hands of the government for the first time ever as well U.S. taxpayer dollars at risk—the Federal Reserve and Treasury Department will loan up to $85 billion to AIG in return for convertible warrants, giving the U.S. government an approximate 80 percent stake in the insurance company. The deal also called for AIG CEO Robert Willumstad to be succeeded by Edward Liddy, the former head of fellow insurance giant Allstate.

The deal came two days after the U.S. government decided not to bailout crumbling New York-based investment bank Lehman Brothers, resulting in Lehman filing Chapter 11. This led some industry observers to believe that AIG would suffer a similar fate. But at the 11th hour, the Feds decided that the markets, though able to endure the bankruptcy of Lehman, could not handle the liquidation of AIG.

AIG dials 911

On September 15, 2008, shortly after AIG requested $40 billion from the Federal Reserve in a bid to raise capital in the light of three quarterly consecutive losses, the firm received a $20 billion loan from the state of New York. The announcement of the loan, which New York Governor David Paterson said would not affect the state's taxpayers, temporarily stopped AIG's stock from dropping further—it had fallen 46 percent on the morning of the 15th. It also gave AIG some temporary breathing room in order to shore up more capital to stay in business. By the end of the 15th, the firm's credit ratings had been downgraded by Standard & Poor's and Moody's.

On the morning of September 16, 2008, AIG's stock plummeted another 60 percent, as Goldman Sachs, Morgan Stanley, JPMorgan Chase and the Federal Reserve were scrambling to provide the firm with a $75 billion credit line and prevent it from entering into bankruptcy. According to insiders, AIG's ultimate amount of write-downs may end up anywhere between $60 billion and $70 billion.

Made in China

New York-based American International Group operates in 130 countries around the world. AIG also provides financial services and asset management, as well as auto insurance, mortgage guaranty, annuities and aircraft leasing.

AIG was founded in 1919 in Shanghai, China, by Cornelius Vander Starr, a former U.S. Army veteran. At first, the company offered only fire and marine insurance. In 1936, it opened a New York office specializing in insuring risks incurred outside the country by U.S. companies. World War II forced the company to move its headquarters to the U.S. and focus on the life insurance markets in North and South America. In 1967, Maurice "Hank" Greenberg replaced Starr as the head of AIG (Greenberg was forced out of the firm in 2005). Two years later, the insurer went public. Greenberg's policy on underwriting profits has been credited for much of the company's success, preventing AIG from suffering during the insurance industry price wars in the early 1980s. During the 1990s, the company became the first established insurance agency to enter the Vietnamese market, the first foreign company in Pakistan in two decades and the first major foreign investor in the Russian insurance industry.

In 2001, AIG established life and general insurance operations in India; it also bought American General Corporation for $23 billion, by far its largest acquisition. In November 2006, AIG agreed to acquire London City Airport, with Credit Suisse Group and General Electric. Under terms of the deal, AIG took 50 percent of the airport's equity. Insider's speculated that the value of the deal was about $1.4 billion. In 2007, AIG took on two more companies: 21st Century Insurance Group, and Wurttembergische und Badische Versicherungs-AG (Wuba), its major subsidiary DARAG Deutsche Versicherungs und Ruckversicherungs-AG (DARAG) and other minor subsidiaries from entities associated with J.C. Flowers & Co. LLC.

AIG's stock is traded on the New York Stock Exchange, as well as stock exchanges in London, Paris, Switzerland and Tokyo.

It's not easy being Greenberg

In March 2005, Maurice "Hank" Greenberg, who had been with AIG for over four decades, was forced out of his CEO position by the company's board of directors, due to state and federal investigations into the company's accounting practices. He was replaced by Martin J. Sullivan, another longtime AIG veteran. Also pushed out was former CFO Howard Smith, who

Visit the Vault Finance Career Channel at www.vault.com/finance — with insider firm profiles, message boards, the Vault Finance Job Board and more.

VAULT CAREER LIBRARY   37

was replaced by Steven J. Bensinger, formerly a senior VP, treasurer and comptroller at AIG. In November 2006, former top Citigroup official Robert Willumstad was elected chairman of AIG.

Greenberg's departure was only part of the fallout related to a spate of bad publicity endured by AIG. An investigation by former New York State Attorney General Eliot Spitzer and the Securities Exchange Committee revealed that a reinsurance deal with Berkshire Hathaway's General Reinsurance unit in 2001 led to an artificial boost in AIG's balance sheet. In May 2005, Spitzer's team of state insurance regulators filed civil charges against AIG, Greenberg and Smith, accusing the men of engaging in fraud to falsely inflate stock price; Greenberg denied the allegations.

AIG restated its earnings in 2005 because of questions raised by these transactions and, in February 2006, agreed to pay $1.64 billion to resolve allegations that it used deceptive practices to mislead investors. That settlement required that the company amend its business procedures to guarantee proper behavior in the future. AIG has thus retained an independent consultant to review its internal controls as part of the 2006 settlement.

Starr Wars: Greenberg strikes back

The situation between AIG and Greenberg has had so many developments, they can be hard to keep track of. Here's a quick timeline:

On August 7, 2006, Hank Greenberg sued three AIG employees alleging that they tried to destroy the four companies he now heads under C.V. Starr & Co— Starr Tech, Starr Aviation, C.V. Starr & Co. and American International Marine Agency. He charged that the staffers misappropriated confidential information, stole employees and tried to discredit Starr. While Greenberg was chairman of AIG, there was a cozy relationship with the Starr agencies, and those agencies had all of its policies underwritten by AIG. When Greenberg left AIG, that relationship was severed. By latest count, C.V. Starr owns about 47 million shares of AIG, while affiliate Starr International Co. owns more that 300 million. Starr's complaint came in response to a July 2006 suit filed by AIG against two former AIG Aviation employees now employed by Starr. AIG alleged the two staffers used confidential information to recruit more than 20 AIG staffers to Starr Aviation.

In March 2007, an independent committee appointed by the Starr Foundation, which Greenberg controls, cleared him of any wrongdoing. The report addressed Spitzer's allegations from the year before; in a statement to The New York Times, current New York State Attorney General Andrew Cuomo said, "We are not surprised that a foundation controlled by Greenberg issued a report attempting to resolve him from wrongdoing."

Then in June 2007, Greenberg offered, in a court filing, testimony from three AIG employees who he said would discredit any allegations of wrongdoing of which the state of New York had accused him. In his filing, Greenberg explained that the state accused false information from him as the reason behind the drop in market price of AIG stock.

Later that month, AIG sued Greenberg and former CFO Smith, seeking $1 billion in a suit alleging that AIG was "exposed to liability for violations of the federal securities laws and potential criminal liability." The lawsuit claims that the two executives should be responsible for legal costs incurred, an internal investigation, a city fine of $100 million, and two settlements totaling $825 million.

Hit hard

A slew of financial giants reported billions in write-downs in the third quarter earnings of 2007, and AIG was no different. The insurance giant attributed the troubled mortgage market as its reason for the $2.2 billion reduction in value of the company's investments.

Net income for the quarter fell a whopping 27 percent to slightly more than $3 billion, and analysts were concerned that the worst wasn't over. AIG execs expected a possible write-down of $550 million in the fourth quarter of 2007. Bloomberg News reported that the sour results might help "shake up" AIG, which it said was the third-worst performer in the Dow Jones Industrial Average in 2007.

Heading into the 21st century

In September 2007, AIG completed its acquisition of the 21st Century Insurance Group, acquiring nearly 40 percent of 21st Century that it did not previously own. The acquisition made 21st Century a wholly owned subsidiary of AIG. The insurance giant paid $22 per share or $813 million for 21st Century, whose board of directors unanimously approved the merger in May 2008. The newly merged company will be called aigdirect.com and it will be headquartered in Wilmington, Del., and Woodland Hills, Calif. Bruce Marlow, CEO of 21st Century, will take the helm as president.

Visit the Vault Finance Career Channel at **www.vault.com/finance** — with insider firm profiles, message boards, the Vault Finance Job Board and more.

VAULT CAREER LIBRARY   39

The acquisition would seem to be a hit for AIG, but some of the insurer's employees were singing the blues. AIG has incorporated its auto unit with 21st Century, a move that eliminated roughly 600 jobs, or about 11 percent of the combined workforce. A spokesman for AIG said that most of the layoffs involved call center staff, claims handlers and administrative workers.

Taking over the world

AIG acquired 21st Century in 2007, but the finance and insurance company didn't stop there. In mid-August 2007, AIG entered into a deal to acquire Wurttembergische und Badische Versicherungs-AG (Wuba), its major subsidiary DARAG Deutsche Versicherungs und Ruckversicherungs-AG (DARAG) and other minor subsidiaries from entities associated with J.C. Flowers & Co. LLC.

Wuba offers property and casualty, marine, personal lines, and accident and health insurance through 2,500 broker relationships throughout Germany. The acquisition was completed in October 2007.

Taking account

AIG had told investors that through November 2007, it was due to write-down about $1 billion in assets related to losses on subprime mortgages. But in February 2008, an internal audit from PricewaterhouseCoopers found "material weakness" in AIG's internal accounting standards and assessed these write-downs at $4.88 billion. The news constitutes a major blow for AIG's reputation on Wall Street, which has been shaky ever since the accounting scandals of 2005.

If Wall Street was steamed before, it was absolutely flabbergasted when AIG ended up writing down $11.1 billion on the year, a sum $10 billion greater than originally forecast. These write-downs contributed to AIG's largest quarterly loss ever, $5.3 billion, and cut year-end profits by more than 50 percent year-over-year: AIG earned $6.2 billion in 2007, as opposed to $14 billion in 2006. The same day AIG released these earnings, CEO Martin Sullivan announced that Martin Cassano, chief of the financial products unit responsible for the write-downs, was retiring from AIG, effective March 2008.

A new chief

In June 2008, AIG ousted Sullivan, naming Robert Willumstad, who had served on the firm's board of directors since 2006 as CEO. AIG was hoping that Willumstad, a former president and chief operating officer of Citigroup, would be able to turn around its flailing financial state. In the first quarter of 2008, AIG booked a $7.8 billion loss, mostly due to defaulted loans stemming from the subprime mortgage crisis.

Over and out

In July 2008, AIG announced that its board director Richard Holbrooke was resigning. Holbrooke joined AIG's board in 2001, formerly served as a U.S. United Nations ambassador and is currently vice chairman of Perseus, a private equity firm. Holbrooke, whose resignation was effective immediately, did not give a reason for leaving, but told *The New York Times*, "I didn't feel I could continue to give [the position] the time it deserved."

The third loss

The second quarter of 2008 brought about AIG's third quarterly loss, due mostly to the frail housing market and still-bleak credit markers. The net loss of $5.36 billion was a stark contrast to the $4.28 billion in net income the firm posted in the 2007 second quarter. Revenue for the quarter was also down, decreasing to $19.9 billion from $31.2 billion in the previous year. Following the posting of these results, things went from bad to worse for AIG, culminating in the Federal Reserve bailout.

GETTING HIRED

Discover the culture

Learn about AIG's culture, benefits, diversity hiring policies and career development efforts at www.aig.com/careers. Job openings are available on the site, too, and applicants can send or e-mail resumes to addresses listed in the "career opportunities" sections. Qualifications and requirements for applicants vary by department. For more information, applicants can call AIG's job hotline. Potential hires should be pleased to know that the company offers a variety of

Visit the Vault Finance Career Channel at **www.vault.com/finance** — with insider firm profiles, message boards, the Vault Finance Job Board and more.

VAULT CAREER LIBRARY   41

benefits, including extensive medical, life and disability insurance (naturally), as well as work/life benefits such as public transportation subsidies, parental leave, back-up child care and, for the children of employees, assistance in choosing and applying to colleges. One insider says that AIG "rarely" recruits from schools, and usually culls candidates from recruiting firms instead. Interviews are "conducted by HR, the hiring manager and usually another manager." One insider notes "the interview process was rather short, which is not typical for an analyst role." Usually, you'll "meet with the senior manager of the department, supervisor and analyst." Just beware—sometimes "management makes roles more glamorous than they are," and "promises numerous things and fails to deliver." Either way, if you accept a job at AIG, expect to buck up—when you arrive you are expected to perform.

OUR SURVEY SAYS

Mind your Ps and Qs

Working at AIG can be "very formal," one insider reports, adding that frequently, "you must ask for authority directly up the chain without going over anyone's head." This can be "good, because there is structure and you always know who to go to," but there is also "a lot of red tape and therefore it is sometimes hard to get things done because of the amount of people that have to approve every decision." While the corporate culture is "several notches below investment banking" in terms of intensity, it's still "intense for the insurance field."

Sources note that "working at AIG has its benefits and drawbacks like any other global financial services firm." One insider calls the culture "very results-oriented," but another says the culture is "starting to get like Wal-Mart in the sense of 'How cheap and how fast can it be done?'" The source adds, "Like any shop that uses this thinking, you get short-term gains, but in the long run, the process and product suffer."

In part due to the decentralized organized structure, insiders say that AIG engenders an entrepreneurial environment. "AIG encourages entrepreneurship and rewards it," reports one contact. "If you made a wrong decision, and if you had AIG's best interest in mind, there will be no adverse consequences. But don't make the same mistake twice." Another respondent concurs that "as a very strong company, AIG can permit you to create something by yourself if you play the game."

The loose environment unfortunately doesn't extend to AIG's dress code, which "is corporate—men in suits, women in suits and dresses." Not everyone is comfortable working for a large global corporation however, with one source saying, "It's obviously a very large company, and in a lot of ways it seems way too structured." But where one sees too much structure, another sees opportunity. A contact notes, "AIG is a large company with a diverse workforce and offers lots of work locations for business types." Another notes that while "the company is an ideal place if you are mid-career ... if you are young, motivated, bright, ambitious and want to develop a career, this might not be the best place for you."

Putting in the time

Face time required depends largely on your location. One insider says, "Hours are very good—at the home office in New York it is 9 to 5, and by 5:01 p.m., you could hear a pin drop since everybody has left for the day." The source adds, "Many people come in late and take one-and-a-half- or two-hour lunches, and nobody seems to notice or say anything." Another, though, says, "AIG is not a 9-to-5 company. If you want to be really successful, you must be willing to go the extra mile." One contact says that the company has a "Work 'til you drop" culture. And yet another says that he and his colleagues "work hard," but management "will often buy lunch for employees if under deadline." An insider reports that the New York offices offer a perk in the form of the company cafeteria "which is cheaper than most of the restaurants in the area." Another gives the "stock purchase plan" a thumbs-up.

Reports yet another worker, "Since AIG's headquarters are in New York, the environment is a little more tense and intense than it might be otherwise." But there is a method to this system. AIG employees are willing to work hard, because, well, they can get rich doing so. "They do pay well, and there's a lot of room for growth," says one. Adds another, "There are a lot of very rich people working for AIG. I'm not talking about the get-rich-quick thing you hear about Silicon Valley. You may not see instant gratification for your efforts, but in the long run, the rewards can be great." Several respondents report that there's an unspoken rule at the firm—"if you make it to two years and want to continue, then you are a lifer. A perfect fit."

Needs some polish

Insiders report that the company's diversity efforts leave quite a bit to be desired, especially diversity efforts with respect to women. One respondent reports that "like at most companies, diversity is just an HR-driven program," and "as a male, even I found the jokes to be crude, reflecting a lack of emphasis on education and polish found at other financial firms." A female source admits that she feels

Visit the Vault Finance Career Channel at www.vault.com/finance — with insider firm profiles, message boards, the Vault Finance Job Board and more.

VAULT CAREER LIBRARY   43

"angry, frustrated and upset" regarding her treatment at the firm, adding that AIG "is the only place I have ever experienced discrimination." The contact goes on to say that she and several female colleagues "were made conscious of [their] age and sex on more than one occasion."

Pretty perky

AIG offers its staff the usual array of benefits, including medical, dental and life insurance, as well as a retirement plan, tuition reimbursement program and a stock purchase plan where employees can buy the company's stock at a discounted rate. The company also offers college coaching for employees' college-bound children and scholarship programs. One contact notes, "My son got a $12,000-a-year scholarship from the company." In addition, AIG offers its staff an adoption assistance program and a pre-tax dependant care reimbursement account, which enables eligible employees to use pre-tax dollars to pay for certain expenses related to caring for dependent children, parents or other family members. And for those in New York in the summer, these rewards include a "blast" of a company picnic.

Although the company is one of the largest insurance providers in the world, some contacts think the plan it offers could be better. "They actually offer surprisingly poor insurance benefits, especially in light of AIG being one of the world's largest insurance companies," says one source. "There's a good 401(k), though, and an OK stock option plan."

AIG also provides a few innovative award programs like its Service Award Program that offers gifts to staffers dedicated to service after specified periods of continuous employment, the Big Idea Program that grants financial awards for ideas outside of an individual's job responsibilities that result in a solution/potential benefit to the company, and the Talent Search award that offers financial rewards to employees for the referral of individuals who are hired for full-time employment.

What's in store

As far as the future of AIG goes, there's no denying that "the company is going through tough times currently given problems in credit markets." But, as one insider points out, "the company is strong" and "as long as there is insurance, there will always be claims." After all, "more people are suing and more claims are coming in—that's job security for claims professionals." Still, "the company has a lot of excess fat" and could "cut back on some of its employees and management."

Alliance Data

17655 Waterview Pkwy.
Dallas, TX 75252
Phone: (972) 348-5100
Fax: (972) 348-5335
www.alliancedata.com

THE STATS

Employer Type: Public Company
Ticker Symbol: ADS (NYSE)
Chairman & CEO: J. Michael (Mike)
　Parks
President & COO: John W. Scullion
Revenue: $2.3 billion (FYE 12/07)
Net Income: $164.06 million
No. of Employees: 9,300 worldwide
No. of Offices: 60 worldwide

EMPLOYMENT CONTACT

See "careers" at
www.alliancedata.com

Visit the Vault Finance Career Channel at **www.vault.com/finance** — with
insider firm profiles, message boards, the Vault Finance Job Board and more.

VAULT CAREER LIBRARY　　45

THE SCOOP

Credit masters

Alliance Data Systems provides transaction, credit and marketing services to over 600 clients, including retailers, oil companies, utilities, supermarkets and financial services companies. Alliance Data is the second largest outsourcer of retail private-label credit cards, with approximately 90 million accounts. Ranked on the S&P 400, Alliance Data's sales have tripled since it went public in 2001.

Alliance Data was the result of a 1996 merger of JC Penney's transaction services business and The Limited Inc.'s credit card bank operation, both of which were acquired by venture capital firm Welsh, Carson, Anderson and Stowe; the two businesses were combined to then create Alliance Data. When the company was freed from its ties to its parent companies, it was able to court outside business.

Almost private

In May 2007, Alliance Data agreed to be taken private by The Blackstone Group, in a deal worth some $7.8 billion—about $81.75 per share, plus the assumption of more than $1 billion of Alliance debt. Alliance's shareholders approved the acquisition in August 2007, and the deal was expected to close in the fourth quarter 2007. However, like so many of the deals taking place as the housing and financial markets were beginning to crumble, this one took a detour through court, as Blackstone failed to stump up the cash to go through with it.

Despite concerns that the deal wouldn't make it past regulators, not to mention the increased level of difficulty in securing any sort of financing in the post-credit crunch world, Alliance Data sued Blackstone on the grounds that the private equity firm pulled out of the deal without good reason. Blackstone refuted the charge, and is currently defending itself to avoid having to pay a $170 million breakup fee.

Contract extensions

In the space of 10 days at the beginning of July 2008, Alliance announced that it had signed deals extending its contract to provide services to two of its major clients. The National Geographic Society extended Alliance subsidiary

Epsilon's contract to continue to host its e-mail platform until 2011. And top 10 customer New York & Co. signed a deal to have Alliance continue to manage its own-label credit card unit, extending a relationship that stretches back more than 12 years.

Outsourcing hat trick

Alliance Data's main focus is—and will continue to be—managing and facilitating interactions between retailers and consumers through the three segments of its business: transaction, credit and marketing services. Transaction services include processing of sales transactions, account processing and billing services. Its credit services business involves private label credit card programs and gift card services. In addition to the processing of these financial transactions, Alliance Data stands out by providing marketing services, thereby allowing clients to outsource management of the entire financial relationship. The company's marketing services includes creating and managing loyalty programs.

Alliance Data's private-label credit card business has been a huge profit generator for the company, with finance charges being a major source of income. This sector has stayed profitable with the addition of new retail contracts, and the renewal of existing ones. In late 2006, the company signed a long-term agreement with Cruise Management International to provide co-branded credit card services for cruise industry customers. Also, in 2007, it signed a multi-year renewal agreement with American Signature Inc., a major furniture retailer. In November 2007, Alliance landed a multi-year agreement to provide payment processing services to more than 5,500 7-Eleven convenience stores nationwide.

Alliance stands apart from the pack of its competitors in its ability to provide marketing services. Most of its closest competitors simply serve as the outsourcing solution for the processing of financial transactions, such as payment and billing processing between companies and its customers. Alliance Data differs in that it handles loyalty programs and marketing strategies.

Alliance Data also runs the Canadian AIR MILES Rewards Program, a coalition loyalty program that more than two-thirds of all Canadian households participate in.

Visit the Vault Finance Career Channel at www.vault.com/finance — with insider firm profiles, message boards, the Vault Finance Job Board and more.

VAULT CAREER LIBRARY   47

Banner year

The third quarter of 2007 was the strongest in Alliance Data's history. Overall revenue increased 14 percent to a record $575.5 million, compared to $506.6 million in the third quarter of 2006. Double-digit growth in the firm's AIR MILES Reward Program in Canada, U.S. marketing (Epsilon) and private label services accounted for the majority of Alliance's revenue and earnings increases.

Big picture

But for the full year, the financial picture was slightly shakier. Annual revenue came in at $2.29 billion, a jump from $1.99 billion in 2006, but net income for 2007 was down to $164.06 million from $189.6 million the previous year. (The costs associated with the Blackstone merger were largely to blame for the losses.) The firm painted a rosy outlook for 2008, however, and so far hasn't disappointed. Alliance brought in $507.2 million in revenue in the second quarter of 2008, up from the $481.8 million it posted for the second quarter of 2007. Net income was also up, to $46.9 million from $44.1 million.

GETTING HIRED

Keep apace

Alliance Data says it has a "fast-paced, friendly environment that supports career advancement," and prides itself in the "diversity of its associates." Also, according to the firm, it's looking for "talented people who are eager to contribute ideas and take action to keep our momentum strong." If you think you're up to the challenge, go to www.alliancedata.com/careers.html and start building your resume through its system. The firm posts job openings with detailed descriptions of duties.

American Express

World Financial Center
200 Vesey St.
New York, NY 10285
Phone: (212) 640-2000
www.americanexpress.com

CUSTOMER GROUPS

Global Business-To-Business
    Business Travel
    Commercial Card
    Merchant Business
    Network Services
Global Consumer
    Consumer Travel
    Customer Service Network
    Prepaid Products
    Proprietary Consumer Cards
    Small-Business Services

THE STATS

Employer Type: Public Company
Ticker Symbol: AXP (NYSE)
Chairman & CEO: Kenneth I. Chenault
Revenue: $27.7 billion (FYE 12/07)
Net Income: $4 billion (FYE 12/07)
No. of Employees: 65,000+
No. of Offices: 650+ in the U.S.

KEY COMPETITORS

Discover
JPMorgan Chase
MasterCard
Visa

UPPERS

- "The quality of the people" you work with
- "Flexible" working hours—the firm is "very accommodating"

DOWNERS

- "Bureaucratic"
- Average salaries

Visit the Vault Finance Career Channel at **www.vault.com/finance** — with
insider firm profiles, message boards, the Vault Finance Job Board and more.

VAULT CAREER LIBRARY   49

THE SCOOP

The rise of Ameriprise

American Express is more than a plastic card. It's also a huge, diversified financial company with about $30 billion in annual revenue. In addition to its well-known line of credit cards, Amex offers customers a wide variety of products and services, including traveler's checks, expense management services and travel services. But with the highest-spending cardholders in the industry, the 159-year-old company has decided in recent years to shed some major business lines and focus on its strength—those well-known plastic cards.

The Minneapolis-based American Express Financial Advisors—comprising more than 12,000 financial advisors and the Platinum Financial Services group—was spun off in September 2005, as an independent publicly traded company, Ameriprise Financial, listed on the New York Stock Exchange under the symbol "AMP." Amex shareholders received all of the common shares of Ameriprise under the terms of the spin-off, with one share of Ameriprise common stock for every five shares of Amex common stock outstanding.

More recently, in early 2008, American Express Bank was sold to Standard Chartered. American Express Bank was Amex's international bank, which offered financial services for wealthy individuals and other banks outside the United States.

Plastic's plight

American Express had a strong 2007. Revenue was up 10 percent from 2006 to $27.7 billion, and net income increased 8 percent to $4 billion—despite a $438 million charge for the fourth quarter of 2007, a slowdown in U.S. consumer spending, and a rise in delinquencies and loan write-offs.

Buffalo '41

Back in 1841, Buffalo, N.Y., was a wild and thriving frontier town. It was the western terminus of the Erie Canal and a bridge for people and goods between the developed eastern states and the wide open Northwest Territory. A man named Henry Wells recognized a need in the boomtown for a service that would provide safe transport of permit goods, valuables and bank remittances in and out of Buffalo. Wells started an express service, first carrying precious metals and securities between Albany and Buffalo (the trip took four days). Wells merged his service with two competitors in 1850 to form American Express. The leadership of the new firm proved accommodating, even though the company's directors nixed an idea for expansion into the then-gold rush state of California, where President Wells and Secretary William G. Fargo started a new firm there in 1852—Wells Fargo—while continuing their responsibilities at American Express.

American Express merged with a competing company in 1868. That year, William Fargo took over the presidency of American Express from Henry Wells. His younger brother, J.C. Fargo, succeeded him. Under the younger Fargo's 33-year tenure, the American Express Money Order was developed. In 1891, the famed American Express Travelers Cheque arrived and by 1901 over $6 million of the checks had been purchased. The firm created a travel department in 1915. When the U.S. government nationalized all express services after WWI, American Express concentrated on its money and travel businesses.

American Express services enjoyed a boost during the increased overseas activity of World War II and its aftermath. By the 1950s, it became apparent that an American Express charge card would be a logical extension of the company's services. Introduced in 1958, the card enjoyed immediate popularity. Within three months, half a million people wouldn't leave home without their American Express card. In the 1960s, when the globalization of markets picked up, sales of American Express Travelers Cheques increased exponentially, and the company established a firm presence in overseas markets.

Focusing on what works

In 2007, American Express decided to focus more on its core business of credit cards, a decision that resulted in the pending sale of its 88-year-old international banking unit (American Express Bank) to a London-based emerging markets bank, Standard Chartered.

Standard Chartered paid for AEB with cash on hand and credit lines. The deal, which closed in 2008, called for Standard Chartered to pay for the net asset value of the bank, plus a premium of $300 million, a total of around $860 million. In addition, the bank will pay dividends to American Express for 18 months beginning in 2008. Standard Chartered, which is currently most profitable in

Visit the Vault Finance Career Channel at **www.vault.com/finance** — with insider firm profiles, message boards, the Vault Finance Job Board and more.

VAULT CAREER LIBRARY   **51**

Asia, expects that the purchase of the bank will save the company about $100 million per year.

Settlements bring total payments to $4 billion

American Express emerged victorious in early November 2007 when Visa agreed to settle in a lawsuit that alleged that Visa and MasterCard had worked with lenders to exclude American Express from the bank-issued card market. Visa agreed to pay $2.25 billion to American Express; under the agreement, which stems from a 2004 antitrust suit, American Express will receive $945 million by the end of March 2008 and then up to $70 million per quarter for the next 16 quarters.

Less than a year later, in June 2008, American Express announced that it agreed to drop a lawsuit alleging that MasterCard had illegally blocked American Express from the bank-issued card business in the U.S. Under the terms of that agreement, MasterCard will pay American Express up to $1.8 billion in quarterly installments over three years.

Subject to certain performance criteria, American Express is expected to receive more than $4 billion for agreeing to drop its claims against the two credit card networks. The combined antitrust settlement is the largest in U.S. history.

Customer satisfaction

A nationwide survey in October 2007 by J.D. Power & Associates placed American Express at the top of the pack when it came to customer satisfaction in the credit card industry. The survey found Amex at the top of the major 10 credit card companies in the United States. Amex brags that it offers many benefits and services at no additional costs to clients, as well as around-the-clock customer service via telephone and online.

Losing their keys

American Express customers who prefer the (somewhat) traditional form of paying with their credit card can breathe a little easier. In March 2008, American Express announced plans to drop its six-year-old "express pay" keychain mini-card, which was available to consumers in certain cities, such as New York and Phoenix. American Express is working on further developing the convenience angle for card users, including expanding the technology behind its "contactless" credit cards and working to get more merchants to use contactless readers.

Expressly unimpressive

Though not posting titanic losses like some of its counterparts, American Express did sink, reporting in July 2008 a second-quarter net income of $653 million, down from the $1.0 billion it brought in the second quarter of 2007. Revenue looked a little better for the company, rising 8.7 percent to $7.5 billion, up from $6.9 billion a year ago. Analysts indicated that Amex's overall results were likely an effect of the weakened economy, which trickled down even to the firm's comparatively affluent customers.

GETTING HIRED

Browse and learn

"The selection process is fairly stringent," says an insider in recruiting. "Ultimately, only one applicant out of 25 gets hired." Generally, the recruiting process begins at www.americanexpress.com, where a detailed career section is maintained. Applicants can search for jobs by function and location or create a job search agent that sends an e-mail when promising openings pop up. "Jobs are posted for one or two weeks," notes a source. "Online applicants are sent notification of receipt of application. Applicants of interest will be contacted rather quickly, once posting ends."

The company also recruits at a broad range of colleges and universities in various regions around the world, including top-tier MBA programs and undergraduate institutions. The campus selection and assessment process involves several rounds of structured interviews, which are focused on candidates answering specific questions based on American Express core competencies.

One insider reports a fairly streamlined interview process, noting, "I first applied online, was interviewed by a panel of three that included the head of HR and then had a final interview with the president." Another describes going through "two interviews, meeting with a manager, a director and a VP." But the interview process can vary somewhat, according to department. One insider reports, "Most people interview with between three and five people,

Visit the Vault Finance Career Channel at **www.vault.com/finance** — with insider firm profiles, message boards, the Vault Finance Job Board and more.

VAULT CAREER LIBRARY   53

including the hiring manager, the hiring manager's boss, peers of the hiring manager and possibly would-be peers of the interviewee." Another contact reports a stress-free process, noting, "I think the reason why I was hired quite easily was because of my experience."

One contact gives a blow-by-blow of his experience landing at American Express. "All available job listings are located on the company web site," he says. "Upon online application I was contacted by the human resources department for a preliminary phone-based interview. After the initial weed out, resumes are forwarded to the hiring manager who directly contacts the candidates they want to interview. The second-round interview is directly with the hiring manager and the third round is with senior management."

The interview questions vary. One insider explains, "At the lower levels, the interview process is basically a test-your-knowledge sort of interview combined with personality matching. No particular questions stand out in my mind, but the general sense of the interview was comfortable and low stress. Just make sure you're very familiar with Excel and PowerPoint, and possibly writing macros." One customer service representative remembers getting "behavioral questions" such as "'Describe a situation in which you gave outstanding customer service' or 'Describe a situation where you had to work with a difficult co-worker.'" Another says that the interviews questions center around four areas: "customers, implementation, results and communication." There are also "standard interview questions" that focus on "your weaknesses and strengths," and "long-term plans."

The more you know

One source who started with the firm as an intern in the risk management department praises the program, adding, "I gained so much valuable knowledge both in the technical area as well as financial." Indeed, veterans of the internship program say that internships help the company try out potential full-time employees—and help interns try out the company for size. "Many interns have special projects during their summers, but I worked in a regular line position in card retention," says a former summer (and now permanent) employee. "I believe it was easier to get a full-time position after having interned here because I demonstrated that I was a good fit. It was also easier for me to get hired at other companies after interning here." In the firm's summer internship, "pay is competitive," and a source says, "It's much easier to get hired after an internship—if you perform well."

OUR SURVEY SAYS

Nurturing Amex

American Express says the firm is a "great company to work for," and has a corporate culture that "nourishes diversity," "values experience" and "mentors its youth." Insiders also call the corporate culture everything from "very relaxed" and "very family-oriented" to "conservative" and "employee-focused." One notes that the "corporate culture is quite good," and although some sources have "culture conflicts," "people are all nice to each other," "with no bias at all." Another contact says, "The most positive aspect of my tenure has been the quality of the people I have worked with," adding, "My current group is comprised of some of the most intelligent and genuinely decent people that I have ever worked with." One insider agrees, saying, "You can develop good friendships with the people at the company, and you're always in a position to move around and try new things. There are many opportunities at Amex."

While the company has "some groups [that] can be much more political and have high school-like cliques," "this is not universal, and even in those groups, you can find a few fantastic people." Another source says the culture is "extremely supportive and conducive to professional and personal growth."

But in a company as large as American Express, it comes as no surprise that insiders have conflicting views of the company's culture. (Amex has operations in all 50 states plus the District of Columbia, so aspects such as pay, benefits and even culture will vary from region to region.) One source uses a slew of adjectives—"smart, analytical, consensus-based, respectful, diverse [and] competitive"—to praise the company. Others paint the picture of a company that is "bureaucratic and closed to new ideas unless those ideas come from upper management," and trying to pull off impossibilities like "changing four tires on a car moving at 90 mph."

One former insider from the Midwest region says the "corporate culture was mostly Midwest in nature with a very strong emphasis on understanding diversity and cultural differences as a positive to the workforce." "I was very impressed with the people at American Express from top managers on down to my team members," says another source. "We were a very diverse group and all groups were very well represented and their needs were addressed in a very professional and caring way." One contact says the company "wants to win in the marketplace," but notes, "Conflicting and overlapping efforts in separate business units often causes silo mentality and passive aggressive behaviors." Another critic calls American Express "a very poorly managed organization,"

Visit the Vault Finance Career Channel at www.vault.com/finance — with insider firm profiles, message boards, the Vault Finance Job Board and more.

VAULT CAREER LIBRARY   55

with "narrow-minded managers who are unwilling to learn from mistakes" and who "preach the latest buzzwords about diversity and teamwork but manage the old-fashioned way." However, the contact admits the firm is "making some progress towards reengineering its processes and systems." Another lauds the office's open seating arrangement, where managers are "visible and contactable at all times," and "are there to help and answer questions—and it's common knowledge that the managers sit below us on the corporate pyramid and are there to support us. Our customers are above us."

Another contact, who has only positive things to say about the firm, brags that "working for Amex is great, especially in the finance department." The source explains, "The finance group consists of some of the best people I have worked with, all dedicated to their jobs, and leading innovation and business profitability using some of the most current theories in finance."

Dressing down

The company allows for year-round business casual dress in most offices. "Dress code is casual except when clients visit," says a source. You'll have to do it by the book, though. "We have a dress policy with specifics on what is acceptable 'business casual' and what is not," says one insider. "No denim of any kind, anytime, on any day." Another says it's "formal always" where she works (in Minneapolis). Still another adds that the dress code is "flexible," and "every Friday and the day before any public holidays are casual days." One source calls the code "generally casual" and adds that "although women aren't supposed to wear flip-flops in the summer, that rule is never enforced." As far as the aesthetics of the firm's offices, one contact notes that it "varies by location," but says, "generally, they're above average."

Pretty accommodating

While working hours "depend on your team leader and your clients," they are "flexible," says one insider, adding that "you don't need to come in at 9 a.m. strictly, and if you're late, you can leave late to make it up." And "the needs of employees are very much attended to," so "if you need to pick up your child early, arrangements are willingly made to accommodate all your needs." Staffers also have the "ability to work from home and teleconference into meetings. Amex prides itself on maintaining a good work/life balance, and it shows."

And although the company expects an honest day's work, respondents say they aren't locked in the office indefinitely. "Most jobs don't have any pressure to bill, and there is no requirement to stick around for 'face time,'" says a source. "However, jobs are meaty and often require long hours. I generally work 55 to 60 hours a week." Others put the target a little lower, and most report never having to work weekends. "Although there were times when extra hours were needed, the leadership model dictates that employees should be able to perform their weekly job functions within 35 hours," remembers one former insider. Special arrangements can be accommodated. "The culture is fairly supportive of flexible work schedules," says one source who takes advantage of the company's generosity in this regard. "Individuals are accountable for themselves."

The 411 on salaries

Insiders have different takes when it comes to compensation. One New York contact says that while "salaries are slightly lower than average for financial services," employees still receive "four weeks vacation, plus holidays and four summer flex days, so it's not too bad." Another source reports that "the salary is competitive with other major firms. Bonuses are paid out on a bell curve so that only so many people will receive the highest possible." Sometimes it pays to come in from the outside. "For experienced hires, salary ranges are wide for similar positions," says an insider. "This is because Amex has to pay market rates for external hires but pays less to people who transfer internally. The result is that external hires make $10,000 to $12,000 more per year in the same position as an internal transfer."

Pay is standard for entry-level hires and is based on competitive regional salary ranges. Though one source comments that "employee benefits should be given more emphasis," the company offers a variety of perks and benefits, which include "tuition reimbursement; a variety of health care options, life insurance, stock options, vacation purchase plan, pensions, 401(k), many employee programs with large retailers, and the opportunity to win tickets to Amex-sponsored events." There's also a "lot of advancement opportunities across multiple lines of business," and an "excellent pay structure with peripheral benefits and perks."

Take the opportunities

American Express is trying to quicken the pace when it comes to training. "For several years, training was sparse," reports one contact. "It is picking up again, mainly because many of the midlevel managers haven't ever attended appropriate training and it's needed." Another insider says, "You are given

Visit the Vault Finance Career Channel at **www.vault.com/finance** — with insider firm profiles, message boards, the Vault Finance Job Board and more.

VAULT CAREER LIBRARY

57

endless opportunities to better your leadership skills and it is encouraged that you take part in a variety of training sessions. Opportunities for advancement depend on the leadership teams working together, but there are always other areas that consider your knowledge and years of experience a bonus to the organization." Another notes that "opportunities for advancement seem hard," and when it comes to promotions, superiors "only consider your management skills, but never consider how long you've been working here."

One contact says that while "opportunities for advancement easily exist for analysts, there are not as many once you get to the director level, and vice president positions are very hard to come by." But another says, "Amex encourages you to move to a new position approximately every year, if you so desire," and "they recognize that things may become stale and a new environment and new challenges can help you grow as an employee," adding that they encourage staffers to explore international opportunities as well. To advance, an MBA might be a good investment. "An MBA is not required for upward movement," says an insider. "However, it seems anyone under 35 has one. So do the math." Another insider notes that "if you have a strong desire to advance," relocating might be an option—especially to Amex's offices in "New York and Phoenix."

Join the club

"There is plenty of diversity in this company," assures one insider, adding that "American Express has diversity clubs and encourages employees to be a part of them." Still, another contact notes that "it should push and promote programs and initiatives that will give equal treatment to women and minorities." That contact adds that the firm should "support and encourage our lawmakers to pass bills that will guarantee employment and security of tenure to women." Another says that the firm is "receptive to all people," and others praise the company's efforts. "My particular office consists of many foreign nationals of both genders," says one employee. "Some of the highest ranking finance officers in the company are women."

Things can be different at a specific location. "Overall, Amex is very diverse, but not necessarily in all locations," notes a source. Another notes that "there are many nationalities, religions and backgrounds." But one insider says that while there is "good diversity in terms of race and sex, you don't see a lot of different opinions or ideas, because almost everyone comes from upper-middle-class or upper-class families and the same few business schools, banks and consulting firms."

Great expectations

Insiders seem to have high hopes for Amex's survival in the marketplace. "I joined Amex because it has an unusual position in the business as a premium product, and the outlook on Wall Street is extremely strong," says one insider. "American Express is known for excelling at innovative product development and strong marketing." Another contact adds that American Express is "one of the top 10 most recognized brands in the world" and "one of the top 100 most preferred employers to work for." Yet another puts it succinctly—"the only place this company is going is up."

Visit the Vault Finance Career Channel at **www.vault.com/finance** — with
insider firm profiles, message boards, the Vault Finance Job Board and more.

VAULT CAREER LIBRARY

59

American Family Insurance Group

6000 American Parkway
Madison, WI 53783-0001
Phone: (608) 249-2111
www.amfam.com

DEPARTMENTS

Actuarial
Claims
Education
Finance
Government Affairs & Compliance
Information Services (I/S)
Insurance
Underwriting

THE STATS

Employer Type: Private Company
Chairman & CEO: David R. Anderson
Revenue: $6.87 billion (FYE 12/07)
Net Income: $82.42 million
No. of Employees: 8,237

KEY COMPETITORS

Allstate
GEICO
Nationwide
Progressive
State Farm

EMPLOYMENT CONTACT

See "careers" at www.amfam.com

THE SCOOP

It all started with a car...

In 1927, in Madison, Wis., insurance salesman Herman Wittwer planted the seed of what eventually grew into American Family Insurance Group, supporting the firm's tentative early beginnings with farmers' premiums as the Farmers Mutual Automobile Insurance Company. After subsequently adding a host of other services, including sickness, accident, farm owners' and homeowners' insurance, the company changed its name to American Family Mutual Insurance Company in 1963.

More than 80 years (and a few name changes) later, the firm has proved that it's in the insurance game for the long haul. After making Fortune 500's list of top companies in 1996 (and debuting at No. 403), it has retained a spot every year since. In 2008, on the most recent Fortune 500 list, American Family Insurance came in at No. 352. Today, the firm offers a host of available policies, which includes everything from annuities to ranch insurance.

Recognizing the progressive

The firm has also managed to harvest a number of awards—including many that honor its progressive ideals. In 2007, Computerworld magazine honored AFIG as one of the 100 Best Places to Work in IT for the eighth year in a row. In the same year, the firm was voted Best Diversity Company by Diversity Careers in Engineering & Information Technology magazine. Hispanic Magazine also honored the firm in April 2007, giving it a spot on its annual "Top 100 Companies for Latinos" list.

Watching from behind the wheel

In 2006, AFIG instituted the TeenSafe Driver Program, a voluntary but free program for clients in 18 states that uses video cameras on the exterior and interior of vehicles driven by teens. The cameras, which record incidents of unsafe driving (such as sudden, extreme acceleration or braking), feed into a secure web site that allows parents and teens to review the videos online and make appropriate changes in driving patterns. So far, the program seems to be producing results—as of August 2007, the group said the program had decreased incidents of dangerous driving by approximately 70 percent since its inception.

Visit the Vault Finance Career Channel at **www.vault.com/finance** — with insider firm profiles, message boards, the Vault Finance Job Board and more.

VAULT CAREER LIBRARY   61

Finally free

After years of a long legal tug-of-war, a federal judge ruled in December 2007 that American Family Insurance had no obligation in a wrongful death lawsuit that had been brewing in the courts since 2003. The families of two teens, Aaron Rollins and Seth Bartell, who were fatally shot by John Jason McLaughlin inside a Minnesota high school, filed a suit seeking to claim damages from AFIG under McLaughlin's parents' policy. While the families' lawyers said that McLaughlin was suffering from mental illness and didn't perpetrate an intentional act, the firm, which had denied coverage for the damages, cited an "intentional-injury exclusion" clause in the McLaughlins' policy that ultimately cleared the company of accountability.

A greater good

Through the firm's corporate giving program, AFIG supplies financial support to charities such as United Way, Second Harvest Foodbank, the Red Cross and Neighborhood Housing Services. The program also awards scholarships, finances youth resources centers and supports employee volunteer hours dedicated to a variety of causes, including after school and mentoring programs. The firm financially assists community events in the 18 states in which it operates, ranging from Phoenix's Chinese Week Festival to local Women Chamber of Commerce programs.

Flood of claims

In 2008, American Family Insurance paid out approximately $8 million in claims to the victims of floods that had ravaged cities in the Midwest. In addition, the firm added that flood victims in Wisconsin will receive up to two months in additional time to make their required insurance premiums. The company currently provides insurance coverage for about 25 percent of all Wisconsin homes.

GETTING HIRED

Get on board

If you're interested in securing a seat on the AFIG train, be sure to point your browser to the "careers" link at www.amfam.com. There, you can check out the firm's "Discover Career Paths" section, which includes information about jobs ranging from the firm's well-known traditional insurance positions to public relations and marketing jobs. The site also includes guidelines on snagging an internship in addition to resume tips and FAQs about the interview process.

During your interviews, insiders say to expect questions "concerning insurance and how you feel about getting your license to help sell." One contact calls the process "very quick," consisting of just two interviews with "competency-based behavioral questions." Just be sure to know what you're talking about. Another insider says that "I remember that when I was asked a question, my answer had to provide a concrete example of what I was demonstrating."

OUR SURVEY SAYS

Reap the rewards

Insiders call the firm "extremely rewarding," "a great company to work for" with "a lot of opportunities for advancement." Hours tend to run "a normal Monday through Friday from 8:30 to 5:30" with a dress code that's "always professional." (Even an independent contractor with the company admits he "always" dresses formally.) Employees seem mostly happy with the corporate culture, which they call "responsive to suggestions."

Diversity, too, gets high marks from insiders, who say that "there is always a diverse group of individuals that work for American Family." The firm also "strives in equal employment opportunities for every race and ethnic background," adds one contact.

Visit the Vault Finance Career Channel at **www.vault.com/finance** — with insider firm profiles, message boards, the Vault Finance Job Board and more.

VAULT CAREER LIBRARY   63

AmeriCredit

801 Cherry St., Ste. 3900
Fort Worth, TX 76102
Phone: (817) 302-7000; 800-284-2271
www.americredit.com

DEPARTMENTS

ACF Investment Corp.
AFS Conduit Corp.
AFS Funding Corp.
AFS Funding Trust
AFS Management Corp.

THE STATS

Employer Type: Public Company
Ticker Symbol: ACF (NYSE)
Chairman: Clifton H. Morris, Jr.
President & CEO: Daniel E. (Dan) Berce
Revenue: $2.34 billion (FYE 6/07)
Net Income: $360.25 million
No. of Employees: 4,831
No. of Offices: 65

KEY COMPETITORS

Capital One
Consumer Portfolio
Credit Acceptance
Discover Financial Services
Wachovia/WFS Financial

EMPLOYMENT CONTACT

See "career seekers" at
www.americredit.com or call (866)
411-HR4U

THE SCOOP

Used cars

Cash America pawnshop executives Jack Daugherty, Clifton Morris and a group of investors created the country's first used-car chain in 1986. UrCarco also offered financing to customers with poor credit ratings, and from these modest beginnings grew a company that would eventually appear on the S&P 400. After a splashy IPO in 1989, the company got into financial trouble due to bad loans and a slumping market. After landing $10 million from Rainwater Management in 1991 and restructuring, the company changed its name to AmeriCredit in 1992.

The company sold off its used cars and beefed up its lending business by teaming up with credit-scoring firm Fair Issac to develop a credit-risk scorecard to avoid making bad loans. The company branched out in 1996 by buying Rancho Vista Mortgage, which became AmeriCredit Corp. of California. The Rancho Vista purchase allowed the company to build a home equity lending business. But three years later, it pulled the plug on its mortgage business and began focusing on car loans. The corporation launched an online network that allows dealers to send loan applications to lenders, called DealerTrack, in 2001.

Looking beyond subprime

The company began a strategy in 2007 to diversity its portfolio and originations to be less dependent on subprime loans, as subprime defaults in the mortgage market caused many casualties on Wall Street. The majority of AmeriCredit's business remains in the subprime credit range, and the fallout in the auto loan market has appeared far more minimal than in the mortgage market. AmeriCredit's leverage has shifted upward over the past year to reflect the decreased credit risk profile of its portfolio. The company's leverage ratio stood at 7.7 managed receivables to equity in June 2007. The change marks a new strategy for Americredit to redefine itself as a full-spectrum auto-finance firm, instead of a subprime lender.

Acquisitions and expansions

In January, AmeriCredit's operating subsidiary AmeriCredit Financial Services completed its purchase of Long Beach Acceptance Corp., which had been an auto finance subsidiary of ACC Capital Holdings. The buy cost

Visit the Vault Finance Career Channel at www.vault.com/finance — with insider firm profiles, message boards, the Vault Finance Job Board and more.

VAULT CAREER LIBRARY

65

AmeriCredit about $282.5 million in cash. In fiscal year 2007, AmeriCredit originated loans totaling $660 million through the LBAC platform.

AmeriCredit plans to relocate Long Beach collections and customer service operations from Orange, Calif., to Arlington, Tex., in January 2008 and to achieve full integration by the end of 2008. Long Beach currently markets its near-prime product to 1,500 dealers, but by the end of 2008, that product will be available to more than 15,000 active AmeriCredit dealers. "With the completion of this acquisition—and out acquisition of Bay View Acceptance last year—we are now a full-spectrum auto-finance company that is building relationships with and creating solutions for auto dealers and consumers across the country," Berce said in a statement.

In May 2006, the company purchased Bay View Acceptance Corp., which offers specific auto finance products, including extended term financings and higher loan-to-value advances to customers with prime credit bureau scores. Bay View operates from offices in Covina, Calif., and serves auto dealers in 32 states. During fiscal 2006, AmeriCredit originated loans totaling $672 million, respectively.

The company hopes that the two acquisitions will strengthen its position with dealers by offering more choices in credit dealers and expects to grow annual originations 10 percent to 15 percent annually over the long term. AmeriCredit expects Bay View's and Long Beach's higher-tier credit products to provide some improved stability and flexibility for the company.

AmeriCredit's average new loan size increased to $18,506 for fiscal 2007 from $17,354 in fiscal 2006, due to loans from the BVAC and LBAC platforms, which are usually higher in quality and larger in size. The average percentage rate for finance receivables purchased during fiscal 2007 decreased to 15.8 percent from 16.7 during fiscal 2006, due to lower average percentage rates on the BVAC and LBAC loans purchased.

"O Canada"

The company moved back into the Canadian market in May 2006 by establishing AmeriCredit Financial Services of Canada in Mississauga, Ontario. The company's underwriters operate from Mississauga with sales reps located across the nation. The company plans further Canadian expansion. AmeriCredit operated in Canada from 1998 to 2003, but left due to restructuring.

Looking to leases

AmeriCredit began a small pilot program offering leases straight to consumers in fiscal year 2007 through franchised dealers. The program currently serves only consumers with relatively high credit and only involves foreign cars. "Looking forward, we are not in a hurry to expand that program. It is a test," Berce said.

Running with the big dogs

The annual Fortune 1000 list of the nation's biggest companies saved a place for AmeriCredit. The firm made Fortune's list of the largest companies in the U.S. in 2008, moving up to the No. 805 spot from No. 916 in 2007. The ranking was based on the $2.34 billion in revenue the firm posted in 2008, up 26 percent from the previous year.

Mid-year report

AmeriCredit's fiscal year might end in the middle of year, but that doesn't mean its results weren't newsworthy. The firm brought in $2.54 billion in revenue for 2008, up from $2.34 billion in 2007. The firm did, however, sustain a net loss of $69 million, compared with net income of $360 million. And the fourth quarter was an especially rough: revenue decreased to $598.4 million from $625.4 million in the previous year's fourth quarter. The firm also posted a net loss of $150 million for the quarter compared with a profit of $87 million. Decreasing restructuring charges and a decline in loans (to $780 million from $2.41 billion on the quarter) largely led to less-than-rosy results.

GETTING HIRED

Play matchmaker

Under the "career seekers" section of www.americredit.com, those interested can view positions by location or position. And through the firm's online PeopleMatch Career Center, applicants can check out potential matches. If you prefer to give the firm a ring, you're in luck. Job seekers can call "The HR Connection" for additional information about positions at 1-866-411-HR4U.

Visit the Vault Finance Career Channel at **www.vault.com/finance** — with insider firm profiles, message boards, the Vault Finance Job Board and more.

VAULT CAREER LIBRARY   67

OUR SURVEY SAYS

No cure for AmeriCredit

The company says it bases its culture around "four fundamental principles: integrity, investment, innovation and information." It seems to be working. One insider says the company "really values its employees and sincerely cares about team member involvement." Another calls the culture "not only evident, but also contagious."

AmeriCredit offers a full array of benefits, from standard options like medical and dental coverage to "floating holidays" and "paid time off for volunteer work through AmeriCredit's Community Investment program."

Arthur J. Gallagher & Co.

The Gallagher Centre, 2 Pierce
Place
Itasca, IL 60143-3141
Phone: (630) 773-3800
Fax: (630) 285-4000
www.ajg.com

DEPARTMENTS

Employee Benefits Consulting
Insurance Brokerage
Risk Management Services

THE STATS

Employer Type: Public Company
Ticker Symbol: AJG (NYSE)
Chairman, President & CEO: J. Patrick
   Gallagher Jr.
Revenue: $1.62 billion (FYE 12/07)
Net Income: $138.8 million
No. of Employees: 9,329
No. of Offices: 250+

KEY COMPETITORS

Aon
Marsh & McLennan
Willis Group

UPPER

- "Relaxed atmosphere"

DOWNER

- Diversity efforts could be improved

EMPLOYMENT CONTACT

At www.ajg.com see "job
opportunities" under "company facts"

Visit the Vault Finance Career Channel at **www.vault.com/finance** — with
insider firm profiles, message boards, the Vault Finance Job Board and more.

VAULT CAREER LIBRARY   69

THE SCOOP

Midwest giant

Founded by its namesake in 1927 in Itasca, Ill., Arthur J. Gallagher & Co. has grown into the world's fourth-largest insurance brokerage and risk management services firm, working through a system of subsidiaries and operating divisions in the United States, United Kingdom, Australia, Bermuda, Canada and New Zealand. The company, which went public in 1984, provides property/casualty and employee benefits products and services, as well as risk management consulting, and claims and information management services. The company's clients include businesses of all sizes, not-for-profits, associations and municipal and governmental entities.

To stay true to its Midwestern values, former chief executive officer Bob Gallagher composed a list in 1984 of 25 shared values for the corporation and its culture. Dubbed "The Gallagher Way," the list still represents an important philosophy for the company, even though the former chief is gone. In August 2006, Bob Gallagher died at the age of 83, after more than half a century with the company his father founded. His nephew Patrick, who was serving as president and CEO, took over as chairman in October 2006.

Balance sheet

For full-year 2007 results, Arthur J. Gallagher brought in $1.62 billion in revenue, up from $1.44 billion the previous year. Net income, however, decreased to $138.8 million from $188.5 million in the previous year. Like many insurance brokers, Gallagher's brokerage operations worldwide were negatively impacted by falling rates and intense competition in the property/casualty market worldwide.

In the first quarter of 2008, revenue increased slightly to $375.8 million, up from the $375 million in the first quarter of 2007. Net income was negative for the first quarter, however, as the firm reported a $6 million loss compared to the $19.8 million gain it brought in a year earlier. According to the firm, the loss was due to the write-off associated with the sale of its worldwide reinsurance brokerage operations.

In the second quarter of 2008, revenue rose slightly compared to the second quarter of 2007, to $428.9 million from $427.6 million. Net income, though, was down to $40.8 million from $43.8 million. The firm said its brokerage segment had put up respectable results, while its risk management unit struggled due to the "current soft market" and "slowing economy."

Acquisition spree

Gallagher has grown through a feeding frenzy, gobbling up small insurance brokers and benefits consultants. Gallagher acquired 19 companies in 2004, 10 companies in 2005 and 11 companies in 2006. In 2007, Arthur J. Gallagher & Co. announced the acquisition of 21 smaller retail and wholesale property/casualty and employee benefit brokerage operations scattered throughout the United States and Canada. In addition, in the first half of 2008, the firm announced 20 acquisitions, including Dallas-based Wm. W. George & Associates Inc.; Marlton, N.J.-based Lance Group LLC; Voluntary Benefits Solutions LLC; and Montclair, N.J.-based Petty Burton Associates.

The corporation views acquisitions, many of which are under $5 million in revenue, as a form of organic hiring, strengthening niches and allowing the firm to expand geographically.

Looking abroad

About 11 percent of the firm's employees and 11.5 percent of its revenue are located overseas in places like the United Kingdom, Australia, Bermuda and Canada. J. Patrick Gallagher has said he see strong expansion potential internationally, particularly in the United Kingdom. About half of the company's revenue in the United Kingdom is in the commercial sector, and half is in the public sector.

GETTING HIRED

Looking for leadership

Like a potential suitor rhapsodizing about the characteristics of its perfect mate, Arthur J. Gallagher lists qualifications for its ideal candidate on the career section of its web site, noting that it's looking for "strong leadership potential," "flexibility," "exceptional drive," "good interpersonal and communication skills," and the "ability to learn and retain new information." Don't pin your hopes on browsing its current openings, however—instead of cataloging specific

Visit the Vault Finance Career Channel at www.vault.com/finance — with insider firm profiles, message boards, the Vault Finance Job Board and more.

VAULT CAREER LIBRARY   71

job opportunities on the site, the firm encourages candidates to contact individual offices to learn about possible open positions. The firm also relies on "word of mouth and some headhunters" to get the word out.

Think fast

Once you're called into the office for a meeting, expect "team interviews" and "quick decisions," says an insider. Another interviewing for an account manager position says that he went through a "first interview with the division vice president that went on for about 30 minutes" and that involved "a Q&A format that was easy to respond to." The second round with HR was "relaxed" and included two tests—a "personality test along with a short general knowledge test."

Make your mark

During the course of the internship, interns get the chance to learn "basic insurance concepts," "what a broker does" and "where Gallagher fits in the world of insurance." According to the firm, in the summer 2008, more than 150 college students participated in its summer intern program in the U.S. alone. The company says it looks for college students who are interested in a career in insurance sales and who will have completed their sophomore year prior to entering the program. Interested parties can fill out an application online, or direct any specific questions to SIP_Info@ajg.com.

OUR SURVEY SAYS

Team spirit

There's a "high esprit de corps" within the company, which also means that there are "aggressive sales" and a strong "emphasis on client service." Gallagher's motto seems to be "if colleagues and clients are happy, the stockholders will be happy." One insider notes experiencing "a lot of support from staff members," adding that the firm promotes "a professional and relaxed atmosphere." Another calls Gallagher "a good company in many ways." Management receives high marks, too. One contact says, "I felt comfortable around upper management, who were personable and approachable." The hours you end up working per week, however, are fairly variable. One insider calls them "outstanding and flexible," but another contact says that "we are grossly understaffed" and due to this, hours "often exceed a normal 40-hour work week." The dress code is "business casual and usually not abused by the staff." And climbing up the corporate ladder seems to be a matter of grabbing the right rung. One insider says that "opportunities for advancement were there if you worked for it." And as for perks, there's the "401(k)," "stock purchase" and, for those in sales, a "car allowance." Plus, the firm "pays for continuing educational classes" related to employees' specific job functions (classes have to be approved by employees' managers).

Equality across the board?

"As far as I can tell," says one insider," "they treat everyone equally." Still, the firm's diversity efforts could stand to be improved, some sources report. The company "does not encourage, recruit, promote or retain qualified diverse employees," says one insider, adding that he had one "profoundly antebellum experience" where "stereotypical comments and actions" occurred. The contact goes on to suggest that "to move beyond the firm's equal opportunity statement to achieve true diversity, senior management should be required to participate in mandatory diversity training." Another insider agrees that there is a "lack of qualified diverse talent at AJG and a culture that is not inclusive" within the firm. But yet another insider says that "my observation is this firm treats women great and gives them many opportunities." And when it comes to gays and lesbians in the workplace, one contact admits, "I have no way of knowing what the orientation of anyone else is" but says the firm's policies promote equality.

Visit the Vault Finance Career Channel at **www.vault.com/finance** — with insider firm profiles, message boards, the Vault Finance Job Board and more.

VAULT CAREER LIBRARY   73

Assurant

One Chase Manhattan Plaza
New York, NY 10005
Phone: (212) 859-7000
Fax: (212) 859-5893
www.assurant.com

BUSINESSES

Assurant Employee Benefits
Assurant Health
Assurant Solutions
Assurant Specialty Property

THE STATS

Employer Type: Public Company
Ticker Symbol: AIZ (NYSE)
President & CEO: Robert B. Pollock
Revenue: $8.45 billion (FYE 12/07)
Net Income: $653.8 million
No. of Employees: 14,000

KEY COMPETITORS

Cigna
Mutual of Omaha

UPPER

• Bonuses "are fairly generous"

DOWNER

• Health benefits "are nothing special"

EMPLOYMENT CONTACT

www.assurant.com/inc/assurant/career
s/index.html

THE SCOOP

Going for the big time

Insurance company Assurant—in the form it exists in today, at least—was officially birthed under its current moniker in 2004. But Assurant's health business can trace its origins to Wisconsin way back in 1892 when it conducted its dealings under the La Crosse Mutual Aid Association. At the turn of the century in 1900, the firm shuffled off to Milwaukee and modified its name to the Time Indemnity Company and then to the Time Insurance Company. Assurant existed under the name Time Insurance Company until 1977, when it was acquired by Netherlands firm N.V. AMEV. In 2004, insurance provider Fortis merged into Assurant as it is today and went public shortly afterward.

Through the years, Assurant's businesses have evolved to try to cover all the bases a potential customer might need. Its Assurant Health group offers a range of health plans to individuals and to groups. Assurant Specialty Property offers plans for homeowners and renters alike. The Assurant Employee Benefits group provides employee benefits for small to mid-sized employers, and Assurant Solutions offers other policies for businesses, such as debt protection, unemployment insurance and even warranties for electronics such as computers.

In 2008, *Fortune* magazine put Assurant in its No. 309 spot on its annual Fortune 500 list, down a few pegs from its previous rank of No. 300. The firm's net income also took a little bit of a dip, falling to $653.75 million from $717.42 million in 2006. However, revenue increased 4.7 percent to $8.45 billion.

The first half of 2008 looked a lot healthier for Assurant. The firm brought in $2.25 billion in revenue in the second quarter of 2008, up from $2.17 billion in the first quarter and also up from $2.06 billion in the second quarter of 2007. Net income for the second quarter was $189.95 million, up from $186.83 million in the first quarter of 2008 and also up from $166.3 billion in the second quarter of 2007. Net earned premiums increased by 11 percent during the quarter, which helped the firm's bottom line.

Keeping up

Assurant has kept on its toes when it comes to acquiring businesses. In October 2007, Assurant's U.K. affiliate acquired building distributor

Visit the Vault Finance Career Channel at **www.vault.com/finance** — with insider firm profiles, message boards, the Vault Finance Job Board and more.

VAULT CAREER LIBRARY   75

Centrepoint Insurance Services Limited. In July of the same year, Assurant purchased mortgage payment protection distributor Swansure Group as well as Mayflower National Life Insurance Company in a separate transaction for approximately $67.5 million. And in the previous year, the firm acquired Safeco Financial Institution Solutions in addition to signing a dental PPO network sharing agreement with Aetna.

ONE plan allows employees to contribute pre-tax dollars towards qualified benefits, such as health insurance and child care, while the company's Single-Point Billing option consolidates billing and financial requirements from multiple insurance carriers into a single overall benefits group.

Cutting its losses—but with empathy

The firm has also faced its share of setbacks recently, including the fallout it felt from the October 2007 wildfires that swept through Southern California. But the firm counted itself as among the lucky ones in the meantime—right after the fires began to race through the state, Assurant's Specialty Property President and CEO Gene Mergelmeyer said he was "humbled at the composure of our customers," acknowledging "there is nothing like standing next to a homeowner, gazing at their home that has been reduced to rubble." In December 2007, the firm announced that its claims from the natural disaster came in at more than $37 million (an amount that incorporates future claims and ones already received). The firm "mobilized our catastrophe team operations in California and adjusted and settled over 90 percent of our claims within 30 days of reporting," Mergelmeyer said in a statement.

A probing issue

In July 2007, the firm placed five of its head executives on a paid administrative leave following the development of a Securities and Exchange Commission inquiry into practices Assurant used with its finite risk products. (The SEC had also served Wells notices to the individuals, which indicate that civil action may be a possibility.) The market immediately reacted to the news—the day the SEC announcement was made, Assurant's shares dropped 12.7 percent, the most severe drop in its history. Assurant, meanwhile, says it is continuing to cooperate with the SEC's review.

Ultimately, a senior vice president and a risk manager who had been placed on leave were terminated by Assurant in August 2007. Also because of the federal probe, Assurant suspended its stock buyback program in September 2007.

Still raking it in

In April 2008, it came to light that Assurant's President and Chief Executive Robert Pollock still received $3.5 million in compensation in 2007, despite the fact that he was on a probe-related administrative leave for much of the year. Pollock also received an additional $1.7 million in stocks and option awards. In comparison, he received a total overall compensation of $3.7 million in 2006 (when he worked the full year), the Associated Press reported.

GETTING HIRED

Get the lowdown

The careers link at www.assurant.com attempts to provide it all for prospective employees, giving workers sections regarding the company culture and people, a detailed list of benefits offered and, of course, current career opportunities with the firm. On the site, you can apply for specific jobs or keep a profile on file with Assurant for the future. Applicants are also encouraged to learn more about each of Assurant's businesses, with links provided for each.

The interview process can vary. One employee already working within the firm describes a "short," "to the point" interview, but concedes that the experience is "probably not typical for someone applying cold."

OUR SURVEY SAYS

Fairly generous

"If a senior underwriter leaves the company," explains one source, "you can post for that job, but that's as far as career advancement goes." On the bright side, however, "managers look favorably on most requests for time off," and "the dress code is business casual—people dress for comfort, not for appearance." Perks, which include a 401(k) plan and an employee stock purchase plan, mostly receive high marks from employees, and annual bonuses "are fairly generous." The health benefits "are nothing special—but nothing terrible either." And even though the firm touts its fair hiring practices and equal employment opportunities when it comes to diversity, not all employees agree with the sentiment. "Assurant has a commitment to diversity that clearly shows in its hiring practices, but doesn't always live up to things after that," admits one employee.

Visit the Vault Finance Career Channel at **www.vault.com/finance** — with insider firm profiles, message boards, the Vault Finance Job Board and more.

VAULT CAREER LIBRARY

77

Berkshire Hathaway Inc.

1440 Kiewit Plaza
Omaha, NE 68131
Phone: (402) 346-1400
Fax: (402) 346-3375
www.berkshirehathaway.com

DEPARTMENTS

GEICO Corp.
Insurance Re
McLane Co.
National Indemnity

THE STATS

Employer Type: Public Company
Ticker Symbol: BRK.A (NYSE)
Chairman, President & CEO: Warren
   Buffett
Revenue: $118.26 billion (FYE 12/07)
Net Income: $13.21 billion
No. of Employees: 192,000

KEY COMPETITORS

Blackstone Group
HM Capital Partners
KKR
Onex

THE SCOOP

Omaha stakes

The "Oracle of Omaha" founded Buffett Partnership in 1956 with $105,000 when he was still 25 and fresh from studying under investing guru Benjamin Graham at Columbia University. Averaging annual returns of more than 20 percent over the next 51 years, Warren Buffett has become the second richest man in the world (following his close friend Bill Gates), according to *Forbes*. The Oracle holds about 40 percent of the company's shares. Not bad for a kid from Nebraska.

Berkshire Hathaway's core holdings are its insurance companies, of which the most significant are GEICO and Gen Re. GEICO is one of the largest auto insurers in the U.S. The company prefers low-risk clients, particularly government and military employees, but has in recent years begun taking on greater numbers of average drivers.

Berkshire Hathaway's simple but successful business strategy involves taking the "float"—cash income prior to claims payouts—from its major interest (its insurance companies) and using the cash to buy undervalued businesses, cheap but promising stock and even simple bonds. Likely profit represents the sole determining factor in acquisitions, but Buffett views profitability as correlating to intelligent, responsible management. Refusing to invest in Internet stocks during the 1990s boom, Buffett had the last laugh during the dot-com implosion. Berkshire Hathaway's subsidiaries employ more than 192,000 people, but only 16, all personal friends and family of the founder, work at the company's world headquarters in Omaha.

Trouble at General Re

In October 2006, General Re received a letter from the U.S. attorney for the Eastern District of Virginia in Richmond saying the reinsurer was not a target in the government investigation of collapsed insurer Reciprocal of America. Government investigators had wanted to know if General Re participated in an alleged program to deceive state regulators and Reciprocal policyholders that led to a jail sentence for the former president of Reciprocal. Four former and current General Re employees who had been subpoenaed were also cleared.

A little over a year later, in February 2008, four other former General Re employees were convicted of criminal fraud, stemming from a deal with the

Visit the Vault Finance Career Channel at **www.vault.com/finance** — with insider firm profiles, message boards, the Vault Finance Job Board and more.

VAULT CAREER LIBRARY   79

insurance firm American International Group (AIG), which had major problems with executive corruption in the early years of the new millennium. The fraud concerned a phony reinsurance scheme in 2000 that General Re and AIG executives conceived to falsely boost AIG's reserves by about $500 million, thus deceiving investors and inflating AIG's stock price. The convicted executives were noteworthy, too—a former General Re CEO, CFO, SVP and assistant general counsel—and they each faced a maximum of 20 years in prison for their crimes. Federal prosecutors continued investigating General Re into early 2008, specifically over CEO Joseph Brandon's role in the scandal. Amid reports that prosecutors were pushing for Brandon to get the sack, he resigned in April 2008 and was replaced by General Re's president, Franklin "Tad" Montross. Brandon was largely thought to be a major candidate for Warren Buffet's title after his retirement.

The numbers, and the confessions

In 2007, Berkshire Hathaway's net income increased 20 percent to $13.2 billion. Revenue also increased 20 percent to $118.2 billion. According to the Buffet's annual letter to shareholders, the firm's 76 businesses "did well overall" in 2007, and the "few that had problems were primarily those linked to housing." The CEO's candid annual letter also documented his own mistakes, including what Buffett called the "worst deal" he ever made: buying the show company Dexter. In the letter, he said the move cost his firm's shareholders $3.5 billion, and instead of assuring investors that it won't happen again, he wrote, "I'll make more mistakes in the future—you can bet on that. A line from Bobby Bare's song explains what too often happens with acquisitions: 'I've never gone to bed with an ugly woman, but I've sure woke up with a few.'"

Speaking of which, the firm's numbers in the second quarter of 2008 sure weren't pretty, as net income fell 8 percent to $2.88 billion. The decline was largely due to poor results in the insurance underwriting unit, whose profit fell 43 percent to $360 million (although earned premiums rose 5 percent to $6.23 billion). The results didn't come as that much of a surprise: in May 2008, Buffett had told shareholders they should not expect similar results as in the past.

Buying businesses

Berkshire Hathaway achieved by minimizing risk, which means that for most of its 37 years, income has exceeded claim outlays, fueling the company's acquisitions. Buffett has backed blue-chip stocks and choice newcomers with spectacular results. However, the chaos in the market in the last decade, generally due to dotcom debacles, has reduced the number of stocks that meet his criteria: favorable economic characteristics, sound management and reasonable prices. In response, Berkshire Hathaway has turned to buying businesses outright.

Berkshire Hathaway tends to buy companies that make practical products such as underwear, paint, steel beams, carpet and hamburgers. The company owns Dairy Queen and is a major shareholder in Coca-Cola and Anheuser-Busch. The company also holds shares in American Express, Moody's, The Washington Post and Wells Fargo.

Berkshire's holdings can be grouped into four rough categories: building materials, clothing and footwear manufacturers, furniture and food.

Buying railroads and utilities

As scores of investors in 2007 abandoned the risky junk bond market, Berkshire Hathaway announced in December a $2.1 billion agreement to buy TXU junk bonds from Goldman Sachs. TXU is an electric utility corporation serving 2.5 million Texans. The investment bolsters Berkshire Hathaway's utility holdings, which include a majority stake in MidAmerican Energy Holdings.

In August, Berkshire Hathaway bought more than 10 million shares of Burlington Northern Santa Fe railroad, increasing its stake to 14.8 percent. In April, the company disclosed a 30.03 million share or 11 percent stake in the company, making it Northern Santa Fe's biggest shareholder. It has also recently bought stakes in Union Pacific and Norfolk Southern. Some analysts expect railroad stock prices to grow as the need to convey coal and ethanol increases as the U.S. emphasizes domestic sources of energy.

All that glitters

In May 2007, Berkshire Hathaway announced plans to purchase jewelry manufacturers Bel-Oro International and Aurafin LLC and merge them into a firm called the Richline Group, which would become the largest jewelry supply group in the U.S. The combined company has 1,200 employees, exceeds $500 million in annual sales and markets to consumers under multiple brands. The companies did not disclose the terms of the deal. In November 2007, Richline acquired jewelry manufacturers Alarama and Prime Time.

Berkshire Hathaway also controls several jewelry retailers, including Borhseim's, Helzberg's Diamond Shops and Ben Bridge Jeweler.

Giving back

In June 2006, Buffett promised to provide Class B Berkshire Hathaway stock gifts to the following five charitable foundations: the Bill and Melinda Gates Foundation, the Susan Thompson Buffett Foundation, the Howard G. Buffett Foundation, the Susan A. Buffett Foundation and the NoVo Foundation. Each year of Buffett's life, the number of shares given to each foundation decreases by 5 percent. In July 2007, the gifts totaled $2.12 billion. Buffett does not partake in the investment decisions of any of the five foundations.

Buffett has publicly stated that he plans to give away most of his fortune before he dies. In 2007, he testified in Congress against the dissolution of the "estate tax," levied by the federal government on the estates of the wealthy after their death.

Buffett to the rescue

When bond insurers Ambac Financial, MBIA and Financial Guaranty Insurance began to deal with a massive amount of defaults in 2007 due in part to subprime mortgage defaults, the last thing they probably imagined was the possibility of billionaire investors offering their services. But that scenario came true in February 2008 when Warren Buffett announced that Berkshire Hathaway would personally back up $800 billion in municipal bonds. Buffett wasn't doing this out of the kindness of his heart, though. "We're doing this to make money," he confirmed. He added that the reinsurance he and Berkshire Hathaway offer will bring the bonds an equitable price—the bonds were being bought at deep discounts due to worries about the fiscal fitness of bond insurers. Although not every firm has committed to the idea (and Buffett hasn't said which ones have), the reinsurance, if accepted, will allow the companies to underwrite the financial stakes they routinely undertake for clients.

The authorized Snowball

The first authorized biography of Warren Buffet will be released at the end of September 2008. The book, which is almost 1,000 pages long, was written by former Morgan Stanley insurance analyst Alice Schroeder, who has supposedly spent thousands of hours with Buffett; she has also spent time with his files and friends. The book will be published by Bantam Dell and called *The Snowball: Warren Buffett and the Business of Life*. The title takes its name from a Buffett quote: "Life is like a snowball. The really important thing is finding wet snow and a really long hill."

GETTING HIRED

Sink or swim

Getting in at a Berkshire Hathaway company may be difficult, but as noted earlier, employment at Berkshire Hathaway headquarters is virtually impossible. The company's homepage doesn't even list openings. To find a position at a Berkshire Hathaway company, job seekers should visit the individual companies' web sites. Also, as noted above, dead wood doesn't float in Buffett's ocean. Employees, particularly managers, are expected to get results wherever possible, whenever possible, even against industry trends. Those who do will be rewarded with the usual perks and benefits; those who don't will be shown the door.

One insider with more than "20 years of experience as a workers' compensation adjuster" reports one such experience, commenting that he was "interviewed and hired by a manager" for a position in Georgia and "asked to come to work as soon as possible." Upon starting at the position, the contact says that technical issues and "password problems" led to spotty "access to the company's computer system" for two days. On the third day, the contact says he was told "by that manager that I was not a senior adjuster and needed to find another job."

Visit the Vault Finance Career Channel at www.vault.com/finance — with insider firm profiles, message boards, the Vault Finance Job Board and more.

VAULT CAREER LIBRARY

83

Capital One Financial

1680 Capital One Dr.
McLean, VA 22012
Phone: (703) 720-1000
www.capitalone.com

THE STATS

Employer Type: Public Company
Ticker Symbol: COF
Chairman and CEO: Richard D.
   Fairbank
Revenue: $14.58 billion (FYE 12/07)
Net Income: $1.57 billion
No. of Employees: 32,000 (approx.)
No. of Offices: 12 (US, UK and
Canada)

KEY COMPETITORS

American Express
Bank of America
Countrywide Financial
Discover Financial Services
Freddie Mac
Wells Fargo

UPPERS

- "Culture is focused on getting the work done, not how many hours you spend doing it"
- Colleagues are "warm, friendly and inclusive"

DOWNERS

- Culture "favors people who can speak loud and make their voices heard"
- "Very diverse at the lower levels, but once you get to the senior levels, it's not"

EMPLOYMENT CONTACT

See "careers" at www.capitalone.com

THE SCOOP

Gaining Ground

Based in McLean, Va., Capital One is the nation's fifth largest issuer of MasterCard and Visa credit cards, and has more than 50 million customers. As well as its card services, the firm provides savings and consumer lending products. Its major subsidiaries are Capital One Bank, Capital One, N.A., Capital One, F.S.B., Capital One Auto Finance and North Fork Bank. Capital One Services, another subsidiary, provides operating and back office services to the company and its other subsidiaries.

The company offers a full range of credit cards, including platinum cards, secured cards and cards for small businesses. Capital One's savings products include certificates of deposit, money market accounts and individual retirement accounts; the firm's lending unit helps consumers purchase everything from cars to homes.

In 2006, the firm delivered another year of solid results and increased its focus on banking with the purchase of North Fork, the credit crisis of 2007 proved more difficult for the company.

Getting out of the mortgage business

Like most other Wall Street financial firms, Capital One's financial statements and overall business health suffered from the mortgage industry crisis. In August 2007, the company announced it would discontinue making residential mortgages and close GreenPoint Mortgage, its wholesale mortgage-banking unit, instantly shuttering GreenPoint's 31 offices and stopping all residential mortgage origination activity. The company said conditions in the secondary mortgage markets would create significant near-term profitability challenges, given the company's "originate and sell" business model.

The total after-tax charge for the closure amounted to about $860 million, with about $650 million of the expenses resulting form the noncash write-down of goodwill associated with the acquisition of GreenPoint Mortgage as part of the North Fork Bancorporation in December 2006. GreenPoint's focus had been on prime, non-conforming and near-prime markets. The choice forced the company to lay off about 1,900 employees in addition to the 2,000 layoffs announced in June.

Visit the Vault Finance Career Channel at **www.vault.com/finance** — with insider firm profiles, message boards, the Vault Finance Job Board and more.

VAULT CAREER LIBRARY   **85**

Capital One expects to lose more than $5 billion in 2008, because of rising delinquencies and home foreclosures. Although Capital One has diversified holdings that include auto loans, consumer credit cards and global financial services, the housing meltdown has represented a growing burden on the company's bottom line.

Acquisition abandoned

Capital One announced in November 2007 it would cease its planned acquisition of NetSpend, an online provider of prepaid debit cards. The companies still plan to create a strategic relationship with each other, under which Capital One will hold a minority interest in NetSpend, options to purchase additional shares of the company and representation on the NetSpend Board of Directors. The companies intend to jointly pursue the distribution of prepaid card products through mainstream retail channels. In August 2007, Capital One had announced plans to purchase NetSpend for $700 million.

Management changes

Larry Klane, president of Capital One's global financial services businesses stepped down from his position in November 2007 to pursue a White House nomination to the Federal Reserve Board. Klane will continue to oversee the company's U.K. businesses through March 1st. President Bush nominated Klane in May 2007, but the nomination remains under Senate review. Klane joined Capital one in 2000, after serving as a management director at Deutsche Bank, where he oversaw global corporate trust and service agencies. Klane has also held positions at The Walt Disney Company, William Kent International, Booz Allen Hamilton and Strategic Planning Associates.

Also in November 2007, the company named Michael W. Azevedo head of its banking operations. Azevedo, a 27-year veteran of Wells Fargo Bank, will supervise national operations and phone-based banking for the company. He will report to Lynn Pike, president of Capital One's banking business.

Cashing in

Fairbank agreed in 1997 to relinquish his salary and financial benefits for the next three years in exchange for massive 10-year stock options. Although the company has hit a financial rough patch, its share prices grew more than 200 percent in the past decade. Fairbank began exercising more than 10,000 options per day in May 2007, and selling his shares, to collect more than $3.4 million before taxes per week.

Settling up

Capital One said in December 2007 it would take a charge of about $80 million in the fourth quarter as part of a $2.25 billion legal settlement reached by Visa USA and American Express Co. in November. The settlement followed a 2004 lawsuit by American Express against MasterCard, Visa and their member banks claiming that the companies illegally blocked American Express from the U.S. bank-issued card business. Visa will pay most of the $2.25 billion settlement, but member banks like Capital One must contribute some payments as well.

All downhill from here?

For 2007, Capital One brought in $14.58 billion in revenue, up from the $12.09 billion it earned in 2006. Net income for the year decreased to $1.57 billion, a downturn from the $2.41 billion it generated in 2006. The overall shakiness of the credit markets industry contributed to the unimpressive income statement.

By the middle of the year, the firm's numbers grew worse. For the second quarter of 2008, revenue dropped about 5 percent to $3.35 billion and net income decreased to $452.9 million from $750.4 million in the second quarter of 2007. Analysts pointed to continued worsening of the credit markets for the poor numbers, along with the $829.1 million in cash the firm had to reserve for the quarter to cover loan defaults.

Getting listed

In the Fortune 500 2008 list, Capital One Financial ranked No. 130, rising from No. 154. Along with that list, the firm regularly ranks in Fortune's Global Top Companies for Leaders survey. The corporation earned accolades for its executive coaching and leadership development programs. Capital One runs numerous programs aimed at cultivating leaders, including its Leaders as Teachers program, executive speaker series, Capital One University Leadership College, Leadership Development Program, Executive Coaching Program and semi-annual Executive Talent review.

In September 2007, Working Mother Magazine, named Capital One Financial Corp one of the 100 Best Companies for Working Mothers. The magazine

Visit the Vault Finance Career Channel at www.vault.com/finance — with
insider firm profiles, message boards, the Vault Finance Job Board and more.

VAULT CAREER LIBRARY   **87**

highlighted Capital One's corporate culture, which encourages advancement or women and the work/life balance of employees. The company offers expansive time-off programs, including generous parental leave options and office flexibility, ranging from telecommuting to flextime.

GETTING HIRED

Exam time

If you're thinking of applying to Capital One, but you're not sure about which position to apply for, never fear—the firm is one step ahead of you. The career section of its site contains tests that "help us predict your fit with different roles" within the firm. Or if you already have an idea of what you'd like to apply for, just check out the site for information on the company's college, MBA and military recruiting process—Capital One looks for former military personnel to fill a diverse array of jobs from fraud investigators to senior managers.

Underlining the variety of schools at which the firm recruits, one insider says the firm recruits from "colleges all over." "We look for the ultimate best and the brightest," says another insider. The interviews can be tough. One insider says, "The process can be rigorous." "We put our applicants through an intense testing, followed by a series of 'power days' to interview," says a source. "Interviews are primarily behavioral-based. Questions are specific to past experiences and 'how would you handle' situations." Another agrees, adding that the firm will "test your skills" and might give you "a case study relevant to the position." "A test is given first, then several interviews," says another contact. One source expands on that description, saying, "You must pass a math test on interpretation of graphs to be given an offer. Interviews are case and behavioral. Case interviews are about calculating outcomes, not about developing strategies."

Yet another respondent says, "The interviews are a combination of cases and behavioral questions. You can expect the cases to closely mirror the type of analyses that are done routinely at the company." One insider notes that the written test "centers around quantitative and data interpretation skills." He admits, "This test was pretty simple for me due to my background, but I guess one needs good numerical skills as well as fast calculation and data comprehension skills." The case interviews, which most but not all candidates will go through "can be difficult, especially if you're not a math wiz." Case interviews are "quantitative" and "have a clear solution rather than some of the consulting cases where the answer depends on the approach."

OUR SURVEY SAYS

Chill out

The culture is "fairly laid-back," "collegial and collaborative," but "Capital One defines its values different than how some other organizations do," some insiders say. "For example, the firm talks a lot about teamwork but I find it to have the least teamwork of any place I've ever worked," elaborates one insider. "Teamwork is more reaching out to colleagues and getting them to buy into your projects." Even so, other sources call the culture "consensus-based and genteel," full of colleagues who are "warm, friendly and inclusive." And others note that Capital One is a "fairly young company with a very young workforce," and say it has "long been known for its entrepreneurial environment and very collegial work culture."

One insider notes that the firm has "a fast-track career development. However, the company is maturing very fast into a big bank-type workplace, which has a lot to do with the industry they are in and the big banks they're competing with." For the time being, "the culture is very collaborative," says another insider. "The company's primary motive is for its employees to enjoy coming to work every day, ensuring a daily challenge and a fun place to work." Others say that the firm has "a culture of encouraging great analysis, and allowing all employees to participate in decision making through good arguments."

Some sources believe that Capital One's culture has been changed by growth. "With the rapid expansion, the company is definitely trying to keep up the internal organization with that pace," observes one source. "The culture within the firm is strong and apparently favors people who can speak loud and make their voices heard." One pleased contact says, "People here are very smart and have a very high level of analytical ability and quantitative skill."

As for managers, one respondent says, "I've had some great managers and some not-so-great managers." He adds, "Regular feedback is encouraged and will help you grow. I've learned a lot. The key to success is to network at the level more senior than yours." Another contact comments, "in general, the working atmosphere is fun and pleasant, and collaboration is essential for success."

Visit the Vault Finance Career Channel at **www.vault.com/finance** — with insider firm profiles, message boards, the Vault Finance Job Board and more.

VΛULT CAREER LIBRARY

89

Depends on where you look

The company has a "diverse culture," notes an insider. But that may not be an attribute that occurs throughout the entire firm. Although Capital One is "very diverse at the lower levels, once you get to the senior levels, it's not," notes an insider. "It's very much a frat boy culture in some departments, as well. The company is working to address this, but they have a long way to go." Another calls the firm "preppy and white bread," saying, "It's perfect for the typical Ivy-Leaguer or MBA who wants to work in a straightforward, hierarchical environment. Your day will be scheduled down to the minute and you'll learn to follow process." However, another source says, "The culture is very open, with associates at all levels able to challenge the status quo and to push on our strategies and latest thinking."

You have great freedom to move horizontally and try out different roles that interest you." And according to Capital One, the firm "works to create an atmosphere of inclusion" through hosting diversity forums with presenters such as Geraldine Ferraro, the first female vice presidential nominee, and Betty DeGeneres, mother of actress and comedienne Ellen DeGeneres. The firm says it has also established associate networks that provide support in the form of programs, resources and tools "enabling Capital One's diverse associates to achieve their full potential in an environment that values the differences everyone brings to the workplace."

Leverage it

Compensation is "very highly leveraged," and the bonus opportunity is anywhere from "zero to 60 percent." And "sign-on bonuses vary a lot," but "you have leverage in working with your recruiter on this." Overall, however, you may get paid the same rate regardless of the area in which you work, some insiders say. One notes, "It seemed like the D.C. and Richmond areas paid the same even though it's cheaper to live in Richmond." The contact adds, "It's easier to get hired if you are willing to work in Richmond." Another source says of his offer, "The base salary was barely enough [but] Capital One interviewers and HR staff will repeatedly tell you how inexpensive Richmond is. The key is Richmond was inexpensive at one time."

Benefits include a generous 401(k) that "matches half of employee contributions up to 6 percent," a "stock purchase plan for employees" and an "on-site fitness center" in some locations. Additionally, the firm offers "educational reimbursement provided for bachelor's or graduate degrees." There is also a "free on-site health center with a doctor in Richmond," "concierge service," "good food service," "discounts to retailers and theaters," "quarterly social events" and "lots of community events." One source points to another nice perk: "three weeks of vacation and four weeks after five years" with the firm. And it doesn't hurt that the dress code is "business casual" and employees "can wear jeans on Friday." The firm also offers an interesting perk—"they give us free coffee and one free week of meals during what is called Month End," one employee says.

Hours tend to "vary a lot by department," but Capital One isn't keeping anybody in the office or demanding face time. "Culture is focused on getting the work done, not how many hours you spend doing it," says an insider. Even so, some sources admit "work hours can be long." Others say hours are "dependent on the current projects you're working on." One contact says that though "hours are very reasonable and mostly you're working 40 to 50 hour weeks, once in a while there could be spikes where you're working 60 to 80 hours per week, depending on projects and roles." The insider adds that "flexible work arrangements are increasingly being encouraged." Either way, "some employees have a lot of flexibility, and can work from home and have flexible hours, but others do not." One insider suggests that "if flexibility is important to you, ask about this before accepting the job so you aren't disappointed." Another contact says, "It is not an up-or-out type of environment—you can cruise, as long as you are competent and get your work done."

Nice outlook

Things are looking rosy for the firm lately. "The company has been doing great lately, and I would expect it to continue growing at a healthy rate," one source enthuses. There's a "positive outlook" among staff, and "morale is generally good, though it varies by department." One insider notes that "the morale was hurt when the company started establishing tighter corporate governance policies and sharpening control of the policies following a memorandum of understanding signed with the Federal Reserve." But others say that the company "continues to manage its credit card business very well and has embarked on an aggressive new product development plan." And it's been "actively acquiring new businesses to ensure that it is fully diversified and continues to have growth opportunities." A contact agrees, for the most part, saying, "Overall business outlook is good, but challenging. The core credit card business is slowing, but Capital One is diversifying into highly fragmented business areas—auto, home equity, retail banking—with excellent growth and consolidation prospects." Indeed, the firm has a "rock solid strategy to expand and diversify," and "very strong leadership and analyst teams."

Visit the Vault Finance Career Channel at **www.vault.com/finance** — with insider firm profiles, message boards, the Vault Finance Job Board and more.

VAULT CAREER LIBRARY   91

CB Richard Ellis Group, Inc.

100 N. Sepulveda Blvd., Ste. 1050
El Segundo, CA 90245
Phone: (310) 606-4700
Fax: (949) 809-4357
www.cbre.com

SERVICE LINES

Asset Services
Brokerage—Tenant & Landlord
   Representation
Capital Markets
Consulting
Debt & Equity Finance (CBRE |
   Melody)
Development & Investment
   (Trammell Crow Company)
Facilities Management
Global Corporate Services
Government and Public Sector
Healthcare
Industrial
Investment Brokerage/Agency
Investment Management (CBRE
   Investors)
Office
Project Management
Research & Investment Strategy
   (Torto Wheaton Research)
Retail
Specialty Services
Transaction Management
Valuation & Advisory Services

THE STATS

Employer Type: Public Company
Ticker Symbol: CBG (NYSE)
Chairman: Richard C. Blum
President & CEO: W. Brett White
Revenue: $6.03 billion (FYE 12/07)
Net Income: $390.5 million
No. of Employees: 29,000+
No. of Offices: 400+

KEY COMPETITORS

CarrAmerica
Cushman & Wakefield
Jones Lang LaSalle

UPPER

• Good advancement opportunities

DOWNER

• "Very conservative" culture

EMPLOYMENT CONTACT

www.cbre.com/careers

THE SCOOP

Rising up the ranks

As a result of a string of acquisitions that have strengthened this commercial real estate services company over the past two years, CB Richard Ellis Group is growing at an exponential rate. In 2007, it jumped from no ranking at all up to 33 on Fortune's 100 Fastest-Growing Companies. Also in 2007, CBRE collected a ranking of Best in Class from *BusinessWeek*. The 100-year-old company (it was founded in San Francisco in 1906) also has considerable clout abroad. In October 2007, it was awarded the Exceptional Achievement Award in the MPF European Practice Management Awards in London just one week after the firm was awarded European Retail Agency Team of the Year and European Industrial Agency Team of the Year at the European Property Awards 2007.

CB Richard Ellis Group already holds the honor of being the world's largest commercial real estate services company. Its offerings include brokerage services, corporate services, consulting, project management, market research, mortgage banking, and asset management and advisory services. With the acquisition of Insignia Financial in 2003, CBRE became the world's largest commercial property manager. CBRE's three geographic segments are the Americas; Europe, the Middle East and Africa (EMEA); and Asia-Pacific.

Public/Private tango

Colbert Coldwell and Albert Tucker started real estate brokerage Tucker, Lynch, & Coldwell in 1906 in San Francisco. In 1962, it was incorporated as Coldwell Banker, which went public in 1968. Sears, Roebuck & Co. bought the company in 1981 for 80 percent above its market price. But by 1991, Sears sold Coldwell Banker's commercial operations to The Carlyle Group as CB Commercial Real Estate Services Group. In 1998, the company acquired REI Limited, the non-U.K. operations of Richard Ellis; it was renamed CB Richard Ellis Services.

The company was taken private in 2001 by a group of investors led by Richard Blum (now CBRE's chairman) and Ray Wirta. Blum Capital Partners bought the 60 percent of publicly traded CBRE that it did not already own. In 2003, CBRE merged with top commercial real estate broker and property manager Insignia Financial. The next year the company changed its

Visit the Vault Finance Career Channel at **www.vault.com/finance** — with insider firm profiles, message boards, the Vault Finance Job Board and more.

VAULT CAREER LIBRARY

93

name to CB Richard Ellis Group and went public once again. In February 2004, CBRE filed for a $150-million initial public stock offering. Richard Blum maintains a nearly 15 percent stake in CBRE through Blum Capital Partners.

Growth through acquisitions

CB Richard Ellis has used acquisitions as a key method for growth in recent years. In July 2006, the company acquired The Polacheck Company, a commercial real estate services firm in Wisconsin, for approximately $20 million. Also in July 2006, it acquired Holley Blake, an industrial real estate services specialist in the United Kingdom, for approximately $22 million in cash. One month later, CBRG and Alfa Capital Partners announced that CB Richard Ellis acquired the remaining outstanding shares (49 percent) in CB Richard Ellis Noble Gibbons, one of Russia's leading real estate services firms, from ACP's investors and other shareholders.

In one of its biggest deals, the company entered into an agreement to acquire its rival, Trammell Crow Company for $2.2 billion in cash. The deal closed in December 2006. The deal increased the company's total number of employees to more than 24,000, and the firm now counts approximately 85 percent of the Fortune 100 among its clients. The combined companies also control approximately 10 percent of the commercial real estate business.

Stock problems

While the company has been busy growing its business with acquisitions around the world, its stock price has languished below what many in the industry feel the company is worth. In March 2007, when the stock was trading at $33.52, Goldman Sachs analyst Jonathan Haberman upgraded the stock from "neutral" to "buy" setting a price target of $42. But over the next several months, as the turmoil from the subprime catastrophe unfolded, the stock price plummeted to $22.68.

Perhaps in an attempt to boost the faltering stock, the company announced that it would buy back $500 million in shares in early November 2007. Just a few weeks later, the board of directors voted to up the repurchase of shares to $635 million. As of August 2008, the share price was hovering around $14.

Worldwide numbers

Full-year revenue for the firm was promising, coming in at $6.03 billion, up from $4.03 billion in 2006. Net income was up as well, increasing to $390.5 million from $318.57 million the previous year. The first half of 2008 looked less promising, however. The firm's revenue for the second quarter of 2008 came in at $1.31 billion, down from $1.49 billion in 2007 and below analysts' estimates of $1.42 billion. Net income for the second quarter fell to $16.6 million from $141.1 million in the previous year. Considerably lessened sales activity and continued bad news for credit markets were to blame for the disappointing numbers.

GETTING HIRED

Picky, picky

Selectivity at the firm is "somewhat variable, but fussy," insiders say. As far as getting in the door goes, referrals help, although resumes can be sent to opps@cbre.com. Alternately, applicants can try their luck emailing the head of corporate human resources at jack.vanberkel@cbre.com. Women interested in working at CBRE will find themselves in good company. A breakfast for female employees organized by Senior Vice President Lisa Konizeczka at the CBRE annual conference in 2001 led to the creation of the Women's Network, now 250 members and growing. The network's main tasks these days are to establish company-wide initiatives for the recruitment, retention and advancement of women. For its efforts in recruiting female employees, CBRE won the Organization of the Year award in October 2004, presented by the Commercial Real Estate Women Network.

The firm operates offices in "virtually all of the world's key business centers," and recruits from "universities and the industry," so candidates can expect interviewing experiences to run the gamut. One insider says he went through "three interviews," including "two with the president."

Visit the Vault Finance Career Channel at www.vault.com/finance — with insider firm profiles, message boards, the Vault Finance Job Board and more.

VAULT CAREER LIBRARY   95

OUR SURVEY SAYS

A little button-down

Insiders report the culture as a "very conservative" one, but the firm's international reach ensures that clients and employees alike have access to every possible resource they might require. "Working for CB Richard Ellis is an awesome experience" says an insider, adding that "the company offers great customer service." One thing that's the same across the board is the dress code, which sources call "business professional." One insider notes, "We have an appearance to uphold." The contact goes on to say that "opportunities do exist for advancement for sales negotiators," and "many of the company's directors have been promoted from within the company over the past 14 years." Plus, there's "no pressure" when it comes to hours and employees often work "what's needed to get the job done" rather than meet a quota. And good news on the diversity front—there is "no discernable prejudice" from the company. Other insiders call the firm "very progressive"—and that includes CB Richard's "treatment of women."

The Chubb Corporation

15 Mountain View Rd.
Warren, NJ 07059
Phone: (908) 903-2000
Fax: (908) 903-2027
www.chubb.com

DEPARTMENTS

Chubb Commercial Insurance
Chubb Personal Insurance
Chubb Specialty Insurance

THE STATS

Employer Type: Public Company
Ticker Symbol: CB (NYSE)
Chairman, President & CEO: John D. Finnegan
Vice Chairman & COO: John Degnan
Vice Chairman & CFO: Michael O'Reilly
Revenue: $14.11 billion (FYE 12/07)
Net Income: $2.81 billion
No. of Employees: 10,600
No. of Offices: 120

KEY COMPETITORS

AIG
The Hartford
Travelers

UPPER

- "Very good" perks

DOWNER

- Dealing with "politics"

EMPLOYMENT CONTACT

See "careers" at www.chubb.com

THE SCOOP

Covering all its bases

Based in Warren, N.J., The Chubb Corporation is a holding company for a group of property and casualty insurance firms known as the Chubb Group of Insurance Companies. The company offers three kinds of insurance: commercial, specialty and personal. The commercial insurance segment offers a range of insurance products, including worker's compensation, casualty and property insurance. Chubb's specialty insurance includes executive risk protection and professional liability insurance for private and public companies, financial institutions, non-profits and health care organizations. Chubb's personal insurance is generally geared toward the rich, offering coverage to those with expensive homes and possessions such as yachts, who are in need of higher limits and broader coverages than those in standard insurance policies. For example, Chubb's Masterpiece Valuable Articles Coverage includes "mysterious disappearance" and accidental breakage. Chubb is also a leader in insuring yachts valued at over $1 million. Additionally, Chubb's surety business offers bid, performance and payment bonds for construction and financial companies.

Chubb's empire includes a host of subsidiaries in property and casualty insurance, insurance underwriting, reinsurance, consulting, licensing, finance, and real estate. These subsidiaries include, among others, Federal Insurance Company, Vigilant Insurance Company, Chubb Insurance Company of Australia, Pacific Indemnity Company, Chubb Insurance Company of Canada, Chubb Argentina de Seguros, S.A., and Chubb Multinational Managers.

Still going strong after more than 125 years

In 1882, Thomas C. Chubb and his son Percy formed Chubb & Son in New York to underwrite marine insurance. The company became the U.S. manager for Sea Insurance Co. and launched New York Marine Underwriters, which became Chubb's chief property/casualty affiliate, eventually known as Federal Insurance Co. In 1939, Chubb bought Vigilant Insurance Co. Twenty years later, the company bought Colonial Life, and then later Pacific Indemnity in 1967. That same year, Chubb Corp. was formed as a holding company. In 1991, three subsidiaries were combined to form Chubb Life Insurance Co. of America. In the 1970s, Chubb worked on expanding its real estate portfolio by acquiring Bellemead Development. In 1997, Chubb sold its life and health insurance operations and parts of its real estate business, and focused instead on its lucrative property/casualty market.

Targeting the top

Chubb takes the business of its high-net-worth customers very seriously and has its sights set on drawing in more of this coveted market in the future. In July 2007, Chubb published the results of an independent study of more than 600 insurance agencies that attempted to glean the most effective sales techniques when targeting high-net-worth clients. The study found, not surprisingly, that high-net-worth clients want agents who come across as having a specialized knowledge of the market—more like a consultant than a salesperson. The study also yielded four bullet points Chubb agents are supposed to keep in mind to target this elite clientele: know their consultant, know their market, know what they need and know them.

Battling identity theft

In November 2005, Chubb partnered with Identity Theft 911 to help customers recover or recreate missing personal identification and documentation after a disaster or other calamity. Homeowners receive free access to the service, which gives them identity authentication and verification as well as access to investment and bank accounts. Theft 911 will also help members replace birth certificates, driver's licenses and passports, Social Security cards, and check and credit cards.

In 2006, Chubb announced that it will provide group-benefits customers with the option to purchase financial protection for child abductions and home invasions. Customers can elect optional coverage of up to $50,000 for medical expenses and wages lost while recovering from the trauma associated with a home invasion or abduction of a child. It can also cover the costs of temporary relocation or security enhancements. Chubb first introduced a broader version of this one-of-a-kind policy to its personal insurance customers a few years earlier. Also in 2006, Chubb broadened its kidnap/ransom and extortion insurance policy in its specialty commercial lines packages for companies, as well as for high-net-worth individuals. The policy helps pay for ransoms, negotiators and security expenses. The policy even includes coverage for cyber extortion.

Visit the Vault Finance Career Channel at www.vault.com/finance — with insider firm profiles, message boards, the Vault Finance Job Board and more.

VAULT CAREER LIBRARY   99

Chubb goes green

Many large corporations jumped on the environmental bandwagon in 2007 and Chubb was no exception. In September, Chubb made the leap into the 21st century by offering ePolicies. The online capabilities of the new ePolicy allowed customers to access their accounts via e-mail, speeding up the policy distribution process and providing a way for policy holders to electronically important documents if their home is destroyed. The new technology was an effort to reduce the amount of paper that Chubb uses in processing its policy. Executive Vice President Andrew McElwee said, "If 20 percent of our customers opt to receive ePolicy renewals and endorsements, we will save approximately 1,000 trees and nearly one million gallons of water and prevent the creation of 46 tons of solid waste and emission of 113 tons of greenhouse gases."

In August of 2007, Chubb formed a "green energy" team, which will focus on creating insurance solutions for environmentally friendly companies. The team will expand its coverage of companies who specialize in power generation (including wind, solar and geothermal), renewable and clean fuels (ethanol, biodiesel and fuel cells), alternative energy devices (solar panels, wind turbines and other devices), energy-efficient products (compact fluorescent lighting, HVAC systems, office equipment and other products), and renewable energy users, including businesses with energy-efficient and environmentally friendly properties.

Slowly but surely

In 2007, the firm brought in $14.1 billion, up from the $14 billion it brought in for 2006. Chubb also pulled in $2.8 billion in net income in 2007, up from $2.53 billion in 2006. But for the second quarter 2008, revenue fell to $3.35 billion compared with $3.5 billion in the second quarter 2007, and net income decreased to $469 million from $709 million. The less-than-stellar results were largely attributed to higher than expected catastrophe losses connected with storms in the Midwest.

Going to CNA

In May 2008, Chubb Chief Operating Officer and Vice Chairman Thomas Motamed announced his retirement. Motamed, who will be become chairman and CEO of CNA Financial Corp., was replaced by John Degnan, formerly Chubb's vice chairman and chief administrative officer. Motamed served as Chubb COO since 2001; in total, he spent 31 years at the firm.

Gel to the rescue

A program created by Chubb and Thermo Technologies LLC may be responsible for saving property and homes. As of mid-2008, about 10,000 policyholders in 13 states had signed up for The Wildfire Defense Service, in which firefighters trained in wildfire prevention spray Thermo's fire-blocking gel product Thermo-Gel onto the property of Chubb policyholders' homes when a fire is approaching.

GETTING HIRED

Let Chubb invest in you

The firm's careers site offers a searchable database of employment opportunities in a variety of different job categories, including accounting, actuarial, appraisal, claims, human resources, information technology, loss control services and underwriting. Job opportunities are available in 20 states and the District of Columbia as well as internationally.

As far as the hiring process goes, you may be "approached by a recruitment consultant working on behalf of Chubb." One insider says that after his first round of interviews, the interviewer "informed me he would provide feedback and would confirm if I was to go to a second interview." The insider goes on to add that some questions were standard, such as "What makes you tick?'" Other contacts say questions can be out of left field, say the firm's hiring method is "very informative" but "slightly over the top." In addition to the rounds of questioning, there are also "some basic personality and skills tests." Another employee gives prospective applicants a tip: "Wear a suit and emphasize how much you are interested in being a generalist in the business world. We hire all degrees—but business is best."

Broadening their horizons

The firm's chief diversity officer cites what could be the firm's credo: "We believe that talent comes in many packages." And it seems that the firm practices what it preaches. The Human Rights Campaign rates Fortune 500 companies on a 100-point scale based on seven key indicators of fair treatment for GLBT employees, including policies prohibiting discrimination based on sexual orientation, gender identity and equal health care benefits.

Visit the Vault Finance Career Channel at **www.vault.com/finance** — with insider firm profiles, message boards, the Vault Finance Job Board and more.

VAULT CAREER LIBRARY **101**

Chubb received the highest possible score on the Human Rights Campaign Foundation 2008 annual report card on corporate America's GLBT employees for the sixth year in a row. The firm also regularly conducts diversity seminars that address women in the workplace issues and sexual orientation discrimination.

OUR SURVEY SAYS

Relationships—but politics, too

The firm is "a good place to work," notes an insider, and while "its culture is a bit hard to describe, it's generally very rooted in relationships." The contact adds that "this is the sort of company that employs people who, by and large, love the firm." But there are "politics" at play as well. "We are overrun by corporate initiatives, which make it hard to get any real work done." One source adds, "The ladder is so packed with VPs that we are constantly bombarded with phone calls and ideas that take us away from our real work while making them look busy."

At the firm's headquarers, the dress code is "business attire from Labor Day until Memorial Day," "business casual in the summer" and business casual on Fridays throughout the year. Other offices have various dress policies, ranging from business attire all year round to business casual all year round. Ours are "easy," notes an insider, adding that "the place is empty after 4:30 p.m. every day." Another contact says that the hours "vacillate between eight- and 12-hour shifts." But as far as advancing within the firm, things might not be so cut and dried. One insider notes that there's a "greater pressure on titles than in the past." Another agrees, adding that there's "no advancement unless you seriously luck out." One contact says that there's "no chance of being promoted" within the firm, and that "in order to get promoted, you have to be a robot and not an independent thinker." Perks offered by the firm, however, are "very good"—although you likely "will have to put up with a lot to get them," say insiders.

CIT

505 Fifth Avenue
New York, NY 10017
Phone: (212) 771-0505
www.cit.com

DEPARTMENTS

Corporate Finance
Trade Finance
Transportation Finance
Vendor Finance

THE STATS

Employer Type: Public Company
Ticker Symbol: CIT (NYSE)
Chairman & CEO: Jeffrey (Jeff) M. Peek
Revenue: $8.61 billion (FYE 12/07)
Net Income: -$111 million
No. of Employees: 5,425
No. of Offices: 50 (North America)

KEY COMPETITOR

GE Commercial Finance

UPPERS

• "Opportunities for advancement are great, and continued education is encouraged for those looking to advance further"
• Reasonable hours, and "face time is nonexistent"

DOWNERS

• Diversity with respect to women could be improved—"there are not as many women in upper management as there used to be"
• Average compensation

EMPLOYMENT CONTACT

See "careers" section of www.cit.com

Visit the Vault Finance Career Channel at **www.vault.com/finance** — with
insider firm profiles, message boards, the Vault Finance Job Board and more.

VAULT CAREER LIBRARY   103

THE SCOOP

All inclusive

CIT Group provides financing and related services to just about everybody, from small businesses to the world's largest multinational corporations. With finance products ranging from acquisition financing and asset management to venture capital and vendor financing, CIT operates across 30 industries in 50 countries, including North America, Europe, Latin America, Asia, Australia and New Zealand. The company, which itself is ranked No. 306 on the Fortune 500, does business with a majority of the Fortune 1000 companies and, by the end of 2007, managed over $80 billion in assets.

CIT's business can be broken down into four main segments. Corporate finance provides lending, leasing, and other financial and advisory services to middle-market companies, with a focus on specific industries, including health care, energy, communications, media and entertainment. The trade finance division provides factoring and other trade and financial products to companies in the retail supply chain. Transportation finance provides lending, leasing and other banking services to the rail as well as aerospace and defense industries. Vendor finance provides financing solutions to manufacturers, distributors and other intermediaries, including Avaya, Dell, Microsoft, Snap-on and Toshiba.

Ups and Downs

Founded in 1908, CIT has weathered a somewhat rocky past under the ownership of numerous companies. It is probably best known for its affiliation with Tyco, which in 2002, embroiled in corporate scandals, spun off CIT. Out from under its beleaguered owner, CIT has grown over the past few years through acquisitions, including units from GE Commercial Services, HSBC Bank and CitiCapital.

Today, it is a global commercial finance company, providing financing solutions, leasing products and advisory services to commercial and consumer clients around the world. Especially strong in factoring, vendor financing, equipment and transportation financing, small business administration loans and asset-based lending, CIT is a Fortune 500 company and member of the S&P 500 Index.

The firm went through some new expansion efforts in early 2007. CIT announced plans to open offices in Shanghai and Singapore, and it bought

Barclays' vendor finance business in England and Germany. It's managed to keep busy in other ways, too. In April 2007, the firm filed an IPO of $275 million for the real estate investment trust Care Investment Trust. Within the same month, CIT Chairman and CEO Jeff Peek told Investment Dealers' Digest about a few other new developments the firm has on tap for the future, such as an agreement to finance Microsoft's software sales and the recent hiring of a loan specialist team "to look for distressed debt when we find something that is of value."

Closing up shop

If things looked rosy in the early part of 2007, they didn't stay that way for long. The company closed its home lending origination business, which was impacted by the market decline in subprime mortgages. All in all a $134.5 million decrease in profits was reported in the second quarter and the stock price continued to decline into the late months of 2007. Closing the home lending business also meant bad news for some CIT employees: 550 jobs were cut in over 25 offices around the country.

Silver linings

It wasn't all bad for CIT Group in 2007—some key deals were still carried out, including the aforementioned collaboration with Microsoft. In the terms of that deal, CIT expanded its vendor financing relationship with Microsoft to the U.S. and in Canada. Before, CIT had been serving Microsoft primarily in European countries such as France, Germany, Italy, Switzerland and the United Kingdom. Separately, the company expanded its global vendor financing division throughout the world, opening offices in Dublin and Shanghai.

In July 2007, CIT acquired an M&A firm called Edgeview partners, in an attempt to branch out into the steadily growing private equity market. Walter J. Owens, president of CIT's corporate finance group, said of the deal, "We are very pleased to have completed this acquisition as it will accelerate CIT's coverage of the rapidly growing private equity community."

Though its home lending business is now kaput, CIT's small business lending remains strong. In fact, CIT Small Business Lending Corporation was named #1 Small Business 7(a) lender for the eighth year in a row. The ranking is based on SBA 7(a) loan volume for the 2007 SBA during which time CIT provided more than $882 million in SBA 7(a) loans to 1,601 small businesses as compared to $872 million and 1,487 small businesses in 2006.

Visit the Vault Finance Career Channel at www.vault.com/finance — with insider firm profiles, message boards, the Vault Finance Job Board and more.

VAULT CAREER LIBRARY   105

Numbers tell a sad story

As for its overall financial results in 2007, the firm's revenue increased to $8.6 billion, up from $6.94 billion in 2006. Net income took a freefall, decreasing from $1.05 billion in 2006 to a net loss of $81 million in 2007. And over the course of the year, CIT's stock price dropped from a high of $61.59 to December lows of $23.05. CIT's home lending and student lending businesses suffered the most, leading to the overall dismal results.

At the half-year mark of 2008, CIT's finances still weren't looking up. The firm earned $1.56 billion in revenue in the second quarter, down from $2.06 billion in the second quarter of 2008. Net income, too, was anemic in the second quarter of 2008—the firm was dealt a net loss of $2.06 billion for the quarter, worse than both the net loss of $249.7 million in the first quarter of 2008 and the net loss of $127 million in the second quarter of 2007. CIT's results were a manifestation of the financial fallout it continued to feel due to the bottoming out of its home lending business.

GETTING HIRED

Getting more selective

CIT recruiters "are a bit choosy," sources say, and they're "looking for individuals who fit into their puzzle and have long-term goals." Selectivity can vary by department; one woman in portfolio management says, "My department is very specialized, so only those with thorough knowledge and the ability to adapt quickly are chosen. Other departments are less stringent." Overall, though, insiders believe the firm's standards have gotten higher in recent years. "It used to be much easier" to land a job at CIT one employee opines.

The company recruits at several schools across the country—"Boston College, New York University, Columbia, Bucknell and Michigan" are some favorites. Other "Northeast colleges" are targeted, especially for the New York-area offices. But CIT doesn't just recruit on campus—it also relies on "job boards and staffing agencies" as well as job fairs, external recruiters and referrals from current employees."

No tricks

Candidates interviewing for a position in another city should expect several preliminary phone interviews before traveling to their potential job site. Sources report two to four interview sessions in total. "I had four interviews—two with managers above me, one with a peer and one with a subordinate," a man says. A woman in the loan division recalls, "I met with the hiring manager, someone I would be working closely with and a vice president. It helped that I did some research into FELLP lending before the interview."

Another employee who "met with a bunch of my future employees" during the interview process believes that some CIT departments "seem to favor the group interview, where four to eight people are in the room asking questions."

The questions are "fairly straightforward in nature," and cover things like "your background, experience in the industry and examples of deals you may have worked on in the past." There is an emphasis on "personality questions," like "How do you handle stress?" and "Why do you want to work here?" According to one source, first impressions make a real impact at CIT: final interview rounds are "more of a business formality—after the first interview they know if they want to hire you or not."

Prove yourself

CIT offers internships, and also accepts interns "through INROADS" (a national program that links minority candidates with internships). The internship "is a good foot in the door," but "it is not vital" for landing a full-time job. It's also "not a guarantee for a job," says an investment manager. "We just let an intern go because he was not up to speed."

The firm's financial analyst program is another entry point; to be eligible, candidates must have recently obtained an undergraduate degree in finance or accounting, with a minimum 3.2 GPA. This program begins with a six-week training program at CIT headquarters in New York City, where they learn modeling, analytical, communications and sales skills. From there, candidates are assigned directly to business units. CIT recruits on-campus for the financial analyst program, and posts an updated recruiting calendar on its careers web site.

Visit the Vault Finance Career Channel at www.vault.com/finance — with insider firm profiles, message boards, the Vault Finance Job Board and more.

VAULT CAREER LIBRARY

107

OUR SURVEY SAYS

Still evolving

The CIT environment is "collegial and performance-oriented," but one source says the company is "still trying to figure out its culture, which is not an easy task since it is an international corporation." "Evolving and varied" is how one longtime employee describes CIT. "A new CEO came in about four years ago and has surrounded himself with executives hired from the outside. The company is pretty decentralized, so I think that the culture is more regional as opposed to corporate. I also think the culture is perceived differently by those who were with the company prior to the new CEO's arrival because they have a basis for comparison."

Another employee who's been at CIT for several years says that on the plus side, "Opportunities for advancement are great, and continued education is encouraged for those looking to advance further." She adds, "Self-expression is not frowned upon, within the bounds of good taste." "In the past couple of years, the company has made great strides in shedding its image as a sleepy factoring/traditional ABL firm," adds an insider. The new CIT image is that of "a more robust specialty finance firm offering a broad array of products and services." A recent hire notes that one obstacle the firm faces is "not being a large commercial bank or affiliated with a AAA-rated company." This "can sometimes limit liquidity or capital outlay, which in turn can lead to not winning certain deals."

Keeping the balance

CIT Group insiders agree: their company is "not a sweatshop." "We are in at 8:30 a.m. and out at 5:00 p.m.," says a portfolio manager. "There is no real pressure from where I sit." "A typical work week is 50 to 55 hours," a longtime member of the client lending department says. Of course, "hours, including potential weekend work, vary depending on the stage of a particular deal you're working on, as well as the state of the market." Still, "face time is nonexistent here." "Some groups work bankers' hours," adds an insider, while other groups or departments put in longer hours. "It all depends on leadership, the competence of those in the group and your ability to say no." "There is more than enough work to work 60-hour weeks," concludes a source. "However, with rare exceptions, you will not be requested by management to work more than 40."

Employees give the company just average marks on compensation, and one source says "The compensation policy changed last year, for the worse. We used to receive a target bonus percentage at certain salary bands, but we moved to a discretionary system by which bonus dollars are taken away from the entire pool to be given to high performers. It's really a demotivator to not be able to count on a percentage for working hard and meeting job standards, which are set to a high standard to begin with."

Perks and benefits include "good 401(k) matching," though one source says there "are not enough funds to have safe returns." Employees get "reimbursement, up to a stated amount, for gym memberships; paid parking in some offices; company cars for business development officers; and free bottled water." One investment manager says, "Managers usually buy dinner on the last day of the month if we end up working past 8 p.m."

In good taste

Office space is "functional at best" at most CIT locations. "As with much of corporate America, basic color schemes and pseudo-ergonomic chairs abound," says a source in the Jacksonville office. "However, if you chose to cover your space in the latest clippings from Vogue or Popular Mechanics, that's okay too." Recent upgrades "in New York and Chicago" earn high marks from sources, but many employees in New Jersey complain about "dingy" conditions. "The main office has tiny, low cubes, but a great cafeteria," a source in Morristown, N.J., says. Over in Livingston, N.J., employees bemoan the "old furniture, sinking chairs and worn carpets" as well as the "potholes in flooring and mold in bathrooms."

The CIT dress code is business casual, except for client contact; "casual Fridays" are enjoyed in some locations. A source in the Sunshine State says, "No jeans are allowed, but here in Florida, golf shirts are always acceptable." In Los Angeles, "jeans are allowed every Friday." Bottom line? Just "keep it tasteful," one source advises.

Working on diversity

"There are few, if any, minority managers in this firm," a source says. "From what I can tell it's not for a lack of looking, but upper management does seem to be primarily white males." "The culture here accepts the glass ceiling and acquiesces to it." While there is a women's council at CIT, one employee describes it as "just window dressing," and a woman says the firm still has hallmarks of "a boys' club." Another female employee says she wishes CIT

Visit the Vault Finance Career Channel at **www.vault.com/finance** — with insider firm profiles, message boards, the Vault Finance Job Board and more.

VAULT CAREER LIBRARY

109

did more to "provide a respectful and inclusive environment where people are encouraged to share their diverse perspectives and backgrounds while working toward a common set of goals." One suggested change? "Modify the contracts that start with 'Gentlemen.'"

One man says that when it comes to ethnic diversity, there's "high representation of minorities in the rank and file, but not in management and the board of directors." An openly-gay employee notes that CIT "does provide health benefits to life partners for those employees who need it," but adds, "I would like to see a GLBT employee in a management role."

Speak up for training

There is "an open-door policy" at CIT, and sources say that most managers are "interested in treating employees well." "High respect for subordinates is the norm throughout the company," according to one insider. As a result, "managers and subordinates seem to all get along quite well," but some "CIT policies" and layers of red tape can interfere. One man reports the frustration of "having to be micromanaged," and a woman says the management mentality seems "stuck in the times of 25 years ago," with decision-making in the hands of "top-echelon executive vice presidents. They don't need to make all the decisions, especially the very mundane ones."

Opinions vary on CIT's training, and "depending on who runs the training, the experience varies wildly." "Formal training is run of the mill," says one source, "but the online learning center is like a college at your fingertips, for free." An investment manager suggests, "You are not always offered training, so sometimes you have to ask."

Countrywide Financial Corp.

4500 Park Granada
Calabasas, CA 91302-1613
(818) 225-3000
Fax: (818) 225-4051
www.countrywide.com

DEPARTMENTS

Banking
Capital Markets
Corporate
Global Operations
Insurance
Loan Closing
Mortgage Banking

THE STATS

Employer Type: Subsidiary of Bank of
America
Chairman & CEO: Angelo R. Mozilo
President & COO: David Sambol
Revenue: $6.06 billion (FYE 12/07)
Net Income: $-0.70 billion
No. of Employees: 54,655
No. of Offices: 800

KEY COMPETITORS

Fannie Mae
Washington Mutual
Wells Fargo

UPPERS

- "Nice people and great co-workers"
- "Ethics-driven [culture] with a focus on productivity"
- Good relations with managers

DOWNERS

- Culture can be "very corporate" and "rigid"
- Opportunities for advancement aren't easy to obtain"
- Sale to Bank of America = uncertain future

EMPLOYMENT CONTACT

www.countrywidecareers.com

THE SCOOP

Hard times

In 2007, tough times fell upon Countrywide Financial Corporation, the largest U.S. mortgage lender. With the market in freefall, and banks declaring new waves of massive write-downs every day throughout the tumultuous summer, one word was on everyone's lips: subprime. Unfortunately for Countrywide, and the mortgage business in general, subprime loans were one of the main forces that was driving its stunning revenue in the housing boom of the last several years. The party came to a screeching halt and the beleaguered Countrywide struggled to regain a steady footing.

Things came to a boil in January 2008, when Bank of America announced it would be acquiring Countrywide for approximately $4 billion in stock. The price valued the troubled Countrywide at $7.16 per share; under the terms of the deal, Countrywide shareholders would receive 0.1822 of a Bank of America share in exchange for each Countrywide share.

Prior to the announcement of the deal, Countrywide's foreclosure rate had doubled, it recorded its first quarterly loss in 25 years and rumors flew that it was on the verge of bankruptcy. So why would BofA make the acquisition? For one thing, the bank already owned a 16 percent stake in Countrywide (BofA paid $2 billion for the share in August 2007), and part of its stakeholder rights was the ability to beat any other bid for the lender. In communications about the deal, BofA noted it stood to gain significant capabilities, including Countrywide's proven distribution and technology operations. In addition, the merger would position BofA as a leader in the effort to help keep more Americans in their homes and ensure that more Americans have the opportunity to achieve home ownership.

Although Countrywide's subprime mortgage issues topped headlines, revenue in its core business—its loan servicing portfolio—remained steady (subprime-related mortgages only account for 10 percent of its portfolio). Analysts also noted that BofA's proposal was priced at a discount and that in 10 years, BofA could turn it into a profitable piece of its pie.

But in March 2008, Countrywide's planned sale to Bank of America ran into a snag. A federal inquiry from the U.S. Justice Department and the F.B.I. into possible securities fraud at Countrywide resulted in BofA receiving pressure to withdraw its proposal that Countrywide president and COO David Sambol take over the combined mortgage company once the purchase was completed.

(In addition to Countrywide's activities, the criminal inquiry encompassed 14 other firms in the mortgage industry.) Despite the investigation, a Bank of America spokesman said in an interview with Thomson Financial News that the acquisition still "remains on track." And it did remain that way, for the most part. The deal finally closed in July 2008.

Take five

Countrywide is organized into five major divisions: mortgage banking, capital markets, banking, insurance and global operations (a joint venture in the United Kingdom launched in 1999). The mortgage banking segment is comprised of three divisions: loan production, loan servicing and loan closing services. Loan production originates prime and non-prime mortgage loans through a national distribution system. Loan servicing services mortgage loans on behalf of Fannie Mae, Freddie Mac, Ginnie Mae and various private and public investors in return for an annual fee. Loan closing services provides credit reports, appraisals, title reports and flood demonstrations to the loan production sector and other third parties.

The banking segment's operations are made up of Countrywide Bank, N.A. and Countrywide Warehouse Lending. Countrywide Bank offers depository and home loan products to consumers. Countrywide Warehouse Lending provides temporary financing secured by mortgage loans to third-party mortgage bankers.

The capital markets segment is a fixed-income investment banking firm comprised mainly of the operations of Countrywide Securities Corporation (CSC), a registered broker-dealer and primary-dealer of U.S. treasury securities. CSC primarily engages in the sales, trading and underwriting of mortgage, U.S. treasury and other asset-backed securities, as well as related research and advisory activities.

Insurance activities are conducted through Balboa Life and Casualty Group, whose companies are national providers of property, life and casualty insurance; and Balboa Reinsurance, a captive mortgage reinsurance company. Global operations' primary unit is Global Home Loans, a majority-owned joint venture that provides loan origination processing and loan sub-servicing in the United Kingdom.

Visit the Vault Finance Career Channel at **www.vault.com/finance** — with
insider firm profiles, message boards, the Vault Finance Job Board and more.

VAULT CAREER LIBRARY   **113**

Humble beginnings

In 1969, Angelo Mozilo, who began his career as a 14-year-old messenger for a Manhattan mortgage company, and David Loeb launched their own mortgage company, Countrywide Credit Industries. Before the year's end, Countrywide went public, trading at less than $1 per share. The offering did not raise much capital but, undeterred, the two New York bankers left the Big Apple thereafter and opened an office in Los Angeles amidst a booming housing market.

During its initial years in business, the company offered Federal Housing Administration and the Veterans Administration loans through a commissioned sales force. Countrywide has always focused on the multicultural community and is the largest lender to minorities, including being the top lender to African Americans, Hispanics and Asians, as well as the leading lender in low- to moderate-income communities.

However, the firm's founders believed that its existing business model did not provide the proper type of customer service, and decided they needed to move in a new direction. Over lunch one day, the two came up with a model that would revolutionize the way they do business. Namely, the company would open branch offices without sales people, where customers could receive retail bank-like service. The first branch was opened in 1974 in Whittier, Calif. Over the next 10 years, loan production and branches grew steadily, and by 1980, there were 40 Countrywide branches in nine states. Eventually, the firm further expanded lending operations into conventional loans that could be sold to Fannie Mae and Freddie Mac.

Growth continued and Countrywide rose up in the ranks of mortgage lenders in the United States. In 2006, the company became the first mortgage lender to surpass $1 trillion in servicing,

Trouble before the credit crisis

In September 2006, without giving a reason or a departure date, the company's president and COO for more than a decade, Stanford L. Kurland, said he was leaving the company. Kurland was believed to be the heir apparent to Mozilo, who was expected to step down as CEO at the end of the year but remain as chairman. The move was inexplicable at the time, but in retrospect, it seems to be a gloomy harbinger of the chaos about to break loose upon Countrywide.

Things continued spiraling downward in September 2006 when the company announced it planned to sell up to $4.5 billion in new debt as a result of faltering home prices. Chairman and CEO Angelo Mozilo warned investors that he had to prepare the company for the "worst that could happen in the market," adding that he had never seen a soft landing in 53 years. In April 2007, the worst seemed to rise to the surface: the company announced that it planned to cut 108 positions in its wholesale lending unit's subprime division.

Unfortunately for Countrywide, these problems in the spring were only a small taste of the misfortune that was about to unfold. Countrywide's central philosophy of making loans available to low and middle income class families, combined with a bad ratings system that overestimated the value of subprime loans, caused a blowback that resulted in thousands of delinquencies and defaults on loans. In August 2007, Countrywide was forced to access its emergency credit line for $11.5 billion just to maintain liquidity.

With the company in shambles, the industry was buzzing about Countrywide's ability to sustain itself in such catastrophe. But in August, 2007, it received a pick-me-up from its own personal white knight, Bank of America, which pumped $2 billion in capital into the failing company, temporarily bailing it out. In exchange, Bank of America received $2.4 billion worth of preferred convertible shares.

By the third quarter of 2007, Countrywide had to admit that its losses were significant enough so that in order to pull the company out of the looming shadow of bankruptcy, it would have to cut some of its workforce. In September 2007, it did more than just lay off "some" employees: Countrywide announced that in the next three months, it would trim its labor force by 10,000 to 12,000 jobs. At the time of the announcement, this number represented approximately 20 percent of Countrywide's 60,000 employees. The layoffs were directed at mortgage underwriters and back-office operations, leaving those in the banking and insurance divisions relatively unscathed.

Lawsuits, lawsuits, lawsuits

After it became apparent that Countrywide was in dire straights, many investors became understandably upset about the company's misrepresentation of its financial stability. Five separate lawsuits were filed, and in December 2007, a federal judge consolidated them all together and appointed New York's Common Retirement Fund and New York City Pension fund as the lead plaintiffs. The company's third quarter losses were $1.2 billion and the stock price had lost nearly 75 percent of its value in the past year. At the time that the consolidation of the lawsuits was announced, the stock was trading at $10.68, far lower than its 52-week high of $45.26.

The troubles continued to mount in December when a national labor union that represents more than 450,000 called on its constituents to boycott Countrywide as a result of its high level of foreclosures. The union, called UNITE HERE, represents workers in the apparel manufacturing, hotel, restaurant and retail industries, and has called for its members to aggressively e-mail Countrywide regarding its foreclosure policies and also to refuse to make deposits into its banks.

More bad news

In July 2008, Florida's attorney general filed a lawsuit against Countrywide and five other companies he said used dubious business practices in their mortgage practices that might constitute fraud. Attorney General Bill McCollum said Countrywide saddled customers with mortgages they couldn't pay for. Legal Services of North Florida's Marc Taps also alleged that that the firm "accepted applications which were patently fraudulent and reflected no ability on the part of the borrowers to make the required payments."

GETTING HIRED

No snail mail

Submitting a resume online is the "fastest and most efficient way to express interest in job opportunities," according to the firm, as it "no longer accept resumes via e-mail, mail or fax." Insiders say the firm recruits "nationally," but there seems to be a focus out West. One source cites "UCLA, Stanford, USC and Pepperdine" as major hunting grounds. Even so, the firm does go coast to coast, visiting schools such as Boston University, the University of Illinois at Chicago, Kent State (in Ohio), Arizona State University, UNLV and the University of North Texas, among others. On-campus recruits could have as many as five interviews. One risk management insider who went through that many adds, "It took about three months to get the offer." Another, who works in sales, only went through "three interviews" and ranks the firm about average when it comes to selectivity.

At the firm's careers site, candidates can search for openings by job category and location. They can also read about the firm's programs in tuition reimbursement, career development, mentoring and diversity. There's also a link to the firm's on-campus recruiting events and a place for candidates to sign up to be reminded about events in their area.

Several ways in

Depending on position and location, the interview process tends to vary. "I was contacted directly by the hiring manager who found my resume online," says one contact. "I was surprised that the hiring manager didn't want to do a phone screen prior to bringing me in." The source adds that when he did go in, "the interview was fairly pleasant. The hiring manager spent several minutes describing his department and the various functions in it, as well as the function he wanted me to perform. We had some very basic Q&A and it went quite well." The source does admit that he felt "very uneasy about the fact that I was fairly isolated during the entire interview process. I was not even casually introduced to anybody in the halls."

Another respondent says that it "was one of the easiest interviews I've ever had," adding, "I met the hiring manager for lunch on a Saturday, then met with his manager the following Wednesday for about an hour and received my offer letter the following week. During the interview, there were no tough questions, just the standard, 'Where do you see yourself in five years?' 'What are your strengths?' and 'Tell me about a time when ...'" An insider who went through several interviews says, "I was interviewed by a senior recruiter in HR, the EVP of sales, the EVP and SVP of operations, the EVP of compliance, and the director of the division at the corporate office. I was also interviewed by the regional sales manager and the regional operations manager in the hiring location." In addition, he was "interviewed via telephone twice and in person four times," adding that when applying for a senior vice president-level position, candidates will be asked questions "primarily directed at management style and experiences in other organizations similar to the position. The interview process seemed more like they were selling the company to me than vice versa."

But there are a variety of questions you can expect to be asked during your interview process. One insider reports being asked "What do you see yourself doing in the future?" Another contact who went through two interviews to land her job was asked, "If you could describe yourself in one word, what would it be?" Another reports going through an "easy interview with two people who would become my bosses" before landing the job. A business analyst lays out a four-tier process: "The first interview is with a recruiter who asks you why you want to work here and the basic behavioral

Visit the Vault Finance Career Channel at **www.vault.com/finance** — with insider firm profiles, message boards, the Vault Finance Job Board and more.

VAULT CAREER LIBRARY   117

questions. The second one is with the head of the group who was also the hiring manager and who asks questions about work experience. The third is with the same person as the second, and it's a technical interview with a written exam. The last interview is with an executive who asks behavioral questions." If you're made an offer at the end of the process, you can also expect to go through a "credit check" and a "reference check" prior to your hiring, say insiders, who call the whole process an "extensive and time-consuming" one.

OUR SURVEY SAYS

Make the corporate sale

The Countrywide culture can be "sales-oriented" and "very corporate," insiders say, while others call it "excellent" and "ethics-driven with a focus on productivity." "The culture is a bit rigid, but fast-paced," says one respondent. "I enjoyed working with my colleagues more than anything," admits another. Either way, "it's a culture of accountability where employees are expected to work hard." Yet another source says, "I really enjoy my job and co-workers." "Nice people and great co-workers," says a contact describing the culture. "And my group is very diverse." Others, though, are less pleased. "This is a good company, and it tries to institute a noble culture, but with some of the managers in place, the culture cannot take hold." The contact adds that for advancement "it depends on who you know." Another source says, "I was promised training and never received it. They are full of broken promises." Yet another says, "For a long time, I really enjoyed our work environment. My co-workers were fun, and our branch manager fostered an open, friendly environment. Then the regional sales manager got involved, and everything went downhill." Manager relations, though, generally receive good marks. "My manager is great," says one source, who concedes, though, that "it does all depend on the individual manager."

The comp and the extras

Sources give compensation and benefits average ratings. "Stock options, 401(k) with matching, and an on-site gym and cafeteria" are among the extras provided. Others include two weeks of vacation per year for the first five years (higher-ups receive more), increasing to three weeks after that, eight paid holidays, one floating paid holiday and six sick days. An employee stock purchase plan is also available. One insider laments, however, that there are "no monthly or year-end bonuses, ever."

Required employee dress is "business casual"—or, more specifically, "nice business dress," "with some unique rules." For women, shoes "must be closed in either the front or the back—no dress sandals allowed," and "if you wear a sleeveless blouse, you must keep your jacket on all day." Another insider says that staffers are allowed to wear "jeans only on the last day of the month."

Hours can be harsh depending on your work cycle. "All employees are expected to be at their desks by 8 a.m. every morning and not leave until after 5 p.m.," says one. "If lunch is taken, it should not be more than an hour." A risk manager puts his normal hours as "50 to 60" per week and, during crunch times, as "60 to 70." He adds, "Even if you're here until 1 a.m. working on something, you're still expected to be in first thing in the morning." He does, though, report "rarely" coming in on the weekends. Another contact says that "nearing the month-end, our work hours increased to 48 to 50 hours." And when it comes to advancing, be aware that "the opportunities for advancement aren't easy to obtain" and "they don't promote often. If they do, there was hardly a raise given when being promoted."

The office space is just average, report insiders. One says that "only VPs receive offices, and the cube walls are very, very low," making it "difficult at best to have any type of a private conversation or view anything private on your computer." And one respondent notes that while "diversity efforts are big, it's not a top priority."

Tough times

The outlook for Countrywide, is looking a little "difficult" and "grim," insiders say. The firm's "credibility is shot—as is their credit rating." One contact predicts "massive layoffs yet to come either way" with "little or no severance money for the white-collar people who actually do the work day in and day out." Another employee confirms the tough times for Countrywide. "My marketing position is being eliminated in California due to cost-cutting techniques to transfer all Countrywide Insurance Service operations to Arizona and Texas." The contact adds that potential employees should "be wary before jumping onboard—I joined thinking I would find a home for a few years, not realizing that my permanent, full-time job would be shortened to a year-and-a-half" due to the rounds of layoffs." Yet another worker warns to "watch the news—Countrywide will be lucky if they survive this downturn in the market," adding that employee "morale is extremely low."

Visit the Vault Finance Career Channel at www.vault.com/finance — with
insider firm profiles, message boards, the Vault Finance Job Board and more.

VAULT CAREER LIBRARY   119

Daimler Financial Services

Eichhornstraße 3
10875 Berlin, Germany
Phone: +49-30-2554-0
Fax: +49-30-2554-2525

27777 Inkster Road
Farmington Hills, MI 48334
Phone: (248) 427-6300
Fax: (248) 427-6600
www.daimler-financialservices.com

DEPARTMENTS

Business Vehicle Financing
Consumer Leasing
Credit Cards
Dealer Financing
Fleet Financing
Municipal Financing
Owner-Operator Financing
Personal Insurance
Vocational Financing

THE STATS

Employer Type: Subsidiary of the Daimler Group
Chairman: Jürgen H. Walker
President & CEO, Americas: Klaus D. Entenmann
Revenue: €8.71 billion (FYE 12/07)
No. of Employees: 6,500
No. of Offices: 100

KEY COMPETITORS

Ford Motor Credit
GMAC
JPMorgan Chase
Toyota Motor Credit

UPPER

- "The people"

DOWNER

- Better diversity needed

EMPLOYMENT CONTACT

See "jobs & more" section of
www.daimler-financialservices.com

THE SCOOP

New name

In October 2007, DaimlerChrysler Financial Services, the financial services department for the Daimler Group, announced it would begin operations under the new name Daimler Financial Services AG, which includes Mercedes-Benz Financial, Daimler Truck Financial, Mercedes Benz Financial Services Canada and Daimler Financial Services Mexico. The name change followed DaimlerChrysler's sale of its Chrysler division to American private equity firm Cerberus for about $7.4 billion in May 2007. Chrysler had been losing money due largely to costs associated with rising pension and health costs. As a result, Chrysler Group announced a restructuring plan that would cut about 13,000 jobs. Under the plan, the firm does not expect to turn a profit until 2009. Outside of North America, Daimler Financial Services will remain the exclusive financial services partner for the brands Chrysler, Dodge and Jeep.

Daimler Financial Services Americas announced in December 2007 that it would retain its U.S. headquarters in Farmington Hills, Mich., following the DaimlerChrysler de-merger. "At Daimler Financial Services Americas, our commitment to the region is clear—we believe in the long-term potential of Michigan and want to facilitate job growth in the area as well as strengthening the community in which we live," president and chief executive officer Klaus Entenmann said.

Financial driver

A worldwide financial services provider, Daimler Financial Services AG represents one of the world's largest financial services providers outside the banking and insurance industries. Headquartered in Berlin, Germany, it offers flexible financial solutions customized to suit the requirements of individual customers of all vehicle brands within the Daimler Group, as well as cross-brand fleet management. Globally, the company manages a portfolio of approximately €65 billion through its operations in more than 40 countries; every third Daimler vehicle sold is financed or leased by Daimler Financial Services.

In the U.S., Mercedes-Benz Financial offers a range of financing plans to customers looking to buy Mercedes-Benz vehicles. More than 400,000 U.S. drivers enjoy the benefits of leasing or financing their Mercedes-Benz vehicles through Mercedes-Benz financial. Daimler Truck Financial serves

Visit the Vault Finance Career Channel at **www.vault.com/finance** — with insider firm profiles, message boards, the Vault Finance Job Board and more.

VAULT CAREER LIBRARY   **121**

as a captive financial services provider for the Freightliner LLC family of commercial vehicle products, including Freightliner, Sterling, Western Star, SelecTrucks, Springer, Thomas Built Buses, Unimog, Setra and others. The division serves more than 10,000 commercial vehicles in the U.S. Overall, Daimler Financial Services in the U.S. employs more than 450 people managing contracts worth more than $23 billion.

Late 1980s discovery

The tale of Daimler Financial Services began in 1989, when the board of then Daimler-Benz AG decided to establish a financial arm, initially called Debis. In 1990, Debis became official and divided into five business units: Systemhaus, Financial Services, Insurance Brokerage, Trading and Marketing Services. In 1991, together with Metro trading company and NYNEX, Debis founded Debitel, a network-independent telecommunications provider. In 1993, Debis played its hand at aviation, when it started an aircraft fund for private investors for the financing of A340 airbuses. By January 2005, Debis generated 50 percent of its revenues with customers outside of Daimler-Benz.

Debis' focus became more centered in 1998, when Daimler-Benz AG and Chrysler Corp. merged, creating Daimler Chrysler. The next year, DaimlerChrysler announced it would fuse its worldwide financial services under the umbrella of Debis. In 2001, the division became known as Daimler Chrysler Services. Also in 2001, the division found presence in the German banking market by changing the Mercedes-Benz Lease Finanz Group's name to DaimlerChysler Bank.

Expanding in Texas, contracting in Illinois

In response to the de-merger, Daimler Financial Services Americas announced plans in November 2007 to expand its Westlake, Tex., customer service, collection and remarketing operations of the Mercedes-Benz Financial business unit to embrace similar functions for the Daimler Truck Financial business unit by summer 2008. The employee base of about 44 people at the Texas location expanded to include 180 positions from the Daimler Truck Financial operations in Lisle, Ill., and another 35 employees from Mercedes-Benz Financial locations throughout the country.

To accommodate the expansion in Texas, the company plan to build a three-story, 160,000-sqaure-foot facility near Forth Worth that can accommodate up to 800 employees. The move represents the leaner company's strategy to grow and service its loan portfolio in the U.S., which support the sales of

Mercedes-Benz cars and Freightliner, Sterling and Western Star heavy duty trucks. "The de-merger has given us the opportunity to take a clean sheet of paper approach to our operations and re-engineer the way we serve our dealers and retail customers in the U.S. market," Entenmann said in a press release.

Reorganizing for regions

In April 2007, Daimler Truck Financial announced a fresh regionalization initiative aimed at improving service to Freightliner, Sterling and Western Star dealers and all industry segments across the U.S. Under the initiative, four departments (sales, credit, dealer credit and a new small business credit department) will begin operating regionally to serve the eastern, central, southern and western portions of the country. The newly formed small business credit team will handle fleets with less than 11 trucks or less than $500,000 line of credit with Daimler Truck Financial, while fleet credit will service larger fleets.

The reorganized sales and credit teams will allow the company to create credit buyers for specific regions, facilitate daily internal communication between sales and credit departments, and allow for team visits to dealerships to fortify communication.

Reaching Russia

In November 2007, DaimlerChrysler Bank Rus opened in Moscow. The company, which changed its name to Mercedes-Benz Bank Rus, offers loans to private and commercial customers for new and used vehicles, allowing Daimler dealers in Russia to broaden the range of financial services they can offer customers.

The company has set up electronic point of sale systems at local dealerships, allowing the whole loan application to take place electronically and ensuring quick decision-making when it comes to approving credit applications and processing contracts. The bank will also offer dealers financing for their inventories.

Best in overall satisfaction

In 2007, J.D. Power and Associates ranked Mercedes-Benz Financial as the best in overall satisfaction in its dealer financing satisfaction study. The company also took the top spot in floor planning and prime retail credit. It came in second place in retail leasing and account management.

Visit the Vault Finance Career Channel at www.vault.com/finance — with insider firm profiles, message boards, the Vault Finance Job Board and more.

VAULT CAREER LIBRARY   123

Ten years of fleet management in Germany

In July 2007, DaimlerChrysler Fleet Management celebrated its 10th year providing passenger car fleet management services in Germany. The company's portfolio includes about 680 fleets with a contract volume of more than €850 million. Daimler Fleet Management began in July 1997 as debit Car Fleet Management, offering cross-brand fleet management to fleet operators.

In addition to service leasing, customers also could take advantage of driver support, claims management, online reporting and online order processing. The company's uniform FleetPlus product package combines leasing and service components for operators of small and mid-sized fleets with 10 to 30 vehicles. Customers with larger fleets can create their own service packages.

Slight fall

For the second quarter of 2008, Daimler Financial upped its contract volume by 4 percent versus the same period a year earlier to €60.4 billion. But earnings dipped to €183 million for the quarter from €220 million in the second quarter of 2007. The higher cost of risk during the year was cited as a factor in the lower numbers. An overall bigger contract volume, however, helped to counteract the fallout slightly.

GETTING HIRED

They'll find you

If you're interested in the firm and you have the right background, you can rest assured that Daimler Financial Services will find you—the company recruits using "the Internet," "newspaper ads" and "headhunters," insiders say. Then there's the standby of checking out their website as well. At the "jobs and more" section of its web site, candidates can search for open positions on the firm's job board. Daimler Financial Services recruits through events and campus visits at colleges throughout the U.S. One insider says the company also recruits through "the Internet, newspapers and headhunters."

What to expect

You can expect to go through two—maybe three—rounds of interviews with the firm. One insider reports fielding questions that "focused on my previous experience and education." Another contact says interview questions "centered on writing abilities—I had to provide samples—and my strategic vision for the position." You might also be asked about "previous work experience and education." Yet another insider reports an all-day interview in an "assessment center" with "six to seven group exercises as well as individual interviews."

And once you're extended an offer on the salaried side, watch out for "HR bluffs," one insider warns. "HR played the 'bad cop' and said that they were a 'first offer is the best offer' company, and the terms offered could not be changed. I found out after I was hired that this was not true."

OUR SURVEY SAYS

Daimler pride

Insiders seem pretty proud of their culture. One insider says the firm "thinks all the time about integrating us to its labor culture with events and diverse activities." The firm has "a culture of talking and politics," says another insider. Yet another employee says that "it's a pretty good place to work," but the specific company culture "varies by department, since each department has the leeway to set the standards for hours, dress code, opportunities for advancement, etc." One employee agrees, adding that "hours and dress code are left up to individual department management."

The dress is "generally business casual," reports one insider, who adds that "the hours are also good. As long as you take care of the work you are responsible for in the time frame it needs to be done, flex-time is accepted." Other perks include the "Christmas bonus," "company-provided meals" and cars provided for work.

Move on up

Advancement opportunities are available, but employees "have to manage their own careers" and "take the initiative if the opportunity is there," says one insider, adding that "people rarely stay in the same job or department for their entire career." It's also expected within the firm that "you move to

Visit the Vault Finance Career Channel at **www.vault.com/finance** — with insider firm profiles, message boards, the Vault Finance Job Board and more.

VAULT CAREER LIBRARY   **125**

a different position every three years or so." Employees are "the drivers for opportunities for advancement," notes one insider. Another contact says that "opportunities for advancement are multiple, since DaimlerChrysler is a very global company and has many interesting departments." And largely, the culture seems to vary from department to department. While "some departments have totally empowered workers to do the job and make decisions," others "have a more traditional, 'you-must-get-your-boss'-approval' type of management." But "generally speaking, any employee can express their opinion respectfully to any of the company's officers--they are visible and accessible."

More progress needed

The firm needs to move beyond lip service when it comes to diversity, some employees say. One employee says that "we have the same opportunities," though another says that "diversity and work/life balance are talked about as being valued by the company, but while progress is being made, there is still a ways to go for females and minorities." Another employee reports that "diversity is heavily talked about, but even though one woman and one African-American are officers, the top of the company is still overwhelmingly white males."

That said, according to the firm, of the 12 top leaders profiled on its corporate web site, three are women or an ethnic minority. In addition, the company is engaged in a number of diversity initiatives, such as a diversity council made up of senior executives within the firm as well as respected community and business leaders from across the U.S. The firm says, "The council serves as a sounding board as the company works toward a more diverse and inclusive workplace."

Discover Financial Services

2500 Lake Cook Rd.
Riverwoods, IL 60015
Phone: (224) 405-0900
Fax: (224) 405-4993
www.discoverfinancial.com

DEPARTMENTS

Credit Cards
Electronic Payment

THE STATS

Employer Type: Public Company
Ticker Symbol: DFS (NYSE)
CEO & Director: David W. Nelms
Revenue: $2.89 billion (FYE 11/07)
Net Income: $588.63 million
No. of Employees: 12,000
No. of Offices: 11

KEY COMPETITORS

American Express
MasterCard
Visa

EMPLOYMENT CONTACT

See "careers" section of
www.discoverfinancial.com

Visit the Vault Finance Career Channel at **www.vault.com/finance** — with
insider firm profiles, message boards, the Vault Finance Job Board and more.

VAULT CAREER LIBRARY   127

THE SCOOP

Here comes the sun

Discover Financial Services is the fourth-largest credit-card issuer behind Visa, MasterCard and AMEX. The Discover Card was unveiled during the 1986 Super Bowl when a "Dawn of Discover" commercial featured a rising sun and a simple message: "Very few things cost you nothing to get and pay you back every day. But now the Discover Card does."

The company pioneered new features, stepping up as one of the first companies to offer cash rewards and no annual fees. Discover has evolved into one of the United States's most recognized financial brands, with its well-known "It pays to Discover" tagline and more than 50 million card members. Discover is also known for its electronic-payment services—the firm is the only credit-card issuer whose payment-network operations include both credit and debit functionality. The networks, Discover Network and PULSE, processed more than three billion transactions in 2006.

In addition to its Riverwoods, Ill., headquarters, Discover Financial Services has offices in Arizona, Delaware, Ohio, Tennessee, Utah and Texas. The firm employees over 12,000 people.

I-banking and credit cards are a different breed

Until the third quarter of 2007, Discover was part of Morgan Stanley, the revered New York-based investment bank. That relationship dates back to 1997, when Morgan Stanley merged with what was then known as Dean Witter, Discover. Although the Discover unit made some respectable contributions to the investment bank's bottom line, Morgan Stanley's soul was never in the credit card business. When the bank announced plans to spin off the Discover unit, *The New York Times* reported, "The decision represents a tacit recognition that the future of [Morgan Stanley's] success lies with the traditional heart of the firm, its lucrative trading and investment banking business."

But Morgan Stanley didn't want to cut the unit loose only to see it fail completely. The firm spent 2006 whipping it into shape, resulting in record net revenue of $4.3 billion, a 24 percent increase from 2005. Discover's credit quality and bankruptcy rates improved as well, and delinquencies and loan losses were at 10-year lows. It also launched a new debit card program, and entered into several new agreements with merchant acquirers in an effort to increase Discover's acceptance at small- and midsized businesses. The spin-off was completed in the third quarter of 2007.

Technology innovator

Discover's place at the forefront of electronic-payment systems has resulted in several technology-related awards. The firm's technology department ranked in the top 200 of America's most innovative companies on the 2007 InformationWeek 500 list. Discover also was recognized by CIO magazine in 2007, with a CIO100 Award for being one of the top 100 organizations that exemplify operational and strategic excellence in information technology. Finally, Computerworld selected Discover Financial Services as one of the top workplaces for information technology professionals for the fifth year in a row. Discover was ranked No. 45 on the 2007 Computerworld Best Places to Work in IT list, and No. 73 on the 2008 list.

Goldfish swims away—for a bargain

In February 2008, Discover announced that it was selling its U.K. credit card business, Goldfish, to Barclays Bank for about $70 million. Barclays plans to integrate Goldfish into its own credit card arm, Barclaycard. Amid worsening credit quality in Britain, the abandoned business is being offloaded at a big loss. Goldfish, which lost nearly $600 million in 2007, has been under Discover's wing since February 2006, when then parent Morgan Stanley acquired it from Lloyds TSB Group for $1.68 billion.

"Yep, that's $1.6 billion, or 96 percent of the original purchase price, up in smoke," said a Seeking Alpha commentator following the sale announcement. "In fact, Discover has lost significantly more than its original purchase price, since Goldfish has been losing money hand over fist ever since Discover bought it."

Indeed, Discover got nailed in the fourth quarter of 2007 on account of its slippery Goldfish unit. The firm reported a net loss for the fourth quarter of $84 million, including a non-cash impairment charge of $391 million related to Goldfish. Excluding the impairment charge, the company earned $195 million, 4 percent more than the same period in 2006. For the full year, Discover reported net income of $561 million. Without that pesky impairment charge, net income would have been $840 million.

Discover CEO David Nelms continued to look on the bright side: "The sale will free up capital, enhance Discover's net income and bring even sharper focus to our profitable and growing U.S. card and third-party payments businesses,"

Visit the Vault Finance Career Channel at **www.vault.com/finance** — with insider firm profiles, message boards, the Vault Finance Job Board and more.

VAULT CAREER LIBRARY   **129**

Nelms said in a statement. An analyst for Sandler O'Neill & Partners, L.P. agreed, telling Reuters, "The sale is a net positive, given that it eliminates a drag on earnings and frees up capital, which we estimate to be $190 million."

Buying Diners

In July 2008, Discover completed the acquisition of Diners Club International from Citi for $165 million. The deal—which CEO Nelms said "provides us with a path to achieving global acceptance, establishing new international partnerships and generating higher payments volumes"—brings more than $30 billion per year in spending volume outside of North America, deals with 44 licensees that issue Diners Club cards, and a network in 185 countries and territories worldwide. Diners Club launched the first general purpose credit card in 1950, and since has grown a wide-reaching global payments network.

Recent results

For the second quarter 2008, Discover booked $234 million in net income, a nice rise versus the $209 million it reported in the second quarter of 2007. CEO David Nelms pointed to increases in managed loans and third-party payments as the reasons for the rise.

GETTING HIRED

Discover a new job

Interested in becoming part of the Discover team? Then surf on over to www.mydiscovercareer.com, where job-seekers can find out detailed information regarding the staffing process and the company culture. Or if you'd prefer to cut straight to the chase, you can go to the career search page and peruse listings for any area or unit. The site even offers the option of subscribing to a RSS job feed to help keep you abreast of when your dream job is posted. Additionally, prospective employees can sign up for Discover's career newsletter to be delivered by email.

The firm also offers internships for students who are enrolled in college full-time (and who maintain a 3.0 or higher GPA). Discover offers campus recruiting and posts an online calendar so students can prepare for when the company comes to town looking for the university's finest.

DST Systems

333 W. 11th St.
Kansas City, MO 64105
Phone: (816) 435-1000
Fax: (816) 435-8618
www.dstsystems.com

DEPARTMENTS

Brokerage Subaccounting
Business Process Management
Distribution Support & Financial
    Intermediary Solutions
Healthcare Solutions
Integrated Customer
Communications & Output
International Asset Management &
    Portfolio Accounting
International Shareholder & Investor
    Recordkeeping Solutions
Outsourcing Solutions
Retirement Plan Solutions
U.S. Mutual Fund Shareholder
    Recordkeeping
Wealth Management

THE STATS

Employer Type: Public Company
Ticker Symbol: DST (NYSE)
President & CEO: Thomas (Tom) A.
    McDonnell
Revenue: $2.30 billion (FYE 12/07)
Net Income: $874.7 million
No. of Employees: 9,000

KEY COMPETITORS

Misys
PFPC
SunGard

UPPER

• Culture is "unified," "really friendly,"
  "open" and "motivating"

DOWNER

• Diversity hiring practices need
  improvement

EMPLOYMENT CONTACT

See "careers" section of
www.dstsystems.com

Visit the Vault Finance Career Channel at **www.vault.com/finance** — with
insider firm profiles, message boards, the Vault Finance Job Board and more.

VAULT CAREER LIBRARY   131

THE SCOOP

DST is No. 1

Founded in 1969 as a division of Kansas City Southern Industries, DST Systems was established to develop an automated recordkeeping system for the mutual fund industry. Throughout its almost 40 year history DST has grown to become the largest provider of third-party shareholder recordkeeping services in the U.S.

DST Systems operates in two segments: financial services and output solutions. The financial services segment provides information processing, and computer software services and products to mutual funds, investment managers, insurance companies, healthcare providers, banks, brokers, financial planners, health payers, third-party administrators, and medical practice groups. Its software systems include mutual fund shareowner and unit trust recordkeeping systems for U.S. and international mutual fund companies; a defined-contribution participant recordkeeping system for the U.S. retirement plan market; and investment management systems to U.S. and international investment managers as well as fund accountants. This segment also provides a business process management and customer contact system to mutual funds, insurance companies, brokerage firms, banks, cable television operators, healthcare providers, and mortgage servicing organizations; record-keeping systems to support managed account investment products; health care processing systems and services to health payers, third-party administrators, and medical practice groups; and recordkeeping systems to support consumer risk transfer programs.

The output solutions segment provides integrated print and electronic statement, and billing output solutions. It also offers various related professional services, including statement design and formatting, customer segmentation, and personalized messaging tools. The output solutions segment also provides electronic bill payment and presentment solutions, and computer output archival solutions.

A paperless world

In May 2007, DST received excellent news courtesy of the Securities and Exchange Commission. The SEC announced that it had passed a new rule called "Internet Availability of Proxy Materials" (which is colloquially referred to as the "Notice and Access" rule) that will allow mutual funds to conduct proxy campaigns via the Internet. As a result of the ruling, DST's California affiliate DST Output will create integrated solutions that help mutual fund companies transition into this new phase of technological development.

This decision bodes well for DST Systems and their subsidiaries, which are already leaders in the e-commerce world. As consumers and institutions continue to turn to their computers for everyday tasks like bill paying, DST pledges to be there to snap up the financial opportunities this will create.

Adding Amisys

In October 2006, DST Systems' Birmingham-based DST Health Solutions subsidiary completed the acquisition of Amisys Synertech (ASI) for an undisclosed sum. Amisys, an enterprise software developer, software applications service provider and business process outsourcer for the commercial healthcare industry, employs about 1,400 people at three offices in Pennsylvania, Maryland and India. The company reported 2005 revenue of $103.4 million and, as of September 2006, had amassed more than $65 million year-to-date. Following the close of the deal, the integrated companies began operating as DST Health Solutions.

Subtracting Asurion

DST unloaded a large stake of its ownership of the Nashville, Tenn..-based wireless handset insurance company Asurion in July 2007, yielding a gain of $996.3 million before taxes. On its third quarter earnings report, DST announced that it used the majority of the proceeds from the transaction to pay down debt. DST will retain approximately 6 percent of its share in Asurion. The shares it sold are now owned by a private equity firm. Prior to the sale, DST owned a 37.4 percent equity interest in Asurion.

For the full year of 2007, the firm brought in $2.3 billion in revenue, down from the $2.4 billion it earned in 2006. Net income, however, rose to $874.7 million, up from $222.8 million in the previous year. The sale of Asurion gave DST a little boost for 2007, helping them to report a consolidated net income of $811 million.

Halftime report

The firm reported net income for the second quarter 2008 of $49.9 million compared to $72.8 million for the second quarter 2007 and $72.2 million for

Visit the Vault Finance Career Channel at **www.vault.com/finance** — with insider firm profiles, message boards, the Vault Finance Job Board and more.

VAULT CAREER LIBRARY

133

the first quarter 2008. Revenue was up slightly, to $572.9 million from $567 million in the second quarter 2007 and $587.8 million in the first quarter 2008. The sluggish credit market and higher mutual fund processing fees were partly to blame for the downturn.

GETTING HIRED

Search it

The careers section of www.dstsystems.com allows applicants to search current openings for all DST groups, from DST Systems positions to DST Health Solutions and DST Realty jobs. Job seekers can also submit their resumes to the company for consideration for potential openings. The career site also lays out the training programs, advancement opportunities, benefits and diversity efforts offered.

The interview process entails "the usual interview questions," such as "What are your strengths and weaknesses?" and "Why do you want this job?" If you are selected, you'll be notified by the hiring manager and receive an official letter. But one insider suggests that you "make HR and the hiring manager put all agreements in writing," because "once you take the position, they conveniently forget or deny agreements."

OUR SURVEY SAYS

All for one

The work culture at DST is "unified,""really friendly," "open" and "motivating," and the overall positivity "makes working in such a demanding profession rather easy." But the culture does seem to vary from department to department. Work hours "are left to your manager's discretion," and "the workload is highly variable among employees." There's also "no compensation for extra hours or days of work if you are an exempt employee." The fact that the culture seems to differ by department means that the treatment of employees is ultimately "left to the discretion of management to determine fairness." And "although this is logical on the surface, this policy is grossly abused by some managers and supervisors," admits one insider. But not everyone agrees. "I like the way the management takes care of the employees," says one insider. "Hierarchies matter little and creativity matters a lot."

Insiders seem pretty happy with their pay, too. "The payout at DST is really good." "It's the most competitive compensation I've seen in this field," an insider says. Plus, "since their products are doing really well, I could expect compensation to grow more." "It will hardly be a surprise that your salary will increase very rapidly after a few years of work with the company." And the perks are "great"—even if offices have only "basic creature comforts." "DST's idea of a lunch or break area is some small space containing a coffee maker, ice maker and fridge—with no place to sit."

Up the effort

Diversity efforts by the firm seem a little patchy, insiders report. One contact working out of the Kansas City office says, "The ethnic mix of employees does not represent that of the Kansas City area." Also, "what few people of color or non-U.S. origin there are always seem to be in the lowest-level positions and do not seem to remain for long." And while "DST is gay-friendly in terms of hiring," one worker says, "I'm aware of instances of abusive behavior towards some employees which was consciously ignored by upper management and HR." And "the greatest proportion of employees, by far, seems to be mid-30s and younger" and "the smallest proportion is over 50." One insider reports that "one manager I know of was severely chastised for hiring someone in their 50s," and "employees that are 50-plus seem to chronically fear having their job eliminated." There's not much by the firm in the way of actively recruiting those with disabilities, either. "Oddly, in all the years I've been at DST, I have seen only one employee with a physical limitation—and that person lasted about two weeks," says one employee.

What lies ahead

Employees have mixed views regarding the future of DST. One insider says that DST's recent acquisition of other companies "is its only possibility for market share." The firm's "home-grown technology is horrible, and the executives that work at the base company are the reason for the antiquated business plans and technology strategy." Not everyone at the firm feels that things are quite so bleak, however—another worker says simply, "This company is going to grow big."

Visit the Vault Finance Career Channel at www.vault.com/finance — with insider firm profiles, message boards, the Vault Finance Job Board and more.

VAULT CAREER LIBRARY   135

The Dun & Bradstreet Corporation

103 JFK Pkwy.
Short Hills, NJ 07078
Phone: (973) 921-5500
Fax: (973) 921-6056
www.dnb.com

DEPARTMENTS

Business Development
Finance
Global Technology
Human Resources
Marketing
Product Management
Sales Operations
Strategy

THE STATS

Employer Type: Public Company
Ticker Symbol: DNB (NYSE)
Chairman & CEO: Steven W. Alesio
Revenue: $1.6 billion (FYE 12/07)
Net Income: $298.1 million
No. of Employees: 4,400

KEY COMPETITORS

Acxiom
Equifax
infoUSA

UPPERS

- "Exciting" and "positive atmosphere"
- "Benefit package is generous compared to similar companies in its industry"

DOWNERS

- "There's not a whole lot of diversity"
- "Tremendous turnover" at times

EMPLOYMENT CONTACT

See "jobs @ D&B" at www.dnb.com

THE SCOOP

D&B is B-to-B

Ranked No. 1 in the financial services segment on *Fortune*'s list of America's Most Admired Companies in 2008, the Dun & Bradstreet Corporation mainly provides business-to-business insight on public and private companies. The company, known as D&B, aspires to "be the most trusted source of commercial insight so [its] customers can decide with confidence." And it's currently focusing on three major areas to improve its customer service: information quality (such as increasing the number of company records in its database; it now has 130 million), customer experience (it's trying to answer all customer calls within 10 seconds) and product innovation (like its web-based interactive risk product DNBi). Information is culled from a variety of sources, including management interviews, accounts-receivable information, state filings and news services. D&B sells this business-credit information, and offers marketing information and purchasing-support services.

Customers can derive information from four different sets of tools: D&B Risk Management Solutions help to increase profitability and cash flow, D&B Sales & Marketing Solutions allow clients to boost revenue from current customers, D&B E-Business Solutions provide research to help turn prospective clients into permanent clients, and D&B Supply Management Solutions protect customers from risk and reaps savings from customers' suppliers.

D&B's D-U-N-S (Data Universal Numbering System) system was developed and is regulated by D&B. The system assigns a unique numeric identifier to a single business entity. The number provides information about the company, including addresses, sales, number of employees, market research, mailing lists, new product development and corporate family trees. A D-U-N-S number is required for many government transactions.

Two pioneers merge

The history of Dun & Bradstreet begins in 1841, when Lewis Tappan, a noted abolitionist, formed his Mercantile Agency in New York. This agency served as a way for wholesalers and importers to rate customer credit. In 1859, this business was taken over by Robert Dun, whose Dun's Book listed information on over one million businesses by 1886. The company's biggest

Visit the Vault Finance Career Channel at www.vault.com/finance — with insider firm profiles, message boards, the Vault Finance Job Board and more.

VAULT CAREER LIBRARY   137

rival at the time was the John M. Bradstreet Company. In 1933, the two companies merged, and took on the name Dun & Bradstreet in 1939.

Some of Dun & Bradstreet's notable acquisitions have included Reuben H. Donnelley Corp., publisher of the Yellow Pages, in 1961. In 1962, Moody's Investor Service became part of D&B. Moody's eventually developed the largest private database in the world, and this information was used to create Dun's Financial Profiles in 1979.

In the 1970s and 1980s, Dun & Bradstreet bought additional information and publishing companies, including AC Nielsen, Hoover's Inc. and McCormack & Dodge.

By the 1990s, however, poor performance suggested D&B had overreached. The company began to shed its subsidiaries, including AC Nielsen, Cognizant (which included Nielsen Media Research and IMS Health and Nielsen Media Research), R.H. Donnelley and Moody's.

After spinning off subsidiaries, D&B returned to focusing on providing business insight, helping businesses manage credit exposure, find profitable clients and convert prospects to clients. Customers include over 90 percent of the Fortune 1000 companies, as well as thousands of small and medium-sized businesses.

Changing of the guard

In October 1999, Chairman and CEO Volney Taylor retired amid shareholder pressure to put the company on the block. Allen Loren was then brought in to serve as chairman and CEO, and succeeded in making strong headway, which ultimately resulted in a steadily rising stock price. In January 2005, Loren passed the CEO baton to then-president Steve Alesio. Later that year, Loren completely retired from D&B.

Web presence

Since then, the company has started to focus heavily on web-enabled information tools. The 2003 acquisition of Hoover's, a subscription-based business information company, is one example of this strategy. D&B has also given its traditional products a stronger web-presence—the company's credit reporting business is now largely web-based.

In December 2007, D&B acquired AllBusiness.com, an online publisher and business resource, for $55 million. AllBusiness.com reportedly has more than 2 million users who access the site's 2 million articles, blogs, videos and other resources that offer business owners and executives guidance.

D&B reasoned that AllBusiness.com would help boost its Internet presence and beef up its small-business coverage. AllBusiness.com is a well-known site for all business types, but especially for the small-business market. The site will be a wholly owned subsidiary of D&B, and Kathy Yates, CEO, will continue at its helm.

The Associated Press reported that D&B hopes the acquisition will produce upwards of $10 million in incremental revenue in 2008.

Just two months before the acquisition of AllBusiness.com, D&B purchased Purisma, a commercial data integration software solutions provider, for $48 million. The company expects that Purisma's software and services will help to facilitate the transfer of information and data between D&B and its customers.

More global endeavors

In 2005, D&B increased its risk management business when it acquired LiveCapital, a provider of online credit management software, for $16 million. International operations, both by acquisition and divestitures, are also a large part of D&B's current focus. A series of purchases in Italy, such as the 2003 acquisition of controlling interests in three Italian real estate data companies, have strengthened D&B's position in that country.

Also, D&B sold its operations in Denmark, Finland, Norway and Sweden to Bonnier Business Information in 2003. Bonnier now operates those businesses under D&B's name, and provides D&B access to its business information databases.

In November 2006, D&B announced that it signed an agreement with Huaxia International Credit Consulting Co. Ltd., a provider of business information and credit management services in China, to establish a joint venture that will trade under the name Huaxia D&B China.

Japanese joint venture

In October 2007, D&B announced that it had expanded its risk management business in Japan. D&B will be the main shareholder in a joint venture with its Japanese partner, Tokyo Shoko Research. D&B hopes that the partnership

Visit the Vault Finance Career Channel at **www.vault.com/finance** — with insider firm profiles, message boards, the Vault Finance Job Board and more.

VAULT CAREER LIBRARY   139

will increase the company's presence in the large-business market in the East. The partnership will commence its business operations in 2008.

By the numbers

For the fiscal year 2007, the firm brought in $1.6 billion in revenue, up from $1.47 billion in 2006. Net income for the year came in at $298.1 million, an increase from the $240.7 million the firm earned in 2006. The December 2007 sale of the firm's Italian real estate business certainly helped push up its overall results—the sale brought $60.5 in revenue and $5.4 million in net income.

Halfway through 2008, the firm kept the momentum going for the most part, booking $427.7 million in revenue for the second quarter, up from $380.8 million in the second quarter 2007. Net income, however, dipped a little to $84.2 million from $87.6 million. Harsh industry conditions continued to plague the firm, which affected its results. But increases in revenue in its risk and management, sales and marketing, and Internet solutions units helped keep the firm well in the black.

GETTING HIRED

Pick a category, any category

Go to the Jobs at D&B link at www.dnb.com, and search job listings in categories such as sales, technology, marketing, finance, operations, customer service and human resources. While you're there, in addition to applying for positions, you can learn about the firm's company culture ("focused on winning in the marketplace and creating shareholder value") and the benefits offered.

The site's job listings aren't the only way to get hired, however. One insider explains being hired on full-time after coming on "through a temp agency." After a while at the firm, the contact reports, "The sales manager interviewed me and said she wanted me on her team."

OUR SURVEY SAYS

Exciting times

On the whole, D&B is a "great place to work" with a "positive atmosphere" that's also "exciting"—plus, "the exposure to different companies is amazing." One insider explains that the firm "organizes team events and tries to spread morale and motivation throughout the floor." The "good casual environment" that's "generally business casual" with "casual jeans days" probably helps to boost the office morale as well.

The firm is "good with flexibility and work-at-home" options, says one New Jersey insider. Since "there are many employees commuting from New York or Pennsylvania," the culture is "very supportive" of working at home. Opportunities to advance vary, however. One contact says that "there have been some years where I have had no people reporting to me and my prospects seemed slim. Then, other years with a different leader, it was completely different. It also really depends on what kind of year the company is having as well as who you work for." Morale tends to get down at times, reports an insider, who explains, "The worst part of working here is that they have tremendous turnover. I have probably been though more than six rounds of layoffs and restructuring since I've worked here, and many employees are left wondering when they will be next."

Perks get generally good marks, though. One insider says that "D&B's benefit package is generous compared to similar companies in its industry." The firm also "pays for college up to $5,000 a year." The office space gets a thumbs-up, too. The cubes are "fairly decent and everyone except the senior leadership team is in them, so it's not so bad." But the firm's diversity efforts could be better, sources say. One insider notes, "There's not a whole lot of diversity compared to other companies I have worked at."

The final verdict

By and large, "D&B is a great place to work at," says one insider. "The information and data that D&B has collected over the last 170 years has be the root of its success." And when it comes to securing its future as a trusted company, the firm seems to be playing by the book, too. "D&B not only has laws and regulations to abide by, but they are also enforced by Sarbanes Oxley." Overall, the "main focus is doing what's right for the company," says one contact.

Visit the Vault Finance Career Channel at www.vault.com/finance — with insider firm profiles, message boards, the Vault Finance Job Board and more.

VAULT CAREER LIBRARY   141

Equifax

1550 Peachtree St. NW
Atlanta, GA 30309
Phone: (404) 885-8000
Fax: (404) 885-8055
www.equifax.com

DEPARTMENTS

Marketing Services
North America Information Services
Personal Solutions

THE STATS

Employer Type: Public Company
Ticker Symbol: EFX (NYSE)
Chairman and CEO: Richard (Rick) F. Smith
Revenue: $1.84 billion (FYE 12/07)
Net Income: $272.7 million
No. of Employees: 6,900
No. of Offices: Locations across 14 countries

KEY COMPETITORS

D&B
Experian Americas
TransUnion

UPPER

- "People are very friendly"

DOWNER

- Average salaries

EMPLOYMENT CONTACT

See "careers" under "about Equifax" section of www.equifax.com

THE SCOOP

Securing customers for over a century

In business since 1899 and called Equifax since 1975, this Atlanta-based company enables and secures global commerce through its information management, marketing services, direct-to-consumer, commercial and authentication businesses. In plain English, Equifax is a credit-reporting agency. It gathers, compiles and processes data, utilizing its proprietary software and systems to distribute data to customers in various formats. Equifax's products and services include consumer credit information, information database management, marketing information, business credit information, decisioning and analytical tools, enabling technologies and identity verification services.

The company's mission is to enable businesses to make informed decisions about extending credit or service, mitigate fraud, manage portfolio risk and develop marketing strategies. Equifax also helps consumers manage and protect their financial affairs through a portfolio of products that it sells directly via the Internet and in various hard copy formats. As one of the nation's top three credit reporting agencies, Equifax has information on more than 400 million credit holders worldwide. It services clients across industries, including financial services, retail, health care, telecommunications/utilities, brokerage, insurance and government industries.

Equifax reported $1.55 billion in revenue in 2006, up from $1.44 billion in 2005. Net income also rose to $274.5 million from $246.5 million a year earlier. Equifax Chairman and CEO Richard F. Smith said that the firm "met or exceeded the guidance provided in all areas."

Financial techies

In November 2007, Equifax was named to the 2007 FinTech 100 list by *American Banker* and *Financial Insights*. The company placed No. 24 (up from No. 26 the year before) on this annual listing of technology companies that derive more than one-third of their revenue from the financial services industry. Companies are selected based on their primary business, key application solution or vertical industry, and total annual revenue.

Equifax has earned a strong reputation in the marketplace for its continued investment in new technologies. Nearly 1,000 organizations, including some

Visit the Vault Finance Career Channel at **www.vault.com/finance** — with
insider firm profiles, message boards, the Vault Finance Job Board and more.

VAULT CAREER LIBRARY   **143**

of the world's largest banks, financial institutions and many of the top utility companies use Equifax technology. In fact, 30 of the top 50 banks, and four of the top-five telecommunications companies rely on Equifax's decisioning solutions.

In November 2007, Forrester Research cited Equifax as a top leader in its industry, noting the firm's "superior client service, flexible and pragmatic database management and mid-market specialization." Of 144 companies surveyed, Equifax was one of only 12 to meet Forrester's criteria.

Adding TALX, Austin-Tetra

In May 2007, Equifax acquired TALX Corp. in a stock and cash transaction valued at approximately $1.4 billion. Based in St. Louis, TALX provides employment verification and related human resource/payroll services, serving over 9,000 clients in the U.S., including 385 companies in the Fortune 500. TALX provides a wide variety of products and services, including employment and income verification, pay reporting, hiring and employment tax management services. The company said the acquisition of TALX and its 1,900 employees is aligned with its long-term growth strategy of expanding into new markets and acquiring proprietary data sources.

In October 2006, Equifax expanded its commercial information business by acquiring Fort Worth, Tex.-based Austin-Tetra, a privately held provider of business-to-business data management solutions for Fortune 1000 companies and government agencies, in an all-cash transaction. Austin-Tetra leverages a proprietary database of more than 30 million global businesses, with information aggregated from more than 300 information sources. In a third-quarter 2006 earnings release, Equifax CEO Rick Smith called the Austin-Tetra acquisition "an integral part of our long-term growth strategy, complementing our commercial information business."

Equifax in 2010

Rick Smith went into more detail about the company's long-term strategy at a September 2006 investor conference. At the event, Equifax brass outlined how the company plans to build on the strengths of its current core business model and, then building from that core, implement a long-term strategy based on four pillars: deepen its relationships with existing customers, provide unique and differentiated data, build on its capabilities to offer enabling technologies and predictive sciences, and target emerging opportunities through organic growth, acquisitions or geographic expansion.

The company identified initiatives with potential incremental revenue in each of those areas, and outlined the application of the corporate strategy to its North America Information Services, Marketing Services, Personal Solutions, Europe and Latin America business units. By 2010, the firm hopes to achieve compound annual growth in revenue of 7 to 10 percent from organic market growth, core organic growth initiatives and new markets, adjacencies and mergers/acquisitions; earnings-per-share growth in excess of 10 percent; and cumulative cash from operations in excess of $1.9 billion.

Theft protection

Identity theft has become a huge problem in the U.S. Thankfully, in October 2007, Equifax announced that its customers nationwide would have the ability to freeze their accounts. Equifax volunteered to offer its customers in 11 states and Puerto Rico the option to freeze an account; customers in the other 39 states already have state laws that protect them from identity theft.

Freezing an account prevents someone from fraudulently opening a new account, even with a customer's account information. "File freeze has emerged as another option for consumers to use in the battle against identity theft," said J. Dann Adams, president of Equifax U.S. Consumer Information Services in a press release. "In the absence of one national standard for file freeze, we are closing the loop and allowing consumers in those states that do not have laws in place to take advantage of this type of protection."

Seasoned pros

Lee Adrean was appointed Equifax's CFO in October 2006, replacing the retiring Donald T. Heroman. Adrean, who most recently was CFO for NDCHealth Corporation, officially took over when Heroman's retirement began on June 1, 2007. Prior to NDCHealth Corporation, Adrean held senior level positions at such companies as EarthLink, First Data Corporation, Providian Corporation, Bain & Company, and the former Peat, Marwick, Mitchell & Co. (now KPMG).

A mixed year

Full-year 2007 results were a mixed bag for the firm. Revenue jumped to $1.84 billion from $1.55 billion in 2006, but net income decreased to $272.7 million from $274.5 million. The lethargic economy certainly didn't help the firm's results. And although revenue in most of the company's sectors were up from

Visit the Vault Finance Career Channel at www.vault.com/finance — with insider firm profiles, message boards, the Vault Finance Job Board and more.

VAULT CAREER LIBRARY   145

17 to 37 percent, Equifax's consumer information unit saw sluggish growth, only rising to $969.7 million in revenue from $968.1 million the year before.

The numbers don't lie

Things were looking fairly bright for Equifax halfway through 2008. Its second quarter revenue increased 10 percent to $501.9 million, and though net income didn't see explosive growth, it did grow 1 percent to $70.8 million from the year before. Still, the frail economy kept Equifax from doing as well as it could have—as a possible result of consumers' financial prudence, sales in its consumer information unit decreased 9 percent to $228 million.

GETTING HIRED

Peruse it all

Under the careers link at www.equifax.com, you can stock up your job cart on positions ranging from accounting and consulting to financial resources and research across the U.S. and Canada. You can also save your profile on the site and log in to check out the status of your current application.

If asked to come in for an interview, keep in mind that it's a large firm with many offices, so there's no cookie-cutter hiring route. One insider says that after being "contacted by a tech recruiter," a telephone interview was set up within 24 hours. "The phone interview was very simple and straightforward—mainly a screening. Then I got a face-to-face interview the following day." And though the contact says she "only interviewed with the hiring manager," the turnaround was quick. She says, "I was notified I had the job before I got home, and after taking the drug test and the reference checks," the deal was sealed.

OUR SURVEY SAYS

No worries

Insiders seem pleasantly surprised by the workplace culture. One hire admits being "a bit concerned about coming to a large corporate environment having always worked at small companies," but adds that once she began working there, "the experience hasn't been bad at all." Another insider in the Alpharetta, Ga., office calls the corporate culture "fair," adding that "the people are very friendly" and while it's "fairly laid-back," it may be due to the fact that there's "primarily tech folks" in that particular office.

The dress code is "casual always, unless you go to headquarters at midtown, which is rare." One insider notes that the code "isn't stringently enforced" anyway and "as long as your dress is business casual" you shouldn't run into any problems—just "stay away from blue jeans," she warns. Employee hours are "flexible" and "there seems to be more working from home recently."

Compensation and salaries get average marks from employees. One insider notes that although the "base salary for business analysts and project managers vary," the range tends to be "from mid-$60K to over $90K." The contact goes on to add, "I was offered between $85K to $90K with an annual bonus of 10 percent, which was based partly on performance incentive and partly on company incentive. But there were no signing bonuses or anything like that." Another worker notes that annual bonuses "have run between 10 and 15 percent." Vacation time, however, "starts at three weeks per year and increases to four weeks—after 10 years."

The future is uncertain

"There aren't a lot of minorities in senior management," comments one insider. Another says that "there are other kinds of diversity now that so many employees from India are at Equifax now, because of the outsourcing. So in that sense, there are other kinds of diversity."

The company's immediate outlook, however, seems to be mixed, at least according to insiders. "Under the current atmosphere, continued employment is a concern," confesses one insider. Another contact calls the firm's business outlook "good," adding that "there is a new management team that has been doing some corporate restructuring" and Equifax has also "introduced a couple of new products in the past year that have been doing well." But then again, "the downside is that the company is committed to outsourcing" and because of this, "it appears that a good number of people are in an uncertain state."

Visit the Vault Finance Career Channel at **www.vault.com/finance** — with insider firm profiles, message boards, the Vault Finance Job Board and more.

VAULT CAREER LIBRARY   **147**

Fannie Mae

3900 Wisconsin Ave., NW
Washington, DC 20016-2892
Phone: (202) 752-7000
Fax: (202) 752-6014
www.fanniemae.com

THE STATS

Employer Type: Government Entity
Chairman: Stephen B. Ashley
President & CEO: Daniel H. Mudd
Revenue: $44.77 billion (FYE 12/07)
Net Income: $-2.05 billion
No. of Employees: 6,600
No. of Offices: 78

KEY COMPETITORS

Countrywide Financial
Freddie Mac
Wells Fargo

UPPERS

- Professional environment
- "Excellent benefits and vacation days"
- Well-known name

DOWNERS

- "Pay is "slightly less than competitors"
- Promotions are difficult but not impossible
- Current turmoil

EMPLOYMENT CONTACT

See the "careers" link at
www.fanniemae.com

THE SCOOP

The "American Dream" turns into a nightmare

Fannie Mae company's slogan proclaims, "Our Business is the American Dream," and its mission is to increase opportunities for home ownership among low- and middle-income Americans. Short for Federal National Mortgage Association (or FNMA), Fannie Mae is the leading source of financing for home mortgages, and it owns or guarantees about 20 percent of the home mortgage market in the U.S. Since 1968, the company has provided more than $7 trillion in financing to over 73 million families.

Fannie Mae was created as a government agency under Franklin D. Roosevelt's New Deal in 1938 to boost and replenish the supply of loan money for mortgages, thereby helping to stimulate the economy in the wake of the Great Depression. The firm later became a private, shareholder-owned company—and a large one at that. But recently, after the subprime mortgage market tanked and the firm booked billions of losses, it was forced to return to its roots: the palm of Uncle Sam.

In September 2008, the U.S. government took drastic measures to attempt to stop the ongoing losses experienced by Fannie Mae (and its cousin company Freddie Mac) by seizing control of both entities. U.S. Treasury Secretary Henry Paulson said the government will take control of the firms and supplant each of the firm's CEOs with new heads. (After staying on for a transition stage, Fannie's current head Daniel H. Mudd will be replaced by former TIAA-CREF chairman Herbert M. Allison Jr.) Additionally, the Treasury will obtain $1 billion in preferred shares for both Fannie and Freddie and will provide about $200 billion in funding. Paulson indicated that allowing either of the giants to fail would "cause great turmoil" for domestic and international financial markets. To this end, his predictions seemed accurate; stocks rallied after the takeover announcement was made.

As far as the big picture for future funding goes, the Treasury will also restrict the size of each firm's mortgage portfolio to $850 billion. As of September 2008, Fannie had approximately $758 billion in mortgages and securities.

The old setup

Before the U.S. government regained control of the firm, Fannie Mae had operated under a federal charter, which granted it special rights and responsibilities. Under the charter, the company was required to increase

Visit the Vault Finance Career Channel at www.vault.com/finance — with insider firm profiles, message boards, the Vault Finance Job Board and more.

VAULT CAREER LIBRARY

149

liquidity in the residential mortgage finance market and promote access to mortgage credit throughout the country. In return, Fannie Mae was exempt from SEC registration requirement as well as state and local income taxes, and enjoyed other privileges as well. Fannie Mae and its corporate cousin Freddie Mac (created in 1970 to break Fannie Mae's monopoly) were the only two Fortune 500 companies not required to report any sort of financial difficulty to the public. In July 2002, Fannie Mae registered with the SEC voluntarily and irrevocably in response to federal pressure on corporate leaders to step up their financial disclosures. However (and partly as a result of this concession), Fannie Mae securities remained exempt from registration.

First in the secondary

Fannie Mae operates in what is known as the secondary mortgage market. The primary market consists of institutions like mortgage companies, commercial banks, savings and loan associations or credit unions. These groups are the ones that conduct transactions directly with borrowers. The lending institution then has the option to either hold the mortgage in its portfolio or to sell the mortgage into the secondary market. By selling the debt to another entity, the primary lender recoups its money and is able to extend another loan. Some of Fannie Mae's rivals in the secondary mortgage market include pension funds, insurance companies, securities dealers and other financial institutions. By setting certain restrictions on the size and terms of the mortgages that it purchases, Fannie Mae encourages primary lenders to make more funds available to low- and middle-income borrowers.

House of cards

The troubled housing market sucker-punched Fannie Mae in 2007, and net income for the first three quarters of the year fell by 57 percent to $1.5 billion (compared with $3.5 billion from the previous year). The whopping loss was attributed to mortgage delinquencies, also responsible for a third-quarter loss of $1.39 billion.

Mudd told Bloomberg News that he didn't see things getting better; he said he expected housing prices to fall by another 2 percent in 2007 and by 4 percent in 2008. The depressed housing market led to more action by Fannie Mae in December 2007—this time the sale of $7 billion in preferred stock and slashing its dividend by 30 percent to increase its capital base. "Fannie Mae has a responsibility to serve the mortgage market in good times and in times like these," Mudd told Reuters. "The steps we are taking today are designed to enable us to meet that responsibility."

Early in the year, rumors surfaced that Fannie Mae would let go several hundred employees in addition to cutting its operating expenses by as much as $200 million. The company also vowed to withhold more than $44 million in bonuses for 46 of its top executives, past and present, because of overstated earnings from 2001 to 2004.

Not a great time to be Fannie

For the fourth quarter of 2007, Fannie Mae booked a net loss of $3.56 billion, quite a slide compared with the $604 million in net income it booked for the same period a year earlier. The firm also reported negative revenue of $2.25 billion, compared with (positive) revenue of $1.75 billion in the fourth quarter of 2006. In a press release announcing its earnings, Fannie Mae said that it expected the housing market "to continue to deteriorate and home prices to continue to decline" in states such as Florida and California, and on a national basis.

Shortly after Fannie Mae filed its latest earnings, the Office of Federal Housing Enterprise Oversight announced that it would be repealing a ceiling for Fannie Mae's and Freddie Mac's investment portfolios as of March 1. The end of the cap, introduced in 2006, meant that the firms would have freedom to buy more mortgages. Head of OFHEO James Lockhart said that the firms' return to filing of "timely, audited" financial statements contributed to the lifting of the cap.

Rescue operation

In July 2008, the firm's troubles as a result of the housing crisis came to a boil, and Fannie Mae's and sister firm Freddie Mac's stocks lost half their value—an event that some analysts said was worse for the financial markets than the collapse of Bear Stearns. (Fannie had lost about $7.2 billion since mid-2007, following a flood of homeowner defaults.) Following the stock nosedives, the U.S. Treasury finagled a few favors from Congress on behalf of the agencies, including a temporary increase in a credit line for Fannie and Freddie and temporary authority to purchase equity in one or both of the mortgage companies.

U.S. Treasury Secretary Henry Paulson spearheaded the plan to save Fannie and Freddie, assuring the Fed and the Federal Reserve Bank of New York that

Visit the Vault Finance Career Channel at www.vault.com/finance — with insider firm profiles, message boards, the Vault Finance Job Board and more.

VAULT CAREER LIBRARY   **151**

any loans to Fannie or Freddie would serve only as an "interim step," not a permanent solution. In the meantime, however, analysts indicated that the steps the government plans on taking to assuage worries about financial backing haven't actually upgraded the economy's overall dreary outlook.

Previous troubles

Investors got jittery in October 2003, when Fannie Mae announced that it had miscalculated its mortgage equity by $1.2 billion and would have to restate its third-quarter earnings. In late 2003, the company's regulator, the Office of Federal Housing Enterprise Oversight (OFHEO), launched an investigation into the firm's accounting practices. In its report, OFHEO alleged that Fannie Mae was manipulating its figures in order to report steady earnings, meet targets and entitle top management to bonuses. In February 2004, former Federal Reserve Chairman Alan Greenspan expressed concerns about the size and power of Fannie Mae and its corporate cousin, Freddie Mac, which had been under investigation for its accounting practices since 2003.

In September 2004, the SEC launched an inquiry into Fannie Mae's accounting practices. While downplaying the issue, Fannie Mae delayed its reporting of third-quarter earnings. In addition, the Justice Department started a criminal investigation of the company, and at the request of lawmakers, the inspector general at the Department of Housing and Urban Development investigated the possibility of political influence on the OFHEO report.

The results were stunning. The SEC demanded that the firm restate three and a half years of earnings reports. And federal regulators fined Fannie Mae $400 million in May 2006 for allegedly cooking the books to boost the bonuses of the firm's executives. Three months later, after millions of man hours and an army of consultants sifted through the mountains of data, the company announced that 2004 losses would be "significantly smaller" than its previous estimate. Fannie Mae completed the restatement and filed its 2004 10-K with the SEC in December 2006.

Six months later, in May 2007, the company filed its 2005 10-K. That same month, Fannie Mae announced that although its 2006 profits were expected to be slightly lower, its 2005 profits had risen 26 percent. The announcement was the first result of the restatement, in which the company lost $6.3 billion of previously reported profit from 2001 to 2004 and was forced to redo its books.

Changes at the helm

Daniel H. Mudd replaced CEO Franklin Raines, who was forced to retire in December 2004. Mudd, the former president and CEO of GE Capital, Japan, was first named as an interim replacement before being named permanently to the post in June 2005. To address the obvious problems with internal control over financial reporting, Mudd and the management team dumped KPMG as the company's auditor and replaced it with Deloitte & Touche, reorganized the company's finance area and hired a new controller, a new chief audit executive and several new senior accounting officers.

Robert Blakely took on the daunting task of Fannie Mae's finances as CFO in 2006; Stephen Swad, a former CFO at AOL, became CFO in 2007. "Bob Blakely came to Fannie Mae with a daunting job—to serve as chief financial officer at a critical moment for our company, to lead our new financial organization, and to oversee a large, complex financial restatement. He did it all with great skill and confidence," Mudd said in a statement.

New efforts

In late July 2008, Fannie and Freddie announced that it would be upping fees the firms pay loan companies to avoid foreclosures. Fannie and Freddie have indicated that their goals are to allow families to stay in their homes, but analysts say this might prove to be difficult given the current industry climate.

Down for Fannie

As expected, Fannie Mae posted huge losses for the second quarter 2008, booking a net loss of $2.3 billion compared with $1.95 billion in net income for the second quarter of 2007. Revenue, however, saw a slight increase to $4 billion from $3.8 billion. Despite this, the company indicated that its losses would likely continue—if not increase—during the remainder of the year.

Shaking it up

In August 2008, with its stock down 90 percent since the beginnning of the year due to the subprime mortgage crisis, Fannie Mae endured a few management changes, as the firm's chief financial officer, chief business officer and chief risk officer all stepped down. (Fannie Chief Financial Officer Stephen Swad had only been with the firm for a year before a replacement stepped in.) Meanwhile, the firm's Vice President of Capital

Visit the Vault Finance Career Channel at **www.vault.com/finance** — with
insider firm profiles, message boards, the Vault Finance Job Board and more.

VAULT CAREER LIBRARY   **153**

Markets Peter Niculescu took on even more duties; he'll head up the firm's single-family mortgage guaranty, capital markets and housing development groups.

A big deal

In September 2008, Fannie Mae sold $7 billion in two-year notes to investors after receiving about $9 billion in orders (which helped defray Fannie's financing charges for the notes). U.S. investors comprised most of Fannie's buyers, purchasing 63 percent of the notes, while investors from Asia obtained 12 percent. Analysts called the record deal a successful one, especially in light of Fannie's recent government rescue.

GETTING HIRED

Dream a little dream

Fannie Mae outlines its "American dream commitment" on its web site, and if your version of the American dream happens to include an interest in helping people find affordable housing, Fannie's got plenty of opportunities available for you. But beware: according to one insider, the firm is "very selective and only looking for people with several years of experience." Expect several interviews. "The initial interview is with an HR person," says one source, "then you'll meet with a line manager, and then you'll have several interviews with peers." Another contact went through an "interview with the hiring manager in the central program management office" before landing a job. Specific questions he received included; "Describe your background in financial services and comfort using analytical tools to understand and communicate the big picture;" "Describe specific examples where you led projects throughout the lifecycle;" "Describe your level of expertise using Excel, MS Project and other MS Office tools for analysis and reporting;" and "Describe your willingness to often work beyond 5 p.m."

A source who went through three rounds describes the process at length: "First I had a phone interview with a recruiter, who asked basic recruiting questions and was quick to the point and very resume-based. The second round, I had [a] personal interview with the recruiter followed by an interview with the prospective manager who asked about previous work experience as pertained to the job. The final interview was with a VP in HR that was more of a formality than an actual interview." The contact adds, "It seemed important that the applicant know and ask about the company and its vision, and understand their place in the mission."

At the "careers" section of the firm's web site, candidates can search for available positions and apply online. In addition, they can read extensively about the firm's career development opportunities (think lots of internal training and tuition reimbursements), health benefits, financial benefits (an equally long list with offerings such as an "employer-assisted housing benefit to help defray the cost of purchasing a home") and family benefits (i.e., "time off for new parents includes 10 to 12 weeks' paid maternity leave, four weeks paid paternity leave and four weeks paid leave for adoption"). Those eligible can also take 10 hours per month to volunteer in the community. In addition, candidates can download a brochure that outlines the pluses of working at Fannie Mae, along with the benefit offerings. But remember that competition is pretty fierce from the inside as well. One insider admits that "many people move within the company, leaving less spots for external candidates."

OUR SURVEY SAYS

They're pros

The culture at Fannie Mae is a "generally positive" and "very professional" one, insiders say. Other contacts say Fannie Mae has a "strong competitive advantage in the mortgage securities markets due to asset size, market position, diversity of products and use of technology products that help mortgage bankers make loan decisions more quickly." Sources also note that "while it's prestigious to work for Fannie Mae," "the firm doesn't offer the most competitive salaries," and the culture can be "hierarchical" and "very bureaucratic" at times. One insider simply says that Fannie Mae is "not a well-run organization at all." However, the "new CEO, Dan Mudd, is on an internal campaign to refresh the corporate culture towards an openness to bring issues to the table and make decisions, eliminating as much as possible the big-company bureaucracy." Indeed, the corporate culture is "very governmental, inflexible and consensus-oriented, but it is changing due to continual and meaningful efforts by upper management."

Visit the Vault Finance Career Channel at **www.vault.com/finance** — with insider firm profiles, message boards, the Vault Finance Job Board and more.

VAULT CAREER LIBRARY   **155**

Excellent and accepting

The "work/life environment is excellent," says one source, "with great acceptance and understanding of family and personal time." Plus, "the company sponsors a number of fun events—including cricket games—during the summer." And the dress code is "casual and relaxed," as are the hours." Indeed, the hours are "reasonable" and sources report "rarely" working weekends. (One insider says he works "less than 45 hours a week.") Some sources, though, aren't so pleased with managers. One insider says, "Unfortunately, management is out of date with cutting-edge management techniques." Another adds that "if upper management can flush out the middle management inefficiencies within, then the company looks like an extremely promising place to work in the coming years." Another insider says, "My boss was incredible," and adds that while it "seemed like there were some other decent managers," there are also a few bad apples that work their way into the company. "I won't forget one director who came off as quite insincere and apparently didn't think much of bothering people during vacation," he confesses. And there are also "times when it seemed that upper management did not communicate well to my direct managers" and "didn't really know what was going on."

The deal on diversity

Fannie Mae receives high marks for diversity with respect to women. But with respect to minorities, diversity receives merely average grades. "There's lots of talk about diversity, but there's the same old group of white guys at the top."

The future's uncertain

Overall, one source says the best thing about working for Fannie Mae is definitely the "benefits." He adds, "I also personally feel good about our core business and how it affects others." The company's future, however, receives mixed reactions from insiders—some of whom lament that the "outlook is quite bleak until housing market picks up." Others, however, say that Fannie Mae is a "significant and necessary vehicle in the U.S. economy that will be around for years to come—particularly given the recent turmoil in the mortgage markets and the U.S. economy in general."

Fidelity National Financial

601 Riverside Avenue
Jacksonville, FL 32204
Phone: (888) 934-3354
www.fnf.com

BUSINESSES

Claims Management
Specialty Insurance
Title Insurance

THE STATS

Employer Type: Public Company
Ticker Symbol: FNF (NYSE)
Chairman: William P. Foley II
CEO: Alan Stinson
Revenue: $5.52 billion (FYE 12/07)
Net Income: $129.77 million
No. of Employees: 17,800
No. of Offices: 1,500

UPPER

- "In solid financial shape"—"cash is abundant"

DOWNER

- Treatment of employees needs improvement

EMPLOYMENT CONTACT

www.fnf.com/FNF/careerops.htm

Visit the Vault Finance Career Channel at **www.vault.com/finance** — with
insider firm profiles, message boards, the Vault Finance Job Board and more.

VAULT CAREER LIBRARY   157

THE SCOOP

New name, new structure

In November 2006, Fidelity National Title Group (FNT) changed its name to Fidelity National Financial (FNF). Fidelity National Financial had been the name of FNT's parent holding company; the name change followed a decision to eliminate the holding company structure and create an independent company. Fidelity National Financial has approximately 1,500 offices in 49 states and the District of Columbia, plus agent operations in Guam, Puerto Rico, Canada, Mexico and the U.S. Virgin Islands.

Headquartered in Jacksonville, Fla., Fidelity National provides title insurance, specialty insurance, claims management services, real estate solutions and information services. Its title insurance underwriters (Fidelity National Title, Chicago Title, Ticor Title, Security Union Title and Alamo Title) make up the Fidelity National Title Group. Fidelity's specialty insurance business, Fidelity National Property and Casualty Insurance Group, offers homeowners, auto, personal and flood insurance. Fidelity National Real Estate Solutions is one of the top providers of data and services to the multiple listing service industry. FNF's claims management services (including workers' compensation, disability and liability and claims services) are operated through its minority-owned subsidiary Sedgwick CMS, which serves corporate and public sector entities. Another minority-owned subsidiary, Ceridian, provides information services in the human resources, retail and transportation markets.

Undaunted by disaster

The giant that is Fidelity National Financial was born in 1847 when a young Chicago law clerk named Edward Rucker created a system for tracking documents and legal proceedings related to real estate titles. Rucker's system saved attorneys the laborious task of searching official records in connection with transfers of real property. This service helped develop what would later become Chicago Title. One year later, over in California, a San Francisco notary public named C.V. Gillespie began the company that would eventually become Fidelity National Title Insurance.

Both men's firms played important roles in American history: Chicago Trust employees risked their lives to save records from the devastating 1871 Chicago fire (their efforts led to the creation of the Cook County land records system). And when the great earthquake struck San Francisco in 1906, Gillespie's successors and their wives rescued huge bundles of title records—a good thing, as San Francisco's own Hall of Records and City Hall were completely destroyed. Chicago Title and Fidelity underwent a series of mergers and acquisitions in the ensuing decades; in 2000, their paths came together with Fidelity's purchase of the Chicago Title Corporation and its many subsidiaries. This merger made Fidelity the biggest title insurance entity in the world.

Change in the air

In May 2007, Alan L. Stinson, a co-chief operating officer with Fidelity, was promoted to the role of CEO. The other co-operating officer, Raymond R. Quick, and president Brent B. Bickett were named co-presidents. Former CEO William Foley now sits at the head of the board as its chairman.

The going gets rough

A monstrous third quarter 2007 ended with the announcement that 1,700 employees had been laid off, a figure that included 14 percent of Fidelity National Financial's field staff. "This quarter presented challenging operating environments for several of our businesses," Chairman of the Board William P. Foley, II, said in a statement. "Obviously, the mortgage and real estate markets have impacted volumes in our title insurance business and we have responded with significant staffing reductions."

Total revenue for the 2007 was $5.5 billion, down from $9.4 billion in 2006. The losses included the result of an $81.5 million charge to boost the reserve for claim losses. Net income, meanwhile, plummeted to $129.7 million from $437.7 million a year earlier, due largely to the abysmal mortgage market. And Fidelity's job situation didn't look much better. BusinessWeek reported that since 2006, Fidelity had eliminated 4,000 jobs; that figure includes the third-quarter layoffs, but not the 600 in October 2007.

Shop around

Despite the company's financial woes, 2007 was a banner year for acquisitions. February saw the acquisition of Advanced Total Imaging, Inc., a document management company. Terms of that deal were not disclosed. Also in February, Fidelity subsidiary Fidelity National Real Estate Solutions bought Go Apply, a mortgage lead generator whose customers include 30 mortgage lenders and more than 2,500 mortgage brokers.

Then in March, Fidelity National Real Estate Solutions snapped up Realigent, a California-based company that offers software for real estate professionals. Terms of that deal were also kept quiet.

In August 2007, ATM Holdings, whose primary subsidary is a title insurance agency, was acquired by Fidelity. One of the benefits of the acquisition is ATM's relationships with eight of the top 50 mortgage originators in the United States.

Finally, in November 2007, Fidelity—along with its partner, Thomas H. Lee Partners—completed its acquisition of Ceridian Corporation for $5.3 billion. Fidelity will have a 33 percent ownership stake in Ceridian. Ceridian offers a variety of human resources services, including payroll processing, tax filing, benefits administration and other services.

A steady decline

Fidelity cut another 1,600 jobs during the second quarter of 2008, during which the firm's net earnings decreased 92 percent to $6.9 million from $84.8 million in 2007's second quarter. During 2008, the firm eliminated 1,200 positions up until June and then cut an additional 400 positions, which FNF attributed to decreasing volumes of new sales. Revenue, meanwhile, also took a hit, tumbling 21 percent to $1.18 billion.

GETTING HIRED

Just the facts

Though the firm doesn't provide a lot of information regarding career opportunities on its web site other than a listing of open full-time and temporary slots and descriptions, candidates can check out available positions by job title as well as location at www.fnf.com/FNF/careerops.htm. And for those who prefer a slightly more personal touch, the firm has you covered—it lists its national human resources number as (800) 815-3969.

OUR SURVEY SAYS

Old-school

Insiders say the culture has an "old-school mentality." Some employees also say work conditions could be improved, calling them "dismal at best," adding that the firm "will promise you that the hours will be reasonable" but "you might work 70 hours a week and Sunday through Friday every week." One insider dryly suggests that "if you have kids, you should go ahead and install video cameras in your house so you can watch them grow up while you sit at work." The firm does, however, offer insiders a host of benefits, including health insurance, a 401(k) and employee stock purchase plans, and a purchase program that gives employees discounts on hotels, rental cars, wireless services, gifts, office supplies and more.

In terms of its future, it appears the company will persevere. "They will never go under," says one insider. "Cash is abundant" at Fidelity and "they are in solid financial shape."

Visit the Vault Finance Career Channel at **www.vault.com/finance** — with
insider firm profiles, message boards, the Vault Finance Job Board and more.

VAULT CAREER LIBRARY

161

First American Corp.

1 First American Way
Santa Ana, CA 92707
Phone: (800) 852-3643
Fax: (714) 250-3000
www.firstam.com

DEPARTMENTS

Analytics & Modeling
Appraisals/Valuation
Insurance & Home Warranty
International & Offshore Services
Investment Management
Mortgage Services
Property & Ownership Information
Screening & Risk Mitigation
Technology Solutions
Title & Settlement

THE STATS

Employer Type: Public Company
Ticker Symbol: FAF (NYSE)
Chairman & CEO: Parker S. Kennedy
Revenue: $8.20 billion (FYE 12/07)
Net Income: -$3.12 million
No. of Employees: 35,000
No. of Offices: 2,100

KEY COMPETITORS

Fidelity National Financial
LandAmerica Financial Group
Old Republic International

UPPER

- "Lots of training opportunities available"

DOWNER

- Average pay

EMPLOYMENT CONTACT

www.firstam.com, "careers"

THE SCOOP

Biggest business information provider

With roots back to 1889, First American Corp. combines complex analytics with its vast data resources to supply businesses and consumers with information products to support major economic events, including getting a job, renting an apartment, buying a car or house, securing a mortgage, and opening or buying a business. A Fortune 500 company (coming in at No. 312 in 2008), First American represents America's largest provider of business information. The First American family of companies operates within five primary business segments: Title Insurance and Services, Specialty Insurance, Mortgage Information, Property Information and First Advantage.

The Real O.C.

When Orange County, Calif., separated from Los Angeles in 1889, two firms opened to handle title matters in the new county. Five years later, businessman C.E. Parker merged the two companies and became president of the combined Orange County Title Company. (Orange County Title Company represents the immediate predecessor of today's First American Title Insurance Company, the largest subsidiary of First American Corp.)

In its first 70 years in existence, the company remained a local firm, experiencing modest but steady growth. When C.E. Parker's grandson Donald Kennedy Parker (current chairman emeritus) graduated law school in 1948, he joined the company and promoted its expansion beyond the borders of Orange County. In 1957, the board authorized an expansion plan aimed at making the corporation a strong player in Southern California. By the time Donald Kennedy Parker became president in 1963, the company had changed its name to First American and had operations in four states.

In 1966, the company underwent a restructuring to become a general holding company, The First American Financial Corp., which conducted title operations through First American Title Insurance Company and trust business through First American Trust Company. It continued to expand and, by the 1980s, had operations in every region of the country. In 1984, First American incorporated several new companies, including a home warranty subsidiary, a real estate tax service, a credit reporting company and a flood certification company.

In December 1993, First American moved its shares onto the New York Stock Exchange. At the turn of the century, it changed its designation to First

Visit the Vault Finance Career Channel at www.vault.com/finance — with insider firm profiles, message boards, the Vault Finance Job Board and more.

VAULT CAREER LIBRARY   163

American Corp. to reflect its diverse business mix. The company began an international expansion with operations in Canada in 1988 and currently has operations in almost 70 countries. It became the first title insurance provider in Mexico, Korea and Hong Kong and has leading title market share in Australia and England.

Appraisal accusations

In November 2007, New York State Attorney General Andrew M. Cuomo filed suit against eAppraise IT (a subsidiary of First American) alleging that the appraisal management company colluded with the savings and loan Washington Mutual to employ a list of preferred "proven appraisers" who inflated appraisals on homes. WaMu profited from the higher appraisals because it could close more home loans at greater values, the suit states. Cuomo alleges that executives at eAppraise IT intentionally broke the law to secure future business with WaMu.

The suit seeks to stop the practice and recover illegal profits, although it does not provide a dollar amount sought. First American has denied the allegations and moved to dismiss the suit, arguing Cuomo cannot bring enforcement action in the area of mortgage-loan origination by federal savings and loans, which fall under the Office of Thrift Supervision. First American claims the attorney general's allegations stem from several e-mails taken out of context. The matter will go to court in February 2008.

Settling payment probe

In November 2007, First American agreed to a $5 million settlement to resolve a Florida probe alleging it had made improper payments to real estate agents and mortgage brokers to gain business. Florida Insurance Commissioner Kevin McCarty said the company had funneled the payments through joint ventures. The settlement also requires a review of First American's business practices for one year.

Diversifying

In November 2007, First American announced it had expanded its efforts to guarantee greater diversity and inclusion throughout its organization. The company also announced the appointments of Karen J. Collins as vice president, chief diversity and inclusion officer; Michelle Cheney Donaldson as corporate director of diversity and inclusion; and Stephanie M. Swenseid as corporate director of supplier diversity. The company hopes to increase diverse leadership at all levels of the organization and to create greater supplier diversity.

New face

In December 2007, First American appointed Elise Luckham its vice president, director of corporate real estate. With almost 20 years corporate real estate experience, Luckham will supervise the development of strategies to optimize First American's real estate assets. Prior to joining First American, Luckham served as vice president, corporate services for New Century Mortgage, where she oversaw a real estate portfolio of 360 buildings, totaling about 3 million square feet.

Buying businesses

In January 2008, First Advantage purchased the assets of CredStar a mortgage credit reporting business unit. The purchase expands First Advantage's market leadership in the U.S. mortgage credit reporting industry, where it already services 19 of the top 20 lenders. The companies did not disclose the terms of the acquisition.

A rough year

For the full year 2007, the firm reported $8.19 billion in revenue, down from $8.52 billion in 2006. Net income fell as well—First American actually recorded a net loss of $3.12 million in 2007 compared with the $287.68 million in net income it recorded in 2006. The firm's exposure to the credit crisis, along with $6.5 million in losses in its insurance segment related to its wildfire exposure, led to the paltry results.

By the second half of 2008, though, the firm brought in a bit of a mixed bag of results. First American posted $42 million in net income for the second quarter compared with a $66 million net loss in the second quarter of 2007, due in part to the $500 million the firm earmarked for claims over the last two years. The firm's revenue, however, dipped to $1.7 billion from $2.1 billion in the second quarter 2007. The decrease was due largely to a 25 percent dip in revenue in First American's title insurance group. The poor results led First American to eliminate about 700 positions in the quarter, followed by another 300 in July.

Visit the Vault Finance Career Channel at www.vault.com/finance — with insider firm profiles, message boards, the Vault Finance Job Board and more.

VAULT CAREER LIBRARY   165

GETTING HIRED

Make your own success story

At www.firstam.com/careers.cfm, potential candidates can read "success stories" of longtime employees or just search current job openings. Descriptions are fairly thorough and include whether a position is exempt and the percent of travel the job might require. Job-seekers can also send on a job listing to a friend, create a search agent or simply submit a resume.

Prior to receiving that elusive offer, however, be prepared to be patient. One insider calls the interview process "painfully slow", adding that it took "three months to get hired" and that "you have to do extensive follow-ups with them." Your process may vary, but you could expect an "HR phone screening," followed up by another phone screening, an "immediate supervisor interview," "VP of department interview," "additional interview with immediate supervisor and then other VPs within the company." If you get an offer and accept, notes one insider, your hiring hinges upon successfully passing a drug screening.

OUR SURVEY SAYS

Care for customers—and employees

The firm is "very customer-service oriented" and is "a firm follower of insurance commissioner statutes," contacts say. From employee reports, the firm seems to care about its workers—First American has "lots of training opportunities available" along with "great health insurance benefits," "a great 401(k) program that matches up to three percent of employee contributions," a "subsidized on-site cafeteria" and even "a nursing home insurance plan." The dress is "business casual," and "there are opportunities to telecommute" (one insider adds that "since I telecommute, my home Internet connection is paid for by the company," and the firm "provides me with a laptop and Blackberry"). Generally hours are "flexible," but "it depends on your job." While "many work a standard eight-hour day," this does not apply "if you are at any level of management."

Though pay is just "similar to other title companies," this is somewhat offset by the firm's generous promotion trajectory for employees. One insider says he has advanced "three times since my hire" and "every opportunity has provided a chance to grow as well as learn." Opportunities are also readily available for workers of all backgrounds—insiders describe the firm's diversity regarding ethnic minorities as "excellent."

First Data Corporation

6200 S. Quebec Street
Greenwood Village, CO 80111
Phone: (303) 967-8000
Fax: (303) 967-6701
www.firstdata.com

BUSINESSES

First Data Commercial Services
First Data Financial Institution
  Services
First Data International

THE STATS

Employer Type: Private Company
Chairman & CEO: Michael Capellas
Revenue: $8.05 billion (FYE 12/07)
No. of Employees: 29,000

UPPER

- "Wonderful benefits" and
  "competitive compensation"

DOWNER

- Not very cohesive culture due to
  mergers

EMPLOYMENT CONTACT

www.firstdata.com/careers/index.htm

Visit the Vault Finance Career Channel at **www.vault.com/finance** — with
insider firm profiles, message boards, the Vault Finance Job Board and more.

VAULT CAREER LIBRARY   167

THE SCOOP

Change with the times

In September 2007, First Data Corporation was acquired by private equity firm Kohlberg Kravis Roberts & Company for $26 billion, resulting in the second largest leveraged buyout in history. First Data, known as one of the first companies to process credit card payments, serves more than 5 million businesses and 1,900 card issuers. It's now a wholly owned subsidiary of KKR.

Chairman and Chief Executive Officer of First Data Ric Duques was replaced by Michael Capellas, a 30-year IT-industry veteran with a reputation as a "corporate turnaround artist." Capellas told *BusinessWeek* in July 2007 that First Data will be "the healthiest business I'll have run."

The company expects revenue to increase from 8 to 10 percent in 2008. Analysts suggest that First Data has a lot of work to do before it achieves its goals. *BusinessWeek* noted that the high purchase price of $26 billion will weigh down the company with $22 billion in debt, a fate made worse by a shaky economy. Critics agree that the newly private company will allow for execs to make necessary changes without public scrutiny. Still, the company is considered one of the leading credit card processors, and its third-quarter 2007 revenue increased 16 percent from the same period the year before.

A child of the '60s

The Mid-America Bankcard Association (MABA), a nonprofit bank card processing cooperative, was launched in Omaha in 1969. In 1971, First Data Resources (FDR), a for-profit processing service made up of 110 employees, was created to serve MABA. FDR was bought by American Express Information Services Corporation in 1980; First Data was spun off from Amex and went public in 1992. Three years later, it merged with First Financial Management Corporation (FFMC). This new entity had three business units: card issuers' services, merchant services and consumer services. Western Union, the famed wire transfer and telegram company, became part of First Data in conjunction with the FFMC merger.

First Data expanded rapidly from 2001 to 2005, engaging in a series of acquisitions overseas and in the U.S. A 2004 merger with Concord EFS brought the STAR Network (with 2.1 million ATM and retail locations) under the First Data umbrella. The company also grew its international businesses, launching operations in Europe, Asia and Latin America. Today, First Data is based in Colorado with offices in 35 states, plus employees who telecommute and work at vendor sites. Globally, First Data has a presence in 38 countries across six continents.

The nature of the businesses

First Data's business in the United States is conducted through two core groups, First Data Commercial Services (FDCS) and First Data Financial Institution Services (FDFIS). FDCS offers credit card processing, debit card processing (through the STAR Network), gift and pre-paid card issuing (through ValueLink), electronic check guarantee and verification services (through TeleCheck), payroll cards (through MoneyNetwork) and Internet commerce and mobile terminal solutions.

FDFIS is made up of eight separate product lines: First Data Resources (which offers comprehensive card transaction processing), output services (responsible for mailing company offers and reports, as well as plastic card printing and embossing), First Data Debit Services, Integrated Payment Systems, REMITCO (remittance processing, including electronic deposit services), First Data Voice Services (which develops and implements speech recognition software), First Data Health Care Services and First Data Utilities.

First Data's clients include grocery stores and pharmacies, gas stations and convenience stores, restaurants, retailers, financial institutions, travel and entertainment companies, e-businesses, automotive companies, professionals, government agencies, health care companies and utilities.

Telegrams: stop

On January 26, 2006, First Data announced that it would spin off Western Union, allowing it to become an independent, publicly traded company. The next day, Western Union announced that it would no longer provide telegraph and communications services: e-mail and fax services had put a dent in that century-old business. Instead, it would focus on its money transfer businesses, which reaps nearly $3 billion in revenues each year. Western Union began trading independently in October 2006; First Data reasoned that the decision to split would boost the value of its financial service businesses.

Visit the Vault Finance Career Channel at **www.vault.com/finance** — with insider firm profiles, message boards, the Vault Finance Job Board and more.

VAULT CAREER LIBRARY   **169**

Talk Turkey

In October 2007, First Data officially opened its first office in Turkey. The Istanbul location is an attempt to latch on to the world's major markets. First Data will provide Turkish institutions with a range of credit card and loan processing options, ATM management, fraud and risk management, and other services. According to a statement from First Data, credit-card issuing in Turkey has increased 25 percent annually for the last five years.

Year wrap-up

In 2007, the firm brought in $8.05 billion in total revenue, up from the $7.07 billion it posted in 2006. But First Data also posted a net loss of $907.2 million for the year compared with $1.5 billion in net income in 2006. Costs associated with the firm's merger with Kohlberg Kravis Roberts & Co. in late 2007 contributed to the poor results, which included $499 million in costs related to the buyout.

The first quarter of 2008 looked a little better for First Data, at least on the revenue front. The firm posted revenue of $2.13 billion, a 16 percent jump from the $1.84 billion it pulled in for 2007's first quarter. A net loss of $221.7 million for the quarter came as a blow, however, especially compared with the $175.2 million in net income the firm posted in 2007's first quarter. Continuing arduous market conditions combined with fallout costs from the merger led to the heavy losses for the firm.

GETTING HIRED

Stop on by

If you're looking for a new gig, drop by www.firstdata.com/careers/index.htm, where the firm lets you search relevant current openings—or lets you just submit a resume if nothing happens to strike your fancy. But if you have contacts within the company, milk 'em—insiders say the best way to get an interview with First Data is to name drop. One respondent reports applying "several times for positions, but I failed to get even one interview or callback until I had someone that I knew who worked there intercede on my behalf." The tactic seems to work wonders. "Once they had my name, they pursued me actively." Another source reports being "recruited by the sales manager who knew me when we had worked together previously" and therefore, "there was no interview." One insider (without a friend within the firm) reports going through three interviews, "one with the application and a test, and then later, two interviews with two different HR coordinators," adding, "All were very professional."

Another contact paints a different picture of the hiring process, calling the interviews "very informal" and the process "loose and disorganized." Ultimately, says the insider, the company "took forever to make a decision," and "then the offer letter had a different amount than the verbal offer, and we had to work through that." Yet another reports having gone through a "phone interview first, then an in-person panel interview was scheduled, but only one of the panel interviewers showed up. I was also warned by the interviewer how difficult the 18-month probationary period would be."

OUR SURVEY SAYS

Running the gamut

The firm culture "varies by location," says one insider. "First Data has purchased so many companies and has not done a very good job of blending the cultures." Another says, "Because of the poor job of combining their many 'companies' into a cohesive 'team,' many employees feel neglected, not treated with equal respect, and pressured to work long hours and to not take their paid-time-off days."

Yet another says, "The job is extremely stressful due to the nature of our business of credit and debit card processing. If one of the merchants is down and cannot process, we have a time-critical situation on our hands." One contact gives kudos to the culture, however, calling it a "flexible and corporate" one that "cares about employee satisfaction."

The "wonderful benefits," "competitive compensation" and "lax" dress code all get high marks. But insiders have a beef with the "limited advancement opportunities." One insider expounds, saying there's "not much opportunity for advancement," but "lots of opportunities to learn." The hours, however, are long. An insider who works from home reports working "at least 12-hour days." Others say there are "lots of over 40-hour weeks for all levels," and "overtime for exempt salaried employees is expected without question." And one insider notes that staffers are "frequently assigned to new positions without consultation." Diversity efforts could also stand a little work, employees say. Although one insider reports that there's a "diverse workforce," another calls the culture "male-dominated."

Visit the Vault Finance Career Channel at **www.vault.com/finance** — with insider firm profiles, message boards, the Vault Finance Job Board and more.

VAULT CAREER LIBRARY   171

Fiserv

255 Fiserv Drive
Brookfield, WI 53045
Phone: (262) 879-5000
Fax: (262) 879-5013
www.fiserv.com

BUSINESSES

Depository Institution Processing
Financial Institutions
Insurance
Investment Support Services
Payments & Industry Products

THE STATS

Employer Type: Public Company
Ticker Symbol: FISV (NASD)
President & CEO: Jeffery W. Yabuki
Revenue: $3.92 billion (FYE 12/07)
Net Income: $439 million
No. of Employees: 25,000
No. of Offices: 275

KEY COMPETITORS

Fidelity National Information Services
Metavante
Total System Services

UPPER

- "Great co-workers"

DOWNER

- Needs to beef up diversity hiring efforts

EMPLOYMENT CONTACT

www.fiserv.com/careers.htm

THE SCOOP

Data processing pioneers

Fiserv began as a merger of two small companies which combined to become a giant international corporation in a span of twenty short years. In the early 1980s, Sunshine State Systems was a regional data processing company serving small banks in sun-washed Tampa, Fla., and First Data Processing was its Milwaukee equivalent. The companies came together to form Fiserv in 1984 and went public two years later, launching an effort to become the United States' first national data processor.

Fiserv continued to grow, adding Minnesota On-Line to their growing company in 1988, which expanded their business into credit union services. In 1990, Fiserv acquired GTE EFT Services Money Network and GTE ATM Networks, and in 1992, it gained key access to the card fulfillment market by buying Data Holding, Inc. Securities transaction processing services were added in 1997 with the acquisition of BHC Financial. Fiserv then entered the insurance industry and the health benefits market, acquiring Network Data Processing in 1998 and BenefitPlanners in 2001.

Today, Fiserv's clients included some of the country's biggest financial institutions, and its services still include all of its acquired bits and pieces, including electronic funds services, card fulfillment, insurance, business process outsourcing (BPO), software and systems solutions and health benefits administration. Fiserv is headquartered in Wisconsin with approximately 245 offices nationwide and more than 16 offices internationally. International operations are carried out through its Fiserv CBS Worldwide unit, which serves clients in 50 countries.

In 2008, Fiserv made the Fortune 500 list at No. 468, up from its No. 486 spot the year before. As of 2008, Fiserv reported serving more than 21,000 clients throughout the world. Fiserv operates in two segments: financial institution services and insurance services.

Beefing up

The acquisition spree that made Fiserv the giant corporation it is today didn't abate when the company entered the 21st century. In fact, in the past few years, Fiserv's appetite for acquisition has proved to be virtually insatiable.

Visit the Vault Finance Career Channel at **www.vault.com/finance** — with insider firm profiles, message boards, the Vault Finance Job Board and more.

VAULT CAREER LIBRARY   **173**

In 2005, it snapped up mortgage banking software business Del Mar Database, the U.S. e-lending business of Emergis, electronic bill services firm BillMatrix and underwriting software provider VerticalPoint, among others. This trend continued in the first half of 2006 with Fiserv's purchases of CareGain, a consumer health plan software provider; the Missouri-based Jerome Group LLC, a provider of critical business communications solutions; Insurance Wholesalers, a California company that generates leads for mortgage and life insurance sales; and the assets of CT Insurance Services & CCH Wall Street. In the second half of 2006, Fiserv purchased InsureWorx and Innovative Cost Solutions. In 2007, Fiserv purchased anti-fraud and compliance company NetEconomy to delve deeper into the risk, compliance and anti-fraud financial services area.

CheckFree checks in

In December 2007, Fiserv reached the apex of its buying prowess when it acquired Georgia-based CheckFree Corp., one of the largest providers of online banking and electronic payment technology for $4.4 billion. The merger is the largest acquisition in Fiserv's history. CheckFree's shareholders received a payout of $48 per share for the transaction. The deal was financed with $2.5 billion in proceeds from a five-year term loan and $1.75 billion in proceeds from publicly issued five- and 10-year notes. Jeffrey Yabuki will remain CEO of the combined company; former CheckFree CEO Steve Kight will serve as vice-chairman.

Trimming down

With CheckFree on board, Fiserv is making some key changes to the way it does business. One major adjustment is that the company has shed its Investment Support Services business, selling the majority of it in a transaction with TD Ameritrade worth $225 million plus "contingent cash consideration of up to $100 million based on the achievement of revenue targets over the next twelve months." Fiserv ISS Group President Bob Beriault acquired the remaining accounts and net capital of the company for $50 million in cash.

In November 2007, the company announced that it would also be selling much of its health businesses to UnitedHealthcare for $775 million in cash. The deal will include Fiserv Health Plan Administration, the nation's largest Third Party Administrator (TPA) of self-funded health plans; Fiserv Health Plan Management, an outsourcing service for mid-sized health plans and health care payer organizations; Innoviant, a prescription benefits administrator; Innoviant Pharmacy, a prescription mail-order service; Avidyn Health, a care management company; and four other components of Fiserv Health's ancillary businesses. Not included were Fiserv's worker compensation services organization and CareGain, Inc. which will remain part of the organization.

Fiserv 2.0

Fiserv responded to client demand for better online bill payment systems in August 2006 with the launch of its proprietary Paytraxx system, designed to help financial institutions manage online payments quickly and securely. Paytraxx was a sign of significant changes in the company described as Fiserv 2.0, a company initiative to make its 75 business units work more closely together to serve clients' needs. Fiserv 2.0 was the creation of President and CEO Jeff Yabuki, who spent six months reviewing the firm's business, policies and culture before unveiling the program September 2006. According to the firm, Fiserv 2.0 is "changing the way we do business. We're breaking down internal silos, and focusing on our clients' needs. We have restructured our divisions, and hired a number of top executives in the last year from outside the firm."

Paytraxx seemed to be on track in 2007, as an early progress report showed that the system had gained almost one hundred new financial institutions as customers in its inaugural year. In addition, CEO Jeffery Yabuki was awarded the Innovator Award of 2007 from Bank Technology News in November 2007 in recognition of his campaign to make the company more client oriented. The increase of revenue combined with superior customer service was cited as the reason the award was given to Yabuki.

Selling off

In July 2008, Fiserv announced that it was selling off most of it stake in its insurance businesses. Private equity fund Trident IV acquired 51 percent of the Fiserv Insurance Solutions, investing $205 million in equity and $335 million in debt. Fiserv will retain 49 percent of the businesses, and its current employees will also stay on after the transaction closes.

Visit the Vault Finance Career Channel at **www.vault.com/finance** — with
insider firm profiles, message boards, the Vault Finance Job Board and more.

VAULT CAREER LIBRARY   **175**

GETTING HIRED

Check out Fiserv's server

Those interested in employment at Fiserv can log on to www.fiserv.com/careers.htm, where candidates can learn about benefits the company offers and day-to-day life at the firm—along with, of course, the all-important job listings. The firm notes, however, that while its online openings are updated on a regular basis, general applications and resumes from candidates won't be accepted.

Insiders report that the hiring process at the firm "varies by position," but has one thing in common—having "financial services industry experience is an important criteria." Another says that "the interview process itself was fine, but the information provided to me over the phone from the HR office in California was different from the actual information, such as the place I was to show up for my interview." And after the interview, "it took a very long time for HR to get back to me on the decision, and even longer to get the necessary paperwork mailed back and forth." According to Fiserv, a new executive vice president of human resources came on board in April 2007, with plans to update the HR practices and streamline the hiring process.

OUR SURVEY SAYS

Entrepreneurial culture

The company culture is "very entrepreneurial." One contact notes, "I really enjoyed working with my specific co-workers and enjoyed the actual work we produced, even though the hours were horrid." Another source says he has an "outstanding" relationship with his manager, and one respondent says the best aspects about the firm are "the great co-workers" and "opportunity for advancement." Not everyone feels the same, though. One insider says the firm "does not like 'new blood,'" and "there are opportunities for advancement only through longevity and being a favorite." And others say the firm needs to beef up its diversity efforts. But according to the firm, with the introduction of its Fiserv 2.0 initiative in September 2006, it is "ramping up our diversity efforts," and two recent hires (Rahul Gupta, group president of payments, and Bridie Fanning, executive vice president of HR) are "great examples of it."

Fitch Ratings

1 State Street Plaza
New York, NY 10004
Phone: (212) 908-0500
Fax: (212) 480-4435
www.fitchratings.com

DEPARTMENTS

Algorithmics
Derivative Fitch
Fitch Training

THE STATS

Employer Type: Subsidiary of Fimalac
President & CEO: Stephen W. Joynt
No. of Employees: 2,400 (worldwide)
No. of Offices: 50 (worldwide)

KEY COMPETITORS

DBRS
Moody's
Standard & Poor's

UPPER

- "Very easygoing" culture

DOWNER

- Recent negative news due to subprime crisis

Visit the Vault Finance Career Channel at **www.vault.com/finance** — with
insider firm profiles, message boards, the Vault Finance Job Board and more.

VAULT CAREER LIBRARY   177

THE SCOOP

Making the grades

Founded by John Knowles Fitch as the Fitch Publishing Company in 1913, Fitch was one of the early leaders in providing financial statistics. The Fitch rating system of "AAA" to "D," introduced in 1924, has become the standard for the financial community. Fitch, one of the four major credit-rating agencies (the others are Moody's, Standard & Poor's and DBRS), is the leader in providing ratings on debt issued by companies, covering entities in more than 80 countries. The firm is dual-headquartered in New York and London.

In 1997, Fitch became a subsidiary of Fimalac, a large French business support services company, when it merged with London-based IBCA Limited, Europe's largest rating agency. In 2000, Fitch acquired both Duff & Phelps Credit Rating Co. and Thomson BankWatch, thereby boosting its coverage and international personnel.

Super subsidiaries

Fitch Ratings is a part of larger Fimalac company called the Fitch Group, which (excluding Fitch Ratings) is comprised of three main subsidiaries: Derivative Fitch, Algorithimics and FitchTraining.

Derivative Fitch is a rating agency dedicated to providing ratings and services for the collateralized debt organization and credit derivatives markets. A wholly owned subsidiary of Fitch Ratings, Derivative Fitch has over 1,700 global credit derivatives under surveillance.

Algorithmics, a member of the Fitch Group, is the world's leading provider of enterprise risk solutions. More than 300 financial institutions rely on Algorithmics' software, analytics and advisory services to make risk-aware business decisions, maximize shareholder value and meet regulatory requirements. Supported by a global team of risk experts based in major financial centers, Algorithmics offers solutions for market, credit and operational risk, as well as collateral and capital management.

London-based FitchTraining was established in 1987. It provides financial analytic training with a specialization in credit, corporate and structured finance.

Prism

In May 2006, the firm launched a commercial real estate collateralized debt obligation group headed by Jenny Story, a senior executive in the commercial mortgage-backed securities group. The company uses an economic capital model, called Prism, in its analysis of life, nonlife and health insurers in the United States, United Kingdom, France and Germany. Prism uses simulations to create thousands of economic scenarios. The key selling point of the system is that it can compare companies in different regions and businesses.

Bad credit

The field of one credit rating is one that is controversial and sometimes politicized. Despite the standard disclaimer that warns that credit ratings shouldn't be used as the only vehicle for making investment decisions, financial professionals put a high premium on the grades of these industry soothsayers. As a result, companies like Fitch are subjected to an intense spotlight when they aren't delivering spot-on ratings. But among the "big three" ratings firms, Fitch has earned a reputation for trustworthiness—it was the only one to admit to its mistakes in the Russian debt-default crisis of the late 1990s.

But the Russian ordeal was just the tip of the iceberg for controversy in the credit rating agencies. The Enron scandal rocked the credit rating agencies in 2001. The rating agencies, in turn, claimed that Enron had provided them with misleading information. In 2002, during the Senate hearing on the crisis, the SEC announced plans to launch a thorough investigation into the practices of the three agencies. And later in 2002, similar scandals erupted at WorldCom and Global Crossing, and the agencies were once again questioned for their failure to expose the problems. In late 2004, corporate CFOs, as well as lawmakers, were putting pressure on the SEC to increase governmental oversight of credit-rating agencies.

Despite the criticisms and intense scrutiny surrounding credit agencies over the last two decades, scandal roiled their hallowed halls once again in 2007 when the news broke about the unreliability of subprime bonds that had almost universally been given the trusted AAA rating.

Visit the Vault Finance Career Channel at **www.vault.com/finance** — with
insider firm profiles, message boards, the Vault Finance Job Board and more.

VAULT CAREER LIBRARY   **179**

The blame game

In the aftermath that followed, everyone's head was on the chopping block. Banks were writing down billions of dollars, dreading the lowering of the AAA ratings, which vanished as fast as a rabbit in a magician's hat. The banks blamed portfolio managers, the portfolio managers blamed the ratings agencies, and the rating agencies blamed Alan Greenspan. A chaos spread over the financial industry which still looms large in 2008.

The credit ratings agencies have, for the most part, remained silent as to their complicity in the subprime catastrophe that took hold of the market in 2007. Fitch Ratings web page says little about the ordeal; even a section labeled "subprime and the state of the credit markets" does little to affirm or deny guilt in the matter. But industry insiders say that credit ratings had a large role to play in allowing financial organizations to maximize their tranching of collateralized debt obligations to create the highest ratings. Only in time will the financial market see the full implications of the fall of these subprime mortgage securities. Subprime loans were estimated to be worth approximately $100 billion of the $375 billion in CDOs sold in 2006.

Bad news on the horizon

In July 2008, Fitch released a study reporting that while credit card issuers have had a rough time of things recently, the industry is only likely to get worse. The Fitch report stated that "credit losses have approached, and in some cases surpassed, five-year historical average," and because of it, "many management teams are predicting worsening metrics for the latter part of 2008." The report also predicted that the industry troubles may continue well into 2009.

GETTING HIRED

Take a flyerx

In the careers section of Fitch Ratings' official site www.fitchratings.com, prospective applicants can not only search for job opportunities all over the world, but they can also download a recruiting brochure complete with all the facts they might need to know about the company. The site also provides a link to information on the firm's U.K. graduate recruitment program, a two-year rotational program in corporate finance, structured finance or financial institutions in London. According to the firm, program participants "will be provided with extensive formal and informal training and development, given the opportunity to study for the Chartered Financial Analyst qualification, and participate fully in the day-to-day operations of the company." Additionally, depending on a participant's progress, "advancement into an analytical role on completion of the program may be available."

Prospective candidates for the program can download an application online. According to one insider, analysts can expect to go "through three rounds of interviews: the first with the department head, then with other analysts and finally with a managing director." Another reports going through a "phone interview, then in-office interviews with five people holding different positions within the firm, from analyst to managing director."

OUR SURVEY SAYS

Taking it easy

The company culture is "very easygoing," says one respondent. Others note that the firm is steadily staking its own claim on the ratings frontier. "Since Fitch is the result of mergers and acquisitions of four smaller rating agencies, the corporate culture has only recently become more unified." Insiders say the new Fitch might be more "title-oriented in its structure and more bureaucratic" than its predecessor firms, but "as a much larger organization now, Fitch is paying more attention to in-house training." The firm "provides tuition reimbursement for relevant course work and covers the costs associated with taking the CFA" exam. The working hours are "reasonable," with some saying they put in the "occasional late night," but "not usually more than once a week."

The company dress code also gets high marks, with insiders calling it "casual always except for client contact" and "business casual unless you have a meeting or are traveling outside of the office for meetings." Additionally, the firm offers all the standard benefits, and then some. "One great special perk is a very subsidized membership at New York Health & Racquet," says a source, "which is across the street from Fitch's offices." Insiders say "as a worldwide organization, Fitch has a diverse workforce," and "among analysts, Asians are probably the most prominent minority group."

As for advancement opportunities, "there are a lot of really qualified, great analysts at Fitch, and advancement depends on having the opportunities to excel in various situations, and these opportunities vary from department to department."

Visit the Vault Finance Career Channel at www.vault.com/finance — with insider firm profiles, message boards, the Vault Finance Job Board and more.

VAULT CAREER LIBRARY   181

Freddie Mac

8200 Jones Branch Dr.
McLean, VA 22102-3110
Phone: (703) 903-2000
www.freddiemac.com

THE STATS

Employer Type: Government Entity
Ticker Symbol: FRE (NYSE)
Chairman & CEO: Richard F. Syron
Revenue: $43.10 billion (FYE 12/07)
Net Income: -$3.10 billion
No. of Employees: 5,398
No. of Offices: 12

KEY COMPETITORS

Citigroup
Countrywide Financial
Fannie Mae

UPPERS

- "Very good" benefits package—"they give you a lot of options to choose from."
- Fairly diverse workforce

DOWNERS

- Work environment is "highly political"
- Current turmoil

EMPLOYMENT CONTACT

www.freddiemac.com/careers/index.html

THE SCOOP

Taking center stage

Professionals in the finance industry would have had to be living under a rock to avoid reading or hearing about Freddie Mac in 2007 and 2008. Short for The Federal Home Loan Mortgage Corporation, Freddie Mac has been atop many a headline as of late, and not in a good way. It reported billions in losses in 2007, becoming one of the prime casualties of the subprime mortgage collapse that rocked domestic and international markets. The potential risky loans that made this government supported mortgage lender so powerful quickly became its biggest liability.

The firm and its cousin Fannie Mae (Federal National Mortgage Association) had been publicly traded enterprises until their troubles came to a head in September 2008, forcing the feds to come to the rescue. On September 7th, the U.S. government officially seized control of Freddie Mac and Fannie Mae, in an attempt to stop the ongoing losses experienced by the firms. In addition to taking control, U.S. Treasury Secretary Henry Paulson said the government would supplant each of the firm's CEOs with new heads. (After staying on for a transition stage, Freddie's current head Richard F. Syron will be replaced by Carlyle Group senior adviser David M. Moffett.) Additionally, the Treasury will obtain $1 billion in preferred shares for both Fannie and Freddie and will provide about $200 billion in funding. Paulson indicated that allowing either of the giants to fail would "cause great turmoil" for domestic and international financial markets. To this end, his predictions seemed accurate; stocks rallied after the takeover announcement was made.

As far as the big funding picture goes for the future, the Treasury will also restrict the size of each firm's mortgage portfolio to $850 billion. As of September 2008, Freddie had about $798 billion in mortgages and securities.

From better to worse

Freddie Mac purchases conventional mortgages from mortgage banks, mortgage companies, credit unions, online lenders and thrifts (including savings banks and savings and loan associations), and then securitizes these mortgages. By doing so, the firm transfers the financial risk from those lending institutions, and as a result, helps increase homeownership in the U.S. This, in turn, lowers mortgage rates across the board, increases the number of

Visit the Vault Finance Career Channel at www.vault.com/finance — with
insider firm profiles, message boards, the Vault Finance Job Board and more.

VAULT CAREER LIBRARY   183

mortgage finance options to homebuyers and attracts investors to support America's mortgage lending needs.

While this strategy had been highly successful in the past, it hit its breakpoint in 2007, when credit rating agencies gave their triple A ratings to securities that later fell apart. Freddie Mac reported losses of $2 billion in its third quarter of the year. At a conference in December 2007, Freddie Mac Chairman and CEO Richard Syron told investors that the housing market is going to get "worse before it gets better." And it did, resulting in even worse results for Freddie.

Freddie meets Uncle Sam

Freddie Mac was born during a tumultuous period much like today. In the late 1960s, the U.S. mortgage market was highly volatile, due to a wide disparity in interest rates from city to city. Also, due to the risky nature of mortgage loans, banks were conservative in their underwriting of properties, making mortgage loans harder for the average citizen to get. Neither the government nor the private banking sector alone could address the nation's housing finance needs.

In 1970, just two years after chartering the Federal National Mortgage Association (Fannie Mae), Congress chartered The Federal Home Loan Mortgage Corporation (Freddie Mac), both loosely named after their acronyms. Freddie Mac, along with its sister company, was formed "to provide stability in the secondary market for residential mortgages; to respond appropriately to the private capital market; to provide ongoing assistance for the secondary market for residential mortgages; and to promote access to mortgage credit by increasing liquidity of mortgage investments."

The firm purchases single-family and multifamily residential mortgages and mortgage-related securities, which it finances primarily through the issuance of mortgage pass-through securities and debt instruments in the capital markets. By buying mortgages, Fannie Mae and Freddie Mac increase the amount of capital in the housing market. Together, Fannie and Freddie provide approximately half of the mortgage market's cash.

In 1992, Congress, concerned about the dramatic growth of Fannie Mae and Freddie Mac and the massive effect the firms could have on the housing market, created the Office of Federal Housing Enterprise Oversight (OFHEO) to regulate the two companies' safety and soundness; the Department of Housing and Urban Development regulates their housing mission activities. Although Freddie Mac's charter exempted it from SEC registration, the company had voluntarily committed to register once it became timely in its financial reporting. Freddie Mac was not exempt from the investor protections provided under the antifraud provisions of the federal securities laws (that is, investors in Freddie Mac securities had the same stringent protections under federal law that investors in all other companies have).

Capital losses

In November 2007, Freddie Mac was forced to take some drastic measures to neutralize its losses in the subprime market. The struggling company sold $6 billion of preferred stock and cut its dividend in half to 25 cents. The move came shortly after the company's disastrous third quarter numbers surfaced, exposing the fact that the fair value of net assets attributable to common stockholders before capital transactions decreased by approximately $8.1 billion. Its net loss for the quarter was $2.0 billion.

The company refused to let the disaster overwhelm them completely, however. In addition to selling preferred stock and cutting dividends, Freddie Mac also adopted new restrictions for which mortgages it will take on in the future. In December 2007, Freddie followed in their sister company Fannie Mae's footsteps by announcing it would charge an additional fee of .25 percent for securitizing company guaranteed mortgages. CEO Richard Syron seemed cautiously optimistic about the company's future. "We have reported really ugly numbers," Syron said in a press release. "But we reported really ugly numbers at a time when the business coming in has got terrific returns to it."

Though charging an additional fee for guarantees on securities may seem a safe move for Freddie Mac, not everyone was happy with the decision. On December 7, 2007, National Association of Home Builders Chief Executive Officer Jerry Howard called the fee "a broad tax on homeownership that ultimately will be passed along to consumers", adding that it was the "exact opposite" of what needs to be done to save the housing market.

"Standing with furniture on the lawn"

At the end of 2007, Freddie Mac Chairman and CEO Richard Syron predicted that high rates of foreclosures will continue well into 2008 and beyond. He estimated that in the next several years, the company will lose somewhere between $5.5 billion to $7.5 billion more. At the same time, he predicted a dire future for those who would be most affected by foreclosure and eviction saying, that he has not yet seen "pictures of people standing with furniture on

Visit the Vault Finance Career Channel at **www.vault.com/finance** — with insider firm profiles, message boards, the Vault Finance Job Board and more.

VAULT CAREER LIBRARY   185

the lawn … As that begins to happen, and it will happen, I am afraid of the impact that this has."

Freddie's flailing

In February 2008, Freddie Mac released its 2007 results, which disappointed all around, mostly due to the ongoing chaos created by the industry's subprime defaults. For the fourth quarter of 2007, Freddie Mac reported a $2.45 billion loss. (The day before, sister firm Fannie Mae stated a $3.56 billion loss for the quarter.) For the full-year 2007, Freddie reported a $3.09 billion loss, compared with a (positive) net income of $2.33 billion for 2006. CEO Syron said that the firm is "extremely cautious as we enter 2008," adding that if the economy continues to deteriorate, "it will have a further negative effect on homeowners across the country and drive credit costs higher."

Treasury to the rescue

In July 2008, Freddie Mac and Fannie Mae's stocks lost half their value—an event that some analysts said was worse for the financial markets than the collapse of Bear Stearns. (Freddie had lost about $4.6 billion since mid-2007, following a flood of homeowner defaults.) Following the stock nosedives, the U.S. Treasury finagled a few favors from Congress on behalf of the agencies, including a temporary increase in a credit line for Fannie and Freddie and temporary authority to purchase equity in one or both of the mortgage companies.

U.S. Treasury Secretary Henry Paulson spearheaded the plan to save Fannie and Freddie, assuring the Fed and the Federal Reserve Bank of New York that any loans to Fannie or Freddie would serve only as an "interim step," not a permanent solution. In the meantime, however, analysts indicated that the steps the government plans on taking to assuage worries about financial backing haven't actually upgraded the economy's overall dreary outlook.

It's a shame about Freddie

A month later, in August 2008, Freddie Mac posted a net loss of $821 million—a far cry from the $729 million in net income the firm pulled in for the second quarter of 2007. Revenue, meanwhile, dropped 28 percent to $1.69 billion (but was slightly ahead of analysts' estimates, which had predicted a loss of $2.19 billion). The steep overall declines were due mostly to credit-loss provisions of $2.5 billion and a securities-related write-down of $1 billion.

GETTING HIRED

Meet the Mac

Learn about the firm's career development plan, read employee testimonials and learn about benefits the firm offers on the career section of www.freddiemac.com. Candidates can also search for positions by location and job category. The firm lists its extensive benefit offerings, career development programs and upcoming events for prospective employees at various colleges.

Freddie Mac runs a summer internship program for college students pursuing careers in finance, economics, accounting and IT. To recruit for its internship program, Freddie Mac visits several universities, including Duke, Carnegie Mellon, Hampton, James Madison, Maryland, Virginia, Virginia Tech and the University of Puerto Rico. Additionally, the firm advertises its internships at numerous other schools.

Make sure you clear your calendar when it comes to interviews; it's not uncommon to "spend all day here interviewing" with the unit you'll be working with. For full-time seekers, "there could be different numbers of interviews for different people going for the same job," says one insider. Another source went through "one round of interviews with staff, a manager, and a VP who I would be working with." He says, "The interviews were pretty standard and behavioral-based, looking for information on my experience, ethics and how I approach problem solving." An analyst agrees, adding, "If you use common sense, they're easy."

OUR SURVEY SAYS

They know you have a life

The culture at Freddie Mac is "very prestigious" but "relaxed" with a "respect for work-life balance." It's also "very friendly, intelligent and easygoing," and a "great place for serving both the communities and Wall Street." But insiders have varying opinions on Freddie Mac's corporate culture. Some say it's "very academic and not strategic at all," while others think it's "pretty open and very intellectual." At least one insider calls it "family-friendly," and

Visit the Vault Finance Career Channel at **www.vault.com/finance** — with insider firm profiles, message boards, the Vault Finance Job Board and more.

VAULT CAREER LIBRARY   187

another says, "Morale is very low, especially in the HR, single family and multifamily divisions, and it's become worse since several senior executives were ousted."

The one thing most sources agree on is Freddie Mac's at least somewhat "political" nature. One insider even goes as far as saying, "For someone seeking employment there, I would advise that he or she is aware that the environment is highly political, and to keep any new ideas under wraps until very strong relationships have been secured with key players." A few other sources echo this opinion. One observes, "Opportunity depends on [how tenaciously you] network and how visible your work is, as well as who you work for." Another says that while "the mainstream employees are great, mostly kind and educated," management "treats everyone like babies—so all the hard work done by others only results in photo ops for the upper management." Another insider adds, "Accountability is rare, so if you want to get tenured, this is a great place to work. But if you are looking to make a difference, look elsewhere."

Good choices

The benefits package is described as "very good," and "they give you a lot of options to choose from." Vacation time "starts at 10 days" and "increases the longer you stay with the company." Dress is "business casual" except for client contact. The firm does offer flex working schedules, though one source warns, "Only select people are allowed to participate." According to the firm, other benefits include "a free on-site wellness center, free on-site fitness center, near-site child care and back-up care, elder care, a home benefit program, and an on-site sundry shop and dry cleaner, to name a few." Additionally, Freddie Mac says employees "can also take advantage of an easily accessible online concierge service to locate a variety of services including travel, tourist and city information, dining, entertainment, maid service and even grocery delivery services." Other benefits include educational tuition reimbursement, employer-paid professional or trade association membership, computer purchase loan program and an on-site employee assistance counselor. One insider says, "The employees, the nice cafeteria, the free gym, the attractive work spaces and a great philanthropic spirit amongst the staff" are all perks.

Sources have mixed reactions when it comes to salaries at Freddie. "My salary was fair," says one director. Another respondent says, "Salaries vary widely even by position. For the highest levels, don't expect much over $100,000 a year. But the total package is good." One insider says, "Pay raises are lousy, except for those in management, who rate each other highly and then tell support staff that their salaries have to be compared against others in similar positions." The source adds, "So while one person works their butt off and the other does nothing, you can't get a decent raise or promotion because you 'have to compare your salary to others in your position.'" Hours seem standard, with not much overtime. Even so, depending on position, there will be some weekend visits to the office. Some insiders report making "frequent" weekend trips, "at least once a month."

They're trying

According to Freddie Mac, "Minorities make up approximately 45 percent of the company's workforce, and over 50 percent of this workforce is women." The firm also showcases a "2008 Diversity Strategy" that incorporates diversity training, recruitment and retention and a number of employee networks for women, minorities and gays and lesbians in the workplace.

Visit the Vault Finance Career Channel at **www.vault.com/finance** — with insider firm profiles, message boards, the Vault Finance Job Board and more.

VAULT CAREER LIBRARY   189

Genworth Financial, Inc.

6620 W. Broad Street
Richmond, VA 23230
Phone: (804) 281-6000
Fax: (804) 662-2414
www.genworth.com

DEPARTMENTS

Mortgage Insurance
Protection Insurance
Retirement Income & Investments

THE STATS

Employer Type: Public Company
Ticker Symbol: GNW (NYSE)
Chairman: Michael D. Fraizer
CIO & SVP, Operations & Quality:
  Scott J. McKay
Revenue: $11.13 billion (FYE 12/07)
Net Income: $1.22 billion
No. of Employees: 7,000

KEY COMPETITORS

AIG
MetLife
Prudential

UPPER

- "A true meritocracy"—"committed to rewarding those that make meaningful contributions"

DOWNER

- "High-stress environment"

EMPLOYMENT CONTACT

www.genworth.com/employment

THE SCOOP

Ups and downs

This powerful insurance company had a roller coaster 2007, with mounting losses on insurance on home loans. However, the year also brought significant gains in the company's extension of its money management business, as the completed acquisition of AssetMark brought in massive net inflows of capital.

Based in Richmond, Va., Genworth Financial ranked No. 233 on the Fortune 500 in 2008, and is among the leading insurance holding companies in the U.S. Formerly part of General Electric Corp., it now has operations in 25 countries and offers primarily consumer-focused products. The company has three business segments: protection insurance, mortgage insurance and retirement income and investments. The company's May 2004 initial public offering on the New York Stock Exchange raised $2.8 billion.

Genworth's Protection insurance group includes term life insurance and universal life insurance, long term care insurance, and group and individual life and health insurance, as well as payment protection insurance, which is offered in 18 countries and helps consumers meet financial obligations should their incomes be interrupted. The company's mortgage insurance group helps users buy homes and offers loan payment counseling and household protection discounts. Genworth's retirement income and investments division offers annuities to provide income in retirement. Also, a money management business offers asset management services.

Trailblazers

Genworth can trace its history back all the way back to 1871 with the first sale of a policy by The Life Insurance Company of Virginia. Genworth's founding company sold its first fixed-life policy business in 1955, and expanded from there over the next 50 years into long term care insurance, mortgage insurance and universal life insurance.

In 2003, the company became GE Financial Insurance, acquiring General Electric's life insurance, long term care insurance, group life and health benefits, retirement planning and mortgage insurance business in the U.S., Australia, Canada and Europe. After going public, GE's ownership of Genworth dropped below 50 percent, which allowed Genworth to be considered fully independent of GE.

Visit the Vault Finance Career Channel at **www.vault.com/finance** — with insider firm profiles, message boards, the Vault Finance Job Board and more.

VAULT CAREER LIBRARY

191

In March 2006, Genworth announced GE's secondary public offerings were priced at $32.75 each. Genworth was not to receive any proceeds from the sale. The company also said that it would buy back 15 million shares of Class B stock from GE for $479 million. Following the completion of the transaction, GE no longer owned any shares of Genworth's common stock. GE said it would receive net proceeds of $2.8 billion from these transactions. GE sold its remaining stake in Genworth Financial to focus on faster-growing markets.

Hitting the mark

Since Genworth successfully acquired AssetMark Investment Services, an investment management and consulting firm, for $230 million (plus performance-based payments of approximately $100 million over the next five years) in 2006, it has been successful in significantly growing its money management business. But AssetMark brought more than just investment cachet to Genworth—the acquisition of the company brought in approximately $8 billion in assets and a team of skilled financial advisors. AssetMark continues to be a strong contributor to Genworth's growth. In June 2007, it launched a new series of no-load mutual funds called the AssetMark Fundamental Index which will be sub-advised by Research Affiliates. The company's combined assets under management nearly doubled in just one short year, shooting up from $13 billion in October 2006 to $21.7 billion at the same time in 2007.

So far, so good

Though Genworth has been affected by the subprime market, it has had an easy road compared with other companies that are connected to the mortgage business. The stock of Genworth dropped approximately 11 points over a one year period in 2007, from a high of $37.16 to a low of $23.26. The company also predicts that its domestic mortgage insurance unit could have a loss in 2008 of anywhere up to 25 cents a share. However, for a business that insures mortgages in a market where home foreclosures are soaring, Genworth is doing better than expected. This is partially due to increased income from its money management business and partially due to a strong showing in its international segment. The latter increased mortgage insurance sales by 15 percent, partially shielding them from losses in the tanking domestic market. Genworth also has announced plans to buy back approximately $1 billion of its common shares between now and 2009.

Going down?

The firm continued to feel the aftershocks of the nadir of the housing market well into 2008. For the second half of 2008, the firm pulled in $2.4 billion in revenue for the second quarter, a decrease from $2.76 billion in the second quarter 2007 and also a drop from $2.75 billion in the first quarter 2008. Genworth recorded a net loss for the quarter of $109 million compared with net income of $379 million in the second quarter 2007 (and $116 million in the first quarter 2008).

But the bottom line wasn't Genworth's only concern in 2008. In August 2008, the firm disclosed that attorneys general in two states had subpoenaed one of its subsidiaries regarding alleged antitrust abuses. The attorneys general, who represent Florida and Connecticut, aren't the first to subpoena the unit—the SEC and the Justice Department also did so in 2006. Genworth has denied the charges and said it plans to "vigorously" defend itself against the cases.

GETTING HIRED

Point of contact

Get online and join what the firm terms on its web site as the "The Genworth Employment Experience." Submit your resume or apply for open positions online (in departments such as investments, mortgage insurance, protection, and retirement income and investments). "If your resume is selected," according to the firm, "your first point of contact should be with a Genworth recruiter in the staffing center or in a local office." Expect an "initial assessment either via phone or in person," and then anticipate more on-site interviews if your recruiter decides that there's a "possible fit." Once you've been called in, you can expect a hiring process that may last up to "six rounds" with meetings from employees in "HR" to the "divisional CEO."

OUR SURVEY SAYS

Reap the rewards

Genworth Financial is a "great place to work," with "a corporate culture built on rewarding those whose contributions improve the bottom line," insiders

Visit the Vault Finance Career Channel at **www.vault.com/finance** — with insider firm profiles, message boards, the Vault Finance Job Board and more.

VAULT CAREER LIBRARY   **193**

say. It's also "a true meritocracy," and "the firm is committed to rewarding those that make meaningful contributions to the organization." The firm also has a "great training program for recent grads from college." Although one Virginia insider calls the corporate culture "pretty relaxed," she adds that it's also a "high-stress environment that you experience in places like NYC."

Hours of work "vary by department," and the "official hours" "are 8 a.m. to 5 p.m., but the reality is 8 a.m. to 6 p.m. under two to three multiple projects." And "about a third of the time, hours are 7:30 a.m. to 7 p.m." Make sure you're on time. "Your manager will talk with you each time you are more than five minutes late." One insider notes, "During holidays and vacations, they will try to get you to stay a few extra days to help cover for other employees who are out on vacation." Another contact says that "everyone one to two levels above entry level are expected to work a little overtime," and "senior management is expected to work 10-plus hours of overtime a week." Yet another insider paints a worse picture when it comes to hours, commenting, "They expect us to work 70 to 80 hours or more a week every week for their advancement, and we get a $500 bonus each year in return."

Benefits get high marks from insiders, who call them "the most competitive in the industry" and add that "great emphasis is placed on providing support for its employees." The firm's business casual dress code, which falls along the lines of a "nice long-sleeve shirt" and "pressed Dockers with nice shoes" is a little more flexible, but one source says, "The better you dress, the better you'll be treated by management."

For the future

Genworth's immediate outlook is bright, contacts say. "I think that Genworth Financial is poised to see tremendous growth in a number of its business segments," reports one insider. "Due to our scale, we are able to leverage our distribution channel relationships across business lines as well as product lines." And happily, "employee morale is strong despite challenging market conditions." This might be because "the firm is growing" and is "committed to dominating in all areas in which it competes." Really, everybody wins. The current business climate is "a great situation for those that are looking to grow in their career and see upward movement potential."

GMAC Financial Services

200 Renaissance Center
Detroit, MI 48265
Phone: (313) 556-5000
Fax: (313) 556-5108
www.gmacfs.com

DEPARTMENTS

Auto Financing
Banking
Investing
Insurance
Real Estate & Mortgage

THE STATS

Employer Type: Private Company
CEO: Alvaro G. De Molina
Revenue: $9.47 billion (FYE 12/07)
Net Income: $-2.33 billion
No. of Employees: 31,400

KEY COMPETITORS

Bank of America
Ford Motor Credit
Toyota Motor Credit

UPPER

• Good training

DOWNER

• Tough hours

EMPLOYMENT CONTACT

See "careers" section of
www.gmacfs.com/us

Visit the Vault Finance Career Channel at **www.vault.com/finance** — with
insider firm profiles, message boards, the Vault Finance Job Board and more.

VAULT CAREER LIBRARY   195

THE SCOOP

Taking the "GM" out of GMAC

The General Motors Acceptance Corporation (GMAC) was the financial services arm of General Motors until GM sold 51 percent of the company to a private investor group led by Cerberus Capital Management. GMAC started out offering financing to GM dealerships and their customers. However, the company has moved beyond simply providing automotive financing, maturing into diversified financial services company, selling insurance, mortgage products and real estate services in over 40 countries. As of June 30, 2008, GMAC held more than $30 billion in assets but the ongoing poor economy led to a net loss for 2007 of $2.3 billion.

Cars and mortgages

GMAC is divided into three main units: financing, insurance and mortgage. While GMAC finances new and certified used GM vehicles, within the company's automotive financing division is Nuvell Financing Services. Nuvell finances rival auto companies that do not have a financial arm, as well as used cars from dealerships that use bank financing. Kia Motors America is among the auto companies that use Nuvell for their new vehicle sales.

The company's mortgage subsidiary, ResCap Holding, is the umbrella for GMAC's residential mortgage business, which offers residential real estate loans, invests in mortgage-backed securities and packages single-family home loans for sale to investors. GMAC insurance offers commercial and personal auto insurance. GMAC also owns ditech.com, an online mortgage lender, known for its humorous television ads with their catchphrase "Lost another one to Ditech." GMAC Home Services is the parent for GMAC Real Estate, which was formed by the purchase of Better Homes and Garden's Real Estate in 1998, GMAC Global Relocation Services and GHS Mortgage.

Waiting at the end of the assembly line

GMAC was formed in 1919 to provide GM auto dealers with the necessary financing to maintain large vehicle inventories. At the time, most dealerships carried only a few cars, as they were required to buy their stock in cash. The invention of the assembly line allowed for the rapid production of large quantities of cars. Thus, the factories wanted dealers to buy larger quantities of cars to keep factory operations running smoothly. So, the General Motors

Acceptance Corp. was formed to provide dealers with the financing necessary to keep these large inventories. GMAC initially operated in Detroit, New York, Chicago, San Francisco and Toronto. By 1920, GMAC expanded to the U.K. and by 1928 had sold about four million retail contracts.

In 1999, GMAC bought Bank of New York's asset-based lending and factory business to create its commercial finance group. In 2000, the company launched SmartAuction, an online auction site for used GM vehicles. GMAC expanded to China in 2004, becoming the first foreign-based financial services company to offer vehicle financing. Also in 2004, the company opened the GMAC Automotive Bank, which raises money from FDIC-insured certificates of deposit. The bank allows the company to diversify funding sources and gives GMAC access to lower-cost sources of funding.

Bank of America to the rescue

In order to raise money for a reorganization, General Motors has been divesting many assets, including GMAC. This divestiture was prompted by investor Kirk Kerkorian and Jerome York, his former representative on GM's board. In July 2005, GMAC announced that Bank of America agreed to purchase up to $55 billion worth of GMAC retail automotive contracts for a five-year period. BofA made an initial purchase of $5 billion and agreed to purchase up to $10 billion of GMAC's U.S. retail auto finance contracts every fiscal year.

In August 2005, the company sold a 78 percent stake in its commercial mortgage operations, GMAC Commercial Holding, for $1.5 billion cash, to an equity group that included Kohlberg Kravis Roberts & Co., Five Mile Capital Partners and Goldman Sachs Capital Partners. Its mortgage operations unit is one of the company's most profitable, and this subsidiary seeks to obtain a stand-alone credit rating to enhance its ability to fund operations.

Also in 2005, GMAC restructured its residential mortgage operations, creating a new wholly owned subsidiary named Residential Capital Corporation. This allowed GMAC to up its credit rating, apart from GM.

Life after GM

GMAC's credit rating has been downgraded in recent years, mostly due to its beleaguered parent GM. On November 30, 2006, a group of investors led by Cerberus Capital Management—including Citigroup, Aozora Bank Ltd. of

Visit the Vault Finance Career Channel at **www.vault.com/finance** — with insider firm profiles, message boards, the Vault Finance Job Board and more.

VAULT CAREER LIBRARY   197

Japan and a subsidiary of PNC Financial Services Group—agreed to purchase 51 percent of GMAC from GM. The sale raised nearly $14 billion for the cash-strapped parent company. GM continues to own the remaining 49 percent of GMAC and collects a dividend from its holdings. The deal has served to lift GMAC's rating to the top speculative grade rung, after nearly a year on the S&P'S CreditWatch list.

Housing crisis strikes again

Like so many other financial service firms, GMAC was forced to lower the axe to contend with the ongoing housing-market crisis. In October 2007, the firm announced that it would streamline operations and revise cost structure in its mortgage operations, Residential Capital (ResCap). GMAC said the move would enhance ResCap's flexibility, allowing it to scale operations up or down more rapidly to meet changing market conditions.

The restructuring plan called for a 25 percent reduction—3,000 jobs—in the firm's worldwide workforce; the majority of reductions occurred in the fourth quarter 2007. The reductions were in addition to the 2,000 jobs eliminated in the first quarter of 2007.

The fourth-quarter reductions included a range of administrative and managerial positions. Business units most affected by lower mortgage market origination volumes incurred the most reductions. All eligible associates affected by the workforce reduction were provided severance packages and outplacement assistance.

Feeling the heat

Given the hard times that have befallen ResCap, it's not surprising that the unit's CEO and CFO decided to hit the road. In April 2007, ResCap's CEO, Bruce Paradis, announced his retirement after a 24-year career with the GMAC. Jim Jones, ResCap's COO and president of its U.S. residential finance group, was tapped to take over for Paradis.

Jones joined ResCap in March 2007 to lead ResCap's U.S. residential finance group. Jones had previously served as CEO at Aegis Mortgage Corporation. He also served as president of banking and insurance, as well as head of consumer credit, at Bank of America, and previously worked in senior leadership positions at Wells Fargo and Citigroup.

Paradis announced his retirement just a few weeks after ResCap's CFO, James Giertz, resigned. GMAC's CFO, Sanjiv Khattri, was handed Giertz's responsibilities on an interim basis.

New status means new strategy—and CFO

Turns out, the CFO gig at ResCap became permanent for Khattri. The role came as part of a package deal when GMAC created a new role to help contend with its status as a standalone firm— executive vice president of corporate development and strategy. Khattri was named to the position and will continue as CFO of ResCap.

GMAC poached Robert Hull, CFO of Bank of America's global wealth and investment management and principal investing divisions, to take over for Khattri as CFO. Hull joined Bank of America in 2001 as the senior vice president for strategy and financial planning and following that position was named CFO of the card services division. Prior to joining Bank of America, he served as CFO of Investorforce Holdings, Marvel Enterprises and Wise Foods Holdings.

Taking on more risk

Now out on its own, GMAC thought it wise to create another new position, this one for handling risk. Samuel Ramsey, a 25-year vet of Bank of America, was named to the new chief risk officer post in December 2007. In the role, he has responsibility for global risk management and treasury activities, including funding and balance sheet management. He reports to the company's COO, Al de Molina, another role that was created following GMAC's break with GM.

Ramsey had joined GMAC in September 2007 as treasurer. Prior to that, he spent over 25 years at Bank of America Corporation, most recently serving as chief financial officer of global corporate and investment banking. Prior to his role in finance, Ramsey was a member of the risk management organization holding several positions including chief risk officer for consumer and small business banking, chief risk officer for commercial banking, and enterprise credit and market risk executive.

By the numbers

GMAC was hit with a $2.3 billion net loss for full-year 2007 compared with net income of $2.1 billion in the previous year. Revenue was also down in

2007, to $21.18 billion from $23.1 billion in 2006. Ongoing trouble in the housing, mortgage and credit markets helped pull down the results, along with "increased funding costs."

The first half of 2008 didn't look much better for GMAC. The firm endured a $2.5 billion net loss in the second quarter 2008 compared with the $293 million in net income it brought in during the second quarter 2007. Net revenue for the quarter slipped down to $1.3 billion from $3.28 billion in the first quarter 2007. In the first quarter 2008, net revenue came in at $2.4 billion and the firm endured a net loss of $589 million. An ongoing weak economy was mostly to blame for the losses—though within the second quarter, a $716 million write-down in auto operating lease assets certainly didn't help.

Resident slashes staff

Due to the housing market slump, GMAC's home loan unit Residential Capital has been plagued with losses recently, and in September 2008, it announced plans to cut 5,000 employees and shutter all of its 200 retail mortgage offices. The job losses amount to 60 percent of Residential Capital's total employees.

GETTING HIRED

All levels welcome

Whether you're an experienced pro or fresh out of college (that is, a "salaried employee-in-training," according to the firm), GMAC has a niche waiting for you. At www.gm.com/careers, candidates can read about the various career paths available at GMAC, the firm's corporate culture, benefits, training, what life in Michigan is like and where else the firm operates throughout the world. GMAC also posts a recruiting calendar, showing the various events it will be holding on campuses. In addition, candidates can search for openings and apply online. GMAC offers undergraduate internships, which the firm says give "full-time college students on-the-job experience where they get exposed to real-world work situations and polish their business skills."

Brace yourself when it comes to the interview process. One insider says the interview process includes "interviews with five people" along with fielding some "technical questions." Another contact reports being flown in to "interview twice." During the trip, "hotel and flight was paid for," and "the benefits of the job such as bonuses and other perks" were outlined. On the interview question front, "we were asked our strengths and weaknesses and how we'd handle a situation if accused of not handling information correctly." Also expect to be asked "basic personal questions." And be prepared with a few questions of your own. One contact says, "Little information was given about the work environment and actual work hours."

OUR SURVEY SAYS

Same faces?

As far as the workforce goes, expect "college graduates" who are "primarily single" and in their "mid to late 20s." One insider says drolly that this "created a unique yet boring environment." Hours also receive middling marks from insiders. One contact even says outright that "hours were the reason I quit." The source adds, "Hours could and did change—when I began work, we only had to work Monday through Friday, but by the time I quit we were required to work weekends."

On the bright side, dress is "business casual," although "we never see the clients." Some sources say training is "the best part of the job," although workers "need more to do our job at the best level." Other insiders complain about the (lack of) opportunities for advancement. "There were not ways in which you could advance," says one worker. "I asked if there was anything else I should be doing and nothing was ever noted as a way to improve my work skills."

Turn the profit

As far as the future of GMAC, employees believe "it will continue to make profit—but at the expense of clients and employees." Overall, "the benefits of the job did not overcome the harassment employees received from calls." All in all, "more consideration of employees needs to be made at all levels of the job—not just the corporate level."

Visit the Vault Finance Career Channel at **www.vault.com/finance** – with
insider firm profiles, message boards, the Vault Finance Job Board and more.

VAULT CAREER LIBRARY   201

Guardian (The Guardian Life Insurance Company of America)

7 Hanover Square
New York, NY 10004-2616
Phone: (212) 598-8000
Fax: (212) 919-2170
www.guardianlife.com

DEPARTMENTS

Disability Income Insurance &
  Specialty Life Products
Employee Benefits
Guardian Trust Company, FSB
Individual Life Insurance & Business
  Protection

THE STATS

Employer Type: Private Company
President & CEO: Dennis J. Manning
Revenue: $7.65 billion (FYE 12/07)
No. of Employees: 5,000
No. of Offices: 6 (excluding sales offices)

KEY COMPETITORS

MassMutual
Nationwide
New York Life

UPPER

- "From the top down, our firm encourages hiring women"

DOWNER

- Opportunities for advancement could be increased

EMPLOYMENT CONTACT

See "careers" section of
www.guardianlife.com

THE SCOOP

Guarding America with its life

The Guardian Life Insurance Company of America is a Fortune 300 mutual company wholly owned by its policyholders, and the fourth largest mutual life insurance company in the United States. New York-based Guardian has over a century of experience in the insurance industry, employing more than 5,000 employees and 2,900 financial representatives nationwide, and providing mutual life insurance, disability, health and dental insurance products to individuals and businesses. The company also offers 401(k)s, trusts and other financial products. Most recently, Guardian acquired a majority stake in RS investments, a San Francisco-based investment management firm specializing in mutual funds and institutional accounts.

Guardian—which had $41.3 billion in assets as of June 2008—was ranked No. 259 on the 2008 Fortune 500 list. For the full year 2007, Guardian's total revenue, including premium and investment income, was $5.86 billion, up from $5.05 billion in the previous year. Net income also improved: the firm booked $122.76 million in net income for the year compared with a $217.49 million net loss the previous year.

Forceful across many fields

Guardian offers a full display of risk protection, investment, and wealth management products and services, sold through its subsidiaries and affiliates. These include the Berkshire Life Insurance Company of America; First Commonwealth; Guardian Baillie Gifford Limited; The Guardian Insurance & Annuity Company, Inc. (GIAC); Guardian Investor Services LLC (GIS); Guardian Trust Company; Innovative Underwriters, Inc.; Park Avenue Life Insurance Company; and Park Avenue Securities LLC.

To sell its insurance and financial products, Guardian has built a commanding field force of experts in areas ranging from financial products to employee benefits. These professionals use a relationship-driven approach with clients, using tools such as the Living Balance Sheet, a recently implemented technology that provides customers with an integrated view of their financial picture. The online tool provides Guardian field representatives with automatic notifications of financial events or changes, and stores copies of important personal documents.

Visit the Vault Finance Career Channel at www.vault.com/finance — with
insider firm profiles, message boards, the Vault Finance Job Board and more.

VAULT CAREER LIBRARY   203

German refugee finds a home in Manhattan

It's no wonder Guardian founder Hugo Wesendonck had such a keen eye for safety and stability. Fleeing post-revolution Germany, he landed in the U.S. in 1848. After pooling start-up funds from fellow German refugees, he opened Germania Life Insurance Company in 1860 in New York to cover the growing number of German immigrants arriving on American shores. Two years later, he opened a branch in San Francisco, and business spread quickly across the country, reaching territories like Colorado, New Mexico and the Dakotas.

After steady growth, the company set up headquarters in New York City's Union Square in 1911. In 1917, the company changed its name to Guardian, in response to a break with the fatherland—and some anti-German sentiment in the U.S.—after WWI. In 1925, it became a mutual company owned by policyholders, eliminating stockholders and private owners. Guardian relocated in 1999, when, after branching out into financial services, it sent its headquarters downtown to Wall Street. In addition to its Manhattan office, the company has primary locations and regional offices in Appleton, Wis.; Bethlehem, Pa.; Spokane, Wash.; Pittsfield, Mass.; and Bridgewater, Mass.

Life insurance-awareness advocate

Guardian Life has conducted several public awareness campaigns in the past, conducting research on public safety and urging Americans to live healthier, safer lives. Most recently, the company targeted the younger generation's lack of life insurance, launching a public awareness campaign featuring NFL running back Warrick Dunn of the Atlanta Falcons. Dunn completed a radio media tour to promote Life Insurance Awareness Month in September of 2006. And in 2007, Guardian teamed up with Tony Gwynn, former Major League Baseball All Star for the San Diego Padres and latest member of the National Baseball Hall of Fame, to educate Americans about the importance of life insurance. Gwynn's partnership with Guardian included a national radio media tour.

Private equity whiz on board

In May 2007, Guardian hired David Turner, a veteran private equity investment manager, to lead its private equity investment initiative. Turner joined the company from WestLB Mellon Asset Management, Private Equity Group, where he served as general partner and, most recently, chief executive officer and chief investment officer. In his new role at Guardian, Turner is in charge of expanding the company's private equity portfolio.

Prior to his work with WestLB Mellon Asset Management, Turner spent 17 years with the State of Michigan Retirement Systems, where he served as a senior portfolio manager and then head of the alternative investment division.

Senior execs poached from competition

Guardian hit up one of its biggest competitors for talent in June 2007, when it poached MassMutual's chief life and large corporate markets actuary. Barbara Snyder, who was named Guardian's chief actuary, works with executive management on a wide range of areas, including risk management, capital management, economic capital, product pricing and design, reserve adequacy, financial reporting, and reinsurance for all Guardian product lines.

Prior to her tenure at MassMutual, Snyder served as senior vice president and product line officer at Mutual of Omaha and chief actuary at Jackson National Life, and held consulting posts with E&Y, Tillinghast, and Lewis & Ellis. She is a member of the American Academy of Actuaries, the Society of Actuaries (SOA), and is a regular participant of the Conference of Consulting Actuaries.

Earlier, in June 2007, Guardian grabbed two ex-Prudential Financial executives. Maria Umbach was hired into Guardian's individual markets division as vice president and chief marketing officer. At Prudential, Umbach was vice president, life insurance product marketing. Andrea Csaszar joined Guardian as vice president of group operations. She was vice president, operations and systems, at Prudential.

Looking out for its women

In October 2007, Guardian held its annual Women's Leadership Summit, an event that provided over 100 of the company's leading female financial representatives, marketing directors, and long term care/disability income specialists with a forum to network and share best practices to help take their careers to the next level. The goal of the event was to ensure the professional growth and future success of Guardian's female financial representatives by facilitating connections with other Guardian advisors and guest speakers, providing interactive workshops for optimum knowledge-sharing, and offering opportunities for networking and mentoring.

Guardian starts early when it comes to supporting female entrepreneurship. In September 2007, the company launched the 2008 Girls Going Places

Visit the Vault Finance Career Channel at www.vault.com/finance — with insider firm profiles, message boards, the Vault Finance Job Board and more.

VAULT CAREER LIBRARY   205

Entrepreneurship Award Program to recognize and reward girls ages 12 to 18 who demonstrate exceptional entrepreneurship. Guardian will kick-off the annual program with three Girls Going Places Entrepreneurship Conferences. The conferences are designed to encourage financial literacy and educate young women about entrepreneurship and financial independence. Successful local businesswomen will share their ideas and experiences as conference mentors.

"These conferences give us an opportunity to educate young women on the range of entrepreneurial opportunities that are available to them," said Viner, in a company statement. "Today, more than 40 percent of businesses are women-owned. Girls Going Places inspires young women to be financially independent and cultivates the ideas behind the successful businesses of the future."

Guardian in 2008

In the first quarter of 2008, Guardian Life brought in revenue of $1.36 billion, up from the $1.31 billion it posted in the first quarter of 2008 but down from the $1.85 billion it brought in for the last quarter of 2007. Net income for the quarter came in at $52.02 million, up from the net loss of $226.19 million it endured in the first quarter 2007. All of Guardian's operating units performed well worldwide, the firm said in its latest earnings release.

GETTING HIRED

What's open

Applicants can check out Guardian's job listings under "list of open jobs" under "careers" on its web site, or they can just submit a resume (it's "not required" that you submit a cover letter, the firm notes), and a member of the firm will contact you "if your skills and qualifications match what we are looking for." Candidates can peruse corporate openings by job title, location and business organization. Job titles can include accounting, actuarial, administration, communications, equities, finance, group insurance products, human resources, information systems, marketing, Park Avenue securities, retirement services, training, trust company, underwriter and warehouse. Those interested in a field sales position are also encouraged to apply online.

Brace yourself

For entry-level candidates, there are at least "two rounds" of interviews to weather, insiders say, complete with a "technical test to filter out unwanted candidates." Prepare for the test if you can—it's "a bit difficult and, "in many cases, students who may not have had a good day may not be able to qualify for HR interview number two." Once you do, however, expect to be asked "about undergraduate course work." You may very well have to "walk through your entire resume." And remember, project self-assurance—"they look for a certain confidence level in candidates." Sources add that interviewers are "helpful" and "aware that most of us had no prior interview experience."

OUR SURVEY SAYS

Premium blend

The corporate culture at Guardian is "a proper blend" of "professional" and "casual," insiders say. Plus, "people always help one other while in crisis." It's also "businesslike" and "offers training and moral support." One insider also lauds the "detailed" training, adding that the firm's "progress monitoring" also gets a stamp of approval. But company perks, says another, aren't given in the traditional sense of the word. Instead, "all expenses are tax-deductible as business-related expenses, so the company doesn't need to provide 'perks.'"

One insider who has "worked at Guardian for many years" has "seen many changes" recently, adding that "older employees do not get treated well and have to work three times harder because more is expected of them." The contact goes on to note that the firm "used to be a great place to work and used to be very understanding and flexible when it came to family," but now requires many staffers to "to fill out Family and Medical Leave Act papers to protect their jobs." Another contact says, "The atmosphere is pretty charged up, but it is enjoyable simply because they are waiting on you to pull in a big account and for them to get paid." One field representative says, "You're your own boss, and that's either a good thing or a bad thing depending on your work ethic."

Another contact says, "Managers monitor sales and conduct training to increase sales, but they don't have to do 'motivational' activities," and adds

Visit the Vault Finance Career Channel at **www.vault.com/finance** — with insider firm profiles, message boards, the Vault Finance Job Board and more.

VAULT CAREER LIBRARY   207

that "they are very supportive." Generally, management seems to receive praise all around. "They never give us menial tasks," says one insider. "They respect our positions and titles, and involve us in the decision-making process." You can also expect feedback on your work with "semi-annual formal feedback sessions" where "our core competencies and weaknesses were pointed out." But "if we were deserving, we were nominated for a promotion." The firm also hosts "monthly informal feedback sessions so that they can gauge our level of involvement in the projects and mentor us for future."

As far as moving up the ladder, an insider says, "Opportunities for advancement are limited to who you know," and "unless you are really liked, you can forget getting promoted unless it's a job no one else wants or they can't fill the position." Although several sources enthuse about the firm's casual Fridays, one in the Baton Rouge, La., office says, "High-quality business suits are the daily work attire." Another simply calls it "strict."

Benefits and perks, however, receive fairly high marks from employees. Guardian provides "free monthly coupons to get beverages and food through company catering" and "food was pretty decent." There's "a variety of traditional and international dishes in one month," and employee dietary requirements are honored with "a special section for vegetarians."

The spice of life

When it comes to diversity, the company "hires people from a whole variety" and has "huge diversity," insiders say. One contact says, "From the top down, our firm encourages hiring women," and there are "special programs within the firm" for female staffers. Guardian also "helps pay female employees' membership in national women's organizations." In regards to the hiring of minorities, one contact is "unsure of the percentage of minorities," "the encouragement and support is the same as for women." Treatment of gays and lesbians within the firm also receive high marks. One insider says, "I have never heard of a policy either way on this issue," and "believe it is left up to each local agency who they hire and they are probably unaware of sexual orientation."

Hartford Financial Services

Hartford Plaza
690 Asylum Avenue
Hartford, CT 06115-1900
Phone: (860) 547-5000
Fax: (860) 547-2680
www.thehartford.com

BUSINESS LINES

Group Benefits
Individual Life
Middle Market
Personal Lines
Retail Products Group
Retirement Plans
Small Commercial
Specialty Commercial

THE STATS

Employer Type: Public Company
Ticker Symbol: HIG (NYSE)
Chairman & CEO: Ramani Ayer
Revenue: $25.92 billion (FYE 12/07)
Income: $2.95 billion
No. of Employees: 31,000
No. of Offices: 429

KEY COMPETITORS

AIG
Allstate
Berkshire Hathaway
Chubb
Genworth Financial
Liberty Mutual
Manulife
MassMutual
MetLife
Nationwide
Principal Financial
Progressive
Prudential Financial
State Farm
Travelers

UPPER

- "Many opportunities for advancement"

DOWNER

- Dealing with some "politics" and "bureaucracy"

EMPLOYMENT CONTACT

See "careers" section of
www.thehartford.com

Visit the Vault Finance Career Channel at **www.vault.com/finance** — with
insider firm profiles, message boards, the Vault Finance Job Board and more.

VAULT CAREER LIBRARY   209

THE SCOOP

Going stag

Founded in 1810, The Hartford Financial Services Group, known widely as The Hartford, is one of the largest investment and insurance companies based in the U.S. Under its prominent red stag logo, The Hartford sells products to individuals, institutions and businesses through nearly 11,000 independent agencies and more than 100,000 registered broker-dealers in countries around the world, including Japan, Brazil and England. The company trades on the New York Stock Exchange under the "HIG" symbol. In 2008, The Hartford ranked No. 95 on the Fortune 500.

Under its life operations, the company sells retail investment products, particularly fixed and variable annuities, mutual funds and 529 college saving plans; retirement plans, including 401(k)s and 403(b)s; products for institutions, such as institutional mutual funds, structured settlement annuities, and private placement life insurance; individual life insurance; and group benefits. International clients are managed by a separate international division, which provides wealth management, retirement and financial protection products to individual investors outside the U.S., in Japan, Brazil and the U.K. The Hartford's property/casualty business offers a variety of personal and commercial property/casualty insurance products, including homeowners, auto, general liability insurance, marine insurance and workers' compensation.

Insurance to the stars

The Hartford has a celebrated history, with a client list including two U.S. presidents and American legends such as Babe Ruth and Buffalo Bill. The company has survived several national disasters (including the Great Chicago Fire, the San Francisco Earthquake and the September 11th attacks), paying out hundreds of millions of dollars in losses. With nearly 200 years of experience under its belt, The Hartford gives the impression that it can truly handle anything thrown its way.

The company has its roots in the Hartford Fire Insurance Company, which was incorporated by the Connecticut General Assembly in 1810. Yale University was among its first customers, as was the 16th U.S. president, Abraham Lincoln, who purchased fire insurance from the company for his home and property in Springfield, Ill. Babe Ruth purchased a "sickness policy" to protect his earnings in case of illness, and Dwight D. Eisenhower, the 34th U.S. President, bought a policy to insure the family farm in Pennsylvania.

The Hartford became a transnational company in 1910, with the opening of its first office in San Francisco. It began offering mutual funds in 1996, becoming the nation's fastest growing retail-oriented mutual fund family to reach $10 billion in assets, which it did in 2000. The firm became a Fortune 500 company in 2005, five years shy of its 200th birthday.

Pick a category, any category

The Hartford has been recognized with distinction in almost every insurance category you can think of. According to its financials at the end of 2007, it is the fourth-largest life insurance group based on statutory assets, the No. 1 seller of annuities in Japan, the No. 3 seller of U.S. retail variable annuities, No. 3 in fully insured group life sales, the No. 1 in variable universal life total premiums, the No. 1 in fully insured group disability sales, the 11th-largest property and casualty insurer based on direct written premium, the fifth-largest commercial insurance carrier and the No. 5 workers' compensation insurer based on net premiums. Recently, the National Association of Wholesaler-Distributors, an association of 40,000 wholesale distribution companies across the country, selected The Hartford as the preferred insurance provider for the marine and management liability coverage.

Industry spokesperson

Ramani Ayer has been chairman, president and CEO of The Hartford since 1997. Ayer joined the company in 1973 as a member of the operations research department; in 1991, he was elected president and chief operating officer of The Hartford's property/casualty operations. Ayer has been a strong leader both at The Hartford and in the industry as a whole, recently announcing his proposal for a comprehensive, long-term solution for homeowners insurance that will safeguard economic stability by creating a stable private-sector homeowners insurance market in coastal regions. His proposal calls for private companies to take on a larger role in areas prone to natural disasters such as Florida, where a state-run agency became the largest insurer by selling insurance below market prices. Ayer poses that the U.S. government provide a sort of backstop by insuring in these areas to prevent huge losses for storms like Hurricane Katrina, which resulted in $57.9 billion

Visit the Vault Finance Career Channel at **www.vault.com/finance** — with
insider firm profiles, message boards, the Vault Finance Job Board and more.

VAULT CAREER LIBRARY   211

in claims in 2005. He also suggests that states watch building codes more closely and place more restrictions on building in coastal areas.

Connecticut's looking green

The Hartford's Simsbury, Conn.-based life insurance subsidiary has been expanding its operations, increasing its Connecticut employee base by more than 50 percent over the past 15 years. To accommodate these additions, Hartford Life built a new 450,000 square feet campus in Windsor, Conn., as part of a $146-million expansion of The Hartford Financial Services Group. The new facility incorporates green technology, including sun control architectural elements, recycled construction materials, and energy-efficient heating and cooling systems. It will house approximately 2,000 Hartford Life employees.

The latest cross-selling initiative

In 2008, The Hartford merged two successful initiatives—the "cross-sell" and the enterprise "small business"—into one, cross-company team called the business solutions group. The group focuses on small business strategies across all of the firm's business segments. While profit and loss responsibilities and product development remain within each segment, the business solutions group will find new opportunities to increase the business of each segment. In addition, the group will continue to increase 401(k), life insurance and group benefits sales through the property and casualty distribution channel.

Underwriting hops over the pond

After six years of handling things from New York City, The Hartford finally got permission to establish a liability-underwriting subsidiary in London. (The firm had been writing international directors and officers liability insurance and other related coverages since 2001 from its New York office.) The new company, Hartford Financial Products International Ltd., began underwriting through broker channels on November 1, 2007. Hartford Financial Products also plans to exercise passport rights under the EU directives, subject to completion of the associated regulatory requirements.

"The extension of our current underwriting capabilities will better position us with our international customers and worldwide distributors," said David McElroy, head of Hartford Financial Products, in a statement.

One for the record books

In December 2007, The Hartford announced plans to buy the record keeping alliance business of Atlanta-based Princeton Retirement Group. The acquisition gave The Hartford a foothold in the business of providing recordkeeping services to large financial firms that offer defined contribution plans to their clients. The deal also gave The Hartford an additional $7 billion in retirement plan assets across over 720 plans and approximately 170,000 plan participants.

"Our ability to grow our retirement plans business depends in part on being able to provide retirement programs under The Hartford's brand while offering our services to companies that offer retirement plans under their own brand," said John Walters, president of The Hartford's U.S. wealth management group and co-COO of The Hartford's life operations, in a statement.

At the close of the transaction, about 200 Princeton employees were offered positions with The Hartford. In addition, the company intends to maintain its current offices in Atlanta and Winston-Salem, N.C.

The Princeton deal was announced one week after The Hartford said it would acquire Boston-based Sun Life Retirement Services (RSI) from the U.S. division of Sun Life Financial. RSI, a provider of recordkeeping and administrative services to defined contribution plans, was formerly known as MFS Retirement Services. On the close of the acquisition, The Hartford added $17 billion in retirement plan assets across 6,000 plans and 465,000 retirement plan participants to its business. The deal also brought The Hartford an expanded national footprint, with new service locations in Boston and Phoenix.

By the numbers

In its fiscal 2007, The Hartford's revenue was down to $25.9 billion from $26.5 billion in fiscal 2006. Net income, meanwhile, grew to $2.95 billion from $2.75 billion. The first half of 2008 did fizzle a little compared to the previous year. The second quarter of 2008 brought in $7.5 billion in revenue compared with $7.66 billion in the second quarter 2007, and net income came in at $543 million, a dip from the previous year's second quarter figure of $627 million. Analysts pointed to bigger investment portfolio losses and more industry competition as factors that limited its growth.

In December 2007, prior to releasing its most recent annual results, The Hartford announced that its earnings for 2008 would fall below analysts'

Visit the Vault Finance Career Channel at **www.vault.com/finance** — with insider firm profiles, message boards, the Vault Finance Job Board and more.

VAULT CAREER LIBRARY   213

expectations. In a statement, the company forecast full-year 2008 earnings to be between $9.80 and $10.20 per share, and for written premiums from its property and casualty insurance business to grow by up to three percent compared with 2007.

GETTING HIRED

Simply the best

"The best people can choose where they want to work," according to the firm. "And we want the best people." If you think you fall within that lofty target demographic, log on to the careers section of Hartford's web site (www.hartford.com), which provides a searchable database of job opportunities, sortable by category and geographic location. The available job categories can include accounting, actuarial, administration, business analysis, claim, contracts and compliance, facilities management, finance, human resources, information technology, insurance, investment management, legal and government affairs, loss control, medical, marketing and communications, quality and process improvement, sales, service/operations, special risk services, training and underwriting. Special information for recent college graduates and current college students is also listed on the site, as well as information about varying career development and benefits.

OUR SURVEY SAYS

Good balance, but bureaucratic

Sources give different takes regarding the firm's culture. One insider says, "The company offers a great home and work balance." However, another notes, "The culture in the P&C part of the company is very political and bureaucratic." Although the company is "well run," reports one contact, "as an employer, the company is very average." Another believes, "The corporate culture is one of complex office politics—even for an insurance company, where this is the norm—and there's posturing and bureaucracy." The source adds, "Decisions are made only by overcoming these obstacles— and the company seems to succeed in spite of its own culture."

Policies seem to be determined largely by department. One insider says, "Hours vary by position—some managers allow flex-time, while some do not." But another says, "The bond department is flexible with hours since the position does require some travel and extended hours for marketing purposes." And although "core hours run from 8 a.m. to 4:30 p.m.," "there is flex-time available, which can be discussed with the office manager on an individual basis." In the call center arena "you can have a shift that goes from 2:30 to 11 p.m."

Not too fussy

Most of the time, staffers don't have to get too formal, insiders report. The dress code is "business casual," but "marketing calls and account meetings normally require a suit and tie." The dress code "really depends on location and manager." An insider says, "I've seen everything from mini skirts and pajama shoes to suits and ties." But the "home office is more structured, and you see a lot of sweater vests and suits."

Advancement also seems to hinge on the department you're in. "Opportunities for advancement vary by position," and "in the senior management ranks, many position openings are not posted because favored employees are already chosen well in advance." An insider adds, "This is succession planning at its worst—candidates do not seem to be chosen by skills or ability but rather by political positioning." Another contact says, "Depending on the territory handled, internal competition for managerial positions can vary." And it may pay to schmooze. "People with political/network connections and those who fall within diversity groups move up faster," one respondent says, "but sometimes high-performing employees who don't fall into these two groups tend to have a harder time getting promoted and compensated." Another notes, "There are many opportunities for advancement, but you have to put the time in and have to go way beyond the call of duty."

Program in place, but not promoted

The firm has "an extensive diversity and inclusion program, but senior leadership is largely white male," says an insider, and "nothing is done to identify and promote high-performing minority employees." Another agrees, saying, "You will find that most in upper management are white males, which I believe sends a message to others trying to move up." The insider adds, "Women asking for raises is a definite 'no-no' from my experience—for some reason it is seen by the firm as being greedy and not thinking about 'the business need.'"

Visit the Vault Finance Career Channel at www.vault.com/finance — with
insider firm profiles, message boards, the Vault Finance Job Board and more.

VAULT CAREER LIBRARY   215

Leucadia National Corporation

315 Park Avenue South
New York, NY 10010-3607
Phone: (212) 460-1900
Fax: (212) 598-4869
www.leucadia.com

DEPARTMENTS

Manufacturing
Real Estate
Medical Products
Winery Operations

THE STATS

Employer Type: Public Company
Ticker Symbol: LUK (NYSE)
Chairman & CEO: Ian M. Cumming
President & COO: Joseph S. Steinberg
Revenue: $1.15 billion
Net Income: $484.29 million
No. of Employees: 1,323

KEY COMPETITORS

Apollo Investment
Berkshire Hathaway
Blackstone Group

EMPLOYMENT CONTACT

Send resumes to:
Leucadia National
315 Park Avenue South
New York, NY 10010-3607
Phone: (212) 460-1900
Fax: (212) 598-4869

THE SCOOP

Finding diamonds in the rough

New York-based Leucadia National is a diversified holding company whose strategy is to buy and increase the value of undervalued or troubled companies, while taking advantage of any tax breaks. The company's style and practical strategy of fixing troubled companies that make common products has led to comparisons with another somewhat famous holding company, Berkshire Hathaway.

Leucadia owns companies in numerous industries, including manufacturing, medical product development, real estate, gaming entertainment, banking, mining and even winery operations. The company is also involved in telecommunications, including local and long-distance telephone services, Internet services, web development and collection services. And Leucadia develops commercial and residential real estate, and provides consumer and specialty insurance as well as reinsurance services.

Leucadia, founded in 1854, has been ranked No. 53 on *BusinessWeek*'s list of Hot Growth Companies and was No. 20 on Fortune's 2006 list of Fastest Growing Companies, up from No. 59 in 2005.

Match made at Harvard

Chairman Ian Cumming and president and director Joseph Steinberg met at Harvard Business School, both graduating in 1970. Both hold about 13 percent of the company's shares. Cumming also serves as chairman of the board of Barbados Light & Power; director and chairman of the Finova Group; director of subsidiary Allcity Insurance; and a director of Skywest, a Utah-based regional carrier. Cumming is also a director of HomeFed and Carmike Cinemas.

In a June 2007 article, Seeking Alpha said of Leucadia's top dogs, "Cumming and Steinberg are extraordinarily versatile investors, and have succeeded in real estate, medical devices, plastics, wineries, finance, telecom, energy, insurance and travel. They'll buy when everyone else hates a business or a sector. Their track record is tremendous, as Leucadia's stock compounded from 1979-2006 at 24.9 percent. When they took [Leucadia] over, it had negative equity of $7.6 million. Today, equity is around $4 billion."

In the habit of buying and selling

Leucadia has kept business sales coming at a fairly vigorous pace during the past few years. In 2005, the company beefed up its manufacturing holdings with the acquisition of NSW, which makes packaging nets, case liners and other types of industrial netting. Another 2005 success was its $133 million bid to buy Idaho Timber Corporation, which remanufactures dimension lumber and specialized wood products. In July 2006, the firm sold Symphony Healthcare Services to RehabCare Group for $107 million, and in September 2006, Leucadia sold ATX Communications to Broadview Networks Holdings, receiving about $85.7 million in aggregate cash consideration. At the end of 2006, the firm ended up with net security gains totaling around $117.2 million, which was mostly derived from selling publicly traded debt and equity securities.

For its fiscal year 2006, Leucadia reported revenue of $862.67 million, up from $689 million from in 2005. Net income was $189.4 million, down from $1.64 billion in 2005, due to the sale of Tulsa, Okla.-based WilTel Communications Group.

In late 2003, the firm bought WilTel (the bankrupt Williams Communications) and its nationwide fiber network for $780 million. WilTel became Leucadia's biggest revenue generator, making up about 70 percent of its sales. But the catch was that SBC Communications accounted for most of WilTel's income, and in 2005, SBC announced that it would buy AT&T and naturally use AT&T's network instead. In late 2005, Leucadia sold WilTel to Level 3 Communications for about $680 million in cash and stock.

Caught between a rock and a hurricane

The firm was dealt a difficult hand when Hurricane Katrina struck in 2005. Leucadia holds a controlling interest in Premier Entertainment Biloxi, which owns Hard Rock Hotel & Casino Biloxi in Mississippi. With just days to go before it was scheduled to officially open, the resort was destroyed in the hurricane, leading Premier to declare Chapter 11 bankruptcy in an attempt to rebuild the casino. And after nearly two years of negotiation with insurers, Premier finally reached a settlement.

Mysterious involvement

Leucadia was called out in December 2007 for its association with ParkerVision, a Florida company that makes wireless radio frequency technologies. In an investigative article by *Barron's*, the company was highlighted for at one time being an investor in ParkerVision, a company that critics say is guilty of making empty promises about its forthcoming technology. The *Barron's* piece said Leucadia is no longer an investor in the company, but revealed that David T. Cumming—the 63-year-old younger brother of Leucadia's chief executive, Ian Cumming—had been defending ParkerVision in online chat rooms.

According to *Barron's*, "David Cumming says he heard about ParkerVision through Parker's patent lawyer, Robert G. Sterne. Cumming was a director at CNA Surety, but he'd previously spent 15 years working at his brother Ian's Salt Lake City-based Leucadia. In 2000, after some due diligence, Cumming convinced the value investors at Leucadia to join with a unit of Tyco International (TYC) in buying 8 percent of ParkerVision for about $30 million, at 30 bucks a share. By October of that year, the stock hit $56, putting ParkerVision's value at $750 million."

According to *Barron's*, while promising a single-chip radio—"the Holy Grail of the wireless industry"—ParkerVision let deals with IBM, Symbol Technologies and PrairieComm slip through its fingers. Unable to convince wireless manufacturers' of the new invention, ParkerVision tried selling its own Wi-Fi cards with the technology. By 2005, the stock's valuation had dropped to $75 million.

A good year

In 2007, the firm brought in a total of $1.15 billion in revenue, up from the $862.67 million it brought in in 2006. Net income for the year was up to $484.29 million from $189.4 million in the previous year. For the second quarter of 2008, the firm brought in $344 million in revenue, slightly up from $$337.55 million. Net income for the quarter was up to $186.78 million from $26.3 million in the second quarter 2007. (The first quarter of 2008 brought in $324.85 million in revenue and a net loss of $95.82 million.)

To the rescue

Leucadia announced in April 2008 that it would be assisting New York-based investment bank Jefferies by acquiring a 14 percent stake in the company for about $434 million. The terms of the deal included Leucadia selling 10 million of its common shares to Jefferies, and Leucadia getting two seats on Jefferies' board of directors. Meanwhile, Leucadia agreed that it wouldn't sell off any Jefferies shares for two years unless it receives the consent of

Visit the Vault Finance Career Channel at **www.vault.com/finance** — with insider firm profiles, message boards, the Vault Finance Job Board and more.

VAULT CAREER LIBRARY   219

Jefferies' board. Additionally, Leucadia said that it wouldn't purchase more than 30 percent of Jefferies' shares.

And two months later, it stayed true to its word—but just barely. In June 2008, Leucadia revealed (in an SEC filing) that it had bought even more Jefferies stock since April, acquiring an additional 17.7 million shares on the open market for about $322 million. This increased Leucadia's share of Jefferies to 48.6 million shares, or 30 percent of the company.

GETTING HIRED

Variety's the spice of life

Sure, Leucadia National does diversified financials, but it has a little bit of everything else on its plate, too—from real estate to wineries. But if you're looking to work for Leucadia, you may have to get creative—its web site is fairly sparse, including only a few links and no information on open positions. So try sending your resume to the firm's corporate office headquarters at 315 Park Avenue South, New York, NY 10010.

Liberty Mutual

175 Berkeley Street
Boston, MA 02117
Phone: (617) 357-9500
Fax: (617) 350-7648
www.libertymutualgroup.com

DEPARTMENTS

Agency Markets
Commercial Markets
Liberty International
Personal Markets

Visit the Vault Finance Career Channel at **www.vault.com/finance** — with
insider firm profiles, message boards, the Vault Finance Job Board and more.

VAULT CAREER LIBRARY   221

THE SCOOP

Policyholders have the reins

A Fortune 500 company with nearly a century of experience, Liberty Mutual is a powerful name in the global insurance industry. The Boston-based company has grown and reorganized since its inception in 1912 to become the Liberty Mutual Holding Company Inc., a holding company for three principals entities: Liberty Mutual Insurance Company, Liberty Mutual Fire Insurance Company and Employers Insurance Company of Wausau. The group is operated as a mutual holding structure owned by its policyholders. The company in its entirety provides a wide range of insurance products and services, including private passenger automobile, homeowners, workers compensation, commercial multiple peril, commercial automobile, general liability, global specialty, group disability, assumed reinsurance, fire and surety.

Liberty has four business units: personal markets, commercial markets, agency markets and Liberty International. No single business unit contributes more than 30 percent of net written premium. Its personal markets affinity program has more than 9,800 sponsored affinity group relationships with employers, credit unions, professional and alumni associations.

Tops in its field

Liberty Mutual holds numerous distinctions as an insurance company. It is the eighth-largest personal lines writer and the fourth-largest commercial lines writer in the U.S. The company also holds a high-ranking spot among corporations in general.

In addition, Liberty Mutual ranked No. 94 on the 2008 Fortune 500 list of the largest U.S. corporations based on revenue, up one spot from its 2007 ranking. As an employer of more than 41,000 people, Liberty Mutual has been recognized as a top 50 employer by *Equal Opportunity* magazine. In May 2008, Liberty Mutual's agency markets unit received an industry leadership award for the third year in a row. And in September 2008, in *BusinessWeek*'s annnual ranking of the Best Places to Launch a Career, Liberty Mutual came in at No. 41, which was quite a jump from its No. 54 finish in 2007.

Home grown in Massachusetts

Liberty Mutual was founded in 1912 as the Massachusetts Employees' Insurance Association (MEIA), in response to a Massachusetts law requiring employers to protect employees with workers' compensation insurance. The first branch was opened in Springfield, Mass., in 1914, and was renamed the Liberty Mutual Insurance Company three years later. In the 1930s, the company expanded to other states, opening offices across the U.S. It surpassed the $2 billion mark in written premiums in 1972, expanding internationally with the opening of its London office. In 2002, the company converted to the mutual holding company structure that it operates today.

Math whiz in charge

Ireland-born Edmund (Ted) F. Kelly became president and chief operating officer of Liberty Mutual in 1992, chief executive officer in 1998 and chairman in 2000. With a PhD from the Massachusetts Institute of Technology, Kelly has a strong talent for mathematics, teaching at the University of New Brunswick and at the University of Missouri. He proved his leadership capabilities early on at Liberty Mutual, increasing the company's profits by 67 percent during his first few years as COO.

As chairman, Kelly expanded the international market for Liberty Mutual, opening offices in Argentina, Australia, Brazil, Canada, Chile, China, Colombia, Germany, France, Hong Kong, India, Ireland, Japan, Netherlands, Poland, Portugal, Singapore, Spain, Switzerland, Thailand, Turkey, United Arab Emirates, the U.K. and Venezuela. Most recently, Liberty Mutual pushed into India through a joint-venture with Dabur GI Invest Corp., forming a non-life insurance company in India. The company plans to provide personal and commercial insurance products through a range of distribution channels such as agents, banks and car dealers. Liberty Mutual began the licensing application process for the new company before the end of the second quarter 2008.

From one came three

CEO Kelly was also a key force in reorganizing Liberty Mutual Group into a mutual holding company. The firm converted to a mutual holding company in 2002, whereby the three principal mutual insurance companies—LMIC, Liberty Mutual Fire Insurance Company and Employers Insurance Company of Wausau—each became separate stock insurance companies. Kelly defended the decision before the Massachusetts Division of Insurance

Visit the Vault Finance Career Channel at www.vault.com/finance — with
insider firm profiles, message boards, the Vault Finance Job Board and more.

VAULT CAREER LIBRARY   223

headquarters in Boston, arguing that the move would make Liberty Mutual more competitive, allowing each company access to more capital. The three companies operate completely independently, setting their own separate business strategies, including acquisitions.

Fighting natural disasters and terrorism

Liberty Mutual was hit hard by Katrina and other hurricanes in 2005, suffering a whopping $1.5 billion in losses during the year. However, revenue was up due to the company's investment operations, as net investment income increased from $78 million to $2 billion. Following the September 11th terrorist attacks, Liberty Mutual became a strong advocate for the Terrorism Risk Insurance Act, in which the government provides a limited federal backstop to insurance companies in the case of a terrorist attack. This program, which was developed by the Bush administration in the aftermath of the attacks, is currently being phased out. Liberty Mutual CEO Kelly spoke before the National Association of Insurance Commissioners in March of 2006, urging them to be a strong voice for terrorism risk legislation. "The threat of terrorism is a security issue for the entire economy," said Kelly, "not just the insurance sector."

Driving sales in Massachusetts

Liberty Mutual announced in November 2007 that it would increase its automotive sales force in Massachusetts by nearly 50 percent. Sixty-one Liberty Mutual sales reps currently offer auto, home and life insurance products from 13 Massachusetts offices. The firm said it planned to hire 30 new reps by the time new insurance regulations and competitive pricing began in April 2008. All Massachusetts offices will see sales force expansion, including growth in firm's downtown Boston office. To find its new reps, Liberty Mutual held a recruitment event at Gillette Stadium, home to the New England Patriots.

Expanding in China

Liberty's reputation as a New England company ought not detract from the firm's international presence. In July 2007, Liberty received approval from the Chinese Insurance Regulatory Commission to establish a wholly owned subsidiary in that country. The subsidiary, Liberty Insurance Company Ltd., is headquartered in the city of Chongqing, where Liberty Mutual has had an office since 2003. The license allows Liberty Mutual to expand its general insurance capabilities, including coverage for individuals and small- and medium-size businesscs.

"A company can't view itself as truly international without a strategy for conducting business in China," said CEO Edmund Kelly, in a statement. "We have experienced strong growth in our international operations and view China as an integral component of our worldwide strategy."

In July 2008, the company was granted approval to establish a branch in Beijing by the China Insurance Regulatory Commission (CIRC). Beijing is the first branch established by Liberty Insurance Company Ltd. in China, and will offer various personal lines products, including auto and a wide range of commercial lines products with a focus on small-to-medium enterprises.

Big in Brazil

In October 2007, Liberty's Brazilian subsidiary, Liberty International Brasil Ltda, signed an agreement to buy Indiana Seguros S.A. When the transaction closed, Liberty Brazil became the 10th-largest property and casualty insurer in the Brazilian insurance market, with a market share of 3.2 percent, a portfolio of more than one million clients and net written premium of $580 million. The transaction also made Liberty Brazil the sixth-largest auto insurer in the market, with a 6.4 percent market share.

Founded in 1943 by the Afif family, Indiana Seguros's main product is private passenger auto, sold through car dealers and retail producers throughout the country. Additionally, Indiana Seguros writes homeowners and life insurance, both individual and group.

Earlier in 2007, Liberty Mutual invested in SIIF Energies do Brasil and Rosa Dos Ventos—collectively, the country's largest wind power plant projects. Liberty has had a presence in Brazil since its 1996 purchase of Paulista Seguros, a long-standing Brazilian property and casualty insurance company. Today, Liberty Seguros, headquartered in Sao Paulo, has 76 branch offices around the country with more than 1,000 employees.

Still doing domestic deals, too

A Brazilian acquisition came just a couple months after Liberty completed the purchase of a company based closer to home. In August 2007, the firm finalized the acquisition of Ohio Casualty Corporation, in a transaction valued at approximately $2.7 billion. Ohio Casualty Corporation is the holding company of The Ohio Casualty Insurance Company and five other

Visit the Vault Finance Career Channel at www.vault.com/finance — with insider firm profiles, message boards, the Vault Finance Job Board and more.

VAULT CAREER LIBRARY   225

property and casualty insurance companies, which are referred to under the marketing brand Ohio Casualty Group. Ohio Casualty Group ranks 50th among property and casualty insurers based upon net premiums written, and sells personal, commercial and bond insurance products through independent agents and brokers.

Ohio Casualty joined Liberty Mutual's agency markets business unit, which consists of regional property and casualty and specialty insurance companies that distribute products and services through independent agents and brokers.

Safeco buy

In another multibillion-dollar buy, Liberty added another company to its agency markets division with the $6.2 billion purchase of Safeco Corp. in April 2008. The deal, expected to close by fall 2008, will create the fifth-largest U.S. property and casualty insurer, and the second-largest surety company. The acquisition of the Seattle-based Safeco isn't a sure thing yet, as both regulators and shareholders must approve the transaction, but Liberty Mutual expects it to go through, and said it would continue to examine acquisition possibilities going forward.

Up and down

Liberty Mutual put up mixed financial results in 2007. The firm's revenue came in at $25.96 billion, a $2.4 billion increase from the previous year, but net income dropped to $1.52 billion from $1.63 billion. Analysts said the fall in income was due to competition in the industry that has forced many companies to lower their rates.

For the first six months of 2008, revenue came in at $13.8 billion, up from $12.4 billion in the first half of 2007. Net income for the first half of 2008, however, declined to $660 million from $689 million the year before. Poor weather conditions (leading to big payouts on policies) and a still-weak economy contributed to the losses.

GETTING HIRED

Everyday life

Read about individual employees' day-to-day activities at the career section of www.libertymutualgroup.com. Or, if you have any further questions about employment with the company, surf on over to the "FAQ" section—or e-mail careers@libertymutual.com. Employees who achieve results for the firm will be rewarded with a "strong pay-for-performance and promote-from-within culture," the firm says. So if you're ready to kick out the results, get online—the firm's career site also details open positions available for experienced hires, students and recent graduates. The site allows prospective applicants to review job descriptions and openings by type, including actuarial, claims (commercial and personal), finance and accounting, human resources, information systems, loss prevention, sales and underwriting. Recent college graduates can also specifically search for entry-level jobs. The web site lists the career fairs Liberty will be attending, primarily in the summer and fall. Liberty recruits from over 100 universities across the U.S.

OUR SURVEY SAYS

Conservative culture

Several sources point to the "conservative," "stuffy" corporate culture, which one notes is "hierarchal and relatively slow-paced," though "employees are generally nice and have strong values and integrity."

But management could still use a refresher course in communicating, insiders say. One notes, "I have consistently experienced a lack of communications within the leadership of the company," and "it is often put upon the shoulders of the supervisors to communicate to their employees what upcoming changes may be taking place or may affect them." The contact goes on to say, "If an employee speaks out or discloses their opinions or ideas, it is often shot down by another employee due to an unhealthy competition that has been created among employees."

One insider notes that staffers "are left to write their own appraisals in third-person style," and wonders, "Is this so the supervisors can receive the credit

Visit the Vault Finance Career Channel at **www.vault.com/finance** — with insider firm profiles, message boards, the Vault Finance Job Board and more.

VAULT CAREER LIBRARY   227

of writing the employee appraisals?" The contact adds, "Employees are not slotted an amount of time to do this—they need to figure it all out and balance it with their own workload."

Cost of living up, but not salaries

"The workload required and the mandatory overtime hours make it impossible for employees to reasonably balance their work and personal lives," says one insider, "and this tends to leave employees frustrated and wanting to leave the department." The firm "prefers to promote from within," though, so if you can stick around your department, you may have a good chance of moving up.

Decent hours, formal dress

There's a "good work/life balance" at the firm, says one insider, noting that the "standard workday is seven-and-a-half hours." Another calls the hours "standard," adding that "most employees arrive precisely at 8 a.m. and leave at 5 p.m. on the dot." But the dress requirements aren't quite as casual as the hours. One source says that "suit-and-tie is required in most offices, including Fridays," although "business casual" dress is allowed in "some offices."

Not great marks

Despite the fact that the company sponsors "many diversity programs during the summer to attract a wide range of college summer interns that represent a variety of races and ethnicities," actual diversity within the firm is "minimal." One source says the firm is "extremely poor on employee diversity," and "even worse as one gets higher on the corporate ladder." The contact goes on to say that "almost all executives are white males, and the females are stuck in departments like human resources. The only diversity in the company consists of white females stuck in middle management positions."

Lincoln Financial Group

1500 Market Street
Ste. 3900
Philadelphia, PA 19102
Phone: (215) 448-1400
Fax: (215) 448-3962
www.lfg.com

DEPARTMENTS

Investment Management
Life Insurance
Retirement Planning

Visit the Vault Finance Career Channel at **www.vault.com/finance** — with
insider firm profiles, message boards, the Vault Finance Job Board and more.

VAULT CAREER LIBRARY   229

THE SCOOP

From life insurance to sports programming

Lincoln National, which operates as Lincoln Financial Group, is a Philadelphia-based financial services firm with more than 10,000 employees. The company primarily does business in the U.S., where it's been operating for over 100 years, but also offers some life and pension products in the U.K. As of June 30, 2008, Lincoln had assets under management of $221 billion.

Lincoln offers retirement planning and life insurance through its Lincoln National Life Insurance, First Penn-Pacific Life Insurance Company, and Lincoln Life & Annuity Company of New York subsidiaries. The company also is active in the investment management business, offering financial services such as pension plans, trusts, and mutual funds through Delaware Investments and other subsidiaries. The firm's investment management arm offers various retail products, including mutual funds to individual investors, as well as investment services to high net worth and small institutional investors through managed accounts. It also provides investment advisory services to various institutional clients, such as corporate and public retirement plans, endowments and foundations, nuclear decommissioning trusts, sub-advisory clients and Taft-Hartley plans.

Lincoln also has broadcast and sports programming operations in the U.S. At the end of 2006, its Lincoln Financial Media segment operated 18 radio and three television broadcasting stations in the southeastern and western U.S. The division produces and distributes syndicated collegiate basketball and football sports programming.

In memory of Abe

The Lincoln National Life Insurance Company was founded in Fort Wayne, Ind., on June 12, 1905. During a time of controversy among big, established insurers, its 33 founders envisioned an insurance company rooted in dependability and honesty. To convey this spirit of integrity, they adopted the name of the 16th President, Abraham Lincoln. Robert Todd Lincoln, the President's only surviving son, gave the founders permission to use his father's name, in July 1905.

Within its first six years, The Lincoln National Life Insurance Company assumed a respected position of expertise among fellow insurers and regulators. In 1911, Lincoln Life reported $6.5 million of life insurance in force with $250,000 in premium income and $750,000 in assets. Through a series of acquisitions beginning in 1914 through the end of the Great Depression, the company expanded at an amazing rate, adding more than $250 million of insurance in force to its ledger. No other insurance company matched this expansion during its first 50 years; from 1905 to 1955, Lincoln Life grew to become the ninth largest life insurance company in the United States.

The company has undergone its most dramatic transformation in the last 20 years. Lincoln National Corporation realigned its business operations, divested its property casualty and reinsurance operations, acquired Delaware Investments and added life and annuity operations from CIGNA and Aetna. In 2006, Lincoln merged with Jefferson Pilot Financial, solidifying the company as one of the largest financial services organizations in the United States.

Banking on the boom

Lincoln Financial Group's current operating model is centered on three critical strategies, all designed to help the company reap the benefits of retiring baby boomers.

The first strategy is wealth accumulation and protection. As an industry leader, Lincoln knows that future success requires excellence not only in its wealth accumulation and protection products, but also in meeting the next generation of market needs: retirement income and wealth transfer.

The second strategy is known as high net worth. Lincoln is a premier provider of wealth accumulation and protection products, financial planning and investment advisory services for the high-net-worth market. The high-net-worth market includes those individuals with investable assets of $1 million or more.

Finally, strategy three is buyer behavior of baby boomers. Approximately 80 million Americans constitute the baby boomer generation. Their economic, social and political influence remains unmatched and planning for retirement is on their agenda; boomers are focused on asset accumulation. However, as retirement nears, their focus will shift to income distribution and preservation. Lincoln is well positioned in these areas and stands ready to serve the baby boomers in their retirement planning needs.

Visit the Vault Finance Career Channel at www.vault.com/finance – with
insider firm profiles, message boards, the Vault Finance Job Board and more.

VAULT CAREER LIBRARY   231

Glass breaks through

Lincoln appointed a new leader in July 2007, when former chairman and CEO Jon Boscia announced his retirement after 10 years of service. The company named Dennis Glass, then-president and COO, to take Boscia's place as CEO, while board director J. Patrick Barrett was made chairman.

As president and COO, Glass was responsible for overseeing Lincoln's primary manufacturing and distribution businesses, including employer markets, individual markets, Delaware Investment Management, Lincoln Financial Distributors, Lincoln Financial Network and the Retirement Income Security Ventures Group. Glass chairs the investment committee for the insurance entities' general account portfolio. Previously, he served as president and CEO of Jefferson-Pilot Corporation, which merged with Lincoln in 2006.

Turning off the TV down south

In November 2007, Lincoln picked up close to $700 million in cash by off loading some of its southern television stations. The company sold three television stations in Charlotte, N.C.; Richmond, Va.; and Charleston, S.C. It also sold its sports syndication business to Raycom Media for $583 million in cash. Lincoln reached a separate agreement with Greater Media to sell its Charlotte radio stations for $100 million in cash.

The company said that net proceeds from the transactions would go toward debt reduction and share repurchases. And in announcing the deals, Lincoln said it would continue to operate and invest in its remaining radio properties while exploring options to divest those assets. The company currently owns 18 radio stations.

Numbers game

In 2007, the firm pulled in $10.59 billion in revenue, up from $8.96 billion in the previous year. Net income, though, dipped to $1.22 billion from $1.32 billion. Halfway through 2008, the numbers weren't looking much better. For the second quarter 2008, revenue slipped to $2.58 billion from $2.67 billion. Net profit, meanwhile, dove to $125 million from $376 million. The poor showing partially had $81 million in realized losses on investments to partially thank, along with some impaired assets losses.

GETTING HIRED

What Lincoln's about

Under the careers section at www.lfg.com, you can seek out current available positions, learn about benefits offered to employees or read about the firm's programs for college graduates. (The firm's professional development program, for example, is a leadership program that trains graduates for three years, while the actuarial development program is a combination work-study program.) And if you conduct a search on the site for job possibilities and don't happen to find anything that matches your background, you can also post a resume for the firm to keep on file just in case.

Visit the Vault Finance Career Channel at **www.vault.com/finance** — with
insider firm profiles, message boards, the Vault Finance Job Board and more.

VAULT CAREER LIBRARY   233

Loews Corporation

667 Madison Avenue
New York, NY 10021-8087
Phone: (212) 521-2000
Fax: (212) 521-2525
www.loews.com

DEPARTMENTS

Insurance
Financial Services
Hotels
Natural Gas
Oil
Watches

THE STATS

Employer Type: Public Company
Ticker Symbol: LTR (NYSE)
President & CEO: James S. Tisch
Revenue: $18.38 billion (FYE 12/07)
Net Income: $2.49 billion
No. of Employees: 21,600
No. of Offices: 1

KEY COMPETITORS

Altria
American Financial
AIG

EMPLOYMENT CONTACT

See "careers" section of
www.loews.com

THE SCOOP

Holding it all together

Loews Corporation is one of the largest diversified holding companies, run by descendants of founders Preston Robert and Lawrence Tisch. The Manhattan-based company, which began as a small family-owned hotel business, thrives on purchasing temporarily undervalued companies in virtually any industry. Loews has interests in insurance and financial services, including the publicly traded subsidiary CNA Financial; luxury hotels, through its Loews Hotels subsidiary; watch distribution and manufacturing, through its subsidiary Bulova; oil and gas, through contract oil-drilling subsidiary Diamond Offshore Drilling, which owns about 44 oil rigs; and natural gas transmission pipeline systems, through Boardwalk Pipeline Partners.

As a holding company, Loews does not interfere with its holdings' operations. It advises subsidiaries on important strategic, financial and capital allocation issues, but its primary motive is to generate wealth through carefully acquiring companies with strong preexisting management teams. Historically, the company has capitalized on dips in the economy, acquiring CNA in 1974 at a fraction of its value. The company's oil tankers were also purchased at essentially scrap value during the oil crisis of the early 1980s. Most recently, the company expanded its model to include natural gas, announcing a $4 billion agreement to purchase natural gas exploration and production assets in Texas, Michigan and Alabama from Dominion Resources.

A family affair

Brooklyn-born brothers Bob and Larry Tisch used their "buy low, sell high" strategy to turn a small family hotel in New Jersey into the modern investment behemoth that is the Loews Corporation today. Prior to his death in 2005, Bob Tisch was co-owner of the New York Giants football team and had a personal fortune valued by *Forbes* magazine at $3.9 billion. He held both CEO and co-chairman positions at Loews Corporation before passing away, after which his nephew James Tisch took the reins as CEO and his son and nephew, Jonathan and Andrew Tisch, became co-chairmen of the company.

Visit the Vault Finance Career Channel at **www.vault.com/finance** — with insider firm profiles, message boards, the Vault Finance Job Board and more.

VAULT CAREER LIBRARY   235

Out from the hurricane eye

Chicago-based CNA Financial is 89 percent owned by Loews Corporation. Insurance products include primarily property and casualty coverages. CNA serves a wide variety of customers, including small, medium and large businesses, associations, professionals, and groups and individuals with a broad range of insurance and risk management products and services. Both Loews and subsidiary CNA suffered losses in 2005 due to the hurricane-related losses and various reserve-related charges at CNA. In 2006, CNA improved its position in the commercial property/casualty insurance market and posted record earnings due to disc implied underwriting, stringent expense controls and solid investment results. But for the full year 2007 and into 2008, CNA's standing had dropped slightly, as it posted losses that were partially due to the fallout from a settlement reached in late 2007 with John Hancock Life Insurance in regards to reinsurance contracts.

Hoteling done right

Loews's travel subsidiary Loews Hotels is one of the top hotel and resort chains in the United States and Canada. The brand has 19 hotels—in cities such as Annapolis, Denver, Las Vegas, Miami Beach, Montreal, Quebec City, Nashville, New Orleans, New York, Philadelphia, San Diego, St. Pete Beach, Tucson, Orlando and Washington, D.C.—and operates three different vacation spots: Portofino Bay, Royal Pacific and Hard Rock Hotel. In 2008, Loews Hotels was voted the No. 4 "upscale" hotel chain by *Business Travel News*.

Under its "Good Neighbor Policy" initiated in 1990 by Jonathon Tisch, Loews Hotels actively seeks to improve its neighboring communities through food donations, by providing spaces and volunteers for adult literacy, and by donating used linens, towels and furniture to local organizations. The Good Neighbor Policy was awarded the President's Service Award for community service directed at solving critical social problems.

Gas and media, an unlikely pair anywhere else

Recent acquisitions highlight the truly diverse nature of Loews Corporation. In July 2007, the company completed the purchase of gas exploration and production assets from Dominion Resources. The properties being acquired are located in the Permian Basin in Texas, the Black Warrior Basin in Alabama and the Antrim Shale in Michigan, with estimated reserves of about 2.5 trillion cubic feet of gas. The price equates to about $1.61 per thousand cubic feet. Prior to that, Loews purchased two interstate natural gas pipelines

(Texas Gas in 2003 and Gulf South Pipeline in 2004), creating a parent company, Boardwalk Pipeline Partners (NYSE: BWP) in 2005.

And in November of 2006, Loews disclosed ownership of 2.61 million shares of The New York Times Co., amounting to $63 million, or about 1.8 percent of the company's Class A stock outstanding. The purchase came at an uncertain time for the Times, which had been under pressure to disband its voting structure that allows the controlling Ochs-Sulzberger family to maintain control. The Sulzberger family owns about 20 percent of the total equity of the company.

Loews on the Hill

In October 2007, some of Loews' political stances became public knowledge. The Associated Press reported that in the first half of 2007, Loews paid a Washington, D.C., lobbying firm $780,000 to lobby Congress on tobacco-related legislation, including a bill vetoed by President Bush that would expand children's health insurance by raising tobacco taxes to $1 per pack.

It was also made known that Loews lobbied in the first half of 2007 on a 15-year extension of a program enacted after the September 11 attacks that would aid the insurance industry in the event of another terrorist attack. The bill to extend the terrorism risk insurance program was passed by the House in September 2007.

Clearing smoke

One of Loews' most important strategic decisions in recent history took place in December 2007, when the firm severed its 40-year-old ties to the Lorillard Tobacco Company, a $14 billion company that makes Newport and Kent cigarettes.

Loews' interest in Lorillard was spun off to Carolina Group, a tracking stock designed to reflect the performance of the tobacco business. Loews redeemed all outstanding Carolina shares in exchange for Lorillard shares. Carolina stockholders will get one Lorillard share for each share they own. The Lorillard stock being distributed makes up about 62 percent of the company's outstanding shares. Loews will then sell the remaining 38 percent of Lorillard outstanding stock in exchange for some of its own outstanding shares if deemed appropriate. If Loews does not view this as a proper transaction, it will distribute the remaining Lorillard stock to Loews shareholders as a dividend. The spinoff closed in June 2008.

Visit the Vault Finance Career Channel at www.vault.com/finance — with insider firm profiles, message boards, the Vault Finance Job Board and more.

VAULT CAREER LIBRARY   237

The deal, which will free Loews from the threat of tobacco litigation suits, is also designed to free up Loews for making new acquisitions. CEO Jim Tisch said that he hoped the change would provide "a dramatic improvement in our perceived risk profile."

Industry analysts expressed mixed emotions. "Getting rid of Lorrilard entirely is a double-edged sword for Loews," according to a December 2007 Forbes article. "While it might attract more shareholders to the remaining operations, the tobacco unit was profitable."

A fit future

Overall, the financial picture looked healthy for Loews in recent times. Total revenue for 2007 increased to $18.38 billion from $17.7 billion, while net income remained flat at $2.5 billion. But by mid-2008, the numbers had picked up considerably for the firm. Revenue for the second quarter of 2008 rose to $3.92 billion from $3.52 billion in the second quarter 2007. Net income for the quarter, meanwhile, swelled to $4.86 billion from $513 million in the second quarter of 2008. (The first quarter of 2008 brought in $3.61 billion in revenue and $555 million in net income.) The high net income was mostly due to a $4.29 billion related to the sale of Lorillard. The transaction, carried out in shares, was a tax-free one for Loews.

GETTING HIRED

Under the Loews umbrella

Positions at Loews Corporation may be available in its corporate office or at the subsidiary level. CNA, Loews Hotels and Diamond Offshore invites those interested in applying for positions to go to the "careers" section of their respective web sites. Those interested in other Loews companies can contact their human resources companies directly.

The recruiting process at Loews is "very efficient and transparent," one insider says. "A recruiter first calls to ask if you are interested in the interview, then schedules an interview, which is typically three to four hours long." The interview is also "broken into half-hour segments, each of which is an interview with one or more people, and the interview questions are situational." And they don't keep you hanging, reports the contact. "Before I left that day, I knew the initial feelings of the first six interviewers and the timing of our next steps."

Marsh & McLennan Companies

1166 Avenue of the Americas
New York, NY 10036-2774
Phone: (212) 345-5000
Fax: (212) 345-4838
www.marshmac.com

DEPARTMENTS

Consulting
Insurance
Risk Management

THE STATS

Employer Type: Public Company
Ticker Symbol: MMC (NYSE)
President, CEO & Director: Brian
    Duperreault
Revenue: $11.35 billion (FYE 12/07)
Net Income: $2.48 billion
No. of Employees: 55,000

KEY COMPETITORS

AIG
Aon
ING

UPPERS

• "Pretty laid-back" atmosphere
• Hours are "great"

DOWNERS

• "Politics rule the company in all
  locations"
• A new CEO and recent tough times
  mean an uncertain future

EMPLOYMENT CONTACT

See "careers" section of
www.marshmac.com

Visit the Vault Finance Career Channel at **www.vault.com/finance** — with
insider firm profiles, message boards, the Vault Finance Job Board and more.

VAULT CAREER LIBRARY   239

THE SCOOP

'MMC' stands for a lot of things

For more than 135 years, Marsh & McLennan Companies Inc. (MMC) has served clients in a diverse range of financial services. The firm today is a multi-billion dollar public holding company for several professional services subsidiaries, holding market-leading positions in all of the areas in which it operates. Subsidiaries include Marsh, a leader in risk consulting, insurance broking and insurance program management; Guy Carpenter, a risk and reinsurance specialist; Kroll, a risk consulting and technology company; and Mercer Consulting Group, a global human resources and management consulting company.

MMC maintains its headquarters in New York, but has offices all over the world, with subsidiaries employing some 55,000 staff, in over 100 countries. The company reported revenue for 2007 of $11.35 billion, up from the $10.5 billion reported in 2006.

Growing through acquisitions

Marsh & McLennan began as an insurance company in 1871. The company expanded to reinsurance broking in 1923, with the acquisition of Guy Carpenter & Company. MMC entered human resource consulting in 1959, upon acquiring William M. Mercer Limited in Canada. In the 1980s, MMC first introduced specialty consulting. Today the specialty consulting businesses under Mercer Specialty Consulting include strategy and operations consulting (Mercer Management Consulting), financial services strategy and risk management consulting (Mercer Oliver Wyman), organizational change consulting (Mercer Delta), economic consulting (NERA), and design and brand strategy consulting (Lippincott Mercer). In 1970, MMC acquired one of the largest mutual fund companies in the United States, Putnam Investments, which established the company's presence in the business of investment management. The most recent addition to MMC's businesses came in 2004, with the acquisition of Kroll, a risk consulting services company providing investigative, intelligence, financial, security and technology services.

Insurance subsidiary becomes more transparent

In 2004 and 2005, MMC made several important changes to its business model, particularly to Marsh, which said it would implement higher commissions and fees with more transparency. Marsh, MMC's risk and insurance services subsidiary, has 26,000 employees and annual revenue about $6 billion. The firm began rolling out compliance initiatives due to a settlement with the Office of the New York State Attorney General and the New York State Insurance Department. The compliance agreement involved the development of transparency standards, related policies, procedures, employee training and compliance monitoring groups.

New CFO to help pick up pieces

In 2005, MMC company divested its interest in private equity subsidiary MMC Capital, selling to former managers of MMC Capital operating under the Stone Point LLC entity. It also sold Marsh's Crump wholesale broking operations and Sedwick Claims Management Services. The company as a whole eliminated approximately 2,600 employee positions in 2005. Despite the changes, the company announced in its annual report that it expects 2006's revenue to be "significantly lower."

To help whip its finances into shape, in 2006, MMC named its vice president and treasurer, Matthew B. Bartley, to the CFO position. Prior to coming to MMC in 2001, Bartley spent nearly 10 years in international treasury and tax positions at PepsiCo, and as vice president of taxes at specialty chemicals and precious metals company Engelhard Corporation.

A leader in climate change

In September of 2006, MMC was recognized by the Carbon Disclosure Project (CDP) as Best in Class on the project's Climate Leadership Index for 2006. Every year, the CDP surveys the world's largest companies on investment-relevant information on climate change risks and opportunities, publishing results in its annual Index. Earlier in 2006, MMC CEO Michael Cherkasky spoke at the World Economic Forum, identifying climate change as one of the most significant long-term issues facing world businesses. MMC has initiated a goal of promoting dialogue, research and new alliances around the issue of climate change.

Visit the Vault Finance Career Channel at www.vault.com/finance — with insider firm profiles, message boards, the Vault Finance Job Board and more.

VAULT CAREER LIBRARY   241

Breaking global ground

In March 2007, MMC announced that it planned to apply for a license from the Qatar Financial Centre Regulatory Authority. Commenting on the application, Robert Makhoul, head of Marsh's Middle East operations, said, "Our plans to set up an office in the Qatar Financial Centre reflect the exciting opportunities available there. We have had solid growth in the region and believe that there will be strong demand for the kind of broking and risk advisory services we can offer companies in Qatar."

And in April 2007, Marsh established a global real estate practice, and named Jeffrey Alpaugh to lead it. Alpaugh, who had been with Marsh throughout his 18-year career in insurance and risk management, held positions of increasing responsibility in the firm's New York, Los Angeles and Boston offices, serving as a broker, global client executive, regional real estate industry practice leader and, most recently, regional client executive practice leader.

So long, Putnam

In August 2007, Marsh agreed to sell its troubled investment management arm, Putnam Investments, to Great-West Lifeco for $3.9 billion. Although Putnam is one of the largest investment management firms in the United States—it had $175 billion in assets under management as of May 2008—the firm has been performing poorly since 2001.

In a statement announcing the sale to Great-West Lifeco, a Canadian financial services holding company, Marsh CEO Cherkasky said that the deal will help "strengthen our ability to focus on our core businesses, and significantly enhance our financial flexibility." Industry analysts, for the most part, agreed.

AIG exec tapped to lead insurance

In December 2007, MMC named Daniel Glaser as chairman and CEO of Marsh, the company's insurance broking subsidiary. The firm had been looking for a new top dog since September 2007, when then-CEO Brian Storms stepped down from the position. Glaser was poached from AIG, where he served as managing director of AIG Europe (U.K.) Limited and as regional president of AIG's American International Underwriters (AIU), U.K./Ireland division.

Glaser began his career in the insurance industry as a Marsh broker in 1982. He worked at Marsh for a decade, serving in roles in New York, London and Saudi Arabia. Thereafter, he spent eight years at Willis, where he served as president and COO of Willis Risk Solutions, the large accounts practice. In 2000, he joined AIG as president of the global energy division and, in 2002, was named managing director of AIG Europe (U.K.), AIU's largest division.

Cherkasky's sent packing

Although hiring Glaser was a significant appointment, given MMC's recent re-focus on its core insurance assets, MMC's biggest personnel decision came later in December 2007, when it ousted CEO Michael Cherkasky. Cherkasky, who agreed to stay on until a replacement was found, had been in the hot seat since 2004, when he took over in the middle of a bid-rigging scandal of which MMC was at the center.

Cherkasky was charged with bringing MMC back to profitability after an investigation led by former New York Attorney General Eliot Spitzer drained the company's bank. But, "Marsh & McLennan's financial performance in 2007 has fallen far short of our expectations," said Stephen Hardis, MMC's non-executive chairman of the board, in a statement.

One theory, told to Bloomberg by Stanley Nabi, of Silvercrest Asset Management Group, is that Cherkasky "was not the right man for the job. He cleaned up the company there legally, but he's not an insurance person." Cherkasky is a lawyer by background and once served as Spitzer's boss in the Manhattan District Attorney's office.

Despite Cherkasky's failure to bolster MMC's sales, his departure was announced with utmost respect. Non-executive chairman Hardis said in a statement announcing the board's decision, "MMC is a venerable institution that might not be here today were it not for Mike Cherkasky. His leadership and crisis management skills in the wake of the New York Attorney General's action in 2004 enabled MMC to weather a perfect storm and positioned the company for future growth. We all owe Mike an enormous debt of gratitude for his invaluable contribution." News of Cherkasky's ouster sparked rumors that MMC was planning to sell off its consulting units.

The new man on top

In late January 2008, Marsh found its next leader, hiring Brian Duperreault as its new CEO. Duperreault was most recently a nonexecutive chairman of Ace Ltd., a Bermuda-based insurance company with significant operations in Philadelphia. He served as CEO of Ace from 1994 to 2004 and, prior to that, worked for AIG for more than 20 years.

Visit the Vault Finance Career Channel at www.vault.com/finance — with insider firm profiles, message boards, the Vault Finance Job Board and more.

VAULT CAREER LIBRARY   243

Atop the 'Power Broker' list

In February 2008, *Risk & Insurance* magazine published a list of Top Power Brokers, the country's top insurance brokerage executives within different industry categories. Of the 151 winners, 17 were Marsh insurance brokerage and risk advisory executives. The list is based on feedback from more than 300 risk managers, who make their selections based on brokers' creativity in solving risk-related problems, industry knowledge and level of client service.

Mixed results

In 2007, the firm pulled in $11.35 billion in revenue, down slightly from the $11.7 billion it booked in 2006. Net income for the year came in at $2.48 billion, up from $176 million in the previous year. By mid-2008, second quarter revenue had risen to $3.03 billion from $2.82 billion and net income had dropped to $65 million compared with $177 million. (In contrast, the first quarter of 2008 brought in $3.047 billion in revenue and a $210 million net loss.) Strong revenue development across all its businesses—especially Mercer and Kroll—helped push the firm farther into the black.

GETTING HIRED

Submit or create

On its career web site (global.marsh.com/careers), Marsh & McLennan lists openings in all cities and categories for all levels of applicants, but if you don't find the specific gig you had in mind, never fear. If you don't happen to find an opportunity that interests you, the company encourages applicants to create a candidate profile to keep on file and "may notify you by e-mail when an opportunity becomes available in your area of interest and/or expertise."

If you are called in for an interview, expect at least "two rounds." It's likely that you'll meet "a hiring manager" and a potential supervisor. Questions you'll field are likely to be "experience-related" and tend to consist of providing "give me a time where…" examples. And be sure that you don't fudge your resume—the firm is looking for a "demonstration of your credentials," so get ready to prove yourself.

OUR SURVEY SAYS

Politics rule the roost

The company culture is "fragmented, and varies tremendously by office and department/practice." One insider says, "Politics rule the company in all locations." Another notes that "a lot of your satisfaction and success will depend upon which division you work in—some are good and some are bad." Others say that while the firm has "great potential and some really nice folks," it also includes "favoritism," and is a "strange company to work for—everything is done by consensus and committee. These people can't make a quick decision on anything."

Chilled out

On the bright side, however, employees report that hours are "great," and tend to be a "35-hour work week." Additionally, it's a "pretty laid-back" atmosphere. "As long as you didn't abuse the system, one-and-a-half-hour lunches, doctor's visits, etc. were fine." The dress code, too, is similarly lax. "The dress code is business casual with occasional jeans days on Fridays if you donated to the elected charity." However, if you have meetings with clients, "business formal is the standard."

Manage it

As far as management, insiders say that "senior leadership is weak," and "Marsh regularly begins initiatives that are started without much input from employees," and "dropped as fast as they are dictated to the troops." One insider says "current management is focused on cost-cutting and immediate results for street analysts, not long-term stakeholders." As a result, he adds, "bean-counting and the slow, traditional insurance perspective are pervasive."

On the diversity front, one source says the firm is "not in a very diverse industry," adding that "white males run the show, and minorities are almost excluded from management ranks." Another comments that "two CIOs from Marsh are no longer here, both of them women, which makes you wonder about the culture."

Fend for yourself?

Marsh's outlook seems to be hanging in the balance. Some call its future "grim" and say "the company is looking to make financial gains through workforce attrition rather than layoffs," and "the key goal is to annoy people until they leave." "All who are still on the ship, head for the life rafts!" cautions one contact. "And recruiters take note: this sinking ship has some people worth saving."

Visit the Vault Finance Career Channel at www.vault.com/finance — with
insider firm profiles, message boards, the Vault Finance Job Board and more.

VAULT CAREER LIBRARY   245

MassMutual

1295 State Street
Springfield, MA 01111-0001
Phone: (413) 744-1000
Fax: (413) 744-6005
www.massmutual.com

DEPARTMENTS

Insurance Services
Investment Services
Retirement Services

THE STATS

Employer Type: Private Company
President & CEO: Stuart H. Reese
Revenue: $18.74 billion (FYE 12/07)
Net Income: $201 million
No. of Employees: 10,000
No. of Offices: 1,800

KEY COMPETITORS

New York Life
Northwestern Mutual
Prudential

UPPER

- Generous benefit offerings, good salaries

DOWNER

- "Its 'mutual' status" means decisions are made "slowly"

EMPLOYMENT CONTACT

www.massmutual.com/careers

THE SCOOP

Large Mass of insurance services

Founded in 1851, the Springfield, Mass.-based MassMutual divides its business into investment, insurance and retirement services. Its investment division includes life, disability income, long term care, annuities, a private client group, structured settlements and trust services. MassMutual's investment products include annuities, structured settlements, income management services, mutual funds, education savings plans, wealth management and trust services. The firm also offers annuities, income management, contribution protection, trust services and retirement plan services through its retirement services practice. MassMutual's clients include individuals, business owners and corporate and institutional markets.

MassMutual likes to remind clients of its corporate motto: "You can't predict. You can prepare." With more than 155 years of mergers and acquisitions under its belt, MassMutual is prepared for business, with subsidiaries and affiliates that include OppenheimerFunds, Babson Capital Management, Baring Asset Management, Cornerstone Real Estate Advisers, MML Investors Services, the MassMutual Trust Company, MML Bay State Life Insurance, C.M. Life Insurance and MassMutual International, the firm's global arm.

At year-end 2007, MassMutual had more than $500 billion in assets under management. And the 2008 Fortune 500 listed MassMutual at No. 99, making it the highest ranking Massachusetts firm on the list.

Out with the dirty laundry

Robert J. O'Connell, who had served as MassMutual's chairman, president and CEO since 2000, was dismissed from his posts in June 2005, following an internal investigation into his actions. The company's board of directors made the decision, saying that investigators (tipped off by O'Connell's suspicious wife) had turned up a laundry list of abuses and misdeeds, including theft of over $30 million, personal use of company aircraft for his family and friends, bribery and other crimes. Stuart H. Reese, a 12-year veteran and CIO of MassMutual, was named president and CEO. A separate, non-executive chairman of the board was selected: James R. Birle, who had spent 13 years on MassMutual's board of directors. The O'Connell scandal

Visit the Vault Finance Career Channel at www.vault.com/finance — with insider firm profiles, message boards, the Vault Finance Job Board and more.

VAULT CAREER LIBRARY   247

brought a run of bad PR, but Reese and Birle were able to reassure clients and keep MassMutual's performance on track.

Turn the dial to MassMutual

What's the best way to keep field agents, sales managers, trainers and recruiters—many of whom spend a significant amount time on the road and away from the office—up to date on company news? For MassMutual, the answer is podcasting. Begun in February 2006 and expanded in May 2006, the company's podcast program is provided by the MassMutual National Center for Professional Development (NCPD). Radio NCPD creates weekly podcasts, available by free subscription to any member of the MassMutual field force. Topics include information about new MassMutual products, underwriting policies and procedures, plus interviews with top sales representatives and tips for success in niche markets.

Targeting women

In August 2006, MassMutual launched a new Selling to Women series, designed to help its agents provide better financial services to women. The exclusive four-part course was designed by MassMutual's National Center for Professional Development and the firm's women's markets department. MassMutual said it was prompted to develop the course after industry research reported that the majority of women, despite being involved in 80 percent of all financial decisions, feel misunderstood by the financial services industry. Selling to Women teaches MassMutual agents about women's market power, buying preferences, business concerns and other needs; the firm also created a special section of its web site to educate women about financial planning, products and services.

Industry standout

In September 2007, MassMutual was named to *Working Mother*'s 100 Best Company list for the ninth year. The annual honor is given to companies that pay particular attention to retention and advancement of working mothers. MassMutual offers flexible schedules, on-site and near-site child care facilities, an on-site credit union, convenience store with a full-service pharmacy, dry cleaner, tailor, jewelry and shoe repair, a barbershop and a hair salon. MassMutual also has a strong commitment to employee health, offering state-of-the-art wellness activity centers, employee health service centers that offer such amenities as personal health assessments, on-site physical therapy, and flu vaccinations, as well as an employee assistance program. In addition, the company offers forgivable $5,000 loans on an annual basis to qualified employees for the purchase of their first home.

"MassMutual not only offers essential benefits like flextime and telecommuting—they go above and beyond with a range of best practices and policies to ease the difficulties for working parents and their families," said Carol Evans, CEO and president of Working Mother Media, in a statement. "Their supportive culture makes a huge difference to employees who want to be great moms and great workers."

Also in the fall of 2007, MassMutual was awarded the No. 1 ranking in the InformationWeek 500 Information Security/Privacy category for its proprietary information security management system. MassMutual's award is one of only five Leaders in Innovation category awards identified by *InformationWeek*. The firm also earned an overall ranking of No. 66 on the InformationWeek 500.

In February 2008, DALBAR, a financial services market research and consulting firm, gave MassMutual an "excellent" rating for its consumer web site for the 15th consecutive quarter.

A payout to remember

In November 2007, MassMutual announced the payment of approximately $1.38 billion in dividends to eligible participating policyholders in 2008—an 11.2 percent increase over the approved payout for 2007 and the largest ever in the company's history. The total approved payout for 2008 reflects a dividend interest rate of 7.9 percent on most of its eligible participating policies, the company's highest rate in five years. The record 2008 dividend payout approved by underscores the value of the company's mutual status and the long-term financial interests of its policyholders. The previous record amount was the 2007 approved dividend payout of $1.25 billion.

"The record dividend payout for 2008 and increased dividend interest rate reflects how, as a 156-year-old mutual company, we remain focused on helping our clients achieve their financial goals over the long-term," said CEO Stuart Reese, in a statement. "Paying competitive dividends is a core aspect of our status as a leading mutual life insurance company. Since we are in the business of helping customers achieve long-term financial security, our mutual status and long history of dividend payouts illustrate our commitment to working in the best interest of our policyholders."

Visit the Vault Finance Career Channel at www.vault.com/finance — with insider firm profiles, message boards, the Vault Finance Job Board and more.

VAULT CAREER LIBRARY   249

Joint operation

In June 2007, MassMutual made its chief operating officer position a shared post. The firm named Roger Crandall, executive vice president and chief investment officer of MassMutual, and chairman, president and CEO of Babson Capital, and William Glavin Jr., executive vice president of MassMutual's U.S. Insurance Group, to the job. In addition to being named co-chief operating officer, Crandall will have responsibility for MassMutual's retirement services division, which offers products and services for corporate, union, nonprofit and governmental employers' defined benefit, defined contribution and nonqualified deferred compensation plans.

Crandall and Glavin will maintain their current responsibilities and continue to report to CEO Stuart Reese. But in their new roles, the two will work with Reese on broad strategic priorities and help ensure that MassMutual is operating at maximum efficiency in each part of the organization. Key priorities for the COOs include increased emphasis on teamwork across the organization, added focus on operational excellence and execution, and enhancing a performance and customer-oriented culture.

"Roger and Bill have provided outstanding leadership in their respective areas," said Reese, in a statement announcing the promotions. "Their broad experience and expertise, proven track record of operational excellence and outstanding execution, and ability to develop and lead high performance teams with a strong customer focus make them ideal executives to serve in this capacity."

Retirement unit nabs one from Prudential

MassMutual Retirement Income (MMRI)—a division of MassMutual that focuses on serving the retail retirement-accumulation and retirement-income market—looked to one of its biggest competitors in July 2007 to find a new COO and CFO. Douglas Russell, who was senior vice president and head of client services for Prudential Retirement since 2004, was named to the job. Russell will assume overall responsibility for finance, compliance, operations and technology at MMRI, and report to the division's head, Drew Dickey.

Russell had been with Prudential Retirement since 2004 via the firm's acquisition of CIGNA Retirement and Investment Services business, which he joined in 2001 as senior vice president in its corporate insurance unit. He had been with Aetna Inc./ING Financial Services from 1995-2001, mostly with its Aetna International business, which included a two-year period as its CFO and a three-year period as the CEO running Aetna Philippines in Manila.

Russell also worked at Fleet Financial Group, Conning and Company, and Wertheim & Company. In addition, he co-founded Northington Partners, an insurance, investment and investment research firm in Avon, Conn.

Taking a risk on Ward

MassMutual appointed a new head of enterprise risk management in November 2007, when the firm's chief risk officer, John Skar, retired. Elizabeth Ward, the former managing director at MassMutual's Babson Capital Management subsidiary, was named to the post.

As head of enterprise risk management, Ward will have responsibility for all elements of strategic risk management, including the identification, measurement, monitoring, coordination and oversight of risk management policies and programs across the MassMutual Financial Group companies. She will also have direct responsibility for risk management as chief risk officer at Babson Capital Management. Ward will report directly to MassMutual's CFO, Michael Rollings.

Prior to joining Babson Capital in 2001, Ward was employed as managing director at MassMutual investment affiliate Charter Oak Capital Management from 1996, and at various investment and insurance areas at Aetna from 1986 to 1996, including Aeltus Investment Management.

On the horizon

In 2007, MassMutual's revenue went up to $18.74 billion from $18.02 billion in the previous year. But net income didn't fare quite as well, falling to $201 million from the $810 million it posted in 2006. Analysts pointed to instability throughout the industry as reason for the downturn.

Despite the rather tepid results, the firm wasn't resting on its laurels. In February 2008, MassMutual agreed to buy the First Mercantile Trust Company from SunTrust Banks for an undisclosed amount. First Mercantile had almost $5 billion in assets under management at year-end 2007.

Visit the Vault Finance Career Channel at **www.vault.com/finance** — with insider firm profiles, message boards, the Vault Finance Job Board and more.

VAULT CAREER LIBRARY   251

GETTING HIRED

Mass appeal

Create a profile to keep on file with the firm for up to a year, or just browse for open positions at MassMutual's career site, which offers separate menus depending on whether prospective employees are searching corporate careers or national sales and management careers. Those interested in corporate careers can search by geographic location or job type, which can include accounting, actuarial, audit, claims, data management, finance, government relations, investments, legal, quality assurance, systems architecture and underwriting.

For candidates interested in national sales/management careers, many options are available. Again, separate menus can be found for those looking to submit resumes for jobs such as financial professionals, sales managers, business professionals (CPAs, JDs, MBAs), experienced producers and internships (for college students). MassMutual's site also includes detailed information about its campus recruiting practices for undergraduates, graduate students and law students.

The interviewing process can be long, so prepare yourself accordingly. It's not atypical to have "two first-round interviews" that are "followed by a half-dozen final round interviews" with "employees from the director to the EVP level."

OUR SURVEY SAYS

Pros and cons

Insiders call the firm "diversified" with "outstanding financial performance" in its "key business units," such as life insurance, investment management and retirement products. But "the company's key strength can also be perceived as a weakness—its mutual status means it is relatively insulated from the pressures faced by its publicly traded peers." So when it's "faced with a key decision, MassMutual usually makes the right call, but does so slowly."

Perks include the "gym," "cafeteria" and "travel services." Contacts also cite the company's "4 percent match for the thrift savings plan" and "no-load mutual funds" as draws. One source notes that perks seem to be based on level of employment. "If you get in as an officer or attorney, the salaries, bonuses, perks, training and upward advancement are great," says the contact, "but if you don't, good luck." Other benefits available to all staff include "flex-time and flexible work arrangements," "child care," "dry cleaning" and even "film processing." Salaries, too, generally receive high marks from insiders and raises "are anywhere from 3 to 8 percent based on individual and business unit performance."

The dress code is "casual except for client contact," and hours can be "very flexible" if you do a lot of business traveling, though "sometimes you have to travel on Sunday in order to be at a meeting on Monday." Office space could stand to be improved, as the cubicle setup offers "very little privacy." Although one insider reports having had "both bad and good managers," management issues may be external. One source comments that the firm "puts too much stock in listening to consulting firms who really don't know our way of business, and then they implement these suggested policies." As far as advancement within the firm, one insider puts it succinctly: "They do not promote from within."

Diversity seems to be improving in some areas. Although diversity with respect to minorities as well as gays and lesbians generally receives good marks, one respondent notes that while "the company does a fair job in recruiting women and minorities," "some male managers can still be rude to women without even realizing that they have an attitude."

Visit the Vault Finance Career Channel at www.vault.com/finance — with
insider firm profiles, message boards, the Vault Finance Job Board and more.

VAULT CAREER LIBRARY   253

MasterCard Worldwide

2000 Purchase Street
Purchase, NY 10577
Phone: (914) 249-2000
Fax: (914) 249-4206
www.mastercard.com

DEPARTMENTS

Corporations
Government & Public Sector
Midsized Companies
Small Business

THE STATS

Employer Type: Public Company
Ticker Symbol: MA (NYSE)
President & CEO: Robert W. Selander
Revenue: $4.07 billion (FYE 12/07)
Net Income: $1.09 billion
No. of Employees: 4,600
No. of Offices: 37

KEY COMPETITORS

American Express
Discover
Visa

UPPERS

- "Very team-oriented"
- "Multicultural"—good diversity programs

DOWNERS

- "We work very hard and long hours"
- "Fast-moving, stressful culture"

EMPLOYMENT CONTACT

See "careers" section of
www.mastercard.com/us

THE SCOOP

World famous

MasterCard Inc., based in Purchase, N.Y., was founded in 1966 as the Interbank Card Association. It is a leading international payments solutions company that offers a range of innovative credit, deposit access, electronic cash, business-to-business and related payment programs. It was renamed Master Charge three years later and purchased by the California Bank Association. A decade after that, it changed its name again, from Master Charge to MasterCard. By 2003, the company had at last succeeded in overtaking rival Visa to become the largest credit card brand in the world, but has since fallen back to the No. 2 spot.

MasterCard, through its principal operating subsidiary, MasterCard International Incorporated, manages a family of widely recognized and accepted payment cards—including MasterCard, Maestro and Cirrus—and serves financial institutions, consumers and businesses in over 210 countries and territories. The company's award-winning Priceless advertising campaign is now seen in over 100 countries, in 50 different languages, giving the MasterCard brand a truly global reach and scope. A historic turning point for the organization came in 2006, when it was listed on the New York Stock Exchange, and pledged its commitment to an open governance structure, seamless organization and new name, MasterCard Worldwide. In 2008, for the second year in a row, MasterCard ranked third in the financial data services category of Fortune's Most Admired Companies in America list.

Setbacks don't stop successful IPO

On May 25, 2006, MasterCard went public, and began trading on the New York Stock Exchange under the ticker MA. "Listing on the NYSE marks a major milestone for MasterCard and reinforces our commitment to continued growth and building value for our customers and stockholders," Robert Selander, the company's president and CEO, told the Associated Press. The market had expected the issue to open in the $40 to $43 range, but MasterCard was at $39 after a series of setbacks delayed the process.

The IPO was supposed to have gone ahead earlier in the year, when market conditions were better, but it was pushed back after Selander discovered he had prostate cancer. The CEO is now back on his feet, but the underwriters were also worried by MasterCard's legal and regulatory problems; the

Visit the Vault Finance Career Channel at **www.vault.com/finance** — with insider firm profiles, message boards, the Vault Finance Job Board and more.

VAULT CAREER LIBRARY   255

company had been embroiled in a legal wrangle as antitrust regulators investigated the credit card industry, and retailers threatened court action to lower the fees they pay on transactions. Merchant groups have already filed a class-action suit alleging unlawful price fixing of fees that hurt both merchants and consumers, but the opportunity to buy shares of one of the world's top financial services brands at a relatively reasonable price was expected to attract investors nonetheless.

And investors in MasterCard have been rewarded. Since the firm went public in May 2006, the stock has zoomed to over $235 per share as of August 2008, making MasterCard one of the most successful IPOs of 2006.

Recognized for contactless-payment technology

In July 2008, MasterCard Worldwide took the overall winner slot in the 2008 HP NonStop Availability Awards, which recognize firms that use best practices. The company also won the top communication award—"The Silver Anvil"—from the Public Relations Society of America in June 2008. MasterCard's "Project Math" corporate giving program seeks to support math students and teachers, and underwrites local educational collaborations and donates new technology.

Opening up down under

MasterCard opened its first office in New Zealand in February 2007, and Stuart McKinlay was named the firm's first New Zealand-based country manager. Formerly based in Sydney as vice president of business development, McKinlay had worked for MasterCard for more than five years, focusing on developing relationships with major banks across both sides of the Tasman.

Organizational realignment broadens executive responsibilities

In November 2007, MasterCard announced an organizational realignment designed to improve performance by broadening executive responsibilities as a result of COO Alan Heuer's retirement at the end of 2008. Heuer was appointed to the Office of the CEO where he now holds the newly created position of vice chairman. He continues to report to MasterCard CEO Robert Selander.

A number of other executives also were appointed to new roles. Gary Flood, former president, global account management, was named to the newly created position of president, products and services. Walt Macnee, former president, Americas, was appointed president, global markets. MasterCard's former CFO, Chris McWilton, was named president, global accounts. Succeeding McWilton as CFO is Martina Hund-Mejean, who joined MasterCard from Tyco International, where she was senior vice president and treasurer since 2002.

Illegal fees in Europe

MasterCard's legal department got handed a boatload of work just before the 2007 holidays. On December 19, 2007, The European Commission ruled that charges MasterCard imposes on retailers are illegal, saying it would fine MasterCard 3.5 percent of daily global revenue in six months if the fees aren't withdrawn. The fees, paid from bank to bank on every cross-border payment transaction, cost consumers about $21 billion a year, according to the European Retail Round Table, a lobby group for 14 retailers.

On the same day that the Commission released its charges, MasterCard issued a statement stating that it would appeal, explaining that "market forces, not regulation, should drive key decisions such as the setting of interchange fees and retailers' choices over which forms of payment to accept." About six months later, though, MasterCard relented, agreeing to drop 40-year-old transaction fees.

Card wars

In June 2008, MasterCard International announced that it would be paying American Express $1.8 billion in a settlement stemming from a 2004 lawsuit contending that MasterCard—along with competitor Visa—had barred some financial companies from distributing cards through American Express. In the third quarter of 2008, MasterCard will make its first $150 million payment to American Express—a practice that will continue for 12 quarters. Meanwhile, Visa, in its settlement, will pay American Express $880 million annually for the next three years.

Most recent numbers

In 2007, MasterCard brought in $4.07 billion in revenue, up from $3.33 billion in 2006. Net income soared, coming in at $1.09 billion in 2007 from

Visit the Vault Finance Career Channel at www.vault.com/finance — with
insider firm profiles, message boards, the Vault Finance Job Board and more.

VAULT CAREER LIBRARY   257

$50.2 million in 2006. But by the second half of 2008, the future looked a little muddled. While revenue for the second quarter of 2008 rose to $1.25 billion from $996.96 million in the second quarter 2007, the firm sustained a net loss of $746.65 million for the quarter compared with a net income of $252.29 million in the second quarter of the previous year. The reason for the loss was largely due to the $1.65 billion pre-tax charge related to the settlement with American Express that came to approximately $1 billion on an after-tax basis.

GETTING HIRED

If you don't schmooze, you might lose

Though there are a few ways to get inside MasterCard, combing your phone book and leveraging your contacts is by far the easiest, sources say. "MasterCard is very selective when it comes to hiring," says an insider. "They get thousands of resumes per week. The best bet for getting a job is through a referral."

If you don't know someone at the firm, the next best way to apply for work with MasterCard is through the career section of its web site, which is simple yet thorough. Applicants can either search for jobs individually, or let the company come to them by submitting their resumes for future openings. The job search engine allows for specific searches to be chosen among dozens of job titles and the firm's many offices worldwide. The site also features a "job cart" that allows prospective employees to apply for multiple positions simultaneously, and it won't tick anyone off. In case a job hunter doesn't see any suitable openings, he or she can also post a resume on the site, which is forwarded to a central database for review against any openings at MasterCard. Once the resume is submitted, the company will send an e-mail immediately confirming the submission. And because all material remains in the database for 12 months, applicants can update their resumes.

What you need

To get hired, "you need the right expertise and cultural attitude," says one source, "as well as openness to work in an international environment." Additionally, it helps if you have some financial services experience. The firm also prefers candidates who can excel in a "team setting" and who are "not too confrontational or aggressive." The company reportedly does "very little campus recruiting." An insider in St. Louis says, "I had three interviews with levels from team leaders to directors and VPs. Questions were team-oriented, project-oriented and technical in nature." One European contact in technology says he went through "only two interviews, because I had the right background for the job that they were looking for." Another insider reports being contacted by an external recruiter who contacted the candidate and set up a meeting. "I met with one executive, four potential colleagues and wrapped up with the hiring manager." Then, the applicant "went back to the executive's office and was handed a written offer and asked to think about it over the weekend— I could get started in two weeks." The process was "very fast and efficient," adds the contact.

OUR SURVEY SAYS

Exciting times

MasterCard is a "great brand" in an "exciting segment of the market," and the company is filled with "highly competent and intelligent people," especially at the "top two levels in the organization." But "who is the typical MasterCard employee?" the firm asks on its web site. "There isn't one," it answers. The firm adds that it defines "diversity from a multidimensional perspective that encompasses our diverse skills, knowledge, viewpoints, culture and national origins." Insiders give MasterCard high marks when it comes to diversity. "We have in place formal diversity and sensitivity training," says a source. Another contact notes, "MasterCard is very dedicated to ensuring all employees receive training to ensure discrimination doesn't happen here. MasterCard is an international company and considers cultural diversity very important."

MasterCard sources enjoy working for an "easily recognizable name" in a "fairly relaxed environment." It's a "multicultural and open" firm, and "very team-oriented," with a "Midwest work ethic—everyone knows what's expected of them and performs at 110 percent." Insiders also say that middle management makes a "concerted effort to orient new employees." Information systems staffers like the fact that "technologically-speaking, we are on the cutting edge."

Visit the Vault Finance Career Channel at **www.vault.com/finance** — with insider firm profiles, message boards, the Vault Finance Job Board and more.

VAULT CAREER LIBRARY   **259**

Hard work

"We work very hard and long hours," says an insider. "It's a fast-moving, stressful culture," reports another. A contact at the company's headquarters notes, "Official work hours are 35 hours, with flex-time in the summer and no telecommuting. The reality is 50 to 60 hours for the ambitious, but telecommuting is common." Sources in networking and information systems comment that they often work "irregular hours," because "the credit business never shuts down for a holiday." A respondent in Europe adds that he "frequently, about once a month," makes a weekend office visit. However, another reports that "all in all, work hours are not tremendous unless you make them that way." And staffers don't have to get all dressed up, either. At MasterCard, dress is "business casual," "basically no jeans or sneakers or T-shirts," and "no suits, except for outside meetings."

Moody's Investors Service

99 Church Street
New York, NY 10007
Phone: (212) 553-0300
Fax: (212) 553-4820
www.moodys.com

DEPARTMENTS

Corporate Finance
Financial Institutions & Sovereign
  Risk
Public Finance
Structured Finance

THE STATS

Employer Type: Public Company
Ticker Symbol: MCO (NYSE)
Chairman, CEO & President: Raymond
  W. McDaniel
Revenue: $2.26 billion (FYE 12/07)
Net Income: $701.5 million
No. of Employees: 2,900
No. of Offices: 33

KEY COMPETITORS

DBRS
Fitch
Standard & Poor's

UPPERS

- "Reasonable" hours
- "Good [minority] representation at all
  levels"

DOWNERS

- Tight deadlines
- Average pay

EMPLOYMENT CONTACT

See "careers" at www.moodys.com

Visit the Vault Finance Career Channel at **www.vault.com/finance** — with
insider firm profiles, message boards, the Vault Finance Job Board and more.

VAULT CAREER LIBRARY   261

THE SCOOP

Rating the world

Founded in 1900, Moody's Investors Service remains among the most famed and widely utilized sources for credit ratings, research and risk analysis on debt instruments and securities. In addition, Moody's provides corporate and government credit assessment and training services, credit training services and credit software to financial institutions, with 9,000 accounts at 2,400 institutions worldwide. The firm's ratings and analyses track 100 sovereign nations, 11,000 company insurers, 25,000 public finance issuers and 70,000 structured finance obligations. Moody's employs more than 1,000 analysts. Moody's began as part of The Dun & Bradstreet Corporation, under which it operated until September 2000. At that point, Dun & Bradstreet split into two publicly traded companies: Moody's Corporation and D&B Corporation. The newly formed D&B comprised Dun & Bradstreet's business information services, and Moody's contained the remaining ratings, and associated research and credit risk management services.

Moody's ratings business consists of four groups: structured finance, corporate finance, financial institutions and sovereign risk and public finance. The firm's main clients include corporate and government issuers as well as institutional investors, banks, creditors and commercial banks. While print traditionally served as the firm's primary medium, Moody's research web site continues to grow in popularity. In addition to research, current ratings and supplemental information are available online at no charge. The company's top shareholder is billionaire Warren Buffet, who holds a nearly 19 percent stake in the company.

Dividing in two

In August 2007, Moody's announced it would reorganize its business into two divisions: Moody's Investors Service and Moody's Analytics. Moody's Investor Service, the company's ratings agency, performs the credit ratings and related research businesses. Moody's Analytics brought together Moody's KMV, Moody's Economy.com and other non-rating businesses as well as the sales and marketing departments for all of Moody's. The restructuring aimed to emphasize the independence of Moody's opinions on debt securities from its sales department.

In a related move in October 2007, the company published an updated Code of Professional Conduct for its employees. The code implements the International Organization of Securities Commissions' Code of Conduct Fundamentals for Credit Ratings Agencies. The revisions focused on the separation of Moody's Investors Service from the company's other commercial activities.

In January 2008, the Moody's said it would slash about 275 jobs or 7.5 percent of its workforce as part of the reorganization.

Subprime spotlight

Moody's and other credit rating agencies came under attack from critics in 2007 for too liberally awarding favorable ratings to subprime securities. In July 2007, Moody's and competitor Standard & Poor's separately announced that they would take negative rating action against close to $20 billion of 2006-vintage subprime mortgage bonds because of escalating delinquencies and foreclosures.

In October 2007, Connecticut Attorney General Richard Blumenthal served subpoenas to Moody's in addition to competitors Standard & Poor's and Fitch alleging anticompetitive practices. In addition, the Securities and Exchange Commission has launched an investigation into Moody's and Standard & Poor's to determine the agencies' role in the subprime meltdown. Twice in 2007, Moody's executives appeared before Congress to testify about the subprime situation.

The European Commission has also launched an investigation into the rating agencies, focusing on conflicts of interest arising from the rating agencies being paid by the issuers they rate.

Promoting competition

The subprime mortgage mess is not the first time critics have taken issue with the rating agencies. Following the accounting scandals at WorldCom and Enron, which received high ratings from Moody's and S&P, corporate chief financial officers and lawmakers began pressuring the SEC to regulate ratings companies. At the time, the SEC only acknowledged five firms as "nationally recognized" credit raters, with Moody's and archrival S&P controlling 80 percent of the market and seeing profit margins of more than 50 percent. The other three agencies are Fitch Ratings, Dominion Bond Rating Services and A.M. Best Co. The Credit Rating Agency Reform Act was signed into law in

Visit the Vault Finance Career Channel at www.vault.com/finance — with insider firm profiles, message boards, the Vault Finance Job Board and more.

VAULT CAREER LIBRARY   263

fall 2006, designed to make the credit rating business more competitive and ensure transparency. The new rules will make it easier for new competitors to enter the market and give the SEC oversight authority. The new regulations also require ratings firms to provide more disclosure of ratings methods and implement policies to avoid conflicts of interest.

Acquiring for expansion

In January 2008, Moody's Analytics, a division of Moody's Corp., announced it had acquired Financial Projections Limited, a U.K- based provider of credit training services. Financial Projections will operate as part of Moody's Credit Training Services, which provides credit training and continuing education services, including seminars, e-learning and workbooks to customers worldwide. "In the wake of recent developments in the credit markets, our customers are seeking to enhance their credit skills and processes," said Dan Russell, executive director and head of the credit training practice within Moody's Analytics.

In December 2007, Moody's announced plans to acquire Mergent Pricing and Evaluation Services, a provider of corporate and municipal bond price information. Mergent's pricing service will become part of Moody's Evaluations, Inc. The companies did not reveal the terms of either acquisition.

Looking to Latin America

In November 2007, Moody's entered into a technical services agreement with Equilibrium, a Lima, Peru-based rating agency that provides credit rating and research services in Peru, El Salvador and Panama. Moody's will give Equilibrium technical support and analyst training based on credit analysis techniques for companies, municipal governments, financial institutions and structured financings. Equilibrium will continue to provide domestic ratings services, rendering opinions on the creditworthiness of issuers and issues within the countries where it operates. Moody's will continue to assign globally comparable ratings for domestic and cross-border financings in those countries.

Bad ratings

In July 2008, the firm announced that Noel Kirnon will be departing the firm following the launch of a company-wide investigation. Kirnon headed up the structured finance department, whose error regarding a ratings model was detected in May 2008 by the law firm Sullivan & Cromwell. Moody's found that correcting the error would have significantly reduced the ratings of 11 debt products called CPDOs (constant-proportion debt obligations). In addition to Kirnon's departure, Moody's said that other employees who work on CPDOs might be fired for not following company procedures regarding the debt product.

Up and down

In 2007, the firm brought in $2.26 billion in revenue, up from $2.04 billion in 2006. Net income, however, dipped to $701.5 million from $753.9 million in the previous year. A restructuring charge of $47.8 million—combined with a shaky credit market—led to the slightly down results.

A dark second quarter

Moody's profit for the second quarter of 2008 decreased 48 percent to $135.3 million versus the same period a year earlier, while revenue declined 25 percent to $487.6 million. Financially, things looked pretty grim across the board for the firm. Moody's ratings unit's revenue decreased 33 percent, its global corporate finance group's revenue was down 23 percent and its global structured finance revenue dropped off by 56 percent. The firm has been deeply affected by the credit crunch, which has resulted in a smaller quantity of securities for the agency to rate and appraise.

GETTING HIRED

Pretty particular

While Moody's uses everything from "internal recommendations" to "recruiting firms" to discover potential candidates, the firm is "very particular on both education and experience." Still, job seekers can check out the "careers" section of www.moodys.com and search for jobs by title, department and location, including international outposts. According to the firm, "If you thrive in a collegial, think-tank atmosphere, you should consider Moody's." The firm says it typically gives junior employees "direct access to senior staff from the start," adding, "The door is open, giving you an unusual opportunity to hone your skills

Visit the Vault Finance Career Channel at www.vault.com/finance — with insider firm profiles, message boards, the Vault Finance Job Board and more.

VAULT CAREER LIBRARY   265

in an informal setting." Moody's offers "opportunity for professional growth in analytics, information technology, marketing and administration."

Be sure to put on a happy face when you go into your interview—it's common for "all team members" to meet with you "to ensure they all like you." Overall, candidates can expect to meet "up to 12 different people in various positions" during the hiring process. "Some interviews are in person, some are over the phone." One contact says his interview consisted of meeting with "a recruitment specialist, then two managing directors, the team leader of the team I was being considered for, another team leader and three analysts." Insiders say the firm is looking for someone who "won't embarrass the firm in front of a client," "can deliver bad news and be responsive to inquiries," can think in a logical way and arrive at a logical conclusion," "is trustworthy and ethical," and "is interested in getting the rating right." Interview questions "typically center on past experiences." One source reports being asked "a range of things, from my motivation and experience through very specific and detailed questions about structured finance." Although not a hard and fast rule, students at top-25 schools are given preference. Interviewing can last several months; the key is to be persistent until you get an answer.

OUR SURVEY SAYS

Cooperative community

The atmosphere at Moody's is "generally collegial and cooperative," says one insider, adding that "there are surprisingly few political tensions and very little hierarchy." But newbies to the firm should take note: "Since most people are highly educated and pretty smart, a new joiner can be a bit intimidated." Another says, "The corporate culture at Moody's is not as conservative as the big banks, meaning there is a very diverse and relaxed atmosphere." And while "analysts work hard," "they all have a life outside work."

Insiders say life at Moody's, while no day at the beach, can be very rewarding. The firm has a "very respected name," and a "team of very smart and savvy analysts." Beware that the firm has a "high turnover rate," and that it "takes six months to get up to speed as to what is expected." It also "takes one to two years to get comfortable and be trusted with tougher assignments, but if you prove yourself, things ease off a bit." "If you can put up with a gossipy environment and crazy deadlines, there is a degree of satisfaction in the work done, and it certainly won't be repetitive." But while there's "no pressure to bill or record time," "sometimes there's a high volume of work and high expectations of what can be done," says an insider. Also, "there is room for advancement, even rapidly, but up to a certain point." Another contact notes, "Opportunities for advancement are hierarchical, so don't count on being promoted until you've put in your years." But don't worry too much about the pecking order. One respondent says, "Moody's values all levels of employees, so don't expect snobbery here," and "employees are very respectful of each other and focus much on team-building."

Perks are decent, say insiders. There are "stock options and shares that form part of the bonus," and "a stock purchase plan with stock sold to employees at a discount." The firm also offers "a car service after 8:30 p.m." and "business class travel." Sources report that although "management can be a bit distant," "there are "generally good relations" between the levels. Training also seems to be improving. One contact notes that although "many people used to feel it was sink-or-swim" when it came to training, "this is changing slowly." Dress code is "business casual unless you have a meeting, then it's business formal."

And the hours are "generally reasonable: 40 to 50 per week." One employee says, "Hours are usually 8 or 9 in the morning until 6 or 7 at night," but "hardly anyone stays past 8 p.m." Travel is "restricted to three or four days per month, sometimes more, sometimes less." "Most are day trips." Although pay doesn't win any awards, "health benefits and vacation time are pretty generous." And get ready to get down. "Moody's throws great parties," reports an insider.

Diversity also gets a pretty good rep at the firm. One source notes that women receive "good representation at all levels," and "there are no real issues" with the representation of minorities. Diversity with respect to gays and lesbians also receives high marks from employees.

Visit the Vault Finance Career Channel at www.vault.com/finance — with insider firm profiles, message boards, the Vault Finance Job Board and more.

VAULT CAREER LIBRARY   267

Nationwide

1 Nationwide Plaza
Columbus, OH 43215-2220
Phone: (614) 249-7111
Fax: (614) 854-5036
www.nationwide.com

DEPARTMENTS

Financial Services
Property & Casualty Insurance

THE STATS

Employer Type: Public Company
Ticker Symbol: NFS (NYSE)
Chairman: Arden L. Shisler
CEO: William G. Jurgensen
President & COO: Mark Thresher
Revenue: $4.53 billion (FYE 02/07)
Net Income: $626.8 million
No. of Employees: 36,000

KEY COMPETITORS

John Hancock Financial Services
MassMutual
Prudential

UPPERS

- Good managers
- Great advancement opportunities

DOWNERS

- "Bureaucratic"—"dealing with headquarters"
- "Slow to make decisions"

EMPLOYMENT CONTACT

nationwide.com/nw/careers

THE SCOOP

On your side

Many people know Nationwide from its "Life Comes at You Fast" ad campaign featuring a rapidly aging Fabio, and sports fans may recognize the company from the Nationwide Arena, home of the NHL's Columbus Blue Jackets. From its humble beginnings insuring farmers in the Buckeye State, Columbus, Ohio-based Nationwide Financial Services, the holding company for Nationwide Life Insurance and other divisions of the insurance giant, is one of the world's largest diversified insurance and financial services firms with over $157 billion in statutory assets with more than 16 million policies in force. Nationwide provides a range of financial and insurance services, including auto, homeowners, life, health, commercial insurance, administrative services, annuities, mutual funds, pensions and long-term savings plans. The firm is ranked No. 108 on the Fortune 500's 2008 list.

Nationwide ranks fourth in homeowner insurance, sixth in auto insurance, and sixth in property and casualty insurance. Nationwide is also the No. 1 provider of qualified retirement plans and sixth in variable life insurance. The firm won a "best in show" award in July 2008 from the Insurance Marketing Communications Association for its recent ad campaign. And in 2007, the company was named a finalist for the American Business Awards for its "success of a new sales process that was developed and implemented across its annuity, life insurance and retirement plans segments" in 2006.

Buckeye nation

In 1919, members of a farmers' collective established their own auto insurance company, the Ohio Farm Bureau Federation, mainly to avoid having to pay city rates. By 1943, the firm operated in 12 states and Washington, D.C., and began to add regional offices in the early 1950s. With westward expansion and the addition of 20 more states, the company changed its name to Nationwide Insurance in 1955. Nationwide continued to grow in the 1960s and 1970s, and in 1978, it moved into its international headquarters, One Nationwide Plaza, a 40-story structure that became Central Ohio's largest office building. The 1980s showed further expansion, as the company added Colonial Insurance of California (1980), Financial Horizons Life (1981), Scottsdale (1982) and Employers Insurance of Wausau (1985). Earnings fluctuated in the 1990s while the company added Wausau and consolidated offices.

Visit the Vault Finance Career Channel at www.vault.com/finance — with insider firm profiles, message boards, the Vault Finance Job Board and more.

VAULT CAREER LIBRARY   269

Nationwide Financial went public in 1996, and the company initiated a reorganization in 2004, splitting the business into segments—individual protection, individual and corporate-owned life insurance; retirement plans, which includes both public and private retirement plan business; individual investments, which includes annuities and advisory services; and in-retirement, made up of other retirement products for individuals.

Planned purchase

In February 2007, the firm announced that it planned to buy NWD Investment Management (formerly known as Gartmore Global Investments). By May 2007, the deal was complete, and Nationwide had forked over more than $240 million in cash for the purchase. Nationwide CEO William Jurgensen said in a statement that the combination of NWD Investment Management's retail mutual fund business with Nationwide Financial's distribution and core investment and packaging capabilities "makes tremendous sense for our customers and shareholders by strengthening our ability to help consumers prepare for and live in retirement."

NWD's name was changed once again—this time to Nationwide Funds, to better match the Nationwide brand. "The ability to offer Nationwide Funds is a natural extension of our core capabilities, and will improve the competitiveness and profitability of Nationwide Financial products," Nationwide Financial president Mark Thresher said. "These new capabilities will ultimately strengthen our ability to help consumers prepare for and live in retirement, while returning value to our shareholders through enhanced opportunities for growth."

Change of plan

In the fall of 2007, Nationwide announced that it would follow in the footsteps of other U.S. life insurers with a plan to subadvise its mutual fund business. The decision meant that an outside company would take over the management of 21 of Nationwide's mutual funds and nine variable insurance trust funds; in September 2007, a deal was inked between Nationwide and Aberdeen Asset Management, Inc., an asset management firm based in the U.K. Aberdeen is currently said to be managing about $7 billion worth of Nationwide's assets.

"This wasn't a profit-driven exercise," John H. Grady, then-president and CEO of Nationwide Funds Group, told BestWire in October 2007. "It was the philosophy of ensuring that we were always putting the best manager in charge of the assets."

Yet, by mid-December, Grady had resigned, and a nationwide search was being conducted to find his replacement. Although Grady reportedly resigned for personal reasons, it's hard to say how much of an effect the takeover by Aberdeen might have had on his decision. Grady continued to head Nationwide Funds after the deal was inked, and more than 40 members of his staff were transferred to Aberdeen to work there. Aberdeen, which has $180 billion in assets, took over the funds for an undisclosed sum.

Third-quarter flop

Nationwide's third quarter 2007 profits dropped 9 percent versus the same period a year earlier, a decrease that the company chalked up to losses on its portfolio of investments. Earnings for the quarter were $147 million, down from $161.9 million in the third quarter of 2006. Due to an increase in the variety of retirement products the company offers, sales skyrocketed 8 percent to $4.4 billion.

News for the year

The full year 2007 results didn't look much better, due to the dull economy, with revenue coming in $4.53 billion for the year, down slightly from the $4.56 billion it brought in 2006. Net income slipped from the previous year to $626.8 million from $724 million.

And for the second quarter 2008, the firm posted $1.08 billion in revenue, down from $1.17 billion in the second quarter of 2007. Net income was down to $85.4 million from $197.3 million in the second quarter 2007. The results were at least a boost from the first quarter of 2007, which brought in $916.3 million in revenue and $44.5 million in net income. The second quarter included a $6.3 million operating loss related to the firms trading portfolio.

On your side

Since 2000, the Nationwide Foundation has donated more than $169 million to nonprofit organizations in the community. That includes a $500,000 donation to the Red Cross Disaster Relief Fund in 2005 as well as the foundation's largest gift yet—a check for $50 million to the Columbus Children's Hospital. The foundation also offered to match all personal contributions of Nationwide employees during the United Way Hurricane

Visit the Vault Finance Career Channel at **www.vault.com/finance** — with insider firm profiles, message boards, the Vault Finance Job Board and more.

VAULT CAREER LIBRARY   271

Katrina Response Fund. Nationwide also dispatched catastrophe response teams of agents, claims representatives and associates from across the country to serve its customers in New Orleans; Nationwide Financial Services helped customers access retirement plan and life insurance assets to cover emergency expenses; and suspended policyholder obligations for at least two months for customers involved in the disaster.

The Nationwide Foundation is an independent corporation that awards grants to nonprofit organizations focused on health and human services, higher education, culture and the arts and civic programs. The company is also a sponsor of all 36 varsity sports at The Ohio State University.

Buyout time

In August 2008, the firm announced that Nationwide Mutual Insurance Co. will buy out Nationwide Financial for $2.4 billion. Nationwide Insurance sold a minority stake in Nationwide Financial in a 1997 IPO. In this transaction, the company will acquire Class A shares of Nationwide Financial for $52.25 per share. The transaction is subject to approval by shareholders but is likely to close by the end of 2008 or early 2009.

GETTING HIRED

Nationwide wants you on its side

Nationwide's careers section (www.nationwide.com/nw/careers) offers a wealth of information for job seekers relating to benefits, university relations. Job seekers are encouraged to upload their resumes and apply for positions online. The company holds resumes in its database for three months, accessing them to match them to newly available posts. Since Nationwide receives over 50,000 resumes annually, its HR department only contacts those whose qualifications best match the needs of the job description. Various career paths at the company include marketing and sales strategy, customer service, financial accounting, insurance, customer solutions center, office service and property management, information systems and technology and human resources.

Not too bad

Expect to come in for several rounds of interviews. One insider reports going in for "four different interviews" with "the same manager who asked the same questions at each one." And don't expect "anything too difficult." Typical questions include "why do you want to work at Nationwide?"

OUR SURVEY SAYS

Opportunity knocks

Nationwide is a "strong values-based organization" that's "family-oriented" and offers "many great aspects" as well as "lots of opportunities." But some insiders report that there's also a "caste system" that can make it difficult to advance "regardless of skill set, educational level or professionalism."

Despite this, "there are many perks" such as an "on-site wellness center," "comprehensive health and wellness programs," and "discounted tickets to various events." Some might consider another perk to be the dress code, which is "business casual with a jeans option on Fridays."

As far as their civic side, Nationwide has a "huge commitment to community service." And on the diversity front, at least they're heading in the right direction—"they are working on diversity but have a ways to go," admits one contact.

Visit the Vault Finance Career Channel at **www.vault.com/finance** — with
insider firm profiles, message boards, the Vault Finance Job Board and more.

VAULT CAREER LIBRARY   273

New York Life Insurance Company

51 Madison Avenue
New York, NY 10010
Phone: (212) 576-7000
Fax: (212) 576-8145
www.newyorklife.com

DEPARTMENTS

Impaired Risk Life & Annuity
Institutional Asset Management
Investments
Life Insurance
Lifetime Income
Long-Term Care Insurance
Sponsored Marketing Relationships
Retail Mutual Funds
Retirement Income
Retirement Plan Services
Securities Products and Services

THE STATS

Employer Type: Private-Mutual
Chairman: Seymour (Sy) Sternberg
President & CEO: Theodore A. (Ted) Mathas
Revenue: $21.12 billion (FYE 12/07)
Net Income: $1.50 billion
No. of Employees: 8,640 (US); 6,207 (abroad)
No. of Offices: Hundreds of U.S. offices (and thousands of career agents)

KEY COMPETITORS

MassMutual
Met Life
Northwestern Mutual
Prudential
TIAA-CREF

UPPERS

- "Very much a feeling of family here"
- Management is "fair, willing to give credit where credit is due"

DOWNERS

- Not much diversity in the upper ranks
- When first starting with the firm, expect "long hours"

EMPLOYMENT CONTACT

See "sales careers and employment" link at www.newyorklife.com

THE SCOOP

Nothing like New York

A Fortune 100 company with more than $280 billion in assets under management as of June 2008, New York Life Insurance Company is the largest mutual life insurer in the United States and one of the largest in the world. Headquartered in New York City, New York Life's family of companies offers life insurance, retirement income, investments and long-term care insurance. New York Life Investment Management LLC provides institutional asset management and retirement plan services. Other New York Life affiliates provide a variety array of securities products and services, as well as institutional and retail mutual funds.

On the investment side, New York Life's affiliates provide institutional asset management and trust services. Through subsidiary NYLIFE Distributors Inc., they offer securities products and services such as institutional and retail mutual funds, including 401(k) products. As a mutual insurance company, New York Life works for the benefit of its policyholders, or members. The company has offices across America, as well as in Argentina, China, Hong Kong, India, Mexico, Taiwan, Thailand and South Korea. And it has earned some of the highest marks for financial strength in the biz; it ranked No. 82 in the 2008 Fortune 500 list of the largest American corporations.

Perhaps its success is best articulated by New York Life Chairman Sy Sternberg: "The primary responsibility of a mutual insurance company is to ensure that the long-term benefits promised to its policyholders are secure and protected. By remaining a mutual, New York Life can continue to manage for the long term, instead of the quarter-to-quarter orientation of the investment community."

History of innovation

New York Life traces its history to 1845 when it opened in New York City as the Nautilus Insurance Company. The insurer changed its moniker to the present-day New York Life Insurance Company just a few years later, in 1849. The company started with assets of just about $17,000, but it wasn't long before its coffers began to swell. Soon, New York Life was making a name for itself through a series of innovative business practices. In 1860, before any state law required it, the company developed the non-forfeiture option, which became the foundation of guaranteed cash values found in

Visit the Vault Finance Career Channel at **www.vault.com/finance** — with insider firm profiles, message boards, the Vault Finance Job Board and more.

VAULT CAREER LIBRARY   275

policies today. This enables a policy to remain in force even when a premium payment is inadvertently missed. By the mid-1800s, New York Life became the first American life insurance company to pay a cash dividend to policyholders, and in 1892, it became the first major company to issue policies with an incontestable clause, setting a time limit on the insurer's right to dispute a policy's validity based on material misstatements made in the application.

The company took a big step in 1894 when it became the first insurer in the U.S. to issue life insurance to women at the same rates as men. In fact, Susan B. Anthony, the 19th-century American social reformer, was an early New York Life policyholder. Then, in 1896, New York Life became the first company to insure people with physical impairments or hazardous occupations. In another industry first, the company issued a policy in 1920 with a disability benefit that presumes total disability to be permanent after a predetermined number of months.

Going to the customer

The company wasn't just forward thinking in terms of how it issued its policies, but also in how it conducted other business-related matters. In 1892, it became the first insurer to organize a branch office system, establishing an integrated network of general offices across the country. Today, these "GOs" serve the company's over 11,000 licensed agents in the U.S. and 41,248 agents internationally. In May 1998, New York Life launched the Virtual Service Center on its web site, becoming the first major life insurer to provide a full range of customer service capabilities on the Web. At the Virtual Service Center, customers can request policy cash, loan and dividend values; download change-of-address and beneficiary forms; report the death of an insured person; and more.

New prez

On July 1, 2008, Ted Mathas assumed the position of chief executive officer of New York Life Insurance Company. Mathas retained the title of president of the company, a post he's held since July 2007. As CEO, he oversees all of the company's U.S. and international operations, including individual life insurance, retirement income, investments and long-term care insurance.

Mathas succeeded Sy Sternberg, New York Life's chairman and chief executive officer since 1997. Sternberg retired after working for the firm for

19 years, including 11 as CEO. Sternberg remains chairman in a non-executive capacity, for a transition period.

Awards galore

There's no lack of diversity at New York Life. The firm took home an International Innovation in Diversity Award from *Profiles in Diversity Journal* in 2008. And the insurer ranked in the Top 50 Corporations for Supplier Diversity in *Hispanic Enterprise* magazine's list for the second year in a row in 2007. For the fifth year in a row, *Family Digest* touted the company in 2007 as one of the 35 Best Companies for African-Americans. It also earned a spot on Hispanic Business' Diversity Elite, which measures the company's commitment to Hispanic hiring, promotion and marketing. *Latina Style* magazine also gave the company a nod, placing it in the top 12 of U.S. employers for Latina execs. The firm also was named to the 100 Best Adoption-Friendly Workplaces in America list for 2008, an award given out by the Dave Thomas Foundation for Adoption.

As if those weren't enough, New York Life also placed on Fortune's 2008 World's Most Admired Companies List (coming in second overall in the life and health sector of the insurance industry category). Previously, in 2007, *BusinessWeek* named it one of the best places to launch a career. And Al Gore advocates will be happy to know that the U.S. Environmental Protection Agency awarded New York Life's headquarters on Madison Avenue with an Energy Star logo, which identifies the office as one of the most efficient buildings in the nation.

Comforting the afflicted

In 2008, the New York Life Foundation continued to make its mark on the community. In July 2008, the foundation gave a $3 million grant to the Comfort Zone Camp, which assists grieving children. The charitable organization, which has donated more than $100 million to nonprofit organizations since 1979, gave more than $300,000 to fund after-school programs in New York, another $310,000 to aid the Brooklyn Public Library and nearly twice that amount to Junior Achievement's Hispanic Initiative. In addition, by the second week of 2008, the foundation had pledged $748,000 to the Child Welfare League of America to help with mentoring programs.

Visit the Vault Finance Career Channel at **www.vault.com/finance** — with insider firm profiles, message boards, the Vault Finance Job Board and more.

VAULT CAREER LIBRARY   **277**

Dominating the Round Table

In 2008, for the 54th consecutive year, New York Life had the most agents on the Million Dollar Round Table, an international association of more than 36,000 of the world's leading life insurance agents and financial service executives. New York Life had a total of 2,167 agents on board—the highest number in the U.S.; the firm also had more female MDRT members than any other U.S. firm. Membership in this prestigious organization is offered to less than 1 percent of those in the industry who qualify.

Good and bad

For 2007, New York Life booked $21.12 billion in revenue, up from $20.98 billion in revenue in 2006. Net income decreased for the year to $1.5 billion from $2.3 billion. Analysts pointed to instability in the financial markets and weak lending practices in the industry as reasons for the declines.

GETTING HIRED

To live and work in New York

Whether you're angling for a long-term position or an internship, your first stop should be the careers section of New York Life's web site, where you can get the skinny on becoming a sales agent with the firm or just find tips on "living and working in New York City." The site also offers links to available opportunities both as an agent and in the corporate office. Potential agents can read about New York Life's training program, benefits package and information about potential income. In addition, the site has a database of job opportunities at New York Life's office locations as well as field positions. Offices are located in Addison, Tex.; Alpharetta, Ga.; Atlanta.; Cleveland; Clinton, N.J.; Dallas.; Leawood, Kan.; Minneapolis; New York; Reno, Nev.; Sleepy Hollow, N.Y.; Stamford, Conn.; Tampa, Fla.; Walnut Creek, Calif.; and Washington, D.C.

During the interview process, "more than anything, they are trying to get a feel for your ability to succeed," confides one insider. So it comes as no surprise that the firm is "extremely selective," notes one source, adding that the firm tends to "interview 25 people in order to hire one." Interview experiences tend to vary depending on department, but one contact says that candidates are normally given a test, and then "at least two interviews to determine suitability. Then they go over compensation and target marketing." There are also "follow-ups on compliance and regulation issues due to the nature of the job." One respondent reports having gone through "a screening interview, a selection interview, a training interview and a compensation interview. Then the company took me and my wife out for dinner." The contact calls the process "very impressive," adding, "They knew—and I knew—that this was the right thing for me to do when the process was completed." You should also be "personable, clean and professional," and it doesn't hurt if "you know how to dress and use a phone."

OUR SURVEY SAYS

All up to you

Insiders report that day-to-day life at the firm is "professional, not stiff" and "great—if you make it." It helps if you start clawing your way to the top from the beginning. "Established agents make a very nice living with great benefits and working conditions," says one contact, but those below the big dogs tend to "battle fiercely" to become an important player within the company. "There is very much a feeling of family here," notes an insider. "The highest level of management is accessible and visible," and "for a company this size, we are a close-knit group." Another says the firm "is stable and keeps its promises to employees," adding, "Since they are not publicly traded, they think long term." Indeed, loyalty seems to run deep as well. One insider "wouldn't consider leaving, even for a $25,000 raise in pay." Management is "fair, willing to give credit where credit is due," "goes to bat for you" and "stands up for you."

When it comes to advancing at the firm, remember that it's a "very unique culture" and consequently, there's "tremendous internal growth." One insider even reports that "very rarely have I seen people come in from the outside." The firm is a very "promote-from-within organization," says another insider, adding that the "best way to get your foot in the door is join the sales force, demonstrate success in sales for at least two years, and then look around the company at other options." Another says, "There is a very clearly defined path into management through the sales area, which is great for someone that would like to recruit, train and coach new hires." The firm also offers a "formalized training program for [the] new salesperson that's highly ranked

Visit the Vault Finance Career Channel at www.vault.com/finance — with insider firm profiles, message boards, the Vault Finance Job Board and more.

VAULT CAREER LIBRARY   279

across all industries." Yet another contact adds, "There are tremendous opportunities for career-minded people who want to work hard." Though, when first starting with the firm, one insider says to expect "long hours along with evenings and weekend appointments occasionally at first."

Be a pro

Dress within the office is "professional" and usually consists of "jackets and ties" for men, although "summer months are a little more lenient—nobody gasps if you lose the jacket and unbutton your collar." Work hours meet with approval. One insider comments that "the hours are more than reasonable"; "generally we're in by 8 a.m. and out by 5 p.m. Sometimes we'll be there until 7 p.m., but there's a lot of downtime." Another employee says "I make my own hours. I tell myself often that if I fail to make it, I have no one to blame but myself." He adds, "New York Life did everything they could to help me, short of handing me hot leads."

Company perks get high marks. There's a "state-of-the-art gym on site," "a company-subsidized cafeteria in the building," "car service and dinner provided if you work late," and "comp days given if you have to work on a weekend." In addition, "continuing education is encouraged"—the firm offers a tuition reimbursement program. New York Life also offers on-site back-up child care and an on-site employees' health department.

A more even playing field

New York Life is "fairly diverse," even if "top-level positions are overrepresented by whites."

And the firm's diversity with respect to women is "getting better," comments an insider. Another says the firm has "specific programs for women, along with those of Indian, Asian, Hispanic and African-American descent." In addition to these areas, the firm has employee network groups for GLBT employees. "The entire industry seems to be dominated by white men, but don't let that discourage you if you are a woman or not white," says one insider. "In my opinion, women have a great chance at success because they're received better by prospects."

Northwestern Mutual Financial Network

720 E. Wisconsin Avenue
Milwaukee, WI 53202-4797
Phone: (414) 271-1444
Fax: (414) 665-9702
www.nmfn.com

SERVICES

Asset & Income Protection
Business Needs Analysis
Comprehensive Financial Planning
Education Funding
Employee & Executive Benefits
Estate Analysis
Investment and Advisory Services
Personal Needs Analysis
Retirement Solutions
Trust Services

THE STATS

Employer Type: Private Company
President and CEO: Edward J. Zore
Net Revenue: $21.36 billion (FYE 12/07)
Net Income: $1 billion
No. of Employees: 5,000 (corporate home office)
No. of Offices: 350+

KEY COMPETITORS

AIG
New York Life
Prudential

UPPERS

- "Flexibility"
- "Our reputation in the industry"
- "The culture is phenomenal"

DOWNERS

- "Wish retention was higher"
- "We could do a better job of attracting women and minorities"
- "You need to come up with leads on your own"

Visit the Vault Finance Career Channel at **www.vault.com/finance** — with
insider firm profiles, message boards, the Vault Finance Job Board and more.

VAULT CAREER LIBRARY   281

THE SCOOP

Happy anniversary

If you thumb through editions of Milwaukee's hometown paper, the *Journal-Sentinel*, you'll note that Northwestern Mutual plays an important part in the business culture of the city. March 2, 2007 marked the company's 150th anniversary in the southeastern Wisconsin city, and the paper responded by publishing a retrospective of sorts, calling it a "key corporate citizen." The paper noted the more than $630 million the insurer has invested in the city.

Northwestern has also been named America's Most Admired insurance company by *Fortune* magazine for the past 25 years. Ranked No. 110 on 2008's Fortune 500 (moving two spots up from 2007), it has $157 billion in assets and a long, storied history. (When 13 of its clients died in the sinking of the Titanic, Northwestern dished out a total of $500,000 for the policies—more than any other insurer.) Even today, Northwestern pays out more in total individual life insurance dividends than any other company in its industry.

There's more to life than insurance

Best known as one of the oldest insurance companies in the United States, Northwestern Mutual (a.k.a. "The Quiet Company") is also the largest direct provider of individual life insurance in the country. Founded in 1857 by New Yorker John Johnston, the company moved to its headquarters on Wisconsin Avenue in 1910 and has been there ever since.

In addition to life insurance, Northwestern provides a variety of investment products and services. The company offers individual and institutional investment management through its Northwestern Mutual Investment Services (NMIS) subsidiary. Its subsidiary Russell Investment Group provides investment management and advisory services, and Northwestern Mutual Wealth Management Company provides financial planning, investment management and trust services. Long-term care insurance is offered through another subsidiary, Northwestern Long Term Care Insurance Company.

Financial firsts

In February 2007, Northwestern announced that it had reached $1 trillion of individual life insurance protection—a first in the industry. The company hit its milestone in January, after adding more than $100 billion of coverage in 2006. "It's interesting that it's coming at a time when we are going to celebrate our 150th anniversary, and comes right on top of probably the greatest year we've ever had when you look at all the metrics of the company," President and CEO Ed Zore told the *Journal-Sentinel*.

The anniversary year seemed to be a good omen for the company. In October 2007, it reached another milestone: its wealth management division, founded in 2001, reached $10 billion in assets under management.

Career power

In November 2007, Northwestern earned top honors in *Selling Power* magazine's annual 50 Best Companies to Sell For survey. It was the fifth consecutive year that the company had placed, but the first time that it came in first for service.

Based on data gathered through extensive surveys of each corporate candidate, *Selling Power*'s list focuses on three key categories: compensation, training and career mobility. Using these categories, the selection committee takes into account such metrics as average starting salaries, benefit packages, company-sponsored sales training, turnover and advancement opportunities. The ranking primarily takes place among companies with sales forces larger than 500.

Good will

There's no shortage of heart at Northwestern, either. The company regularly makes significant donations to charity and the community. The insurer marked its 150th anniversary by pledging to give more than $3 million away, including $265,000 to nonprofit organizations across the Midwest. It also donated $1.5 million—to be split between Goodwill, YMCA, Second Harvest, and Junior Achievement.

In September, Northwestern also threw $1 million toward the Milwaukee Public Museum to aid in its 2008 exhibit, "Body Worlds." The donation marked the largest corporate gift in the museum's history.

Visit the Vault Finance Career Channel at **www.vault.com/finance** — with insider firm profiles, message boards, the Vault Finance Job Board and more.

VAULT CAREER LIBRARY   283

Accolades all around

In 2008, Northwestern Mutual upheld the top ratings in insurance strength from the rating agencies Standard & Poor's, Fitch Ratings, A.M. Best and Moody's. In February 2008, the University of Michigan revealed that Northwestern won the highest customer satisfaction score for life insurers in the college's American Customer Satisfaction Index for the fifth consecutive year.

Its financials looked good, too. In 2007, the company's revenue rose to $21.3 billion, an increase from $19.3 billion in 2006, and net income came in at $1 billion, a 21 percent increase.

GETTING HIRED

Finding the fit

"Whether it is for staff or financial representatives, we go through a several-step recruiting process," a Northwestern Mutual insider says. It's designed to be "a selection process that truly determines mutual fit." "We look to find the best fit for us and the individual," a woman explains. "The candidate needs to want to be here as much as we want them to be here. The need to see themselves being just as successful as we see them being."

As a result, recruiting can be selective. One source estimates that "we meet with about 190 people from the [online application process] to find one person that is a good fit." For candidates who have been referred by someone else in the company, "we meet with about 50 referrals to find the one good fit." Another employee says that the firm's "commission-based compensation structure" can seem daunting to some potential hires— "this scares a lot of candidates away."

Northwestern Mutual accepts resumes submitted through its web site, posts openings on online job boards, and recruits at "local colleges and universities" located near its offices. "Our own financial representatives and staff referrals" play a role, too.

A chance to learn more

"For the financial representative role, there are typically four or five meetings with three or four different people in leadership," sources say. Potential interns have a shorter, "three-step" recruiting process, but the "same questions are asked in the first interview for full-time and intern candidates." After that, "the process becomes more customized." Adds an insider, "The process is a learning process for the candidates and us to find more and more information about them, and also for them to find more information about us."

As candidates progress through the interview rounds, they may meet with "the managing director of the office," "selected financial representatives, the managing partner and staff." Final interviews are held "at the local office they hope to be housed in."

Odds are good

"On average, one in three interns will convert to a full-time career with us," so it's no wonder that "we really advise college students to intern with us first." Northwestern Mutual sources brag that their company offers "the best financial services internship from a perspective of experience and real-world exposure." Interns "can see the career very clearly before they graduate. They do exactly what our full-time representatives do, but normally the activity expectations are a little less." "They are to build their clientele through their natural market, figure out the financial needs of the client and then provide those services."

Internships are offered for "up to 10 weeks each semester—spring, summer and fall" and compensation "is based on three components: base stipend, commission and bonuses."

OUR SURVEY SAYS

Stay free

Though culture can vary by office location, sources say that it's generally "fantastic" and "supportive." "The people here are great to work with," a respondent adds. "Everybody is invested in the others succeeding." That

Visit the Vault Finance Career Channel at **www.vault.com/finance** — with
insider firm profiles, message boards, the Vault Finance Job Board and more.

VAULT CAREER LIBRARY   285

means that co-workers are "very generous of their time to help each other and support the growth of the agency and company." "Northwestern Mutual Financial Network is a large family that really cares about you professionally and personally," a satisfied source says. "We want to see you succeed in both aspects of your life."

The "fun, positive, energetic" vibe is "extremely motivating," and there's an emphasis on "high integrity," "excellent coaching and mentoring." Best of all, sources say, they have "a degree of independence and flexibility, while having a large support network" and other key "resources."

You're the boss

For the most part, Northwestern Mutual employees are happy with their hours. "I schedule my own appointments," says a source. "I know what my activity numbers should be, and I work very independently." Another insider goes even further: "I have total freedom."

According to the company web site, financial representatives work toward minimum earning levels that all are expected to achieve. "For full-time representatives, it is commission-based," an insider reports. "They can earn a training allowance" during the first four years, which provides enhanced commissions on the sales of certain policies and contracts. Still, Northwestern Mutual gets high marks for compensation, and employees like their perks, which include "a profit-sharing plan with safe harbor and a 401(k)." The company also offers medical, life and disability insurance; maternity leave; retirement plans; and assistance plans for employees who need child or elder care plans.

Learning and leading

New hires begin with initial training that, according to the firm, covers "industry and sales training as well as mentoring and joint work programs for hands-on experience." Further down the road, employees can take advantage of online training programs, career development events and opportunities to obtain advanced professional designations. Training and career development is directed by local network offices.

"We have an extraordinary training structure and process throughout the career," an insider raves. "We take a faculty approach; our most successful reps and specialists are teaching and developing our new representatives."

Managers and supervisors are described as "role models," and subordinates say they enjoy "good relationships" across the board.

Take another step

Northwestern Mutual receives mostly high marks on its diversity efforts, but some say it could be more proactive on these fronts. "I think that we could do a better job of attracting more women and minorities into the business," one woman says. "We could speak to women's organizations on the benefits of the career," one source suggests. Another thinks Northwestern Mutual could be "highlighting women and minorities who have been successful, and putting them in leadership positions." According to the firm, it offers leadership training in diversity, as well as career counseling and internal mentoring efforts.

When it comes to getting dressed in the morning, Northwestern Mutual employees say it's "formal always."

Visit the Vault Finance Career Channel at **www.vault.com/finance** — with
insider firm profiles, message boards, the Vault Finance Job Board and more.

VAULT CAREER LIBRARY   287

Pacific Life Insurance Company

700 Newport Center Drive
Newport Beach, CA 92660
Phone: (949) 219-3011
www.pacificlife.com

DIVISIONS

Annuities & Mutual Funds
Corporate
Investment Management
Life Insurance
Real Estate

THE STATS

Employer Type: Mutual Holding
Company President & CEO: James T. Morris
Revenue: $5.04 billion (FYE 12/07)
No. of Employees: 2,900

KEY COMPETITORS

MetLife
New York Life
Prudential

EMPLOYMENT CONTACT

See "job opportunities" at
www.pacificlife.com

THE SCOOP

New President and CEO

Founded in 1868, Pacific Life provides life insurance products, annuities, mutual funds and other investment products and services to individuals, businesses and pension plans. The company counts more than half of the 50 largest U.S. companies as clients. Its subsidiaries include Aviation Capital Group, College Savings Bank, Pacific Asset Funding, Pacific Life Re and Pacific Select Distributors.

In April 2007, it named a new chief, as James T. Morris became the president and CEO of Pacific Life Insurance Company, replacing Thomas C. Sutton who had worked at the company for 43 years, including 17 as CEO. Morris has worked at Pacific Life ever since joining the company in 1982 as an assistant actuary. Since 2006, he served as chief operating officer, overseeing the annuities and mutual funds division, the life insurance division and Pacific Select Group. He has also held positions as executive vice president and chief insurance officer.

Sutton stepped down when he reached 65, the company's mandatory retirement age. He retired as chairman in May 2008 but remains a director on the board. In July 2007, the Pacific Life Foundation, the philanthropic division of Pacific Life, committed $1 million to endow a Thomas C. Sutton Chair in Policy Research at the Public Policy Institute of California to honor Sutton for his contributions to the company.

140 years and counting

In May 1878, 10 years after the firm was founded, U.S. Senator (and Stanford University founder) Leland Stanford and the first president of Pacific Mutual Life received the first life insurance policy from the company, then headquartered in Sacramento, Calif. By 1905, the corporation had grown to operate in 40 states. Headquarters moved to San Francisco in 1881 and Los Angeles in 1906.

The company continued to merge with other insurance companies. In 1966, "Project '66," a group of eight employees tasked with determining the structure of an insurance company in the future. The group decided that the company should transition from a highly clerical staff to a technical staff that could make use of new computer technology. The company purchased land

Visit the Vault Finance Career Channel at **www.vault.com/finance** — with insider firm profiles, message boards, the Vault Finance Job Board and more.

VAULT CAREER LIBRARY

289

in Newport Center in Newport Beach in 1970 and moved into its present office in 1972.

In September 1997, Pacific Mutual Life Insurance completed its change into a mutual holding company structure. The life insurance company, formerly known as Pacific Mutual Life, became a stock life insurance company, renamed Pacific Life. All policy owners are members of Pacific Mutual Holding Company, which ultimately owns and controls Pacific Life. In 2002, Pacific Life bought College Savings Bank, which gave the company entry into the 529 College Savings Plan market. The bank celebrated its 21st anniversary in 2008.

Focusing on life insurance

Life insurance policies remain at the heart of Pacific Life's business. In the past decade, the company increased its life insurance sales by an average of about 11 percent, compared to an industry average annual increase of about three percent. The business maintains its edge by continually introducing new diversified products and riders. In 2007, new product introductions for policyholders included riders that guaranteed annual distributions in retirement, and access to Fidelity lifecycle portfolios.

New structured credit department

In May 2007, Pacific Life announced the formation of a new asset management affiliate, Pacific Asset Management, which focuses on serving the growing market for structured credit. The affiliate serves as a third party in transactions involving investment grade and high-yield corporate bonds, leveraged loans and credit derivatives. Pacific Life will give capital, legal, operational and technical support for the project. Rex Olson, former head of credit research at Pacific Life, will oversee the creation of Pacific Asset Management.

Nesting in Nebraska

In 2005, Pacific Life Insurance Company completed a legal redomestication process under which it moved its official offices to Nebraska to take advantage of tax and other savings available in the state. As part of the process, the company opened a regional business center for 250 employees in Omaha, to house portions of the internal wholesaling, operations, technology and support staff for its annuities and mutual funds division as well as its life insurance division. The Greater Omaha Chamber of Commerce estimated in 2004 that the move would fetch the region about $31.5 million.

Despite the legal change, the company's principal administrative offices remained in Orange County, Calif. In the first quarter of 2008, the company opened a new 246,806-square-foot building there, which houses about 1,000 employees in the life insurance division, in Aliso Viejo near its Newport Beach location.

Flying high

Pacific Life's subsidiary Aviation Capital Group represents one of the top five commercial aircraft operating lessors in the world. In September 2007, the company signed contracts to purchase an additional 35 planes. The group's leases aircraft to 98 airlines in 42 countries. It also provides asset management and remarketing services to aircraft investors and institutional clients.

The latest figures

In 2007, the company brought in $5.04 billion in revenue, a 5 percent increase from 2006. Net income, meanwhile, increased by 16 percent to $654 million. The firm managed to stay afloat despite the choppy financial waters in the industry—it saw growth in nearly all its groups over the course of the year, and its annuity sales unit increased 12 percent in 2007.

Across the Atlantic

In August 2008, Pacific acquired Scottish Re Holdings Limited as well as the U.K. and Asia portions of the international life reinsurance segment of Scottish Re Group Limited. The purchased businesses, which will be rebranded as Pacific Life Re, provide reinsurance services to insurance and annuity providers in the United Kingdom, Ireland and Asia. The headquarters will stay in London, and the Asia businesses will be run from Singapore.

Visit the Vault Finance Career Channel at **www.vault.com/finance** — with insider firm profiles, message boards, the Vault Finance Job Board and more.

VAULT CAREER LIBRARY   291

GETTING HIRED

Go Pacific

Under the "job opportunities" link at www.pacificlife.com, candidates can learn about the company's culture, benefits offered and opportunities to grow within the firm. And of course, Pacific Life also provides a plethora of job openings for experienced hires. But the site isn't geared only toward employees who have several years of workplace experience under their belts. The firm also has a section on its site devoted to college recruitment, including a list of its upcoming campus visits.

Internships are also offered to interested students. Both MBA students and undergrads are encouraged to apply for the internships, which take place over the summer. If you're keen on snagging one, though, make sure you get into gear quickly—Pacific Life notes that recruiting begins in winter and early spring.

The Progressive Corporation

6300 Wilson Mills Road
Mayfield Village, OH 44143
Phone: (800) 766-4737
www.progressive.com

DEPARTMENTS

Commercial Auto
Personal Lines
Other-indemnity

THE SCOOP

That's progress

Most people think of Progressive as the auto insurer that pioneered giving its rates over the phone—in addition to its competitors' rates. True, the Progressive Corporation provides private automobile insurance, but it also has other specialty property/casualty insurance and related services, and operates in three segments: personal lines, commercial auto and other indemnity. The personal lines segment writes insurance for private passenger automobiles and recreational vehicles through both an independent insurance agency channel and a direct channel. The commercial auto segment writes primary liability and physical damage insurance for automobiles and trucks owned by small businesses primarily through the independent agency channel. The other-indemnity segment provides professional liability insurance to community banks, principally directors, and officer's liability insurance. It also provides insurance-related services, primarily providing policy issuance and claims adjusting services in 25 states. The company is headquartered in Mayfield Village, Ohio, and ranked No. 175 in the 2008 Fortune 500 ranking of America's largest companies (based on 2007 revenue).

Joe and Jack

On March 10, 1937, two young lawyers, Joseph Lewis and Jack Green, started Progressive Mutual Insurance Company in order to provide vehicle owners with security and protection. And ever since its earliest days, Progressive has taken an innovative approach to auto insurance. Case in point: It was the first auto insurance company to offer drive-in claims service, as well as the first to accept installment payments in addition to traditional annual payments, an early hint that the company is all about making auto insurance more accessible to more people.

The firm grew through the 1960s, and went public in 1971. Three years later, it relocated its headquarters to the Cleveland suburb of Mayfield Village, and kept growing steadily for the next 20 years. In 1987, it surpassed $1 billion in premiums and was listed by the New York Stock Exchange as PGR. In 1992, it was recognized as the largest seller of auto insurance through independent insurance agents. In 1994, the firm surpassed $2 billion in written premiums and introduced 1-800-AUTO-PRO, a cutting-edge auto insurance rate comparison shopping service. Consumers no longer had to compare different insurers' rates; with one phone call, they could get a quote from Progressive and comparison rates for up to three competitors. If they chose to buy from Progressive, they could purchase a policy right over the phone.

In 1995, when the Internet was just gaining popularity, Progressive stepped ahead of the competition and became the first major auto insurer in the world to launch a web site. It was primarily informational, but soon became more interactive. By 1996, consumers could obtain comparison rates online, and by 1997, they could buy auto insurance policies online in real time.

Today, Progressive is the third largest auto insurance group in the United States., thanks to such innovations as comparison rates and 24/7 customer and claims service. The firm's net income came in at $1.2 billion for 2007, down significantly from $1.65 billion in 2006. Revenue on the year, meanwhile, came in at $14.68 billion in 2007, down just slightly from the $14.79 billion in 2006.

The first half of 2008 looked to be slightly down—but not horribly so, given the problems that have plagued the industry. Revenue for the second quarter 2008 came in at $3.54 billion, down from $3.68 billion the firm booked in the second quarter 2007 but about on par with the $3.59 billion it posted in the first quarter 2007. Net income for the second quarter 2008 came in at $215 million, down from $283 million in the previous year and also down from the $239 million the firm posted in the first quarter 2007. Analysts indicated that the auto insurance industry is suffering because there have been fewer drivers after the nation saw gas prices hit record highs in 2008.

How low can you go?

In March 2007, Progressive decided to lower its prices by about 8 percent for certain auto policies. The cuts, Renwick reported, were effective within 27 states. In April of the same year, the firm announced that it would also be cutting its insurance rates for motorcycles, boats and RVs.

Some insiders said the cuts were spurred on by ongoing competition between Progressive and its major rival, Geico. Indeed, even Progressive CEO Renwick conceded the contention in a press release, commenting that "Progressive is always at its best when it's getting challenged," adding, "I think you're going to find it's a Geico/Progressive fight for a good number of years to come."

Visit the Vault Finance Career Channel at **www.vault.com/finance** — with insider firm profiles, message boards, the Vault Finance Job Board and more.

VAULT CAREER LIBRARY   **295**

But Progressive's plan to sell more premiums at a lower price didn't exactly pan out. According to TheStreet.com, 2007 was the first year since 1999 that the nationwide average cost of auto insurance premiums had decreased. The rate of growth in personal auto premiums was so slow, in fact, that an analyst at Credit Suisse likened it to "watching paint dry or grass grow." In October 2007, Progressive's net income dropped 42 percent from the same period the year before. In November 2007, net income fell 29 percent.

Play ball

Cleveland Indian fans might now have auto insurance on the brain. In January 2008, Progressive signed a 16-year deal that gave the company naming rights to Jacobs Field in Cleveland. The site will now be known as Progressive Field, and Progressive will become the official insurer of the Cleveland Indians.

"This is a story about two Cleveland-based organizations making a long-term commitment to the city, the fans and our people," Renwick said in a statement.

The deal means that Progressive will be required to pay the Cleveland Indians $3.6 million annually for the 16-year period. Joseph Lewis and Jack Green started Progressive just blocks away from the Indians' original stadium.

They're No. 1

Progressive took home some noteworthy awards recently. In May 2008, Progressive was honored by Fortune as one of the 20 Great Employers for New Grads. In the same year, the firm came in as No. 1 for positive Web-based customer experiences according to The Customer Respect Group. And within the first quarter of 2008, the company also came in No. 1 on Keynote Systems' Insurance Carrier Scorecard—which marks the 12th consecutive time the firm has landed the highest spot on the list. But that wasn't the end of Progressive's 2008 accolades—the firm's MyRate program, which gives safe drivers financial incentives, also made Fast Company's 2008 Fast 50 Reader Favorite list in August.

Going to the dogs

Pet owners no longer have to worry that in the event of a car accident, their mutts might not be covered. Progressive's new policy offers insurance for animals who are injured during a collision; as part of the collision coverage at no extra cost, the policy will pay $500 if a pet is harmed during an accident. The company reports that this policy is now available in 46 states and Washington, D.C.; it soon hopes to offer the same deal to residents of North Carolina, New Hampshire, New York, and Virginia soon.

Green moves

In April 2008, the firm unveiled a creative environmental initiative. Those customers who eschew receiving paper statements and sign up for electronic statements will, in exchange, receive a tree planted in their honor. In its replanting efforts, Progressive will also target national forests whose trees have been partially destructed by fires.

GETTING HIRED

Just their type

On its career site, the company says its "type" of employee is the "curious, reliable and driven" sort. If you happen to be one of those (or, says one insider, if you're "very young," which is what the firm "tends to hire"), check out the careers section of Progressive's web site (jobs.progressive.com), where job seekers have the ability to create an account and upload their resumes to apply for positions online. The various career paths available at the company include claims, IT, customer service, inside sales and professional positions that assist customers by offering "superior buying, ownership and claims experiences." Progressive staffers work out of six major locations across the country: Austin, Cleveland, Colorado Springs, Phoenix, Sacramento and Tampa. Additionally, there are links for students and recent graduates to find information of recruiting events where they can speak with Progressive representatives, as well as information on the internships offered.

Calm down

The interview process is "pretty relaxed," but be prepared to have a lot of tales to tell once you're called in. Says one insider, "The entire interview involves you telling stories about how you handle or would handle various scenarios put forth by the interviewer." Another reports receiving "behavior-based questions." Yet another says she went through her first interview with a recruiter via phone, "had to go in and take a logic test by computer," and then had a "second interview with

Visit the Vault Finance Career Channel at **www.vault.com/finance** — with insider firm profiles, message boards, the Vault Finance Job Board and more.

VAULT CAREER LIBRARY   297

two branch managers." And since the second interview went well, "they waived the third interview with two branch managers." One source confirms, "It was a lot of interviewing," but adds that "the process moved very quickly."

As the process progressed, you might be asked an assortment of different interview questions, such as "Name a time that you disagreed with a co-worker," "Name an example of a time that you were able to motivate other people," "Give an example of a time that you had to do something without any directions" and "Give an example of a time that you had to learn something new—what was your process?"

OUR SURVEY SAYS

Treat 'em right

All in all, "Progressive is a great place to work" and "treats its people well." Some employees call the culture "stressful," but others say, "Many of those who complain about having too much to do are unorganized or inefficient." One insider says that Progressive "is probably the best company I have ever worked for," and "the work environment is great." Others add that "advancement can be quick if you are good." Indeed, there's "great opportunity for advancement." Although "turnover can be high," "the possibilities are great if you stick it out."

Perks, too, are great if you're lucky to work at one of the firm's larger centers. At those, Progressive offers a "fitness center," "health services center" and "convenience store." One employee who's worked at Progressive for five years says that "with five years of service, I have 25 days of vacation per year in addition to the six company holidays." As a bonus to traditional perks, "there is essentially no dress code for people who do not work with clients— shorts, jeans, T-shirts and sandals are commonly sported by employees." And "even those who work with customers are only required to wear khaki pants and polo shirts—never suits." "The dress code is business casual, and there's a wide range of how people take that," admits one worker. "I personally wear a solid color shirt and corduroys to work every day, and it's acceptable. Guys mostly wear sweaters, turtlenecks, polo shirts, and button-down shirts paired with khakis." And while "there are people who dress up more, it's really not necessary."

Clocking in and out at reasonable hours

Most employees say it's hard to beat the hours. "Most people in corporate roles work 40 to 50 hours per week"—"the parking lot is empty by 7 p.m." Additionally, "many employees have flexible work arrangements to work as early as 6 a.m. to 3 p.m. or work a few days from home." Other sources report "the hours are long," and "even though you only work 40 hours on paper, it takes about a year-and-a-half to actually become proficient enough to leave within an hour of your quitting time." However, there are conflicting reports. One respondent says, "The workload is large, but not impossible. I have not needed to put in any extra time." Overall employees say, "The workload for most employees is reasonable" and allows "for a nice work-life balance." Even so, "advancement in the corporate world can be difficult," and "many analysts strive to become product managers but are not able to." Instead, "product managers tend to be external people hired from top MBA schools and not promoted from within." Because of this, "many strong analysts leave Progressive after five to eight years to become a product manager somewhere else." But not all employees have a bone to pick with the advancing process. "If there's something you want to do as far as your career, they'll help you get there," says one insider. "I've been working for this company for four years, and I've moved fairly quickly through the ranks."

Managing them well

And when it comes to their current bosses, employees are happy with the way they're treated. "The open-door policy is truly an open-door policy." "The managers are always willing to discuss any situation that comes up, whether work-related or personal. They are very willing to help in any way that they can." One insider says, "The manager that I've been under for about two years has pushed me to apply for promotions and always has faith in my ability to meet new challenges."

The company could give more weight to expanding diversity efforts, sources say. One insider adds, "The minorities at the office pretty much resemble the areas where the offices are located," but another notes, "There is no diversity in management."

Generally, employees seem mostly content with imagining a future at Progressive. "I have been very happy with Progressive and intend to stay with the company for a while," says one insider. "I love that my hard work is recognized and appreciated." Employees report they are "encouraged to

Visit the Vault Finance Career Channel at www.vault.com/finance — with insider firm profiles, message boards, the Vault Finance Job Board and more.

VAULT CAREER LIBRARY   299

Prudential Financial

751 Broad Street
Newark, NJ 07102-3777
Phone: (973) 802-6000
Fax: (973) 02-4479
www.prudential.com

DEPARTMENTS

Benefits & Services
Commercial Property
Institutional Investors
Insurance
Investments
Real Estate

THE STATS

Employer Type: Public Company
Ticker Symbol: PRU (NYSE)
Chairman & CEO: John R. Strangfeld Jr.
Revenue: $34.40 billion (FYE 12/07)
Net Income: $3.70 billion
No. of Employees: 38,853
No. of Offices: 70

KEY COMPETITORS

AXA Financial
Citigroup
MetLife

UPPER

- "Growing and innovative business"

DOWNER

- "Not particularly great or competitive overall compensation"

EMPLOYMENT CONTACT

See "careers" link at
www.prudential.com

THE SCOOP

Rocking the insurance industry

Prudential's logo, the Rock of Gibraltar, is one of the most recognizable corporate symbols. For years, Prudential has tried to capitalize on its image of solidity as one of the largest and most reputable insurance companies in the United States. According to *Fortune* magazine, it is the No. 2 U.S. life insurance company, one of the top insurers in the world and ranked 74th among the 2008 Fortune 500. Prudential's offerings include life insurance, annuities, mutual funds, asset management, and pension- and retirement-related investments and administration. The company also provides brokerage services through a minority interest in Wachovia Securities LLC, a partnership created by the 2003 merger of Wachovia's and Prudential's retail brokerage businesses. The new corporation, 62 percent of which is owned by Wachovia and 38 percent by Prudential, had total client assets of over $1.2 trillion as of June 2008, with approximately 3,800 brokerage locations.

The firm's business is organized into two main units: financial services and closed block. The financial services business operates through three operating divisions: insurance, investment, and international insurance and investments. The closed block business, established in December of 2001 at the time of demutualization, is managed separately from the financial services businesses. Closed block business includes the firm's participating assets and insurance and annuity products that are used for the payment of benefits and policyholder dividends on these products; it also includes other assets and equity that support these products and related liabilities. Due to the demutualization, Prudential no longer offers these participating products.

Solid as a rock

Prudential can trace its history to the Prudential Friendly Society, founded in 1875. The next year, Prudential issued its first death claim, for $10, and adopted the familiar image of the Rock of Gibraltar as its corporate logo. In 1943, Prudential mutualized, becoming a company owned by its policyholders. By 1966, Prudential had grown significantly, outstripping Metropolitan Life as America's largest insurance firm. In 1981, it diversified into the investment business through the acquisition of the securities brokerage firm Bache Halsey Stuart Shields, which led to the creation of Prudential Securities. The 1990s were less halcyon: several states began to investigate Prudential's sales practices, including allegations of "churning"

Visit the Vault Finance Career Channel at www.vault.com/finance — with insider firm profiles, message boards, the Vault Finance Job Board and more.

VAULT CAREER LIBRARY   301

clients. Despite active efforts by the company to correct any abuses, 30 states determined that Prudential had knowingly permitted wrongdoing by 1996, and by 2000, the company had paid out $2.8 billion in settlement fees.

Buying and selling

In addition to the divisional restructuring and the retail brokerage merger of 2003, Prudential has been very active in both acquiring and divesting assets and businesses. In 1998, Prudential sold much of its $6 billion worth of its national real estate holdings, including the its Prudential Center in Boston and the Embarcadero Center in San Francisco to Mortimer Zuckerman's Boston Properties group for $1.74 billion.

It also sold its health care business to the Hartford-based Aetna Corp. in 1999 in a transaction worth $1 billion. Meanwhile, the company acquired insurance firms Gibraltar Life in April 2001 and American Skandia, the U.S. division of Sweden's Skandia Insurance Company, in May 2003. Both have positively affected Prudential's bottom line. More recently, the Prudential Real Estate Investors (PREI) unit acquired Berlin's ewerk office and the Videojet Technologies headquarters building in Chicago in March 2007.

Legal wrangle

In December 2006, Prudential agreed to pay $19 million to settle a New York State investigation into its group insurance business and to change its business practices. The settlement was the latest in a series won by outgoing New York Attorney General Eliot Spitzer (now governor of New York) as part of an investigation into alleged price fixing and bid rigging in the insurance industry. Prudential will pay $2.5 million in penalties to New York State and $16.5 million to certain group insurance policyholders. Spitzer had been fighting to do away with contingent commissions, which insurers offer to brokers who steer business toward their company. The commissions represent a potential conflict of interest for the brokers, who might not be getting the best price for their clients.

Taking the helm

On January 1, 2008, John R. Strangfeld, Prudential's vice chairman and a 30-year veteran of the company, took over as chief executive officer. Srangfeld succeeded Arthur F. Ryan, who retired at the end of 2007. "The board's decision to name John as the company's new CEO and chairman-elect represented the culmination of a thoughtful succession process that began nearly two years ago," Ryan said in a statement.

Strangfeld became chairman of the board when Ryan retired from that position in May 2008. In addition, Prudential Vice Chairman Mark Grier, who controls all of Prudential's international businesses, was named to the board of directors. Grier and Strangfeld will work together to "shape and drive Prudential's strategic agenda," Ryan said.

Going east

In December 2007, Prudential's real estate investment arm, Prudential Real Estate Investors, acquired Round Hill Capital Partners Kabushiki Kaisha, a real estate management firm located in Japan. According to a statement from Prudential, Round Hill—around since 2001—has provided asset management services to PREI for the past five years, including 19 investments worth a total of $1.5 billion.

As Prudential's real-estate market in Japan and Northern Asia continues to expand, the acquisition will aid in building PREI's presence in the area. "As real estate markets and investor allocations have become significantly more global, Asia has become a more important part of PREI's global growth strategy," Victoria Shigehira Sharpe, a PREI managing director and CEO of PREI-Asia, said in a press release.

Terms of the deal were not disclosed; PREI has operated in Asia since 1994 out of its Singapore office.

Make a deal

Prudential Financial is committed to expand its presence in India as well. In December 2007, the finance giant partnered with DLF Group, India's largest real estate developer, to develop a joint venture company. The effort is Prudential Financial's first experience with the Indian mutual fund market. Prudential now owns 61 percent of the joint venture; DLF will own 39 percent. The new company is called DLF Pramerica Asset Managers Private Limited.

Closing time

Prudential made the difficult decision to shut down its equity research group in June 2007. On June 6th, the company said that effective immediately it

Visit the Vault Finance Career Channel at **www.vault.com/finance** — with insider firm profiles, message boards, the Vault Finance Job Board and more.

VAULT CAREER LIBRARY   **303**

would be shuttering the equity research, sales and trading business, and would drop its coverage of the companies and industries that it followed.

An analyst from Keefe, Bruyette & Woods told *Forbes* that rumors about the unit's demise had been floating around. And TheStreet.com reported that Prudential had been shopping the unit around just two months prior. The unit contributed revenue of $260 million in 2006—a drop in the bucket considering Prudential's overall revenue of nearly $32.5 billion. The equity research unit affected nine U.S. offices and four offices overseas—roughly 35 analysts and 80 traders.

Female friendly

The firm regularly picks up honors and awards for its workplace environment.

In March 2008, for the second year in a row, Prudential was named one of the Top Companies for Executive Women by the National Association for Female Executives, which selects top companies based on their representation of women overall, in senior management and on their boards of directors. In addition, in 2008, for the eighth consecutive year, Prudential Financial was ranked by DiversityInc as one of the Top 50 Companies for Diversity. In the latest rankings, Prudential came in at No. 24 for the second consecutive year. Prudential has also been ranked on *Essence* magazine's list of the 25 Great Places to Work for Black Women, *Working Mother*'s 100 Best Companies for Working Mothers list and *LatinaStyle*'s list of the 50 Best Companies for Latinas to Work in the U.S. Additionally, if you're a newbie, never fear: *BusinessWeek* placed Prudential at No. 30 on its 2007 list of the 50 Best Places to Launch a Career.

The volunteers

Prudential's Global Volunteer Day, formerly known as Prudential's National Volunteer Day, grew out of its local initiatives area, which coordinates volunteer efforts by Prudential employees and works to address community needs. The first company-wide Volunteer Day was held in 1995 with 5,000 employees participating in 100 projects. It now includes more than 32,000 participants at about 900 projects in more than 15 countries. The day is organized by employees who independently identify partner organizations or issues to which they want to donate their efforts. Projects range from building homes to tutoring students, running in marathons, collecting clothes and feeding the homeless. Prudential Financial's 13th annual Global Volunteer Day will be held in October 2008.

Looking up ... and down

In 2007, Prudential brought in $34.4 billion in revenue, an increase from the $32.27 billion it posted in 2006. Net income in 2007 came in at $3.7 billion, up from $3.43 billion in the previous year. More recently, for the second quarter 2008, Prudential brought in $7.7 billion in revenue, down from the $8.43 billion it posted versus the same period a year earlier. Net income for the second quarter was $590 million, down from the $846 million it posted in the second quarter 2007. Ongoing poor conditions in the financial markets and decreased asset-based fees led to the poor results.

GETTING HIRED

Only the best

Get ready to dazzle 'em, because "the company is searching for the best talent in the marketplace," comments one contact. Prudential's extensive careers section of its web site allows candidates to search for jobs by department and location, and offers prospective hires the ability to create an online profile, which the firm uses to match up with open positions. The site also describes the culture at Prudential and the benefits the firm offers to staff, and has a college recruiting section that gives graduates an idea of what majors typically go with what positions. Aside from college recruiting and its own web site, the firm also hires through newspaper ads and employee referrals. Insiders report going through at least two rounds of interviews. One source says, "I interviewed with a recruiter, the hiring manager and the hiring manager's superior." It's not easy to land a spot these days. "Labor is abundant and companies are a lot more fussy about looking for the exact fit," adds that contact. "You have to sell your skills in relation to the job. Money is tight all over."

Another contact reports that "the first interview was standard." The contact goes on to say that candidates "are tested on reading comprehension and mathematics" as well as "future plans and career goals." Of course, also expect to be asked about "prior experience." An analyst says he went through "two interviews, one with a director and one with an HR employee." One contact, who went through a headhunter to land a spot at Pru, says, "I interviewed with someone in human

Visit the Vault Finance Career Channel at **www.vault.com/finance** — with insider firm profiles, message boards, the Vault Finance Job Board and more.

VAULT CAREER LIBRARY   **305**

resources first, who asked me salary information on the first interview, and that shocked me. They wanted to know if they could afford me." The next interviews "with a director and a hiring manager" were less shocking. "I hit it off with the director," says that respondent. "We chatted about work scenarios for an hour-and-a-half and in the last 30 minutes went through the typical interview questions—strengths, weakness, 'Why should we hire you?'" The contact adds, "The hiring manager interviewed me for 40 minutes and asked about my work experience." Another insider reports going through four interviews and meeting with "a recruiting manager and department managers."

OUR SURVEY SAYS

Mixed bag

"The corporate culture is remarkably supportive from within the rank and file of workers," says one source. But largely, insiders are split on Pru's culture. Some praise it, and others criticize it. "Although they are a large company and have felt their fair share of pain," explains one source, "there is a general humanity that pervades relationships at the firm. It may not be the most lucrative place on the Street, but you will like your co-workers, you will be able to have a life outside of work, and you will be treated with respect." Another says while "there are obvious advantages, like having well-defined role structures and a total lack of ambiguity around what you are expected to do," the atmosphere "can seem bureaucratic at times, specifically when you'd want to drive change of any kind. Conservatism is just expected from you." And "in terms of work pressure, let's just put it this way—you're unlikely to die of hypertension," says one wry insider. "The environment is clearly not cutting-edge nor is the momentum heart-wrenching. The only exception to this rule could be if you are on the sales side."

One source calls it a "very professional corporate culture" where "employees are treated respectfully." Others call it a "nose-to-the-grindstone" type of place, and a former insider goes so far as to call it "disorganized" and "hostile." Even so, that contact does say, "I genuinely liked two managers, who were always willing to work with you." Another contact says that "managers are not too strict or demanding, and are very welcoming of new employees and interns," adding that "managers are not too stingy with expense accounts, and often treat their teams to lunches and include them at conferences." Another insider says that "dialogue is encouraged" between managers and staff.

The deal on diversity

Diversity is another issue insiders are split on. "In general, Prudential has a very good record on diversity," says an insider. Another says it's "very diverse," and the firm "takes pride in its diversity practices." However, one source paints a different picture. "My first impression was that the company seemed concerned with its diversity representation. Pru wants to have employees who represent the marketplace. Unfortunately, now I do not feel that diversity is valued, even if the numbers may look good." Another says the firm is "diverse with many women and some minorities," adding that it "actively recruits minorities through select programs for impressive minority job candidates." An insider says, "Management and leadership are mostly comprised of white males, leaving the heralding of diversity limited to lower paying and lower status jobs with little to no room for advancement."

Pay seems to be no different: sources have both good and bad things to say. One source says, "To its credit, Pru offers excellent benefits, although not particularly great or competitive overall compensation." Another agrees, calling comp "way below industry average" and says, "Prudential has a history of paying their employees below industry average." Another respondent, though, says of pay, "I think it's appropriate." With the state the economy is in, it comes as no surprise that pay "increases for 2003 were minimal based on performance." Perks include "investment options and a 401(k), but Prudential Securities no longer receives a match on 401(k)," notes one insider.

Varied but reasonable

"The hours vary according to the department and the job function," reports an insider, "but for the most part are reasonable. I worked 9 to 5, Monday through Friday." Several insiders report that their groups allow staffers to make their own hours. "Flexible hours are available for most employees," says a source. Another notes, "Flexible hours were offered to me by my director, but my manager seemed to have a problem with the fact that I worked earlier than 9 to 5. Yet he'd call me at 8 a.m. requesting that I 'look into something' before he arrived." That contact adds, "Slackers left early in my boss' opinion." Another source, who says hours are good (he "never" has to come in on the weekends), explains the overtime, or rather former overtime

Visit the Vault Finance Career Channel at **www.vault.com/finance** — with insider firm profiles, message boards, the Vault Finance Job Board and more.

VAULT CAREER LIBRARY **307**

policy available to some staffers. "Overtime was initially available, but later rescinded. When it was available, it was so difficult to have the time approved, most employees stopped applying." If you put in the hours, you'll get the promotion, says a source. "Opportunities for advancement are really for those who can put in the long hours." Another contact disagrees. "Opportunities for advancement were there, but like most large corporations, it depended on access to a mentor more than hard work." And another source offers yet another take: "The economy has restricted everyone's upward mobility, and at Prudential, it's no different."

Don't dress it up

With the exception of client contact, most insiders report that business casual is typically the law of the land. "The business casual dress code takes the pressure off of dressing to impress," says a former insider, who adds, "We all knew when to dress up if an executive held an important meeting. I was overdressed during the job interview, but was told then that I wouldn't need a suit." Of the casual Friday policy in his office, one source in Philadelphia reports, "The dress code was not enforced; some of the outfits were downright scary."

Sallie Mae

12061 Bluemont Way
Reston, VA 20190
Phone: (703) 810-3000
Fax: (703) 984-5042
www.salliemae.com

DEPARTMENTS

Education Loan Origination
Collections Services
Loan Servicing

THE STATS

Employer Type: Public Company
Ticker Symbol: SLM (NYSE)
Vice Chairman & CEO: Albert L. Lord
President: Charles Elliot "C.E." Andrews
Revenue: $9.17 billion (FYE 12/07)
Net Income: -$896.39 million
No. of Employees: 9,000+
No. of Offices: 17 (covering 12 states)

KEY COMPETITORS

Bank of America
First Marblehead
KeyCorp.
Student Loan Corp.

UPPERS

- Great benefits
- Flexible hours

DOWNERS

- Can be "cost-conscious"
- Culture can be "high-strung"

EMPLOYMENT CONTACT

www.salliemae.com/about/careers_sm

Visit the Vault Finance Career Channel at **www.vault.com/finance** — with
insider firm profiles, message boards, the Vault Finance Job Board and more.

VAULT CAREER LIBRARY 309

THE SCOOP

Paying for college

You may not recognize SLM Corp., but you're almost certainly familiar with the company's nickname, Sallie Mae, especially if you're still paying off student loans. The company manages more than $137 billion in student loans for more than 10 million borrowers. Through its Upromise affiliates, Sallie Mae also handles more than $11 billion in Section 529 college-savings plans.

Founded in 1972 as a government-sponsored enterprise to address problems that arose from the federal Guaranteed Student Loan program of 1965, Sallie Mae initially focused on convincing banks to grant student loans, considered at the time poor risks. For the next two decades, the company remained partially subsidized by the government. But in 1994, President Clinton proposed direct government loans to students, implying the elimination of Sallie Mae. In 1995, Congress granted the company the chance to become private instead of being phased out. This led to a fierce proxy battle, which came to a head in August 1997, with shareholders firing the company's management, putting current chief executive officer Albert Lord and his team in charge and green lighting his privatization plan. The privatization process closed in December 2004. In May 2005, Thomas J. Fitzpatrick took on the role of chief executive officer. Sallie Mae fired its CFO in July 2005 for inflating revenue to receive a higher bonus and named Arthur Andersen vet C.E. Andrews to the post.

Since its early days, Sallie Mae has grown rapidly. Over the past few years, the firm has moved to adopt other financial practices, such as repackaging student loans as securities and making a number of strategic acquisitions. Since 2004, the company has acquired Southwest Student Services Corp., a financial aid firm; Student Loan Finance Association, a student loan originator and secondary market; GRP Financial Services, which buys and sells distressed mortgages; and college savings program Upromise.

Buyout falls through

In April 2007, Sallie Mae agreed to a buyout to the tune of $25 billion, or $60 a share. JC Flowers & Co. led the way (along with private equity firm Friedman Fleischer & Lowe LLC), with a plan to put in $4.4 billion and take a 50.2 percent ownership in the education lender, while Bank of America and J.P. Morgan Chase & Co. planned to put up $2.2 billion each in exchange for

24.9 percent of the company for each bank. The buyout received approval by Sallie Mae's independent board members and shareholders.

The deal began to fall apart, however, in August 2007, when a new law cut billions in subsidies to private student loan lenders and lowered the prices of government-backed student loans. In early October 2007, the buyers reduced their offer to $50 per share. Sallie Mae responded by filing a lawsuit against the buyers in an attempt to force them to either complete the deal or pay a break-up fee of $900 million. Negotiations continued for months. In December 2007, the companies announced that the Flowers-led group no longer wanted to purchase Sallie Mae. The lawsuit will go before a judge in July 2008.

Management shakeup

Chief Executive Officer Thomas J. Fitzpatrick resigned from the firm in May, reportedly as part of an effort by the Flowers group to improve the image of Sallie Mae among legislators in Washington. Following Fitzpatrick's resignation, the board appointed C.E. Andrews, the company's chief financial officer its interim chief executive officer.

In December 2007, the board appointed Andrews the company's president and made chairman Albert L. Lord chief executive officer. Lord served as Sallie Mae's chairman since March 2005. Before that appointment, he served as the company's vice chairman and chief executive officer, beginning in 1997. He got off to a rocky start with investors in December 2007, when Lord became so frustrated during a conference call that he ended it with an expletive. The company's stock price fell more than 20 percent following the call.

Andrews became Sallie Mae's chief financial officer in February 2006, after three years as the company's vice president of accounting and risk management. Before joining Sallie Mae, Andrews spent more than 20 years at Arthur Andersen.

Other changes announced in December include the promotion of Barry Feierstein to lead sales and marketing, and Robert Autor to guide the company's originations, servicing and call center operations, in addition to its information technology group. Feierstein and Autor joined the company in 2004 and 1999, respectively. Kevin Moehn, executive vice president of sales and originations and June McCormack, executive vice president of servicing, technology and sales marketing left the company.

Visit the Vault Finance Career Channel at www.vault.com/finance — with
insider firm profiles, message boards, the Vault Finance Job Board and more.

VAULT CAREER LIBRARY   311

Delaying stock repurchase program

Sallie Mae profited in the past by entering into "equity forward" contracts, which committed it to purchase millions of shares of stock at set prices at specific dates in future years. For years, the agreements have allowed the corporation to buy shares for less than market value, but plummeting stock prices at the end of 2007 has had the lender scrambling to renegotiate agreements that could demand immediate payment if the market price fell low enough, costing the embattled firm billions. In December 2007, the company announced it had amended the terms of its contract with Citibank so that the trigger prices disappear. The new contracts expired in February 2008.

Settling student loan scandal

In April 2007, Sallie Mae reached an agreement with New York Attorney General Andrew M. Cuomo, under which the lender would willingly adopt Cuomo's code of conduct governing student lending and contribute $2 million to a fund devoted to educating college-bound students about their loan options. The agreement stems from Cuomo's investigation of student lenders nationwide that found potential conflicts of interest between colleges and lenders, including revenue sharing agreements, university call center staffing by lender employees, gifts and trips from lender to financial aid directors and stock tips to financial aid officers. The agreement requires Sallie Mae to discontinue call centers or other staffing for financial aid offices, discontinue paying financial aid officers for appearing on advisory boards and discontinue paying for financial aid officers' travel. Sallie Mae is among 12 lenders to reach an agreement with the attorney general.

Praise for female executive development, corporate citizenship

In March 2008, for the fifth time, the National Association for Female Executives recognized Sallie Mae as one of America's Top 30 companies for executive women. The yearly survey measures women's representation among top-paid and top-tier positions at America's largest companies. A year earlier, in February 2007, Corporate Responsibility Officer magazine recognized Sallie Mae as one of the 100 Best Corporate Citizens. The recognition represents Sallie Mae's fifth appearance on the list. The 100 best Corporate Citizens list recognizes companies for implementing best practices in the area of corporate responsibility.

Funding the future

The Sallie Mae Fund rewards high-risk students and students from low-income households with scholarships. In addition, the fund supplies financial support for volunteer programs in its employees' communities. The firm gave away $2.5 million in scholarships to more than 1,000 students in 2007, and has given $12 million in scholarships to over 5,000 students since 2001.

Troubled times?

In 2007 and well into 2008, the firm saw a few setbacks on the financial front. Revenue in 2007 came in at $9.17 billion, up from $8.7 billion in 2006, but net income for the year took a nosedive, as the firm booked a net loss of $896.39 million compared with net income of $1.16 billion in 2006. For the second quarter 2008, revenue dipped to $2.3 billion from $3.3 billion in the second quarter 2007, and net income fell to $265.74 from $966.47 million. Analysts had expected much higher earnings for the second quarter 2008, and even Sallie Mae CEO Albert Lord conceded that the company's funding costs have been "extraordinarily high," adding that funding costs for the rest of 2008 are likely to be a big factor in Sallie's earning potential for the immediate future.

GETTING HIRED

Choosy

The company's choosiness when selecting candidates "depends on the department," says one insider, adding that "in the accounting, finance and legal areas, the company is very selective." Starting with Sallie Mae as an intern may be a good way of getting your foot in the door, however. One former intern notes, "I only had one interview before I was hired."

As for the interviews, a financial services insider says, "There are usually two interviews, one with immediate management and one with VP-level management." According to one source, candidates can "submit a resume online, after which you'll possibly get screened by HR and maybe invited to attend a pre-employment session. If that's successful, then you'll get an interview with a department supervisor and maybe hired." Another contact reports going through "two different interviews during my hiring process."

Visit the Vault Finance Career Channel at www.vault.com/finance — with
insider firm profiles, message boards, the Vault Finance Job Board and more.

VAULT CAREER LIBRARY   313

The first round involved a meeting with a recruiter and "filling out of the basic application and paperwork." Then, the candidate "met with the hiring officer" and "other members of her team." The overall interview "took approximately two hours." The second interview involved "meeting with hiring officer," who spent "about an hour going over the details of the position." "We discussed what I was looking for in a career and if the position would fit those needs."

If you don't see a position listed that happens to catch your fancy at the firm's careers section of its web site (go to "careers at Sallie Mae" under "about us" on the firm's homepage), consider submitting your resume anyway. "If you don't see an opportunity that matches your skills and interest," the company will keep your resume and keep you in mind for future openings.

OUR SURVEY SAYS

They love it

Insiders don't mind sharing that they "thoroughly enjoy working at Sallie Mae." The company culture promotes a "work hard, play hard" ethic, placing an emphasis on "high performance." Sources also call the culture everything from "conservative" and "really interesting" to "high-strung" and "cost-conscious." "It is a meritocracy," notes one contact. "If you are good, you will be promoted quickly." "Performance management process is very important and equally important is employee satisfaction," adds another insider.

Hours, too, are "fairly flexible," but they also "depends on the department." "In my department, there is approximately a three-hour window in which people arrive in the morning, and then they leave eight to nine hours after they come in," reports one contact. Plus, "managers are very understanding of personal situations such as children and long commutes." Employees also feel as though attaining management status is within reach. "Many of our senior executives have been here for many years and started off as low level employees." "The opportunities for advancement are there if one looks for it."

Nice perks

Sallie Mae offers "exceptional benefits, including retirement matching, stock options and a stock purchase plan." It also offers an "in-house gym," "cafeteria," "tuition reimbursement" and "community service benefits." Sallie Mae also has a "business casual dress code," which "promotes the feeling of an informal business atmosphere." And hours aren't so bad, say insiders, though there could be some weekend work; one respondent says he visits the office on a Saturday or Sunday "at least once a month."

One can always hope

On the whole, Sallie Mae's business outlook is "hopeful." True, it's "going through a rough period with new student loan legislation and the declining credit markets," but "senior management remains confident that we will prevail." And "while employee morale is slightly lower than normal, locations do their best to boost it whenever possible through employee recognition awards and social events."

Visit the Vault Finance Career Channel at www.vault.com/finance — with
insider firm profiles, message boards, the Vault Finance Job Board and more.

VAULT CAREER LIBRARY   315

Scottrade

12800 Corporate Hill Drive
St. Louis, MO 63131-1834
Phone: (314) 965-1555
Fax: (314) 543-6222
www.scottrade.com

THE STATS

Employer Type: Private Company
CEO: Rodger Riney
Revenue: $1.03 billion (FYE 9/07)
No. of Employees: 2,300
No. of Offices: 370

KEY COMPETITORS

Charles Schwab
E*TRADE FINANCIAL
TD Ameritrade

UPPERS

- "Management is supportive"
- "Great hours"

DOWNERS

- "Strict Internet and cell phone policies"
- "Too conservative in some aspects of compliance"

EMPLOYMENT CONTACT

See "employment" link at
www.scottrade.com

THE SCOOP

From Scottsdale to St. Louis

It may seem difficult to believe for a company with such a considerable Web presence, but Scottrade started up long before online trading existed. In 1980, Rodger Riney founded Scottsdale Securities in Scottsdale, Ariz. In 1982, he relocated the firm's headquarters to St. Louis, and started branching out—and never looked back. By 1986, Scottsdale Securities had opened its third branch office, in Dayton, Ohio, and by 1990, it had 14 offices with locations in Springfield, Mo.; Southfield, Mich.; Pittsburgh; Oakbrook Terrace, Ill.; Bloomington, Minn.; Irvine, Calif.; La Mesa, Calif.; Milwaukee; Clearwater, Fla.; and Englewood, Colo.

In 1994 and 1995, Scottsdale Securities made it onto *Inc.* magazine's 500 Fastest Growing Private Companies in America list. In 1996, Scottsdale Securities began offering online trading to its already-substantial customer base. The corporation had 100 offices by 1999, and opened 20 more during the year. In 2000, Scottsdale Securities changed its name to Scottrade to reflect the domain name of its web site. Scottrade was born.

At the turn of the century, things really began to take off. By the end of 2001, the firm had 147 offices. It opened 24 more in 2002, including its first in Manhattan, bringing its brick-and-mortar presence to 170 offices. And fast on the heels of its next move—the 2003 launch of Scottrade Chinese, available to customers in the United States, China, Hong Kong and Taiwan— Scottrade passed another milestone, opening its one-millionth customer account. In 2004, Scottrade launched ScottradeELITE, an online trading platform for active traders.

To commemorate its 25th year as a discount brokerage firm in 2005, Scottrade offered a new flat-rate commission of $7 for all online market and limit orders, which remains in place. In 2006, and again in 2008, CEO Rodger Riney rang the Nasdaq closing bell to commemorate the company's partnership with the exchange.

Keeping quiet in the fourth quarter

A private company, Scottrade did not publicly release results for its fiscal year 2007 (ended September 30th). However, for the 12 months ending June 30, 2007, the company's customer assets jumped 25 percent to $62.4 billion, while active customer accounts grew 10 percent to 1.7 million. Trade

Visit the Vault Finance Career Channel at www.vault.com/finance — with insider firm profiles, message boards, the Vault Finance Job Board and more.

VAULT CAREER LIBRARY   317

volumes and active accounts also saw important increases over the previous 12 months. The firm continued to expand its branch offices throughout the year. In July 2007, the company reached 306 branch offices, making it the online broker with the largest branch network in the United States. As of July 2008, the company had 363 branch offices throughout the country.

An eye on traditional banking

In November 2007, Scottrade's application for a thrift charter received approval from the Office of Thrift Supervision. The bank will transfer brokerage customers' cash balances into FDIC-insured deposit accounts. Scottrade expects to broaden its product offerings in the future to incorporate traditional retail banking products and services, including online checking and savings accounts and certificates of deposit.

In December 2007, the company announced two new St. Louis-based hires to oversee the new banking operations. Scottrade appointed George Horn, formerly the executive vice president of treasury management and services for UMB Bank, as senior vice president. The company also hired Rodney Stanley, former chief investment and risk officer at Reliance Bank, as an executive vice president and chief financial officer.

Their people love them

Fortune magazine named Scottrade one of its 100 Best Companies to Work For in 2008, coming in at the No. 58 spot. In June 2008, *Computerworld* magazine named Scottrade No. 16 on its list of the 100 Best Places to Work in IT, and in February 2008, Scottrade won the Online Brokerage Category for the third year in a row from Brand Keys Customer Loyalty Engagement Index. In the same month, *Training* magazine named the company to its Top 125 for "commitment and excellence in professional development."

In October 2007, J.D. Power and Associates ranked Scottrade first in investor satisfaction with online investing services for the seventh time since 2001 in J.D. Power's 2007 Online Investor Satisfaction Study. The business received a satisfaction index score of 825, 41 points higher than the online brokerage industry average score of 784. The study judged brokers on cost, trade execution, web site functionality, information resources and interaction with customer service representatives.

Also in October 2007, Scottrade won the American Society for Training & Development's 2007 BEST Award. The award recognizes organizations that demonstrate enterprise-wide success through employee learning and development. The award recognized Scottrade for its associated development programs, which include an intern learning map and a customer service simulation-training module.

New data center

In December 2006, Scottrade completed a 34,000-square-foot data center in suburban St. Louis, representing the largest technology investment in the company's 28-year history. Innovations at the data center include a layered security approach that strengthens security without compromising rapidity, Internet trading performance and availability. The Data Center features fully redundant electrical, mechanical and cooling systems to ensure the facility can sustain operations for an extended period in the event of an electrical power loss. In September 2007, *InformationWeek* magazine recognized the new facility by placing Scottrade on its annual list of the nation's most innovative users of information technology.

GETTING HIRED

Plenty of opportunities

"The firm was very selective in the hiring process," one source says, "but rightfully so." The company "strives to get the right people, but if you have the attitude they are looking for, they will recognize that and give you the opportunity." Plus, "we continue to experience such rapid growth that we have a large number of openings."

Open positions are posted on the company web site; applicants can submit resumes for specific jobs or to be considered for general employment. "Scottrade uses all of the major job sites, as well as more than 500 colleges and universities" around the country.

Ready to talk?

Most candidates will go through two rounds of interviews, the first of which may be done via telephone, depending on location. The preliminary

Visit the Vault Finance Career Channel at www.vault.com/finance — with
insider firm profiles, message boards, the Vault Finance Job Board and more.

VAULT CAREER LIBRARY   319

interviews are usually conducted by a human resources official; later rounds involve "a direct supervisor" or "branch manager."

The queries are "thorough" but "typical," focusing on "background, product knowledge, customer service and trading." "I was asked several questions about my ability to perform the job and fit into the culture," a source says. Another recalls being asked about his ability to manage conflict on the job, and yet another source notes that questions about past work and education may turn into discussions about "lessons and values I took away from those experiences."

Some say "a securities industry product knowledge test" or "assessments" may be administered, and most agree that the response time is brisk: "I knew in less than a week," says a successful applicant. Because the company tries to move quickly, an employee tips, it's a good idea to go into the interviews with "concrete dates you are available to start work."

Not just for summer

A Scottrade internship is "a good step in the door for a lot of young people," but "you can still get hired here without participating in the program." One source notes, "The internship is not necessarily a summer internship. Most interns work at least two semesters and get to do real work." And "Scottrade is known for promoting from within so once you are a part of the internship program, there is a good chance that other opportunities will follow."

"I was responsible for much of the same work as the full-time employees in the department," a former intern recalls. "I was counted on as a true employee who made significant contributions to the company. After four weeks of interning I was hired into a full-time position."

OUR SURVEY SAYS

A time of change

Employees call Scottrade "a large company with a small-company feel." "This is a company growing rapidly," a source says. "It is experiencing a few growing pains as it shifts from small business to big business. People are forced to specialize, as they can't do it all. The people still try to keep it like a family, but it is getting more difficult for everybody to know everybody. Still, they try." "I have only been here for a couple of months, and I already feel at home in my department," says a recent hire.

Others praise the "interesting work" and "great opportunities to advance," but note that management "adheres strictly to policies and procedures." Some find this "stuffy" and "conservative," suggesting the company is "too strict regarding phone and computer usage." Still, most say it's "a culture of support for individuals who perform," happily free of "a sense of ego-rules." "There is great opportunity here for any individual who has serious intent to work hard to make Scottrade continue to grow and prosper," concludes a source.

The lunch tradeoff

Employees rave about their hours, but there's a catch. "We don't take a lunch hour, but we get to work an eight-hour day instead of a nine-hour day," a source explains. It's "strange, but it works out." Some offices also maintain a "cafeteria on-site to grab lunch and eat at your desk." "I love the hours that I work," a single parent says. "I am able to take care of my daughter and be a part of her life." Weekend work is "rarely mandatory," but can be helpful for those who need "extra time to catch up or get ahead." Overall, "the company understands the importance of a work-home life balance."

As for perks, "the company offers partial tuition reimbursement and a wellness program that includes gym membership reimbursements," plus transit and parking assistance, discounted cafeterias and "many corporate-sponsored employee events." One woman says, "The company has gone above and beyond with their wellness program. There is a specific dollar amount that they will reimburse you each quarter to help employees lose weight and quit smoking. They also have contests that motivate employees to stay on the program." At headquarters in St. Louis, employees can win "ticket raffles for local sporting events."

Could improve

Though women say the company is "receptive" to gender diversity, several insiders say they work "in an office full of men" and "the majority of clients are men as well." Although there are men and women alike in the firm's management, some believe there's more work to be done.

Visit the Vault Finance Career Channel at www.vault.com/finance — with
insider firm profiles, message boards, the Vault Finance Job Board and more.

VAULT CAREER LIBRARY   321

Similarly, while Scottrade employs people from many different backgrounds, one source says, "I don't see as much diversity here, but I also do not feel like there is any reason for it. My feeling is that the firm seeks people to help it grow and who will maintain a supportive environment—whoever they are."

A happy family

After an initial training/orientation process, employees "have access to our company's university, an online training center with hundreds of training opportunities." Scottrade also offers other training courses and some off-site training sessions; while most believe there's ample opportunity for training, especially for those who take advantage of "self-study," one respondent believes that "there needs to be a better system in regards to training and development of new and intern employees. There should be better worker and supervisor guidelines and communication" about such policies.

Speaking of supervisors, Scottrade employees can't praise theirs enough. Managers "treat their subordinates with respect," and everyone's "views and opinions are always welcome." "My managers have been extremely understanding about personal issues, and have made allowances above what I am entitled to," says one contact.

TGI casual Friday

A source at company HQ in St. Louis describes the office as "cubicle-land." Though the digs may be "nothing fancy," employees enjoy "very comfortable chairs," "dual monitors" and plentiful parking. Shrugs a man, "Luxury isn't really a high priority, as I prefer functionality." And while the dress code is "formal" or "business casual" most weekdays, sources say that "casual dress is allowed on the last Friday of the month." Adds one employee, "Dress code varies depending on location and department," with some departments and offices tending toward "less formal."

Standard & Poor's

55 Water Street
New York, NY 10041
Phone: (212) 438-2000
Fax: (212) 438-7375
www.standardandpoors.com

DEPARTMENTS

Credit Market Services
Investment Services

THE STATS

Employer Type: Business segment of
   McGraw Hill
President: Deven Sharma
Revenue: $3.05 billion (FYE 12/07)
No. of Employees: 7,500

KEY COMPETITORS

A.M. Best
Dow Jones
DBRS
Fitch Ratings
FTSE
Moody's Investors Service
Morningstar
Russell
Thomson Reuters

UPPERS

- Laid-back culture
- Good training

DOWNERS

- "Kissing up" is a standard practice
- Poor future outlook

Visit the Vault Finance Career Channel at **www.vault.com/finance** — with
insider firm profiles, message boards, the Vault Finance Job Board and more.

VAULT CAREER LIBRARY   323

THE SCOOP

Poor in name only

When Henry Varnum Poor published his History of Railroads and Canals of the United States in 1860, he likely never dreamed he had begun what would become a global corporation with enormous influence over capital markets and the world economy. However, 81 years later, a 1941 merger of Standard Statistics and Poor's Publishing Company created one of the world's most prominent independent credit ratings, market indices, risk evaluation, investment research and data companies. A quarter-century after that combination, in 1966, McGraw-Hill, the multibillion-dollar publishing company known for its elementary and high-school textbooks and other media businesses, acquired the company.

Today, New York-based Standard & Poor's operates through six main divisions: credit ratings, data services, equity research, funds, indices and risk solutions. Over $1 trillion in investor assets is directly tied to S&P indices, more than all other indices combined. The company has the world's largest network of credit ratings analysts, and its equity research division is the world's largest producer of independent equity research. More than 1,000 institutions—including 19 of the top 20 securities firms, 13 of the top 20 banks, and 11 of the top 20 life insurance companies—license its research for their investors and advisors. Standard & Poor's team of experienced U.S., European and Asian equity analysts assess approximately 2,000 equities across more than 120 industries worldwide. Furthermore, Standard & Poor's funds research offers in-depth mutual fund reports on over 15,000 U.S. domestic mutual funds and ratings on over 1,800 funds worldwide.

In the aftermath of WorldCom and Enron scandals, pressure on the SEC grew to increase competition in the profitable ratings business. Both companies had received high marks from S&P and its main competitor Moody's. There are only five "nationally recognized" credit raters, with S&P and Moody's controlling 80 percent of the market and seeing profit margins of more than 50 percent. Fitch Ratings, Dominion Bond Rating Services (DBRS) and A.M. Best Co. are the only other three.

In fall 2006, The Credit Rating Agency Reform Act established new rules to make it easier for new competitors to enter the market and give the SEC oversight power. In an effort to create new transparency, the new regulations also require ratings firms to provide more disclosure of their ratings methodologies and to set up policies to avoid conflicts of interest. Analysts expect juggernauts S&P and Moody's will probably still dominate the market, but that new competitors will attempt to get some traction by taking different tacks, such as offering ratings paid for by investors of debt issuers and focusing on specific types of debt.

Hitting 500

Financial news reports make reference to the performance of the S&P 500, one of scores of indices compiled by the company to track the latest results of stock exchanges around the world. Unlike the Fortune 500, which lists the biggest companies in the world, the S&P 500 lists large public companies that trade on U.S. stock exchanges. The companies that comprise the list represent different industries. Individual performances receive weights according to their overall size. Together with the Dow Jones Industrial Average, the S&P 500 represents the key barometer of the U.S. stock market. Individual companies and mutual funds frequently measure their performance against these indices. Other S&P indices track specific contents and countries, from India to Australia.

Besides the index business, S&P also earns fees for rating bonds around the world. The credit ratings division turns a profit: Barron's reported that the unit's profit margin is 42 percent and that much of its new business is focused in foreign markets. S&P makes 37 percent of its ratings revenue abroad, and that figure should reach close to 50 percent by 2010.

The company also publishes a wide array of reports. The Dividend Record, S&P publishes the dividend reports on more than 23,000 securities, including 12,000 equity, bond and money-market funds and 450 closed-end funds. Another publication, The Outlook, offers investment advice for individuals and financial professionals. It provides research, investment ideas and market perspective including buy, hold and sell recommendations for the 1,500 stocks ranked according to Standard & Poor's Stock Appreciation Ranking System. The business added a daily two-minute video clip to its web site in November 2005 to give commentary on the economy, markets and industries. The free streaming media service distills S&P's weekly investment research for institutional and private investors as well as members of the financial media.

Subprime testimony

Standard & Poor's Executive Vice President Vicky A. Tillman, testified before Congress in September 2007 to answer questions about the credit

Visit the Vault Finance Career Channel at **www.vault.com/finance** — with insider firm profiles, message boards, the Vault Finance Job Board and more.

VAULT CAREER LIBRARY   325

agency's role in the subprime mortgage crisis. Critics claim that ratings firms failed investors by indorsing mortgage-backed bonds and other risky products in exchange for large fees. "We support Congress' efforts to investigate… abuses and to prevent their recurrence," Tillman said during her testimony. "For our part, we are taking steps to ensure that our ratings and the assumptions that underlie them are analytically sound in light of shifting circumstances."

In October 2007, Standard & Poor's downgraded more than 1,700 bonds tied to mortgages issued within the year. More than three dozen of the bonds had received the agency's highest rating earlier in the year.

New CEO

Chief Executive Officer Kathleen Corbet left the corporation to "pursue other opportunities," the company said in a statement in August 2007. Her replacement, Deven Sharma joined S&P in 2002, and most recently served as the executive vice president of investment services and global sales. Corbet's departure came as the company downgraded hundreds of mortgage-backed securities tied to subprime loans.

Sharma has helped the company develop global growth strategies. He also played a role in identifying and leading several of the corporation's acquisitions, including CRISIL, Capital IQ and J.D. Power and Associates. Sharma holds a bachelor's degree from Birla Institute of Technology in India, a master's degree from the University of Wisconsin and a doctorate in business management from Ohio State University.

Making acquisitions

Standard & Poor's purchased Israeli rating agency Maalot in January 2008 and changed its name to Maalot Standard & Poor's. Standard & Poor's said the acquisition would allow the company to develop analytical services for Israel and international investors.

In November 2007, the company purchased IMAKE Consulting, a provider of software and services to the structured finance market, and ABSXchange, an end-to-end solution provider for structured finance data, analytics and modeling. Both companies are located in Bethesda, Maryland.

In February 2007, the company purchased the Goldman Sachs Commodity Index and two equity index families from the Goldman Sachs Group. Created in 1991, the GSCI includes 24 commodities and provides investors with a benchmark for investment performance in the commodity markets. The index has been renamed the S&P GSCI Commodity Index.

In 2006, S&P formed a 50/50 joint venture with CITIC Securities, one of the two brokerages firms listing in China, to develop benchmark indexes for the Chinese securities market. That year, the company also launched 10 indexes to track housing prices in a variety of regions throughout the United States and a composite index. The S&P/Case-Shiller Metro Area Home Price Indices track the housing markets in Boston, Chicago, Denver, Las Vegas, Los Angeles, Miami, New York, San Diego, San Francisco and Washington, D.C.

Selling divisions

In February 2007, S&P announced it would sell its mutual fund data business to Morningstar, Inc., in order to focus on its analytical services for the global fund industry. The business includes mutual fund data on performance rankings and holdings on more than 135,000 funds in more than 30 countries. The sale includes desktop applications and data feed products. Under the agreement, Standard & Poor's will license mutual fund data from Morningstar for use in its ratings and research products and services.

The company pulled the plug on its Hedge Fund Index in June 2006 because of PlusFunds Group, a hedge funds operator that gathered the data for the index, filing for bankruptcy. The index launched in October 2002.

A new face for ratings

In August 2008, S&P appointed David Jacob to the position of executive managing director and head of structured finance ratings. Jacob, who will be taking over the position's reins from Vickie Tillman (who was promoted to executive vice president), will be overseeing S&P's structured finance unit in his new role. Tillman added that Jacob will also be helping to "improve transparency, build investor confidence, and continue to deliver high-quality, independent analytics."

Visit the Vault Finance Career Channel at **www.vault.com/finance** — with insider firm profiles, message boards, the Vault Finance Job Board and more.

VAULT CAREER LIBRARY   327

GETTING HIRED

Go globetrotting

Interested applicants can search for open positions worldwide within the firm, from Argentina to Venezuela, under the "careers" link under the "about us" tab at www.standardandpoors.com. The firm says it's looking for "bright and enthusiastic" candidates with "diverse educational backgrounds, work experience and personal interests."

The firm hires entry-level employees in all six of its divisions: credit ratings, data services, equity research, funds, indices and risk solutions. Candidates can also learn more about S&P's business lines, read first-person accounts by current insiders about what it's like to work for the firm, and get detailed information on entry-level positions for undergrads and grad students.

In its credit ratings division, the firm typically hires MBA and other graduate students as credit analysts. First-round interviews for these positions are held on campus (if S&P doesn't recruit at your school, you can apply online), and second-round interviews are held at the firm's New York headquarters or a regional office. The second round includes a full day of interviewing, which, according to S&P, includes "rigorous testing of your financial acumen and, for some business units, an evaluation of your ability to create written commentary." In addition to full-time credit analyst positions, the firm offers a 10- to 12-week summer associate program for "candidates who have completed the first year of an advanced degree program." According to S&P, after a one-week training program, summer associates "work closely with a senior analyst and a junior analyst mentor on relevant work assignments that offer exposure to the ratings process."

In equity research, insiders say, "New analysts have traditionally been hired straight out of graduate school," but lately they have come from the industry as well. "Most applicants are chosen from resumes received from Internet postings." Those chosen are then asked back to "sit for a daylong in-house exam," during which they "write a stock report based upon information provided." Those who pass this exam are then "invited back for a two-hour round of three or four interviews." Interview questions "generally revolve around current market happenings as well as two or three stock recommendations," which the "applicant has to pitch to the interviewer." Overall, though, interviews are pretty "nonchalant" experiences. Just be sure to be patient (and persistent, if necessary). "Although the interviewers are generally pretty good about follow-up, sometimes HR is overwhelmed and getting back to you takes time."

OUR SURVEY SAYS

Black or white

True, you can "learn a lot" at S&P, but it largely "depends on your team."
"Some groups are a lot more proactive in encouraging you to move ahead,
while others seem indifferent." Insiders say Standard & Poor's culture is
"laid-back for the most part," but "some departments can be more demanding
than others." The work environment is "a pleasant change from a finance job
on Wall Street," and "a good choice for those interested in a financial services
job that is toned down from investment banking." "I really enjoy working
with my team," says one worker. "The people are laid-back and more
friendly than in a lot of other places." Others call the culture "bad," adding
there are "too many politics and very little good work." Yet another reports
the atmosphere as one of "sycophancy, in which kissing-up and kicking down
are standard practice."

When it comes to moving up, it also seems to hinge largely on who you ask.
One says "opportunities for advancement are pretty good," while another
reports that "opportunities for advancement are very limited, as senior
officers are more or less entrenched in their managerial positions and not
looking to leave, given the relatively attractive compensation packages and
perks for a limited amount of true work."

Employees do agree, however, that it takes "generally two years to make
associate director, and if you are good, two to three years to make director
after that," though "there are very few managing directors." But watch out
for increasing duties, warns one insider. "Responsibilities and compensation
can grow without gaining a change of title."

For the most part, salaries aren't rated incredibly highly by employees. One
insider says, "Pay is increasing, but it's nowhere near the levels you could get
at an investment bank." And while "S&P may not have corrected the problem
with across-the-board salary increases to match the increased work," a source
says, "I do have to give them some credit for making good efforts to move
people along." Bonuses are "meager" and "virtually non-existent," insiders
say, and business travel is occasionally required, but it's "dependent on your
job function—it could be 25 percent of your time if you are a ratings analyst."
All of your time won't be out on the road. "Once you've been there for a
couple of years, there is opportunity to work from home one or two days a
week," notes one insider.

Visit the Vault Finance Career Channel at **www.vault.com/finance** — with
insider firm profiles, message boards, the Vault Finance Job Board and more.

VAULT CAREER LIBRARY   329

Management is also an area that receives varied reviews from workers. "Senior management is pretty deadbeat—the recent shakeup kept all of them in place, while the good ones were let go," says one insider, adding that "the company needs to whittle them down and allow the good people to advance." Another contact says, "Since management dips into the same bonus pool, they try to stiff others. There is way too much corruption at this firm." In equity research, "which is separate from the credit ratings business," "there is very much a publishing mentality." "Management is most concerned with the quantity and timeliness of published research." One source notes that "telecommuting, job sharing and a host of other activities" are options, but "all of these things are entirely dependent on who your boss is." The insider adds, "Get the right boss and work from home three days a week, but get the wrong one and expect to hear some potentially bogus reason about why these arrangements won't work for you."

Melt and blend

Insiders note that "diversity, work hours and dress code are positives." "McGraw-Hill has very liberal corporate policies," and "employees are much more diverse than at traditional Wall Street firms." The dress code is a casual one "unless you have a meeting with a client." One insider says that the dress code is "a fairly informal business casual code, which translates to a nice collared shirt and slacks," adding that "many people wear polo shirts, but I haven't gone that casual yet."

"Hours are increasing because of higher expectations for productivity," but still, they are "flexible." Other insiders report that "working 9 to 5 is accepted as a trade-off for the lower pay," and "hours get busier at the end of the month." In equity research, "new hires are placed into a short formal training session that gravitates more towards the quirks of writing in the 'S&P style,' the editorial process and the in-house publishing systems."

Though the firm is "not a perfect melting pot of cultures," says a contact, "we do have a good mix of people. We just don't have a perfect blend yet." But women are making strides within the company. The insider goes on to note that "while the industry still appears to be dominated by white males, I work for a female managing director, who works for a female managing director, who works for a female executive managing director, who works for a female executive vice president, who works for the female president of Standard and Poor's." Another says that S&P employs "people from all over the world" and "lots of different races," adding that "McGraw-Hill, the parent company, really emphasizes this aspect in its recruiting."

Pretty dismal

Any way you slice it, it looks like S&P is heading down a bumpy road. While "some of the businesses are fundamentally strong and will continue to see strong demand," the firm and its reputation "has taken an irreparable hit." One insider says, "Business is down and should stay down," adding that the company's "reputation has suffered and no one wants S&P ratings any more—and who can blame them?" Another contact says the outlook is "very poor" since the induction of the new CEO and says the firm is "certainly headed downhill." "If you have decent qualifications, just stay far away, since current qualified employees are desperate to get away," says one director. An analyst agrees, begging "go somewhere else, my friend—and please take me with you!"

Visit the Vault Finance Career Channel at **www.vault.com/finance** — with
insider firm profiles, message boards, the Vault Finance Job Board and more.

VAULT CAREER LIBRARY   **331**

State Farm

1 State Farm Plaza
Bloomington, IL 61710
Phone: (309) 766-2311
Fax: (309) 766-3621
www.statefarm.com

DEPARTMENTS

Automobile Insurance
Banking
Health Insurance
Home Insurance
Life Insurance

THE STATS

Employer Type: Private Company
Chairman & CEO: Edward B. Rust Jr.
Vice Chairman, President & COO:
   Vincent J. Trosino
Revenue: $61.6 billion (FYE 12/07)
Net Income: $5.46 billion
No. of Employees: 79,200
No. of Offices: 13

KEY COMPETITORS

Allstate
GEICO
Progressive Corporation

UPPERS

• Flexible hours

DOWNERS

• "Overworked and underpaid"

EMPLOYMENT CONTACT

www.statefarm.com/about/careers/
careers.asp

THE SCOOP

A huge neighbor

State Farm is among the foremost U.S. auto and home insurer. The company also offers life and health insurance, and runs State Farm Bank, a federal savings bank charter, which offers banking, annuities and mutual funds through agents, by phone, mail and Internet. However, insurance is the primary money maker for the company. State Farm insures nearly 20 percent of all U.S. autos, and auto insurance accounts for over 50 percent of its policies and nearly 65 percent of its property and casualty premiums. Homeowners' insurance is also an important part of the company's business. State Farm insures approximately 20 percent of all single-family homes in the United States.

Ranked No. 32 on the 2008 Fortune 500 list of largest companies, State Farm runs more than 755 claim offices countrywide to process the 71.6 million policies currently in force.

Born on the Farm

In 1921, George J. Mecherle was forced to change careers when his wife became ill. A successful farmer, he left his trade and took a job as an insurance salesman. He disagreed with the established practice charging farmers the same rate as others, believing that since they drove less and had fewer losses than those who lived in cities, they should get a better deal on insurance.

So, in 1922, he started his own insurance firm, State Farm Insurance, as a mutual automobile company owned by its policy holders. The corporation charged a one-time membership fee and, as opposed to competitors, offered annual payment plans and determined rates by a seven-class system, not by the standard of having varied rates for each model.

Today, State Farm Mutual Automobile Insurance Company is the parent of several wholly owned subsidiaries, including State Farm Life Insurance Company, State Farm Fire and Casualty Company, State Farm Indemnity Company and State Farm General Insurance Company, among others.

Visit the Vault Finance Career Channel at **www.vault.com/finance** — with
insider firm profiles, message boards, the Vault Finance Job Board and more.

VAULT CAREER LIBRARY   333

Getting recognized

State Farm frequently receives recognition as an employer and as a service provider. The company appeared at number 34 in 2007 on G.I. Jobs' list of the Top 50 Most Military-Friendly Employers and second for its National Guard and reserve policies. In February 2008, *Latina Style* magazine named State Farm one of the 50 Best Companies for Latinas to Work For (the firm has won the award every year since 2001). In July 2008, *Black Enterprise* magazine named the company one of the Best Companies for Diversity.

In February 2008, Automotive Fleet Magazine recognized State Farm Insurance Companies as having the fourth-largest non-governmental alternative-fuel commercial fleet in the country. Since 2004, State Farm has replaced its vehicles with bio-diesel, hybrid-electric and flex-fuel vehicles. The fleet includes 3,166 eco-friendly vehicles.

Katrina lawsuits continue

In November 2007, State Farm Fire and Casualty Co. asked a federal appeals court to turn over a $1 million punitive damage award to a Mississippi company who sued the insurer for refusing to cover Hurricane Katrina damage to their home. The company's lawyers have argued in the appeal that State Farm could not get a fair trial on the Gulf Coast, due to the negative publicity surrounding Katrina insurance claims. In January 2008, a jury ruled the company owed the couple $2.5 million, but the judge reduced the amount to $1 million.

In a separate case, State Farm filed suit in November 2007 against Mississippi Attorney General Jim Hood, accusing him of violating a January 2007 agreement to end a criminal investigation of the company's handling of Katrina-related claims. The suit alleges that Hood reopened a criminal investigation against State Farm to coerce the insurer into settling civil litigation related to the hurricane. The insurer and the attorney general have clashed since the hurricane. "Sadly, it appears that Mississippi's attorney general is more interested in making headlines in an election year than in making headway for the people of Mississippi," Mike Fernandez, State Farm vice president of public affairs, said in a June 2007 press release.

Meanwhile, attorney Richard "Dickie" Scruggs, who had led successful class action tobacco- and asbestos-related lawsuits in the past, filed a lawsuit against State Farm, alleging the firm had denied policyholders' hurricane-related claims. Scruggs, however, was indicted for conspiring to bribe a judge in the case in November 2007. Following Scruggs' indictment, State

Farm filed a motion in December 2007 to ban all the members of Scruggs' former Katrina Litigation Group from all Katrina-related lawsuits. The lawyers maintain that State Farm intentionally miscalculated the amount of wind damage and water damage to homes during the hurricane. State Farm insurance typically covers wind damage but not water damage.

Through a settlement State Farm reached with the Mississippi Insurance Department, State Farm began processing thousands of claim re-evaluation requests. By June 2007, it had made offers totaling more than $10 million, and the company has committed more than $50 million to the process.

In the meantime, Louisiana Attorney General Charles C. Foti Jr. had sued State Farm and other insurance companies, claiming they conspired to limit payments to policyholders after Hurricanes Katrina and Rita. The lawsuit, filed in November 2007, claims that the insurers coerced policyholders into settling damage claims for less than their value by engineering reports, delaying payments and forcing policyholders to sue in order to challenge the estimates.

By June 2007, State Farm had paid more than $3.1 billion to settle more than 99 percent of all Hurricane Katrina claims. But in 2008, State Farm was facing a new challenge—more legal disputes from policyholders in Mississippi affected by Katrina. In August 2008, Mississippi Attorney General Jim Hood helped reach a settlement over the disputes. With the settlement, State Farm agreed to pay more than $74 million to Gulf Coast policyholders.

Despite upheaval, increases

In 2007, State Farm's net income went up by 3 percent to $5.46 billion in 2007. Total revenue for the year was also up slightly to $61.6 billion from $60.5 billion in the previous year. The firm celebrated its fifth profitable year in a row—but it also noted that its property-casualty underwriting gain decreased 79 percent, which made its net income figure lower than it could have been. Reductions in auto rates also negatively affected State Farm's annual financials.

Visit the Vault Finance Career Channel at www.vault.com/finance — with
insider firm profiles, message boards, the Vault Finance Job Board and more.

VAULT CAREER LIBRARY   335

GETTING HIRED

The site's got it

Peppered with interview tips, sample interview questions and hints on "preparing an ideal resume," the careers section of State Farm's web site offers potential job candidates a little bit of everything. In addition, the site offers links to applying for becoming an agent or joining the company in a corporate function. The site also lists a number of recruiting events across North America for college students and recent graduates. State Farm links to its job opening on the Hotjobs web site, and lists job types both at regional departments throughout the United States and parts of Canada, as well as at its corporate headquarters in Bloomington, Ill. Job opportunities can include accounting, administrative services, agency, claims, human resources, insurance support centers, marketing, mutual funds, systems/IT and underwriting.

Slow and steady

Initially getting hired as an outsider can be a "painstakingly slow" process—indeed, even internal placements "seem to take a while as well." The interview process depends on the "level you're applying for" and "the individual culture of the department or zone." One single interview session could be "two or three levels deep" and include "interviewing with the immediate manager and possibly others." But "this is dependent on the position." Either way, "most interviews are behavior-based and require an individual to provide concrete examples where they have demonstrated a particular behavior, skill or competency in the past."

OUR SURVEY SAYS

It's all location

Much like the interview process, corporate culture "depends on the location" and "varies from department to department even in the corporate office." Contacts report a variety of day-to-day experiences with State Farm life. "State Farm is a great place to work," says one. Another agrees that "it's a fantastic company to work for." "Life at the Farm is just grand," beams a particularly happy insider. Another long-term State Farmer says, "I've been an agent for 18 years and have really enjoyed it." But one source says, "Employee morale is pretty low in my office. I'll be leaving shortly after I get all my licenses." Another notes, "There's a lot of talk about family and closeness within the company, but most people don't care about you as a person. State Farm is not the company that it used to be. Their focus is off." One insider believes, "There is somewhat of a culture of mediocrity at State Farm." The source adds, "Managers will tell you that it is virtually impossible to terminate poor performers, even with the best documentation, numerous follow-up meetings, etc. It can be challenging to maintain a climate of excellence amid this culture."

On that front, "opportunities for advancement exist depending on the needs of that particular department" and "promotions based on seniority do not exist." Instead, "business need is the driver." How to get to the top, then? "Mobility for any management position is very important," says one insider. "Continuing education—either an advanced degree or the equivalent professional designations are highly sought after to be competitive for the next level." It also helps to "become involved in extracurricular activities so that you can get acquainted with as many State Farmers as possible. Some activities might be different sports organized by the activities organization. [You can also join] Toastmasters, which develops your public speaking skills, or one of the many clubs."

Making headway in some areas

The company seems to be progressing in many areas, sources say, but not all. For example, regarding dress, one respondent says, "State Farm also allows casual business dress now, something years ago I would never have dreamed they would do." Another notes, "Dress code is based on the business environment that one is in." Although "professional attire" is recommended when meeting with customers, it's always important to "dress for success." "Should one desire to be considered a possibility for the next level, dressing appropriately always puts one in a more positive light," says one insider.

On the topic of pay, sources express some uncertainty but note that "if you work hard, you should be rewarded quite well." But one claims processor notes, "Overworked and underpaid is mostly what I hear when talking to anyone that is not in a management position or has worked there for 15 years." Another insider says, "Salary percent increases are the envy of most organizations even in a down economy."

Visit the Vault Finance Career Channel at www.vault.com/finance — with insider firm profiles, message boards, the Vault Finance Job Board and more.

VAULT CAREER LIBRARY   337

Your hours may vary

Hours will "vary depending on your role." Although "in some circumstances, hours are dictated by the customer need and the hours of operation," in other areas (such as the corporate offices) "hours are dictated by the activity going on." "Manager discretion" tends to determine the flexibility of working hours, say insiders. "Standard hours are 8 a.m. to 4:45 p.m.," and "every three months you can choose to change your hours." One choice available is the option of working four, 10-hour days with a three-day weekend. The flexible hours correspond with State Farm's comprehensive benefits packages, detailed at www.statefarm.com.

And the face of diversity seems to be changing at State Farm, with the number of women and members of minority groups "constantly increasing at the upper-management levels." One insider says that State Farm "makes a good effort to encourage diversity," adding that "many consultants are Indian nationals working on visas."

What's ahead

As far as its outlook goes, State Farm "remains strong" and is likely to "continue its leading position." But "like all large organizations, there is a tendency in some areas for people to be more inclined to advance their own careers as opposed to building a coalition to advance a cause." And "that can be detrimental, and cause individuals to look outside of the company when forced to deal with those styles and types of management."

SunGard Data Systems

680 East Swedesford Road
Wayne, PA 19087-1586
Phone: (800) 825-2518
www.sungard.com

DEPARTMENTS

Alternative Investments
Banking
Benefit Administration
Brokerage & Clearance
Capital Markets
Corporates & Treasury
Energy
Government
Higher Education
Insurance
Institutional Asset Management
Investment Banking
Public Sector
Trading
Wealth Management

THE STATS

Employer Type: Private Company
Chairman: Glenn H. Hutchins
President & CEO: Cristóbal I. Conde
Revenue: $4.90 billion (FYE 12/07)
No. of Employees: 16,000
No. of Offices: Offices in more than
    30 countries

KEY COMPETITORS

ADP
Broadridge
DST
Fiserv
Misys
Thomson Reuters

UPPER

- "Interesting" and "international"
  culture

DOWNER

- "Some politics"

EMPLOYMENT CONTACT

See "jobs" link at www.sungard.com

Visit the Vault Finance Career Channel at **www.vault.com/finance** — with
insider firm profiles, message boards, the Vault Finance Job Board and more.

VAULT CAREER LIBRARY   **339**

THE SCOOP

Rising Sun(Gard)

The largest privately held software company in the United States, SunGard went private in August 2005 in a leveraged buyout valued at $11.4 billion, which then represented the second largest LBO and still ranks as the largest LBO of a software company. With revenue at $4.9 billion in 2007, SunGard remains a leading provider of software solutions for financial services, higher education and the public sector. The firm boasts more than 25,000 customers in more than 50 countries—including the world's 50 largest financial services companies—and ranked No. 472 (moving up from No. 500 in 2007) on the 2008 Fortune 500 list of America's largest corporations.

More than 10,000 businesses and institutions across North America and Europe rely on SunGard to help them keep their people connected with the information they require in order to do business. These customers include corporations and non-profits in nearly every sector of the economy. SunGard's availability services help these organizations reduce their exposure to threats with the potential to interrupt their operations. These threats include breaches of security, network or hardware failures, data loss, power failure and extreme events ranging from natural disaster to terrorism.

SunGard provides software and IT services to institutions in virtually every segment of the financial services industry. These solutions meet a multitude of needs such as increasing efficiency, improving customer service, complying with regulations and capturing growth opportunities through innovation.

SunGard also provides colleges and universities with strategic consulting and technology management services, helping them improve constituent services, increase accountability and give better educational experiences. In addition, the firm serves public sector customers, including municipalities, counties, police and fire departments, and public and private K-12 schools. For these clients, SunGard offers a broad range of services, such as integrated financial and administrative systems, emergency police dispatch, permitting and code enforcement, and class scheduling and report card management.

Getting better

For full-year 2007, revenue increased from $4.32 billion to $4.9 billion. The firm also suffered a net loss of $60 million in 2007 compared with a $118 million net loss in the previous year. Uncertainty regarding the state of the U.S. economy was mostly to blame for the still-not-quite-recovered results.

The first half of 2008 looked to be on an upswing. SunGard reported that revenue for the second quarter increased 15 percent from 2007's second quarter to $1.36 billion. Meanwhile, adjusted income from operations for the second quarter increased 8 percent to $285 million from the second quarter of 2007. The firm's positive results had an uptick in its broker/dealer businesses to thank, along with a two percent increase in the foreign exchange market.

Recent big buys

Since its founding in 1983, SunGard has completed more than 150 acquisitions. In 2006, SunGard's financial systems business completed 10 acquisitions valued at $163 million, including Integrated Business Systems Inc. (IBSI), a Melville, N.Y.-based provider of software solutions and related services to hedge funds, and Carnot, AG. of Frankfurt, Germany, a provider of business process management software. In 2007, SunGard completed acquisitions in its financial services segment in its higher education, public sector systems segment and availability services segment. And in 2008, the firm continued putting acquisitions under its belt, such as its purchase business software company Strohl Systems Group for an undisclosed amount. And in August 2008, SunGard made an offer to acquire the majority of software company GL TRADE for €41.70 per share.

On the list

For the second year in a row in November 2007, SunGard appeared number one on a list of pinnacle vendors in the annual RiskTech 100 Ratings, compiled by research and analysis firm Chartis Research and RiskTech, a specialist risk management consultancy. The rankings stem from more than 750 questionnaires and more than 100 interviews with technology buyers as well as data reviews from more than 20 independent consultants. SunGard, represented primarily by its Adaptiv and BancWare solutions, scored well across criteria including functionality, customer satisfaction and core technology.

SunGard products frequently receive best-in-class industry awards. Other recent awards included: AIIM's Carl E. Nelson Best Practices Award (in enterprise content management); Aite Group Best-In-Class High-Net-Worth Advisor Platform; Global Finance Best Treasury Workstation and Best Receivables Solution; and IQPC Shared Services Vendor Organization of the

Visit the Vault Finance Career Channel at www.vault.com/finance — with insider firm profiles, message boards, the Vault Finance Job Board and more.

VAULT CAREER LIBRARY   341

year. In April 2008, the firm won the Queen Award for Enterprise: Innovation 2008 for its development of a public safety communication system.

Going Green

At the beginning of 2007, SunGard announced a commitment to introduce corporate guidelines on sustainable development. "The customers, communities and environment we do business with and in are increasingly influenced by sustainability issues," the company said.

SunGard formed a Sustainability Work Group with representatives from each business working to create recommendations for corporate guidelines and launched a corporate intranet site with discussions forums for employee opinions. In addition, SunGard became a member of the World Business Council for Sustainable Development and the Green Grid, a consortium of information technology companies and professionals seeking to lower the overall consumption of power in data centers worldwide.

The company has begun to encourage employees to use Web conferences instead of air travel and green stationary and recycled office furniture. For 2008, it also co-sponsored a survey conducted by the Economist Intelligence Unit on attitudes of business leaders toward sustainability.

GETTING HIRED

Inclusive and international

From Sacramento to Stockholm, SunGard offers international positions ranging from application engineer to technical writer in the careers section of its web site. Detailed job descriptions and more are also available via the site. During various points in the interviewing process, job candidates report speaking with managers, HR and, further on in the process, "all of the team." One source notes that during the interview, "most of the questions asked related to the job and teamwork."

Expect an "informal" interview process when you're called in. You're likely to have at least "two rounds of interviews," but possibly more—one insider says you may go through "a great deal of rounds until everyone meets you." And try to be tolerant if the process seems to be stalled—"sometimes you need to wait until the person you need to meet gets back in town."

OUR SURVEY SAYS

No homogeny here

Insiders call the company "interesting but not homogenous," "very diversified" and "international." It's also a "work hard, play hard" culture. One insider says the company is a "steady place" with "some politics" that has progressed; it's "grown up from a mom-and-pop operation" but "still stays so in some areas." SunGard is also called "a good place to be for a long time"—"most people tend to stay there forever, though a few leave after less than a year." Another simply calls it a "good place to work." But one respondent notes that there is a "lack of communication from management so that employees never know where they stand."

Salaries are "decent," but "are less than what you might earn in an IT role at a Wall Street investment bank," insiders say. Perks include "three weeks of vacation," "two personal days," "12 sick days" and "medical coverage." It also doesn't hurt that hours tend to be "normal"—in the 40-hour-per-week range—and the dress code is "smart casual."

Visit the Vault Finance Career Channel at **www.vault.com/finance** — with insider firm profiles, message boards, the Vault Finance Job Board and more.

VAULT CAREER LIBRARY   343

Thornburg Mortgage

150 Washington Avenue
Suite 302
Santa Fe, NM 87501
Phone: (505) 989-1900
Fax: (505) 989-8156
www.thornburgmortgage.com

DEPARTMENTS

Residential Mortgage Lending

THE STATS

Employer Type: Public Company
Ticker Symbol: TMA (NYSE)
Chairman & CEO: Garrett Thornburg
Revenue: $2.62 billion (FYE 12/07)
Net Income: -$1.55 billion
No. of Employees: 400
No. of Offices: 1

KEY COMPETITOR

Wells Fargo

EMPLOYMENT CONTACT

See "career opportunities" under "about us" on www.thornburgmortgage.com

THE SCOOP

Making sense of it all

Thornburg Mortgage's bread and butter is making complicated stuff seem simple. More specifically, the Santa Fe, N.M.-based mortgage lender focuses on single-family adjustable-rate mortgages (ARMs) for affluent borrowers with sophisticated financial profiles. A relative new kid on the block— Thornburg Mortgage was founded in 1993—the company started out as an investor in mortgage-backed securities. Today, it is a fully integrated mortgage lender with $55.2 billion in assets, and a clear head about its identity. It provides a specific type of mortgage product, jumbo and super-jumbo ARMs, to a specific type of client—successful, finance-savvy men and women with superior credit histories. Thornburg Mortgage admits that its strategy is "not for everyone," but contends that it's this very focus that allows it to achieve the following goals: reduce red tape by eliminating much of the paperwork and fees; provide handcrafted loan solutions to address the opportunities and challenges of clients; and apply a common sense underwriting approach with stringent credit quality guidelines and constantly seek out opportunities and innovations.

CEO Garrett Thornburg began developing his empire before he got in the business of adjustable-rate mortgages. He started in 1982 with Thornburg Investment Management. Two years later, Thornburg, who still holds the chairman and CEO titles at all three of his companies, established Thornburg Securities Corporation, a broker-dealer member firm that distributes Thornburg Mutual Funds.

Adding Adfitech

In August 2006, Thornburg Mortgage announced that it would acquire Edmond, Okla.-based Adfitech, a provider of quality control, post-closing audit and document delivery services to the mortgage industry, from a subsidiary of homebuilding company Centex. According to a Thornburg Mortgage press release announcing the deal, all of Adfitech's services will represent a new source of revenue for Thornburg Mortgage.

"This acquisition supports our long-term goal to build a successful mortgage lending operation by expanding our operational capabilities to include an in-house capability that will support many of our back office lending

Visit the Vault Finance Career Channel at **www.vault.com/finance** — with insider firm profiles, message boards, the Vault Finance Job Board and more.

VAULT CAREER LIBRARY   345

operations," said Larry Goldstone, president and chief operating officer of Thornburg Mortgage.

Under the terms of the deal, Adfitech and its 323 employees will become a wholly owned subsidiary of Thornburg Mortgage Home Loans Inc., Thornburg Mortgage's wholly owned mortgage loan origination and acquisition subsidiary. Adfitech will continue to operate as a separate business unit and continue to serve its mortgage lending clients on a business-as-usual basis. It will also continue to function as Thornburg Mortgage's central document repository and provide data input, document imaging and file management to support Thornburg Mortgage's lending business. Thornburg Mortgage and Adfitech will continue to operate from their respective headquarters.

In the right place at the right time

When Merrill Lynch announced in September 2006 that it would buy the mortgage operations of National City for $1.3 billion, Thornburg Mortgage was one of several mortgage lenders whose shares rose after the deal demonstrated that institutional investors and investment banks may be interested in home loans. After the Merrill deal was announced, Keefe, Bruyette & Woods analyst Bose George told The Associated Press, "It seems like the investment banks are willing to buy these companies if they can get them at a moderate price. This deal along with a couple of previous deals does suggest there's interest in subprime volume." The AP explained, "Stocks of mortgage lenders have been very weak for the past year as investors factor in expectations for mortgage-loan defaults amid a slumping housing market and eroding credit quality. While lenders haven't begun reporting large-scale defaults yet, most investors believe it's only a matter of time." After news of the deal broke, Thornburg Mortgage gained 66 cents, or 2.9 percent, rising to $23.21.

Thornburg Mortgage's full-year revenue for 2006 increased to $2.53 billion for the year, up from $1.54 billion the year before. Net income increased as well, to $297.7 million from $282.8 million in 2005. Chairman and CEO Garrett Thornburg said that attributed the solid results to maintaining "a focus on only originating and/or acquiring excellent credit quality ARM assets, hedging our borrowings to offset interest rate fluctuations, and utilizing an array of asset acquisition, financing and capital strategies."

Changing of the guard

In December 2007, Thornburg Mortgage named chief operating officer Larry Goldstone to the position of chief executive. Goldstone, who replaced Garrett Thornburg in the CEO role, will also keep his role as president. Thornburg remained with the company as chairman. (Both men are co-founders of the firm.)

A profit, but not positive news

Things for Thornburg didn't look completely abysmal when the firm ended up with a 2007 fourth quarter profit of $64.8 million (even though this was down from the $80.3 million it posted in the fourth quarter 2006). But the firm's full-year 2007 results brought a net loss of $915.4 million, compared with net income of $286.9 million in the previous year. Investors purchasing traditional mortgages and largely eschewing anything in the subprime realm led to the firm selling out loans at a discount during the year.

Falling down?

In June 2008, Thornburg disclosed that it had received subpoenas from the Securities and Exchange Commission. The firm is being investigated for restating its 2007 financial results and its accounting practices regarding mortgage-backed securities. The year has been a rough one for Thornburg; it posted a $3.3 billion loss in the first quarter 2008 after the worth of mortgages slipped across the industry.

Cooley as a cucumber

In July 2008, Thornburg replaced board of director member Stuart Sherman with Thomas F. Cooley, a dean at New York University Stern School of Business and researcher for the National Bureau of Economic Research. The move may be a way for the firm to make a last-ditch effort to save itself after its heavy losses. Sherman had served on Thornburg's board since 1999.

Keeping its head above water

In an attempt to stay afloat in July 2008, the firm began to offer an exchange program for four different classes of its preferred stock. The deal will allow preferred stockholders to get $5 and $3.5 shares of common stock in exchange. Thornburg is hoping that the arrangement—part of a

Visit the Vault Finance Career Channel at www.vault.com/finance — with insider firm profiles, message boards, the Vault Finance Job Board and more.

VAULT CAREER LIBRARY   347

recapitalization deal—will help shore up $1.35 billion in new capital for the firm. To meet the terms of the exchange offer (which comes through an investment by MatlinPatterson), Thornburg needs to have two-thirds of each four levels of its preferred stock exchanged.

GETTING HIRED

Every job has its Thornburg

At www.thornburg.jobs, candidates can browse all job openings listed by Thornburg Companies, including specific opportunities under Thornburg Mortgage (the firm notes that unless it's specifically listed as otherwise, the positions will be located in the downtown Santa Fe, N.M., offices). Candidates can also check out a listing of benefits offered by the firm. Interested applicants are invited to send off a resume directly to humanresources@thornburg.com.

Toyota Financial Services

19001 South Western Avenue
Torrance, CA 90509
Phone: (310) 468-1310
Fax: (310) 468-7829
www.toyotafinancial.com

DEPARTMENTS

Auto Lending
Commercial Lending
Credit Cards
Warranties

Visit the Vault Finance Career Channel at **www.vault.com/finance** — with
insider firm profiles, message boards, the Vault Finance Job Board and more.

VAULT CAREER LIBRARY   **349**

THE SCOOP

Toyota takes over

Toyota has been climbing the ranks of the world's automobile manufacturers since it first began selling cars 70 years ago. In 2007, this Japanese giant finally reached the apex of its success, surpassing General Motors as the number one largest carmaker in the world. With Ford and GM struggling for over a decade, the great era of the American car manufacturer seems to have finally come to a screeching halt. And that's good news for Toyota Financial Services (TFS), a financial and insurance umbrella for the popular Japanese automaker. Like its parent company, TFS's offerings have been growing for over two decades. In that time, TFS has evolved from a small, eight-person operation to over 3,000 employees and $65 billion in managed assets. It is the third-largest captive loan operation in the U.S. after GMAC and Ford Motor Credit, and the eighth-largest specialty-financing company in the country. TFS is the brand name used to market the products and services offered by two divisions: Toyota Motor Credit Corporation (TMCC) and Toyota Motor Insurance Services (TMIS).

TMCC, which commenced operations in 1983 when it approved a finance contract for a used Toyota Corolla, provides retail and wholesale financing, retail leasing and vehicle protection plans to authorized Toyota and Lexus dealers, as well as to Toyota Material Handling dealers and their customers in the United States. TMIS offers credit insurance, extended service contracts and other vehicle protection plans. In addition to the TMCC and TMIS offerings, TFS provides wholesale financing to Toyota and Lexus dealers, as well as to Toyota's industrial equipment and marine sports dealers.

Virtual cars

In the 21st century, virtual reality is more than just an expression—it's a whole different realm. Just ask the kids who are buying Toyota Scions on Whyville.net, a popular social networking site for children, tweens and teens who get real life experience in a fictitious country on their computer screens. Inevitably, these underage drivers want something they can't yet possess in the real world—a brand new car. Toyota happily obliges, offering Scion xBs for 15,000 to 35,000 clams, the virtual currency of Whyville. Of course, many of the kids can't afford the steep price tag. That's where Toyota Financial Services steps in, providing them with loans and educating them about their "WhyCO" scores, which is the virtual equivalent of FICO scores.

The marketing move is a win-win for Toyota Financial Services. Not only are parents happy that their children are getting an education about the snags and snares of the complicated world of credit, but Toyota is also reaching into the future to implant their brand name into potential consumers' brains. So far, the plan is working. As of July 2007, these impressionable youngsters used the word Scion approximately 200,000 times in the first three months of the program's existence. About 1,200 Scions had been purchased, and children had gone in 140,000 rides in their new cars.

Prius power

In 2007, green became the new black—or at least it became the buzzword that would shoot Toyota into the black, largely due to the success of the hybrid car Prius. Though Toyota resisted government regulation of gas-mileage mandates, supposedly in support of its guzzling Scquoia and Tundra models, it stepped up its innovation and created a new, dynamic model of an energy efficient car. But while Detroit struggles to maximize the efficiency of traditional fuels, Toyota is trailblazing into the future, becoming the first car manufacturer to offer a hybrid car which is cost effective and practical. As of the end of April 2008, the firm had sold more than one million Priuses, which likely has the skyrocketing price of U.S. oil and the ensuing demand for green cars to thank for the upsurge. This, of course, is good news for Toyota Financial Services, since more cars sold means more auto financing needed.

Not recommended

Though Toyota overall had a stellar year in 2007, the car manufacturer did suffer several hiccups along the way. One of the most significant road bumps for Toyota was the unexpected departure of Toyota North America President and COO James Press, who had been with the company for over 36 years. Press was the first non-Japanese individual to hold such powerful positions within the company. But in September, shortly after the company reached its goal of becoming the world's biggest automobile manufacturer, Press jumped overboard to join Chrysler. Although it was a sign of the company's dominance of the market, it was also an indicator that top level executives at the new number one were now vulnerable to poaching.

Another disappointment for Toyota in 2007 was the downgrading of its Consumer Reports ratings. Previously, Toyota had enjoyed the luxury of automatically receiving a "recommended" rating for any new or restyled car. However, due to problems on its Camry, Tundra, and Lexus models,

Visit the Vault Finance Career Channel at www.vault.com/finance — with insider firm profiles, message boards, the Vault Finance Job Board and more.

VAULT CAREER LIBRARY   351

Consumer Reports will now required Toyota to provide a year's worth of data before issuing its decision on whether or not to recommend the models.

For its fiscal 2008 (ending in March, Toyota Motor Credit Corporation booked revenue of $8.19 billion, up from $6.7 billion in 2007. The firm sustained a net loss of $196 million for the year, however, compared with a net income of $434 million in fiscal 2007. The loss was mostly due to cumulative corrective adjustments from a past financial statement.

For the first quarter (ending June 30, 2008) of its fiscal 2009, TMCC's total revenue came in at $2.16 billion, up from $1.92 billion in the previous year's first quarter. Net income for the quarter came in at $420 million, up from $174. The solid results had a lot to do with increases in financing revenue—not to mention the record financing volume for retail and lease contracts.

Giving back

In June 2008, Toyota Financial Services and Toyota Motor Sales donated $200,000 and several vehicles to the American Red Cross to assist workers who were helping those affected by the Cedar Rapids floods. TFS has had a call center presence in Cedar Rapids since 1991, and 600 of its employees work and live in the surrounding areas. TFS also offered payment relief options to customers affected by the flooding.

GETTING HIRED

Applicants wanted

On the careers site (under "about us" at www.toyotafinancial.com), candidates can search for jobs worldwide, apply online and read about career advancement opportunities and benefits. Job listings are sorted by category, country, company and keyword, and each listing provides a thorough overview of tasks, responsibilities and qualifications. Most candidates can expect to go through "a multiple-part interview process, consisting of situational questions asked several different ways by two to three people." The firm also offers summer internships in several areas, including accounting, business technology solutions, commercial finance, financial planning and analysis, risk management and treasury, among others. Internships typically begin in May or June, and the firm says applicants "must have completed their sophomore year of an undergraduate program" and "majors in business administration, finance, management, marketing or other related majors." "Interns must also possess advanced computer skills with MS Word, Excel and PowerPoint."

Buckle down

Interviewees "tend to go through a series of interviews over the course of several weeks." Expect to meet with a "hiring manager," "peer team members" and "HR." "In some cases, [candidates will also meet with] senior leadership and members from other departments." While "the nature of the questions will focus on your work history," Toyota also takes into account "how you work, make decisions and problem-solve."

OUR SURVEY SAYS

All's great

The firm boasts "great benefits" and "great people," report contacts. Additionally, the culture at Toyota Financial is "very business-minded" and "very conservative," note insiders. Daily work at the company "can be very challenging," says one insider, and is frequently complicated by "major reorganizations" and "countless job reshuffles." But since there are "excellent benefits," "most people are willing to put up with the constant change."

Hours are largely driven by customer needs. "We recently extended our hours to meet the demands of our customers," says one insider, who adds, "My particular department is open from 7 a.m. to 10 p.m. Our collections and customer service departments are open from 7 a.m. to 9 p.m., and we are also open until 5 p.m. on Saturdays." But there's some flexibility, too. One insider says, "We offer different shift options that assist some associates with balancing their home and work lives." Dress is slightly less flexible. One source says, "Our dress is business attire, except for our business casual Fridays."

Perks sometimes come in the form of parties. There are "several business functions throughout the year," including the "popular" annual holiday party. "Toyota does not hold anything back for the occasion, and includes great

Visit the Vault Finance Career Channel at www.vault.com/finance — with insider firm profiles, message boards, the Vault Finance Job Board and more.

VAULT CAREER LIBRARY   353

The Travelers Companies, Inc.

385 Washington Street
St. Paul, MN 55102
www.travelers.com

DEPARTMENTS

Business Insurance
Claim Services
Corporate Services
Financial, Professional &
    International Insurance
Personal Insurance

THE STATS

Employer Type: Public Company
Ticker Symbol: TRV (NYSE)
Chairman & CEO: Jay S. Fishman
Revenue: $26.02 billion (FYE 12/07)
Net Income: $4.60 billion
No. of Employees: 33,000
No. of Offices: Operates in more than
    90 countries

KEY COMPETITORS

Allstate
Geico
The Hartford
Progressive
State Farm

UPPER

- "Plenty of chances for moving up
  the ladder"

DOWNER

- "Above middle management, there is
  little to no diversity"

EMPLOYMENT CONTACT

www.travelers.com/careers

THE SCOOP

Launch your career

The Travelers Companies, Inc. is one of the largest property and casualty insurance companies in the United States, providing a range of commercial, personal property and casualty insurance products and services to businesses, government units, associations and individuals. The firm draws upon the traditions of two of the oldest and most respected companies in the industry, Travelers and The St. Paul. The company kept up its strong pattern of growth in 2007, booking revenue of $26.02 billion, up from $25.09 billion in 2006. Net income was solid as well, increasing to $4.6 billion from $4.21 billion in the previous year. Strong customer retention rates helped to push the results solidly into the black.

With business booming along, Travelers is an attractive place to work, and it ranked as the top property casualty insurer on *BusinessWeek*'s Best Places to Launch a Career in September of 2007.

Dynamic Duo

St. Paul Companies was established in St. Paul, Minn., as the St. Paul Fire and Marine Insurance Company in 1853, back when the region still constituted the Northwestern frontier of the U.S. and local businesses had difficulty getting eastern insurers to speed up payments on claims, which created room for a local insurer to pick up the slack. Within a few decades, the company had expanded its business across the country, and was financially sound enough to pay out all the claims from two disasters: the 1871 Chicago fire and the San Francisco earthquake of 1906.

The Travelers Insurance Company was formed in 1864 for the purpose of insuring travelers against loss of life or personal injury while journeying by railway or steamboat. A year later, the company expanded to offer protection against accidents of all kinds.

On April 1, 2004, The St. Paul and Travelers merged to form the St. Paul Travelers. In 2007, the company reacquired the familiar red umbrella trademark, which continues to be most closely identified with Travelers. The company also changed its name to The Travelers Companies Inc. and began trading on the New York Stock Exchange under the new stock symbol "TRV." As of June 2008, the firm's total assets were $113.76 billion, and the firm had

Visit the Vault Finance Career Channel at **www.vault.com/finance** — with insider firm profiles, message boards, the Vault Finance Job Board and more.

VAULT CAREER LIBRARY   355

approximately 33,300 employees. Travelers is headquartered in St. Paul, Minn., and has significant operations in Hartford, Conn.

Curbing climate change

If climate change wreaks even a fraction of the havoc predicted by various scientific studies, insurance companies will be the first to suffer financially as a result. And Travelers, recognizing that the earth's climate may be changing in a way that poses serious challenges to society, has taken action intended to mitigate the negative impacts of climate change, encourage environmentally responsible behavior and conserve natural resources. These efforts are described in an annual report issued by the Carbon Disclosure Project (CDP), a coalition of global investors interested in examining the risks and opportunities facing the world's largest publicly traded companies due to climate change.

Travelers takes a three pronged approach to address the implications of climate change on its business: risk management, insurance products and services, and corporate operations. First, the company is working to lessen the risks to policyholders in "catastrophe-prone regions" by educating them about disaster preparedness to help reduce personal injury and damage to the property. Additionally, Travelers established its own climate change committee to identify emerging risks that may require new underwriting strategies or the development of new types of coverage that are responsive to a changing climate. For example, Travelers was the first to offer an insurance discount of 10 percent on a national basis for any individual who chooses to drive a hybrid automobile. Finally, the corporate arm of the company will continue to institute environmentally friendly operations in its two main campuses in St. Paul and Hartford, both of which have been certified as "Energy Star" by the EPA for energy efficiency. As a result of the company's participation in the EPA's Climate Leaders program, Travelers has pledged to reduce its total U.S. greenhouse gas emissions by seven percent from 2006 to 2011.

Additionally, in August 2008, the company joined up with the U.S. Green Building Council, a group devoted to seeking out sustainable environmental alternatives. Travelers also said its involvement with the group will help it to continue to develop innovations that follow the green movement for building initiatives. In the previous month, the company began another green initiative of its own—it began to offer a discount on boat insurance policies to those customers with electrically-powered boats.

Traveling to the Northeast

Travelers is a nationally known brand, but recently it announced that it would get a little more name recognition in the Northeast. The Premier Insurance Company, a subsidiary of Travelers that serves the personal insurance needs of Massachusetts residents, made the switch to carry the Travelers name on its marquis. As of October 2007, Premier became known as Travelers of Massachusetts, in an attempt to play up the cachet of being involved with its prestigious parent company. Shortly after the change, Travelers of Massachusetts announced that it would be integrating Travelers' 10 percent discount for hybrid drivers, a Good Student Discount on auto insurance, and a Multiple Policy Discount, all in an effort to work towards the state's new system of "managed competition," which went into place in April 2008.

The good and the bad

Travelers' financial results for the second quarter 2008 were not as good as its numbers for 2007. Revenue fell to $6.3 billion from $6.57 billion compared with the second quarter 2007, and net income decreased to $942 million from $1.25 billion. A reduced investment portfolio and still-challenging economy led to the depressed results.

GETTING HIRED

Beyond St. Paul and Hartford

The company encourages everyone from new graduates and interns to "motivated professionals" to apply, and it has positions available across the United States. Though Travelers maintains significant locations in St. Paul and Hartford, field locations account for the bulk of available positions and existing employees. The careers section of Travelers' web site hosts a database of employment opportunities, searchable by geographic location or job category, which can include actuarial, administrative, business analyst, claim, corporate services, executive, finance and accounting, investments, legal, marketing and sales, product management, policy services, risk control and underwriting. Job seekers can apply for positions online.

Accounts regarding interviews with the company vary. Candidates call it everything from a "great process" to "long and intimidating." One contact describes having to take a "placement test to see how well your data entry skills

Visit the Vault Finance Career Channel at **www.vault.com/finance** — with insider firm profiles, message boards, the Vault Finance Job Board and more.

VAULT CAREER LIBRARY   357

and comprehension for insurance measure up," followed by "a four-hour interview" that included "one hour in a call simulation, one hour with HR, one hour with a manager and a one-hour shadow with an employee." Other insiders say to expect at least "two rounds of interviews," mostly "behavioral interviewing," and note that "the process takes about four to six weeks."

One intern says the process is as follows: "I interviewed with two different people, and questions were based solely on my resume. The interviews lasted about one hour and were very easy going. They gave me the opportunity to ask them questions as well."

OUR SURVEY SAYS

Fun work

Travelers "is an awesome company to work for," says one insider, adding that "the people are friendly, and it's just fun work." Another says, "The underwriting operation is the best in the business—and A++ in my book," but adds that "the operations side of our business is a solid C at best." Another calls the corporate culture "very organized," but adds that new hires "must be computer-savvy and ready to buy into the corporate culture of being No. 1, or survival will be difficult." One insider notes that "the company could be more receptive to new ideas."

Laid-back dress, flexible hours

For the most part, sources report satisfaction with the "business casual" dress code. One insider notes that on occasion "Friday is 'dress down day' for $1, which goes into the employee activities committee." (Dress down days are not offered in all locations.) Hours get good marks, too. A contact says, "Standard shifts run either 8 a.m. to 5 p.m., with some flexibility," depending on business need. Another agrees, adding that there's "flexibility to start earlier or later as long as you fulfill the eight-hour requirement." And another notes, "We're let out around lunchtime on Fridays before holiday weekends."

Fore!

Travelers "seems to be very involved with its employees and always tries to offer something for everybody." For example, "there are several teams that employees can join to play competitively," says one source. "It's very easy to get involved, as there's a newsletter e-mailed bi-weekly with updates of what's going on within the company." Additionally, "there are always trips being planned, and parties all the time." In the summer, "the firm sponsors a golf tournament, and holds a 'pitch and putt' event where they give away free T-shirts, hats and bags of goodies."

Getting to the top

"There are plenty of chances for moving up the ladder," an insider says, adding that "you start out in this position as an agency counselor, assisting agents through policies and answering general questions, and you then move up to getting licensed in the other states and deal directly with insureds." Another notes you're "more likely to advance if you're willing to transfer to other locations, consistently give superior performance, are sales-oriented and toe the company line." Yet another contact says, "If you are a hard worker, there is opportunity to advance," but adds, "Some of the local opportunity is due to the relatively high turnover rate at the middle management level." However, management gets generally high marks. One insider notes, "Managers don't breathe down your neck."

Less diversity in higher levels

Although Travelers was recently named a Best Diversity Company by Diversity/Careers in *Engineering & Information Technology* magazine, diversity at the firm seems to differ according to rank. One insider says, "At the entry-level positions, there is moderate diversity," but "above middle management, there is little to no diversity in key positions." Indeed, "most positions with power are occupied by white males." Another comments that "the company doesn't seem to discriminate, but there are very few minorities in the Boston office and other offices I have visited. The higher you go, the fewer minorities you see." The contact goes on to say that gender balance within the company fares better, and "there are a good ratio of females to males on many levels. There's no glass ceiling for women in the company." The company is making an effort, says a contact, pointing out that the firm holds "annual to biannual diversity and sexual harassment training." Travelers also points out that it has a diversity council led by 12 of the company's senior leaders, and recently launched several diversity programs and partnerships with diversity organizations.

Visit the Vault Finance Career Channel at **www.vault.com/finance** — with insider firm profiles, message boards, the Vault Finance Job Board and more.

VAULT CAREER LIBRARY   359

Unum

1 Fountain Sq.
Chattanooga, TN 37402
Phone: (423) 294-1011
Fax: (423) 294-3962
www.unum.com

DEPARTMENTS

Disability Insurance
Leave Management Services
Life Insurance
Long-Term Care
Voluntary Benefits

THE STATS

Employer Type: Public Company
Ticker Symbol: UNM (NYSE)
President & CEO: Thomas R. Watjen
Net Revenue: $10.52 billion (FYE 12/07)
Net Income: $679.3 million
No. of Employees: 10,000
No. of Offices: Major presence in 4 US
    cities, plus 38 field offices

KEY COMPETITORS

Aflac
CAN Financial
Hartford Life
MetLife
Prudential Financial

UPPER

- "Great" benefits

DOWNER

- "Depending on the job and level, hours can be long"

EMPLOYMENT CONTACT

See "careers" section of www.unum.com

THE SCOOP

E pluribus Unum

Ranked No. 251 on the 2008 Fortune 500, Unum is the largest disability insurer in the U.S. It provides disability income protection to people who, thanks to payments from Unum, are able to keep up with their bills and put food on the table should they suffer a debilitating injury or illness and need to take time off from work. The company also offers life, long-term care and supplemental insurance to millions of clients. Unum plans are used by almost one in every five U.S. employers that provide group disability insurance coverage—that equates to more than 11 million American workers covered by income protection disability insurance. Unum also boasts more than one million customers, and a total of 25 million insured policyholders worldwide.

Headquartered in Chattanooga, Tenn., the company also has offices in Portland, Maine; Worcester, Mass.; and Glendale, Calif. In addition, it has subsidiaries in South Carolina (Colonial Life & Accident Insurance Company) and the U.K.(Unum Limited).

After it was incorporated in 1910, Provident Life and Accident experienced several periods of growth and a few subtle name changes. In 1997, Provident Life & Accident Companies acquired Massachusetts-based Paul Revere Life Insurance Company. But a final, major change made the company what it is today. In 1999, Provident, which had a strong foothold in the individual policies market, merged with UNUM, a life insurance company that was established as a main player in group disability coverage and international operations. Thus, the new Unum was born.

When UNUM and Provident united, the top brass discovered they'd have to manage the merger through technology—but they didn't realize the extent of that task right away. The new company's managers had planned to use advanced computer and telecommunication systems, which would reduce the duplication of staffers and offices by letting product lines and specialty groups work nationally. But sorting out e-mail, internal chatter and phone systems didn't run as smoothly or as soon as they'd hoped.

Fortunately, the company found a way to deal with its technological challenges. It came up with a three-pronged solution: a steering committee that put senior techies in charge of strategic decisions; other business transition groups to manage customers' needs; and working groups whose main aim was to hone in on tech and infrastructure problems.

Visit the Vault Finance Career Channel at **www.vault.com/finance** — with
insider firm profiles, message boards, the Vault Finance Job Board and more.

VAULT CAREER LIBRARY   361

U.K. calls in hungover

In December 2007, Unum's U.K. subsidiary published a study it had conducted that showed the number one reason why Britons call in sick is due to hangovers. Scots in particular were key offenders of skipping out on work due to a night out on the town. Unum wants to keep actions like this under control due to long term health risks. According to the chief medical officer of Unum Limited, Michael O'Donnell, "These figures reinforce well-documented and worrying trends that people's drinking habits are impacting on the workplace. From a medical point of view, this is particularly worrying, given that in 2005/06, there were 187,640 NHS hospital admissions among adults aged 16 and over with diagnosis specifically related to alcohol. This has more than doubled from 89,280 in 1995/96. It is vital that employees recognize that hangovers, and any resulting time off work, not only have serious consequences for their health and their families but can also seriously affect their careers."

Debt busters

Unum set its sights on paying down debt in 2007, and at the end of the year, it had retired about $400 million of outstanding debt. The company announced in October 2007 that it had completed the securitization of a closed block of its individual income protection insurance via its subsidiary Northwind. In conjunction with the deal, the company made a goal of reducing corporate debt by $800 million. The goal set for achieving this debt reduction was the second quarter 2008. In order to create liquidity in the midst of its debt paying plan in December 2007, the company managed to establish a $400 million unsecured revolving credit facility through Wachovia Capital Market and Banc of America Securities. The credit facility was a big win for Unum in the midst of the tightened credit market.

Looking up

In 2007, Unum brought in $10.52 billion in revenue, nearly identical to its 2006 revenue of $10.53 billion. Net income for the year, however, came in at $679.3 million, up from $411 million in 2006. Strong results in individual disability, long-term care and voluntary benefits drove the results, giving the firm power as it pushed into 2008.

The firm kept the momentum going through the first half of 2008, bringing in revenue of $2.68 billion in the second quarter 2008, up from $2.66 billion in the second quarter 2007. Net income, meanwhile, jumped to $240.3 million from $153.5 million.

The good results, which beat analysts' estimates, were attributed to a shift in strategy. "What [Unum has] been doing the past few years is trying to right the boat and move things in a direction that is more long-term oriented," Bruce Cox, a Fitch Ratings analyst, told the *Chattanooga Times Free Press* upon the earnings announcement. "The fundamentals of the business are improved, and they are making progress on their plan."

As further evidence of its financial health, shortly before the announcement, Unum's debt was upgraded by Standard & Poor's, which pointed to Unum's continued strength in market share and profitability.

GETTING HIRED

United with Unum

Find recruiting events, get the skinny on benefits or just take your online job cart and do a little career shopping—Unum's site has a little bit of everything. The firm recruits at numerous schools, including Penn State, Georgia, Miami of Ohio, USC, Bentley College, Boston University, Maine, North Carolina and Tennessee.

The careers section of the firm's web site ("careers" at www.unum.com) also enables job seekers to set up an account to create and/or submit a resume, set up automated job agents and search job openings. Jobs are searchable by location and job type, which can include actuarial, administrative, claims, communications, finance, human resources, information technology, legal, product development, project management, sales and underwriting.

An employee in the firm's Tennessee outpost says, "Unum's hiring process is increasingly becoming more selective, as the reputation of the company strengthens. Many applications are submitted for almost every position." He adds that "normal" interview questions include "What can you contribute to the company" and "Give an example of a time that you have had to show extraordinary leadership." When answering, "make sure to highlight your strong points and anything that might set you aside from the crowd."

Visit the Vault Finance Career Channel at **www.vault.com/finance** — with insider firm profiles, message boards, the Vault Finance Job Board and more.

VAULT CAREER LIBRARY   363

OUR SURVEY SAYS

Sharing is caring

"The company is great to work for," says one source. The corporate culture promotes "open communication and sharing information," says another insider. The company also offers "great" benefits (including those for same-sex partners, "very generous" vacation time and "flexible hours"). Though, one insider notes that "depending on the job and level, hours can be long." Contacts do report some "office gossip and brown nosing," as is typical at most large companies.

Sources also laud the dress code ("jeans most of the time" although "no sneakers or T-shirts" are allowed). But compensation is "on the low side of market value," and there's also "marginal opportunity for advancement." One insider notes that advancement opportunities "used to be more prevalent, but now that there have been cuts, there are fewer openings to move up now." And though "opportunities are presented," "you just have to be the most motivated person in order to get there." There is also "a definite cap to the advancement potential, even for someone with an MBA." Another insider agrees, adding that there are "limited opportunities for career advancement unless you're working at corporate headquarters." Perhaps a reason for that is this: "Education is highly valued here, so unless you have a lot of that, it is not likely you'll advance too far."

Unum gets average marks for its diversity efforts. One insider notes that though there's "not much diversity within the Chattanooga, Tenn., area," "in our national offices, we celebrate it."

USAA

9800 Fredericksburg Road
San Antonio, TX 78288
Phone: (210) 498-2211
Fax: (210) 498-9940
www.usaa.com

BUSINESSES

Banking
Financial Planning
Insurance
Investments

THE STATS

Employer Type: Private Company
President & CEO: Major General Josue
  Robles, Jr.
Revenue: $14.42 billion (FYE 12/07)
Net Income: $1.86 billion
No. of Employees: 21,800
No. of Offices: 8

KEY COMPETITORS

MetLife
UnumProvident

UPPER

- "Great" corporate culture

DOWNER

- Very little diversity with respect to gays and lesbians

EMPLOYMENT CONTACT

www.usaa.apply2jobs.com/

Visit the Vault Finance Career Channel at **www.vault.com/finance** — with
insider firm profiles, message boards, the Vault Finance Job Board and more.

VAULT CAREER LIBRARY   365

THE SCOOP

Ten-hut!

One day in 1922, a group of Army officers gathered in San Antonio to discuss a problem: because their military careers meant frequent relocation, their car insurance policies were expensive and difficult to maintain. The 25 officers decided to form a mutual company to insure each other's vehicles, and to create policies tailored to the military life. The United States Army Automobile Association is now known as USAA, and has grown to over 6 million members. It operates from six offices in the U.S. and two offices overseas, in London and Frankfurt.

USAA products and services are available only to members: active duty officers and enlisted personnel, spouses and children of USAA members, National Guard and Selective Reserve officers and enlisted personnel, retired military personnel and officer candidates in commissioning programs.

Business unusual

"We're not a household name," USAA declares on its web site, "and you won't see our logo in a Super Bowl commercial." Indeed, USAA's business is different from conventional insurance companies in many ways. It relies on direct marketing to sell its products and policies; in addition to insurance, banking and financial services it does a brisk business in mail-order catalog sales, offering computers, jewelry, furniture and other items to members wherever they may be posted.

USAA's insurance division provides annuities, Medicare solutions and automobile, home and property, life, business and long-term care insurance. Its investments business includes mutual funds, IRAs, college savings plans, annuities, asset management plans and brokerage services. Members can use USAA's banking services, which include checking and savings accounts, loans, credit cards and CD products. USAA financial advisors provide advisory and planning services tailored specifically for military concerns— how a family might budget for a deployment, for example. (All USAA financial advisors are salaried employees and not commissioned, thus their advice is not based on achieving sales goals.)

Reporting for duty

USAA welcomed new leadership in 2008 due to the retirement of the sitting Chairman and CEO Robert Davis, who left the company in December 2007. Davis had been the president of USAA for eight years, the CEO for seven years, and was named chairman in 2002. Upon stepping down, Davis praised the company and pledged that he would continue to be involved saying, "It has been my privilege to lead this great organization for the past seven years. As I have for the last 40 years, I will continue to be a proud member of USAA."

Davis was replaced in his duties as president and CEO by Josue Robles, a lifelong army man who began his service in 1966. Originally hailing from Puerto Rico, Robles has served the United States in active duty posts in Korea, Vietnam, Germany and the Middle East. He has also been a longtime member of the USAA, serving as a member of the board of directors from 1990 to 1994. In July 2008, Robles was named the Corporate Executive of the Year by the San Antonio Hispanic Chamber of Commerce. The position of USAA chairman was filled by General John H. Moellering, who had served as vice-chairman.

Pushing for more regulation?

USAA's policy to insure Army officers and their families no matter where they live puts them in a precarious financial position when it comes to high-risk areas like Florida or California. Florida represents about 9 percent of its policy holders and approximately 40 percent of its risk. In July 2007, the insurer looked to slim down its exposure to storm sensitive Florida in particular and applied to the Office of Insurance Regulations to approve a 50.9 percent average statewide hike for the region. It also limited its home insurance policy so that it would only insure one home per family with active military duty in Florida. The Office of Insurance Regulation turned down the proposed hike, claiming that USAA's 1,300-page filing was incomplete.

USAA plans to resubmit the filing sometime in 2008, with hopes for better results. In the meantime, however, the company will lobby for a federal charter for insurances, so that the regulations won't have to be decided state by state in the future. Currently, USAA has policy holders located in all 50 states, the District of Columbia and three of the four territories, racking up costs of over $200 million per year to comply with state regulations. Bill McCartney, USAA's senior vice president for insurance regulation, posed the problem like this to the *Miami Herald* in December 2007: "If you have a full

Visit the Vault Finance Career Channel at **www.vault.com/finance** — with insider firm profiles, message boards, the Vault Finance Job Board and more.

VAULT CAREER LIBRARY   367

range of products with USAA—mutual funds, credit cards, checking account, a life insurance policy, and auto and homeowners or renters policies—when you move from Nebraska to Florida, all you need to do is give us a change of address for [everything but the auto and homeowners policies]. We have to re-underwrite and reissue those policies. An auto policy can be 20 to 30 pages long. If you're moving every 13 months, that's a fairly substantial amount of work for us. And since we're owned by our members, it is a substantial expense for our members."

Highly decorated

USAA does more than just its patriotic duty as an insurance provider for the United States military and their families. It also excels in the areas of customer service and employee satisfaction. In 2008, for the second year in a row, *BusinessWeek* ranked USAA No. 1 on its list of Customer Service Champs. And in February 2008, Forrester Research ranked USAA as No. 1 in its Experience That Satisfy Consumers report for Internet and phone customer service. Previously, in December 2007, Representative Martinez Fischer of Texas also honored USAA by passing a resolution (House Resolution 1614) that publicly honors the company for its devotion to its clients. The company has also been included in *ComputerWorld*'s Top Place to Work in IT list, and *LATINA Style*'s list of leading employers for Hispanic women.

Gaining traction

In 2007, USAA brought in $14.42 billion in revenue, up from the $13.4 billion it posted in 2006. Net income was down slightly in 2007 to $1.85 billion from $2.33 billion in the previous year. An all-around harsh economy in 2007 trickled down to the industry, and USAA wasn't exempt from being affected.

Midway through 2008, the number weren't necessarily looking much better for the firm. For the first six months of 2008 until June 30th, USAA had pulled in $7.26 billion in revenue and $729 million in net income. While the results weren't stellar, the firm's net worth rose to $14.8 billion, its highest net worth ever.

GETTING HIRED

Let the search begin

At www.usaa.apply2jobs.com, you can create a profile and apply to positions via that route—or you can paste in your resume and let the database search your skills and match your interests to open postings. Alternately, you can search jobs by area of interest or even by positions that offer relocation assistance.

Par for the course

Reports regarding the firm's interview process vary, from accounts of USAA's style being "standard" to "pretty informal" and "laid-back." Interviewers, in general, are described as "nice."

"The hiring process consisted of an initial phone interview," explains a source, "then an interview with an HR rep, the management team and then an interview with an executive." Be prepared to anticipate everything from "situational-type questions such as 'Give me a time when …'" to "behavior-based questions asking for a situation, action and result." Other questions may include "What are your best qualities?" and "Tell me about a time you faced a problem and how you handled it." In IT, sources say interviews are "ridiculously easy, as management performs all interviews and no peers are involved."

Expect the process to take "a very long time." One insider says, "I interviewed in May, but was not hired until September." Another calls her series of interviews "a long but easy process."

OUR SURVEY SAYS

The core of the culture

"Emulation of the military culture" is a description that tends to crop up when insiders explain the company ethos. But most are upbeat in their accounts, commenting that "the corporate culture is great," and "USAA has excellent core values." Your experience may hinge on your department. With respect to career advancement, one source says, "Although the Phoenix office is growing quite a bit, they keep telling the representatives that there is a lot of potential for growth and advancement, but I didn't see that in the four-and-a-half years I was there." Another source in that office calls the corporate

Visit the Vault Finance Career Channel at www.vault.com/finance — with
insider firm profiles, message boards, the Vault Finance Job Board and more.

VAULT CAREER LIBRARY   369

culture "great," while a former insider in the Phoenix outpost notes that he came across a serious "lack of professionalism."

Meanwhile, in San Antonio, sources call the firm a "very disorganized company" with a "poor" work environment, and say the firm is currently in "turmoil." One source in that office notes that the "corporate culture is very rigid, with rules-based management, procedures for everything and no independent thinking." However, the contact adds that the outpost has "a very diverse work force," with "very nice people to talk to."

The dress code receives higher praise, however. Dress is business casual most of the year, and if a certain percentage of staffers participate in the United Way program, then the company will extend the casual dress beyond the summer.

Good pay and benefits

The "overall pay is good for the hours you put in," explains one source, "but it's not that great compared to most Fortune 500 companies. However, another believes he's "way overpaid for the amount of work I actually do."

In the compensation realm, the firm touts that "benefits start on day one" with 90 percent of the premium paid." In addition, "USAA offers a pretty decent bonus package—two bonuses a year. There's one in February and a Christmas bonus." But getting that pay increase may be tough. While they execute "performance evaluations once a year in February, the average percent increase is only about three to four percent, which in my mind is not very much."

Other perks at the San Antonio campus include softball fields, jogging trails, intramural sports, pilates, salsa dancing, three Starbucks coffee houses and an on-site wellness clinic and pharmacy.

Mixed reports on diversity and future

Regarding the company's diversity attempts, reports are mixed. One insider says that "USAA is diversity-oriented, and therefore we have a lot of culture within the company," but that's not necessarily the collective feeling. "They do recognize ethnic diversity, but they do not recognize diversity with respect to gays and lesbians." One source adds, "You would think that a company that promotes themselves as world class would recognize this."

Although some insiders say the firm has a "great business outlook" and is "very strong financially," others call the firm's future "bleak" and "fair to poor." One source with a positive outlook says there's room for improvement. "USAA will continue to do great as a company," she explains, "but it needs to give more attention to its employees than it has in the past couple of years."

Visa USA

900 Metro Center Boulevard
Foster City, CA 94404
Phone: (650) 432-3200
Fax: (650) 432-3631
www.usa.visa.com

DEPARTMENTS

Brand Marketing
Client Services (Member & Merchant)
Corporate Relations
Finance
Human Resources
Inovant—A Visa Solutions Company
Interchange Strategy & Fees
Legal
Operations & Risk Management
Product Development &
    Management
    (Consumer Credit, Debit &
    Prepaid, Commercial, Corporate,
    Government & Small Business,
    Processing Products)

THE STATS

Employer Type: Private Company (U.S.
    operations of Visa Inc.)
Chairman & CEO, Visa Inc.: Joseph
    Saunders
President & CEO, Visa USA: John
    Philip Coghlan
Net Revenue: $5.19 billion (FYE 12/07)
Net Income: -$861 million
No. of Employees: 5,581
No. of Offices: 13

KEY COMPETITORS

American Express
Discover
MasterCard

UPPER

- "Intense, dynamic, challenging and
  creative" culture

DOWNER

- Long hours—"they have unrealistic
  expectations with respect to time"

EMPLOYMENT CONTACT

www.visa.com/jobs

Visit the Vault Finance Career Channel at **www.vault.com/finance** — with
insider firm profiles, message boards, the Vault Finance Job Board and more.

VAULT CAREER LIBRARY   371

THE SCOOP

Merger accomplished

It's hard to imagine a company with as much international name recognition as Visa getting even bigger, but in 2007 somehow the credit card behemoth managed to do just that. The company's latest growth comes as the result of a series of mergers that combined all of its various subsidiaries (including Visa Canada, Visa USA and Visa International) into one global entity called Visa Inc. The new company brings together the company's U.S. and Canadian operations with those in Asia Pacific, Latin America and the Caribbean, the Middle East and Africa.

The year 2008 has been another exciting one for Visa. After years of operating as a private entity, Visa Inc. has ventured into the public realm. The company filed for its IPO in November 2007, following in the footsteps of its competitor MasterCard which took the plunge in 2005. Visa's IPO made a huge splash when it finally hit in March 2008, raising a record $7.9 billion for its debut.

The newly formed Visa Inc. is already a giant of global commerce. The combined company boasts 16,400 financial institution clients, 27 million Visa merchant outlets, 45 billion yearly transactions processed, and 1.4 billion Visa cards issued. In 2007, $3.8 trillion of business was conducted on Visa cards. Though the company is still headquartered in San Francisco, it now has offices in 30 countries around the world and approximately 5,581 employees.

The Net

Visa's processing system, VisaNet, facilitates over $1.2 trillion in annual transaction volume, including 51 percent of all Internet payments. U.S. consumers carry more than 520 million Visa-branded smart, credit, commercial, prepaid, and check cards that offer unsurpassed acceptance at millions of merchant locations worldwide. VisaNet's global presence is also impressive—it is one of the largest transaction and information processing networks in the world, providing approximately 74 billion authorization, clearing and settlement transactions per year. These transactions operate from three continents which have power data centers allowing the company to process more than 12,000 messages per second.

Circling the globe

San Francisco-based Bank of America created Visa's predecessor in 1958, when it launched what was then called BankAmericard. In 1966, Bank of America formed BankAmericard Service Corporation, which licensed banks outside of California to issue cards to their customers. Four years later, National BankAmericard Inc. was created, and BankAmericard transferred control and ownership of the BankAmericard program to the banks issuing the cards.

In 1973, the company launched the first global electronic card authorization system, BASE I, which reduced the time consumers needed to wait for purchase authorization from more than five minutes to less than one. Wanting to shed its image as a California company to that of a world player, the card changed its name to Visa in 1976. In another first, Visa created a global ATM network in 1983 to provide access to cash around the clock, to cardholders around the world. Today, Visa claims its Visa/PLUS ATM network is the world's largest, giving customers access to local currency at more than one million ATMs in more than 170 countries. Visa also operates the world's largest consumer payments processing system. It has enough communications lines to encircle the globe nearly 400 times, and can process more than 6,300 transactions each second.

Antitrust anxiety

It may seem like lawsuits can go on forever, but eventually you always have to pay up. Visa's time came in November 2007 when it finally settled its antitrust lawsuit with American Express for a whopping $2.1 billion. The settlement is the largest amount ever paid out in an antitrust case. This case goes back to 2004, when both American Express and Discover Financial filed suits against Visa and MasterCard for restricting its member banks from offering their rival's cards to customers. The payout is a reflection of the amount of revenue American Express estimates it lost as a result of being given access to a lower number of potential customers.

The large number is sure to boost Discover's expectations in its $6 billion lawsuit with Visa, which has yet to be settled. Visa paid American Express $945 million in 2007 and is paying the rest in $70 million quarterly installments until the full balance is paid.

Visit the Vault Finance Career Channel at **www.vault.com/finance** — with
insider firm profiles, message boards, the Vault Finance Job Board and more.

VAULT CAREER LIBRARY   373

Mobile mania

In the age of the iPhone, the bar has been raised for what can be done with those contraptions once used exclusively for ringing your mom. Visa hopes to take advantage of the mobile revolution with a platform launched in 2007 which gives clients the ability to make payments and conduct marketing campaigns from their phones. At the Cellular Telecommunications and Internet Association Wireless conference in March 2007, Visa USA's CEO and President John Coghlan laid out the framework for a plan that would have consumers transferring money, using store coupons, and even making credit card payments with just a click of a button on their trusty cell phones.

Visa's field research showed that 57 percent of consumers aged 18 to 42 would be interested in making payments via their mobile phones. Even more auspiciously, the survey showed that of the group who would be interested in mobile payment services, 90 percent would consider paying more for a phone with higher capabilities.

Visa is encouraging the whole mobile phone industry to work towards a goal of a streamlined device that will incorporate many different types of functionality including customized coupon campaigns, mobile offers and promotion programs, and payment capabilities. The digital infrastructure provider VeriSign currently supports the Visa mobile payments platform.

Gooooooooal!

Visa's name recognition is universal throughout the world and much of its latest marketing campaigns have been accomplished throughout something that unites (and sometimes divides) all nations: sports. Visa is an exclusive sponsor of FIFA (Federation Internationale de Football) World Cup, with a firm hold on the partnership through the 2014. The World Cup gains Visa access to millions of customers in virtually every country in the world.

The credit card company also lends its name branding to the Olympics, extending its sponsorship even to the name given to the competitors, or Visa athletes. Visa was the only card that could be used as payment at the Beijing Olympic Games of 2008, and it will be the only card able to be used at the Vancouver Games of 2010 and London Games of 2012.

A good time for the credit industry

Visa's fiscal third quarter of 2008 was a happy one for Visa, whose net income increased 41 percent from the same period in 2007. Revenue also grew, increasing 18 percent to $1.61 billion. The company's encouraging results sprang largely from healthy spending from credit card holders, whose payment volume increased 19 percent to $652 billion. Overall transaction volume, which increased 22 percent for the quarter, also helped push Visa's results up.

Adding to the positive news for the credit industry was a report released from Visa's Commercial Consumption Expenditure index in July 2008. The report said that annual commercial spending on a global scale increased to $77.3 trillion in 2007, up 12.2 percent from 2006. And in the U.S., spending increased to $19.7 trillion, up 5.5 percent from the previous year.

GETTING HIRED

Finding the best

Visa's college hire program recruits university graduates through "campuses, alumni associations, online resources, business/employee referrals and other venues." At the "careers" section of corporate.visa.com, job seekers can also search for openings with any of Visa's six regional operating units around the world (you can also go to "careers" at www.usa.visa.com for jobs in the United States). The link to Visa's U.S. career site offers a list of current openings with that division. However, the links to the other regional units only provide an address and fax number where applicants can send their resumes, and offer no way of e-mailing a resume. The site also contains a detailed list of the firm's benefits, as well as office locations, corporate culture and community involvement.

One insider says the firm is selective when it comes to new hires, and adds that candidates should expect a "minimum of two to three" interviews. Another candidate says to expect to "interview with at least six people." Also anticipate "questions to determine if you will fit with the team, such as why you want to work for Visa, your interests, etc." Other insiders note that "most of the time I got a sense that the interviewer did not read my resume," and "the hiring process can be brutal if you are not just being given a job because you are someone's husband, wife, boyfriend, cousin, etc."

Visit the Vault Finance Career Channel at **www.vault.com/finance** — with insider firm profiles, message boards, the Vault Finance Job Board and more.

VAULT CAREER LIBRARY   **375**

OUR SURVEY SAYS

Intense and rewarding

Sources give the work environment varied marks. Visa's culture is called "intense, dynamic, challenging and creative," say insiders. But it can also be "frustrating." Maybe that's because at Visa, "work hours are hefty," says a risk manager at the firm. "You cannot succeed without heavy dedication inside and outside the office—40 hours is looked at as almost part-time. They have unrealistic expectations with respect to time." The contact reports going into the office on the weekend "at least once a month." A director reluctantly agrees, saying, "Depending on position, you could expect to work 60 to 70 hours per week, weekends and evenings."

Above its peers in pay

As for compensation, one contact, who has more than 10 years of experience in the industry, says Visa pays above average as compared to its peers. Another calls the salary package "very competitive for most positions," but adds that "one mistake I think they have made is to bring employees in at high levels when they can't meet salary requirements." Sometimes this action "results in someone coming into a job they cannot perform," comments the contact. But most don't have many compensation complaints, though one notes, "I am interviewing for a position at a less stressful company that can match Visa's salary compensation." Employee benefits include "gym memberships and other athletic facilities," plus a "two-to-one matching thrift plan," which increases to a three-to-one match after 10 years of service.

As for the future, one source notes that "for Visa to be successful, they will need to modify their business direction, which will put them in direct competition with their board banks."

APPENDIX

Alphabetical Listing of Companies

Visit the Vault Finance Career Channel at www.vault.com/finance – with insider firm profiles, message boards, the Vault Finance Job Board and more.

VAULT CAREER LIBRARY   379

About the Editor

Derek Loosvelt received his BS in economics from the Wharton School at the University of Pennsylvania and MFA in creative writing from the New School. He is a writer and editor and has worked for *Brill's Content* and Inside.com. Previously, he worked in investment banking at CIBC and Duff & Phelps.

Visit the Vault Finance Career Channel at **www.vault.com/finance** – with insider firm profiles, message boards, the Vault Finance Job Board and more.

VAULT CAREER LIBRARY 380

The Editor's "Thank You" Free Gifts Include:

- Two BRAND-NEW romance novels!
- An exciting mystery gift!

Yes I have placed my Editor's "Thank You" seal in the space provided above. Please send me 2 free books and a fabulous Mystery Gift. I understand I am under no obligation to purchase any books, as explained on the back and on the opposite page.

386 HDL DZ6S   186 HDL DZ67

FIRST NAME	LAST NAME

ADDRESS

APT.#	CITY

STATE/PROV.	ZIP/POSTAL CODE

(H-R-06/04)

Thank You!

The Harlequin Reader Service® — Here's how it works:

If offer card is missing write to: The Harlequin Reader Service, 3010 Walden Ave., P.O. Box 1867, Buffalo, NY 14240-1867

BUSINESS REPLY MAIL
FIRST-CLASS MAIL   PERMIT NO. 717-003   BUFFALO, NY

POSTAGE WILL BE PAID BY ADDRESSEE

HARLEQUIN READER SERVICE
3010 WALDEN AVE
PO BOX 1867
BUFFALO NY 14240-9952

NO POSTAGE
NECESSARY
IF MAILED
IN THE
UNITED STATES

ably made him a wonderful person and a loveable father, but maybe not a very practical farmer.'

He nodded. 'That's true.'

'But you *are* practical. I expect you hauled him back from the brink a few times.'

'That's true as well. He was always going after madcap schemes and having to be rescued. You'd think he'd learn.'

Alex shook her head.

'People like that never do learn,' she said gently. 'They're always sure they're going to get it right next time. I think he relied on you completely, and was just a little bit in awe of you.'

'Nonsense, how could my father—?' But Rinaldo checked himself, and a strange, distant look came over his face, as though he were hearing distant echoes.

'Perhaps,' he said after a while.

'You've said that the money helped this place.'

'A lot. Poppa ploughed it into Belluna—he was a good enough farmer for that. The investment has enabled us to prosper as never before.'

'Then don't you see how he must have cherished his secret, the feeling that *he'd* done something to make things right, instead of leaving it all to you? He probably looked forward to surprising you with it one day, rather like a child springing a surprise on an adult and saying, "There, aren't I clever? What do you think of *that*?"'

Rinaldo stared at her, as if thunderstruck.

'Yes,' he murmured. 'That's exactly how he was. I can hear how he would have said it.'

'It isn't his fault that it all went wrong,' she pleaded. 'He couldn't have known what would happen. Maybe it hurt his pride to have to depend on you so much. He wanted you to admire him.'

'You make it sound so convincing,' he said in a low voice. 'If only I could remember—'

'Remember what?'

'Something—anything—just a moment that would tell me what was in his mind. I keep having this feeling that it's there, just on the edge. Like when you see something out of the corner of your eye, but when you turn it vanishes. I dream about it, but it isn't there when I awaken. Maybe it doesn't really exist at all.'

'If it does, it will come back to you,' she said. 'Not now, because your head's all scrambled, but when you feel easier inside.'

His mouth quirked wryly.

'I think I've forgotten what it's like to feel easy inside.'

She looked at his hands, lying loosely clasped. He was a big man and his hands were large in proportion. She could still feel their power where he'd gripped her. Yet now they looked helpless.

'You carry all the burdens for everyone, don't you?' she said.

He didn't answer, and she wondered if she'd taken a risk too far. But his eyes held only a searching look, as though he were trying to fathom her.

From outside came Gino's voice.

'Hey! Anybody there?'

He was coming toward the barn. Rinaldo put his finger to his lips, shaking his head slightly, and hurried out before Gino could enter.

She heard his voice carrying back.

'I was just coming. We have a lot to do today.'

Their voices faded. After a while she slipped out of the barn to find everywhere quiet.

She went indoors and put through a call to David, but there was only his answerphone. They had spoken several times since she came to Belluna. She had apologised for being so long, and he'd encouraged her to stay as long as necessary.

She always finished these calls feeling a little guilty that he was being so nice and understanding. She felt she was taking advantage of his patience to indulge herself.

One thing she was sure of. There was no way she was leaving before the Feast of St Romauld, which took place on June 19th.

'There's a parade of floats through the streets,' Gino told her, 'and we all wander around eating and drinking, and then we dance. I shall dance only with you, *amor mio*. And you must dance only with me.'

'She can't do that,' Rinaldo said at once. 'Montelli and the others will want some of her attention, and you must do what's necessary to keep them dangling, eh, Alex?' He spoke pleasantly, as though this were an accepted joke between them.

'Of course,' she said, playing up to him.

Gino assumed an air of theatrical comedy.

'But why should you need the others when you have us?' he demanded, clasping her waist and leaning over her dramatically.

'Let's say I like some variety,' she chuckled, clinging to him to avoid falling. 'Now, get off me, you great clown.'

When the day arrived, every worker on the farm went to the festival. Families piled into cars, converging on the road to the city so that they ended up in what Gino told her was the Belluna procession.

Alex spent more time choosing what to wear for the festival than she had meant to. Her first choice had been a white dress. But somehow, at the last minute, it seemed wrong.

After trying on one dress after another she came to one of brilliant scarlet that seemed just right. It had a steep V-neck and looked splendid against her light tan.

That was something new. In London she strove to look elegant, businesslike. But not splendid. Suddenly only splendid would do.

One of the hands, who had no family, drove Teresa, Celia and Franca in Rinaldo's old vehicle, while the brothers and Alex went in her shiny hired car.

As they were leaving the house Alex handed her keys to Rinaldo. 'I'm sure you'd rather have these.'

'Be careful Alex,' he said. 'Someone will mistake you for a traditional female, asking a man to drive your car.'

'Nobody who knows me would ever make that mistake,' she said firmly. 'But I can't get used to the steering wheel being on the left when I'm used to the right.'

'Ah, yes, the English drive on the wrong side of the road,' he murmured.

She ignored this flagrant provocation, and said, 'It's probably safer if you drive.'

'I don't believe I heard you say that.'

'Oh, get in and drive,' she said in exasperation.

He grinned and did so. Gino swiftly urged Alex into the back seat, and so the three of them made their way into the city.

The two men were also dressed 'for best' in snowy white shirts with ruffled fronts. Gino was by nature a stylish dresser, but, except for the funerals Alex had not seen Rinaldo in anything but shabby working clothes.

Though alike in features the brothers were different in the impression they made, Gino the more conventionally attractive, Rinaldo the more virile and uncompromising.

It was as well, she thought, that she was 'spoken for',

or these two might have seriously disturbed her equilibrium.

As it was, she was looking forward to spending time at the festival in the company of her two handsome escorts.

It was late afternoon and things were already happening. Alex found it was nothing like the pallid festivities she'd seen at home.

Figures pranced around the streets. They were all outrageously clad, some from history, some from mythology. Saints mingled with demons, sorcerers and clowns.

Several times Alex was seized around the waist and whirled into an impromptu dance, from which Gino had to rescue her.

Rinaldo left them almost as soon as they arrived, but after a while they came across him, deep on conversation with a grave-looking man.

'Bank manager,' Gino muttered.

'In the middle of a festival?' Alex demanded.

'You'd think he could take five minutes off, wouldn't you?'

'Perhaps he's arranging a mortgage on the rest of the property so that he can buy me out quickly.'

'*What?*' Gino was aghast.

'Well, it would solve a lot of problems,' she said, trying to sound cheerful.

'No it wouldn't. You'd go away. I don't want you to go. You don't want to go, do you?'

She didn't answer. She couldn't.

The Loggia of the Boar was filled with stalls selling all manner of foods. Gino bought cakes and wine and they wandered around, hand in hand, like children.

As the natural light faded the coloured lights became

brighter. Tables were set out in the streets and a band began to play.

They strolled about until they found Rinaldo, clearly having finished with the bank manager, sitting alone at a table in the Piazza della Signoria, brooding over a solitary glass of wine.

'Hello brother,' Gino cried. 'Are you having a good time? You don't look it.'

'We don't all have to go crazy to enjoy ourselves,' Rinaldo observed, unruffled, as they joined him at the table. 'The procession should be starting about now.'

Even as he spoke trumpets sounded in the distance, and a cheer went up from the crowd as the first floats appeared. Alex watched eagerly.

Although it was a religious festival not all the floats had that theme. Some were so bawdy as to be almost obscene, some were cruel.

Alex stared as one went by depicting a huge figure with a goat's head and flashing eyes. She knew enough symbolism to recognise that the goat represented not only the devil but also human sexuality at its most rampant and uncontrolled.

Yet in the saint's parade he did not seem out of place. Everything here had a red-blooded gusto that thrilled her.

'Some of those floats are amazing,' she mused. 'That one with the baker and the loaf of bread, is it really as rude as it looks?'

'Oh, yes,' Gino said with relish. 'The ruder the better. That's how we like it. That's really why we celebrate St Romauld at all, because he's a great excuse for rudeness.'

'I've never heard of him,' Alex said.

'He's not one of the better known saints,' Rinaldo agreed, 'but he has the advantage of having been thoroughly licentious before he became saintly. He lived

about a thousand years ago, and to start with he did a lot
of drinking and wenching. Then he reformed and became
a monk, founding a monastery not far from here.'

'But he was constantly plagued by temptation.' Gino
took up the tale. 'Naturally he resisted it, but it means
that his parade can be very colourful. For every one float
depicting him as a saint there are about ten showing
worldly indulgence. Which is about right,' he added ju-
diciously.

Looking at the floats Alex saw that this was true. The
world and the devil were depicted with great imagination,
again and again.

'But isn't it supposed to be a religious festival?' she
laughed.

'Of course,' Gino said. 'People go to church and say
sorry afterwards. But the pleasures of the flesh must come
first, and you must really exert yourself to enjoy them,
because otherwise the repentance wouldn't be real, and
that would be sacrilege.'

Alex poked him in the ribs. 'That sounds a very con-
venient philosophy.'

'Poppa taught it to me. He said it was ancient tradition,
but I think he invented it.'

Rinaldo nodded. 'That wouldn't surprise me.'

Suddenly Alex burst out laughing. 'What on earth is
that meant to be?' she asked, pointing at a float that had
just come into view.

Seated on it was a very beautiful young woman, with
flower-wreathed golden hair that streamed down over her
throne. Behind that throne stood a man dressed in gor-
geous armour, clearly a victorious warrior.

There were two other men, crouching at the woman's
feet. One of them clutched a piglet that squealed and
made constant efforts to escape.

As the float rumbled by the piglet managed to free itself, dashed to the edge of the float and took a flying leap. Alex bounded forward just in time to catch it.

'Come on,' she laughed. 'The road's hard. You don't want to land on it.'

She handed it back to the men on the float who cheered her, crying, *'Grazie, Circe!'*

'What did he mean?' she asked, returning to her seat.

'He called you Circe,' Rinaldo told her. 'That woman on the float is meant to be Circe the witch-goddess. She lured men into her cave and turned them into swine.'

'Hence the piglet?' she guessed.

'Yes, he must have been the best they could manage.'

'She wasn't just a witch,' Gino objected. 'She was a healer too. The legend says she was an expert in herbs and potions, and a woman of wisdom. The man standing behind her was the hero Odysseus, who overcame her with love.'

'Did he?' Rinaldo demanded. 'He thought he had, but she was an enchantress who could blind men to everything else. He was on an important journey, but he forgot it and stayed with her for a year. So who overcame who?'

'You don't like her, do you?' Alex challenged him, laughing. 'Fancy a woman getting him to put her first! Shocking! Rinaldo, this is festival. Lighten up for pity's sake.'

Suddenly there was a cry of, *'Gino, hey Gino!'* and three scantily clad young women descended on them, laughing, kissing him, then carrying him off by main force.

He looked back at the other two, giving a shrug of comical, helpless dismay.

'My brother is very popular,' Rinaldo observed. 'But he is more pursued than pursuing.'

'You don't have to excuse him to me,' Alex said cheerfully. 'I'm glad of the chance to sit quietly for a bit.'

'Let me order you some wine.'

'Not wine, thank you.'

'Mineral water?'

'What I'd really love most of all at this moment,' she said wistfully, 'is a nice cup of tea.'

Rinaldo made an imperious gesture to a passing waiter, spoke a few words of Tuscan and handed over a note. The waiter nodded and scurried away.

'I don't believe it,' Alex said admiringly. 'You haven't managed to summon up tea in the middle of a wine-drenched festival?'

'We'll have to wait and see.'

In a few minutes the tea arrived and she sipped it in ecstasy.

'Nothing ever tasted as good as this,' she sighed. 'Thank you.'

Then her eyes widened in horror.

'Oh, goodness, look! Over there. Montelli. He's been following me around.'

'Shall I leave you free to talk to him?'

Rinaldo made to rise but Alex stopped him with a hand on his arm.

'Don't you dare. I rely on you to get rid of him for me.'

'Thus confirming my poor reputation. Do you know that I'm commonly held to have taken you prisoner and kept you apart from the world?'

'Well, that was the original idea, wasn't it?' she teased.

'I really can't remember,' he said self-consciously.

Montelli reached them, beaming in a way that didn't

hide his anxiety. He would have taken Gino's seat but Alex dumped her bag on it too quickly for him.

'*Signorina*, what a pleasure! It's so hard to reach you these days.'

'Yes, I'm afraid I keep my phone turned off,' she said. 'You must blame this lovely country which is taking all my attention.'

'Indeed, Italy is ideal for a vacation, but perhaps a fair-skinned northerner shouldn't live here permanently.'

'How kind of you to be concerned for my welfare!' Alex said, with a dazzling smile. 'Would it really trouble you if I decided to stay?'

At this hint that she might not sell at all, Montelli paled visibly.

'Well of course we should all be delighted—good heavens, you're drinking tea. Is this fellow too mean to buy you a proper glass of wine?'

'Far too mean,' Rinaldo said in a voice that suggested he might be enjoying himself.

'How shocking. *Signorina*, let me take you somewhere and buy you champagne.'

His hand clutched her arm determinedly. The next moment his yell split the air and he was frantically dabbing hot tea from his trousers.

'I'm so sorry,' Alex exclaimed unconvincingly. 'I can't think how it happened.'

He gave her a look of wild accusation but was too wise to speak, and scuttled away.

'Why didn't you come to my rescue?' she demanded of Rinaldo.

'I never saw a woman less in need of rescue,' he said, with a grin. '*I* could hardly have thrown tea over him.'

'It was an accident.'

'Of course. I've had a few such accidents myself.'

'I'll bet you have!'

Now the procession had finished and the streets were full of revellers. Somewhere in the distance they could see Gino, flowers in his hair, dancing with three partners at once.

'What does he think he's doing?' Rinaldo demanded.

Alex chuckled. 'I think he's making sure that he won't commit sacrilege the next time he goes to church.'

'Shall I fetch him for you?'

'What for? He's a free agent.'

'And you? Are you free? With a fiancé in England?'

'Yes,' she said hastily, struggling to remember David's face. 'I meant that—Gino—'

'Gino and you spend a lot of time together.'

'Only because you put him up to it,' she retorted with spirit. 'Leave him alone. Let him enjoy himself.'

A dancing couple nearly crashed into their table.

'If you've finished your tea, perhaps we should move,' Rinaldo said. 'It isn't very safe here.'

She followed him out of the piazza and down side streets until they reached the river, where a blessedly cool breeze was blowing. He took her arm to steer her to the water's side, and they stood there for a moment enjoying the night air.

Looking down into the waters of the Arno, Alex wondered at the change in herself. Her light tan made her dark blue eyes seem larger. She could see that much in the ghostly figure who looked back at her from the dark water.

No, she thought. Not so much a ghost as an echo of another self that she might have been. Perhaps still might.

'What are you thinking?' Rinaldo asked suddenly.

'About myself,' she said, still looking down into the water. 'Wondering who I am.'

'I too have wondered that. You are not the person I thought at first.'

'Nobody could be that woman,' Alex said, looking at him with a faint smile. 'She came out of a horror story.'

He nodded. 'I never thanked you.'

'For what?'

'Looking after Brutus. Seeing things about him that I ought to have seen. I let him live too long. I should have done it weeks ago, but I blinded myself to the signs because I couldn't bear to part with him.'

'Was that why you asked him to forgive you?'

'Yes,' he said in a low voice.

'He was your wife's dog, wasn't he?'

'I suppose Gino told you.' His lips curved in a tender, reminiscent smile. 'Maria came to our wedding clutching this ridiculous puppy, and she held onto him all through the service because if she put him down he wandered off, and if she handed him to someone else he cried. She said he was the start of our family, that we would have many children and many dogs. But it didn't happen that way.'

He did not add that now he had nothing left of his wife, but Alex sensed that he did not need to. One by one, those he cared for had been taken away from him. Only Gino was left, and despite the brothers' affection she sensed a distance between them, born of the fact that they were opposites.

'You must be so lonely,' she said impulsively, reaching out to touch him.

He looked at her, then at the place where her hand lay on his arm. For a moment she thought he would put his own hand over it, but then a smile came over his face. And when she saw it she knew she had blundered.

It was as implacable as an iron door slammed in her face.

'Not at all,' he said cheerfully, moving his arm away from her. 'Not at all.'

She cursed her own stupidity for going one step too far with this awkward man. At the last moment he had flinched away from her sympathy, as she should have known he would, retreating into mistrust.

Through the silence she was intensely aware of the unease that swept him as he recalled everything he had confided to her, the way he'd lowered his guard, forgetting that she still represented danger.

She thought vainly for something she could say to bring his mind and heart back to her, but it was too late. He had turned and was heading away from her, along the narrow street.

'Let's go and find Gino,' he called back over his shoulder.

CHAPTER EIGHT

'NEVER mind Gino,' she said desperately. 'I don't own him, and he'd be the first to say so.'

'Is that why I see the two of you fooling around together all the time?' He spoke ironically, and there was a touch of the old edge in his voice as he added, 'I wonder what you'll tell your fiancé.'

'I shan't mention it at all. There's no need.'

'What a very cool race the English must be. If you were my woman I'd want to know that you'd been flirting with another man.'

If I were your woman I wouldn't be flirting with another man.

The thought flashed across her mind before she could stop it. Then it was gone, whispering away into the shadows.

'I wonder if you really would want to know,' she said.

'Yes, because then I could do something about it.'

She understood his meaning perfectly. She should stop him here. But she didn't want to.

'I doubt if you could,' she dared him.

The next moment his arm was across her chest, preventing her going any further, urging her gently but firmly back against the wall.

'Listen to me,' he said softly, his hot breath flickering against her skin. 'I will not be played games with, do you understand? Don't try to tease me. I'm not some callow boy to come begging.'

'How dare you accuse me of teasing you?' she demanded in a shaking voice.

'You're up to something. I'm not a fool, Circe.'

'And neither am I. You set Gino on to me, remember? How stupid do you think I am? Now, will you let me go?' She tried to push his arm away but it was like steel across her chest, not pressing her, but implacable.

'Not yet. We have things to talk about,' he said, speaking in the same low voice that sent warmth scurrying across her skin.

'I can't think what.' She tried to keep calm but the powerful body holding her still was communicating its heat to her, and that was mingling with the rising excitement inside herself.

'You did very well tonight,' he murmured.

'I don't know what you mean.'

'Yes, you do. You were subtle, very subtle. Nothing obvious. Just be nice to the brute and watch him melt. And you came close, until you over reached yourself.'

There was a sudden fierce note in his voice.

'Every man has to want you, doesn't he? Gino satisfies your vanity, the man in London satisfies your ambition. And me? What would I satisfy?'

His words were like hot lava pouring over her, illuminating the world, so that for a searing moment she knew the answer to his question. He would satisfy a deep, aching need that had been there, unacknowledged, in her loins, from the very start.

How long could she have gone on refusing to see it if he hadn't forced it on her?

But hell would freeze over before she would let him suspect.

'You flatter yourself,' she snapped. 'If you weren't so

conceited you'd remember I didn't say a word to you that I couldn't have said in front of Gino.'

'I've already admitted that you were clever. Far too clever to be blatant. Circe weaves her spells and has a different face for all of us. Subtlety wouldn't work with Gino, *but it damned near worked with me.*'

She didn't answer. Words would no longer come. A warm languor pervaded her, making her limbs heavy and her senses vague. Yet she was burningly aware of the faint touch of his lips against the skin of her neck.

Pride made her turn her head away but there was no escaping him. Putting her hands on his shoulders she tried to push him off, with no success.

He didn't try to kiss her mouth, merely rested his lips against her throat, then just beneath her ears, causing a storm inside her that was almost alarming in its violence.

He was warning her not to take him on, because if she did, this was what he could do to her. He could make her flesh defy her mind, defy her very self. He could make her want him when she was determined not to. He was daring her to risk it.

Either the heat of the night or her own feverish urgency was making her react in a way she didn't recognise. It took all her strength not to yearn towards him, seeking new and more deeply intimate caresses.

She could not allow this to happen, but it was happening anyway. There was danger everywhere, but suddenly danger was her natural element. The hands she'd raised to push him away changed course and curved, almost touching him but not quite.

But then—yes—her fingers just brushed his neck of their own accord. There was no stopping them. And his lips were on her face, not kissing her mouth, kissing everywhere else, driving her wild with soft, teasing caresses that left her unsatisfied because she they made her want so much more.

They were no longer alone in the street. A laughing, singing crowd swirled by, but nobody took any notice of them. One more pair of lovers among so many!

He drew back a few inches and stopped, breathing hard, his mouth close to hers. He could see her reaction, she thought desperately. There was no hiding the rise and fall of her breasts under the thin red silk, or the pulse beating in her throat. He must be able to feel her breath against his face, as heated as his own.

'Get—away—from—me,' she gasped in a voice that shook.

He did so, stepping back sharply. She saw his face, one instant before the shutters came down, and saw it ravaged, burningly intense.

And afraid. It was too late for him to lock her out and he knew it.

He turned and strode away toward the main street, leaving her leaning against the wall, trying to calm down. After a moment Alex followed him slowly.

When she had nearly reached the Piazza, Gino came flying to meet her, flowers in his hair, not entirely sober. He embraced her eagerly.

'There you are, *carissima*. Why aren't you with Rinaldo? Don't tell me you two are fighting again?'

Alex never forgot the journey home, with Rinaldo driving the car and herself and Gino in the back. Gino was too sleepy to talk, which was a relief, but left her staring out into the darkness, accompanied by thoughts that she didn't want to think.

As soon as they reached the house she bid the brothers a brief goodnight and went upstairs. She needed to be alone to control her feelings, and to understand exactly what those feelings were.

There was anger, partly at him and partly at herself for being caught off guard.

It had been there all the time. Desire. Basic, brutal, almost uncontrollable desire, not connected to any sympathy of mind. Uncivilised. Alien to her well-ordered world. The kind of feeling that she had never really believed existed, waiting to spring out and make a fool of her.

And what a fool! She could have screamed as she realised how evident her excitement must have been. He had made her want him, and he'd known it.

She closed her eyes, fiercely willing herself to hold onto the anger, so that it might defend her from the other feeling, the shattering awareness that tonight she had been alive in every part of herself, truly alive for the first time.

She didn't want to feel like that about Rinaldo, and she would resist it with everything in her power. She pulled herself together. It would be over soon. This was an aberration, that would be forgotten when she returned to England and reality.

A freezing shower made her feel a little better. Then, as she wrapped a towel around her, she grew suddenly alert, wondering what had happened to her wits. The date of the carnival had always seemed familiar, and now she knew why. This was the day of the partners' meeting, at which David would arrange for her to be offered a partnership.

It must have happened this afternoon. He'd probably been trying to get through to her ever since.

She could have laughed aloud at the way Italy had hypnotised her into forgetting something so important.

She had even left her mobile phone behind to go to the festival. All she had to do was check her messages.

She did so, and stared at the result.

There were no messages from David.

But there were four from her secretary at her home number.

She thought of Jenny, a motherly woman and a tireless worker, of whom she was very fond. Why was she making such attempts to contact her when David was silent?

Perhaps the other partners had been awkward about accepting her, and even now David was arguing with them, defending her.

She dialled Jenny's number quickly, and was answered at once.

'Thank goodness you called,' Jenny said in a relieved voice. 'You're not going to believe what I have to tell you. Are you sitting down?'

'Sure. I'm sitting on the bed. Now, tell me.'

'This afternoon David announced his engagement to Erica.'

In the first moment of shock Alex said the only words that came into her head.

'Who the blue blazes is Erica?'

'His secretary. It's funny how nobody knows her name, but that's what she's like. Little brown mouse. Fades into the wallpaper.'

Now Alex remembered a pale, wispy girl she had sometimes seen in David's office. And this little nonentity had ousted the glamorous, high-powered Alex Dacre?

'There's something else,' Jenny said. 'David has vetoed your partnership.'

Alex uttered a very rude word.

'There was a meeting this afternoon. Everyone thought

making you a partner was just a formality, but he wouldn't consider it.'

'What?'

'He said they couldn't rely on someone who stayed away so long—'

'But he told me to stay as long as I needed!'

'I know. We all know. Nobody believes it for a moment. It's just an excuse. He says you can stay on as an employee—'

'He knows I won't do that,' Alex snapped.

'Right. He doesn't want you around after the way he's treated you. He can't fire you, but he can make your life uncomfortable until you leave.'

'What would he have done if I hadn't obligingly come to Italy?' Alex asked grimly.

'He'd have thought of something. His kind always do. But you made it easy for him. All your accounts have been assigned to other people now. Officially it's "during your absence", but—'

'But I'll never get them back. Damn him! Half those accounts only came to the firm because I went out and fought for them.'

'I know, and he hates that. You've become too strong. You've become competition, and David's a very vain man.'

'Thanks for putting me in the picture Jenny,' Alex said, breathing hard.

'What are you going to do?'

'I'm going to plan my revenge in the dark.'

'What?' Jenny gave a gasp of shock.

'I'm part Italian, don't forget. We plot in the night and we keep our stilettos shining. Perhaps you should tell him that. It might give him a sleepless moment or two.'

'Oh, Alex, I know you must be terribly hurt, but is he really worth it?'

'No. I'll call again later.'

When she'd hung up Alex was still for a long time.

In truth, she wasn't hurt at all. She'd agreed David wasn't worth it and it was true. She'd blinded herself to his true nature, but at heart she'd always known the kind of man he was, cool, self-centred, ruthless where his own interests were concerned.

It hadn't mattered because she had believed herself to be the same.

But she knew better now.

She could have laughed aloud at the thought of mourning the loss of David.

Here was the true reason why he'd been so understanding about her prolonged absence. It had exactly suited him. He must have been planning to oust her from the firm even before she left.

She would waste no time in grieving, but swallowing the insult was another matter.

She noticed a small clay figurine by the side of the bed. The next moment the room shuddered under the impact as it hit the far wall and smashed.

She regarded the damage, feeling a great deal better.

'Alex! Are you all right?'

Gino was knocking on her door, calling her.

'I'm fine,' she called out, hurriedly putting on a light dressing gown.

She opened the door. Rinaldo was there too, in the background, but it was Gino who stormed in, grasping her hands, and saying, 'What was the noise? Did something fall? Are you hurt?'

She freed herself and picked up some of the pieces.

'It was only this,' she said.

Rinaldo came in and examined the dent in the wall.

'Impressive,' he said. 'You must have thrown it with some force. Remind me to duck.'

'Don't worry, I'm not aiming anything at you.'

'No, you wouldn't have missed me, would you?'

'Stop trying to provoke me,' Alex said, feeling strangely calm now that she'd gotten it out of her system. 'I'm sorry for the damage to your wall.'

'Was there any special reason for the violence?' Rinaldo asked, 'or did you just feel that way?'

She looked at him, her eyes kindling.

'I just felt that way.'

Nothing on earth would have persuaded her to tell him the truth at that moment.

Gino was alone in the kitchen, tucking into a hearty breakfast when she went down next morning. Alex regarded him sardonically, amused to see that he could hardly meet her eye.

'"I shall dance only with you, *amor mia*",' she tossed his words lightly back at him. '"*And you must dance only with me.*"'

'I know, I know,' he said shamefacedly. 'It was festival. I got carried away—'

'Yes, I saw you being carried away—by three of them. Naturally you couldn't resist.'

He eyed her suspiciously.

'Are you being very nice, or should I prepare for boiling oil to drop on my head?'

'You'll have to wait and see,' she teased.

He seized her hand and kissed it. 'I adore you.'

'No you don't. You adore your three companions of last night. At least, there were three that I saw, but I wouldn't be surprised if—'

'Yes, well never mind that,' he said hastily. 'Truly, *carissima*, it meant nothing. That's how festival is, all those demons and goats—'

'And the wine,' she said, smiling at him fondly.

'Well, the wine plays its part, but it's mostly the atmosphere—the feeling that anything could happen, and you're going to let it happen, and who knows how the evening will end?'

Alex was silent. Gino's words struck home in way he could never imagine. Last night's feeling of heated sexuality had pervaded her too, giving everything a sharper edge, making her feel things it might have been better not to feel, and even rejoice in them.

But now it was the clear light of day.

'I'm sorry,' he said, seeing her face and misreading it. 'I shouldn't have said that.'

'Why not? I do understand. It was festival. You never stick with the person you came with. Otherwise it's no fun.'

'Bless you for a sweet, forgiving darling.'

He planted a swift kiss on her mouth, and Alex let him. It wasn't unpleasant. It wasn't anything.

'You know I adore you more than life, don't you?' he asked. 'You're the one I dream of—'

'Except during a festival,' she couldn't resist saying.

'Can we put that behind us?' he asked, harassed.

'I'm sorry, Gino dear, but I can't help laughing. You're such a ham.'

'I bare my heart to you and you laugh,' he said plaintively. 'Ah, well!' He struck his breast theatrically. '*Ridi, pagliacco, ridi!* Laugh, clown, laugh, though your heart is breaking.'

'Clown is right,' Alex said severely.

Then, with a quick change of mood that was one of

his characteristics, Gino said, 'Don't go back to England, Alex.'

'Gino—'

'You've changed since coming here. I'll bet you don't even recognise yourself any more.'

It was true. Gino's perceptions could be disconcerting, but she wasn't ready to trust him with the truth any more than Rinaldo.

'You can't return to that other life,' Gino urged. 'You don't belong there any more.'

To throw him off the scent she quickly resumed her bantering tone.

'You stop that. I told you, I see through your little schemes.'

'Please, *cara*—' he begged in comical dismay.

'You're as bad as Rinaldo. The two of you set it all up before I arrived. I wouldn't put it past you to have tossed a coin for me.'

It was a passing remark but Gino's alarmed gulp told her everything.

'You *did*!' she accused.

'Yes—no—it wasn't like that.'

'I'll bet it was exactly like that. You cheeky pair!'

'You're not annoyed?'

'I ought to be, but oh, what the heck! I suppose I should just be glad you won.'

Emboldened by her matter-of-fact attitude Gino grinned and said, 'Actually I didn't.'

'*What?*'

'Rinaldo won, but he didn't take it seriously. He claimed he thought I'd been using my two-headed coin or he wouldn't have played. Anyway, he said he wasn't interested and I could have you.'

'Oh, really!' she asked in a dangerously quiet voice.

'But aren't you glad you got me instead? Come on, admit it. You like me better than Rinaldo.'

'I like anybody better than Rinaldo.'

'I behaved badly, leaving you with him last night, didn't I? I'm sorry if he offended you.'

'*I* may have offended *him*,' she said vaguely.

'I wonder if that's why he's gone.'

'What?'

'Yes, he left early this morning. Something about checking out some second-hand farm machinery, but I didn't know we needed any. He just upped and went.'

She should have been glad of the breathing space. Instead she felt as though she'd been dealt a blow.

They had unfinished business. Rinaldo knew that as well as she did. And he'd simply gone off and left her stranded in limbo. For a moment she looked around for something else to throw.

Then she forced herself to calm down and conceal the storm inside. That must remain her secret until she understood herself better.

She took a horse and rode for miles, noticing how the corn had grown since she first saw it, how the olives and grapes were flourishing in the sun.

How she loved the sun! It was as though she had only discovered it in Italy. There was sun in London, but it beat down in fierce strips of ugly road, baking pavements, suffocating. Here sunshine was fresh air and freedom, and a new awakening.

Her options were simple. She could return to England and fight, or she could stay here and fight. It was fighting either way, no question.

The prizes were uneven. A cold, soulless place in the firm, or another firm. There were plenty who would be glad to have her.

Or she could abandon London and everything she had worked for. All those years of striving for the best, the best clients, the best apartment, the best clothes, the best invitations—all gone to nothing.

In exchange she would have a life here, in a country that had seized her heart, in daily contact with a man who was rude, hostile, unrelenting, a man who'd rejected her out of hand without even seeing her, but who also troubled her heart and her restless body.

'Nonsense!' she said aloud. 'I'm damned if I'm going to fall in love with him! *Who the hell does he think he is?*'

After a while she made up her mind. It felt less like taking a decision than facing the inevitable. Mounting her horse she galloped back to the farm and began to pack. The following morning, in the teeth of Gino's protests, she drove herself to the airport.

There she handed the car in at the local branch of the rental company. An hour later she was in the air, on her way to England.

Rinaldo was away for a week. Twice he called and left messages on the answerphone. Eventually the phone was answered by Teresa, who brought him up to date with events, including the fact that Alex had left and would not be returning.

The following evening Rinaldo arrived home.

He found Gino sitting at the desk in his office, frowning as he poured over account books.

'You'll never manage it,' he said, grinning. 'Give up.'

'*Rinaldo!*' Gino leapt to his feet and hugged his brother eagerly.

Rinaldo hugged him back, and for a moment the two brothers thumped each other on the back.

'What's been happening?' Rinaldo asked.

'Alex has gone,' Gino said gloomily.

'So I gather from Teresa.'

'Is that all you've got to say?' Gino demanded, outraged.

'What do you want me to say? She was always bound to go back where she belongs.'

'I felt she belonged here,' Gino sighed.

'That's what she wanted you to think, to keep you off guard. Circe played her games, and we were nearly fooled. Forget her.'

'You as good as told me to make love to her.'

'Yes, and I should have known better. You're no match for her. It's lucky you didn't fall for her seriously.'

'Who says I didn't?'

'You forget how well I know you. Your most death-defying passion lasted a whole two days, I seem to recall.'

Gino shrugged despondently. 'Yeah—well, she's gone now.'

'So forget her.'

'Do you think she really loves him?'

I said forget her.

'Hey!' Gino said, staring into Rinaldo's tense face. 'No need to get mad at me.'

'I'm sorry,' Rinaldo growled, rubbing his eyes. 'I've had a long drive, and I'm not in the best of moods.'

'You do look pretty done in,' Gino said with his quick sympathy.

In fact, he thought, his brother looked as though he hadn't slept for a week. Or if he had slept, he'd had nightmares.

Poor old fellow, Gino thought. The threat to the farm must be troubling him more than he let on.

'Come and have something to eat,' he said kindly. 'And you can tell me about the machinery.'

'Machinery?'

'The stuff you went to buy.'

'Oh, that. No, I didn't find anything. Something to eat sounds a good idea.'

The maids had already gone to bed. Teresa served them in the kitchen, then retired.

Gino noticed that Rinaldo ate as though he barely knew what the food was.

'So what have you been doing these last few days?' he asked.

'Oh—driving around.'

'For a week?'

'Am I accountable to you?'

'If I vanished for a week I'd have some explaining to do.'

'So you would. Now drop it and tell me the news. When did Alex leave?'

'The day after you did. I keep waiting to hear from the lawyers, but nothing's happened.'

'We'll hear when it suits her,' Rinaldo observed. 'She's playing games.'

That was the mantra he'd repeated obsessively during the last few days. She was playing games, which meant he'd done the right thing to get the hell out.

From that first startling moment at his father's funeral he'd known that he couldn't afford to weaken where this woman was concerned. Hard on the heels of that thought had come fierce regret that he'd 'given' her to Gino. He'd said it casually, arrogantly, thinking life was that simple. In truth he'd expected a female dragon who would scare his volatile brother off.

Then he'd met her and known that this was a job for a man, not a boy.

Their antagonism was a relief, giving him a breathing space. But she'd been clever, offering sympathy like water in a desert to a man who'd spent too long being strong for others. The feeling was so good that he'd almost weakened, but he'd escaped in time.

So he'd won, as he made sure he always did. But now he found himself in a wilderness, his victory nothing but ashes.

'I don't think she was just playing games,' Gino said quietly.

'Then why is she back in England now, planning her wedding?'

Gino had no answer. Looking at the weariness in Rinaldo's face made him realise how depressed were his own spirits. The house had been quiet since Alex left, life had lost its savour.

After that there seemed nothing to say. Rinaldo fetched a bottle of old malt whisky, and they sat in companionable silence, sipping slowly, until Gino roused himself to say in a diffident voice.

'There's something I've been wanting to ask you for a while now.'

'Go on.'

'The day Poppa died—you were at the hospital first. By the time I arrived, it was too late. And I always wondered—what happened?'

'Nothing, he was unconscious.'

'I know but—he didn't come round?—even for a moment?'

'If he had I'd have told you.'

'It's just so hard to think of him just lying there, still

alive but not talking.' Gino sighed ruefully. 'You know what a talker he was.'

Rinaldo closed his eyes, and through his memory there passed the picture of his father, terribly still, swathed in bandages.

Like Gino he had felt it impossible that a man so full of life could lie still and silent. At any moment he would open his eyes, recognise his son and speak. There would be—there *must* be, some exchange between them before the end.

The picture swirled, blurred. He struggled to see clearly again but it was gone. As often before, he was tortured by the feeling of something there, just beyond the edge of memory.

Several times in the past he had come to the edge of this moment, but whatever it was always eluded him, driven away by the jangle in his head.

It had happened that day in the barn with Alex. Their brief moment of sympathy had caused a door of memory to start opening. But not far enough. And it would never happen again now. She had gone, and that was all for the best.

He would try to believe it.

'I wish I had something to tell you,' he said heavily. 'I, too, find it hard that he just left us without a word of goodbye or explanation. But there's nothing we can do but accept it. Now let's get some sleep.'

They went upstairs to bed, and the house lay in silence for an hour. Then Gino awoke, uncertain why, but with a feeling that something was up.

Pulling on a robe he slipped into the corridor, where he found Rinaldo, dressed in shorts.

'We have a burglar downstairs,' Rinaldo said softly.

On bare feet they moved noiselessly along the corridor

and down the stairs. Through the door they could make out part of the room illuminated by a bar of moonlight. The rest was in darkness, but they could hear the intruder moving about, then a crash, like a chair overturning.

'Right,' Rinaldo muttered.

He moved fast, not switching on the light but judging the position by sound alone, then launching himself forward, colliding with a body that reeled back, landing on the floor beneath him.

For a moment they fought in silence, gasping with effort and writhing madly together. Gino, coming into the room, heard a yell from Rinaldo as something caught him on the side of the head. Hurriedly Gino put the light on.

Then he froze at the sight that met his eyes.

Rinaldo drew in a sharp breath. 'You!' he said explosively.

From her position on the floor Alex glared up at him. *'Get—off—me!'* she said emphatically.

Breathing hard, Rinaldo pulled back from her, and stood up. Alex rose stiffly, supporting herself on Gino's outstretched hand.

'What the devil are you doing here?' Rinaldo demanded.

'I live here. I went away, now I've come back.'

'I knew you wouldn't just leave us and forget,' Gino breathed joyfully.

'When I left I didn't know what was going to happen,' Alex said. 'I had to see how the land lay. Now I know, and I'm here to stay.'

'What does the English fiancé have to say about that?' Rinaldo demanded, rubbing his face self-consciously. 'Can we look forward to his descent on us? Shall I tell Teresa to prepare a room for him? Perhaps you mean to be married from this house?'

'Oh, put a sock in it,' Alex said firmly.

'Excuse me? Sock?'

'It's an English expression,' she explained. 'It means don't say any more. David's out of the picture.'

'You dumped him?' Gino cried joyfully.

'No, he dumped me. I found out on the night of the festival that he'd vetoed my partnership and got engaged to his mousy secretary. I went back to England to have the satisfaction of telling him a few home truths, face to face.'

'I'll wager you did it in great style,' Rinaldo observed.

'Oh, I did. In front of everyone. I can't tell you how much I enjoyed that. My lawyer will go after the firm for a settlement. I've put my apartment on the market, and after that there was nothing left to do but come back here.'

'You couldn't have notified us that you were arriving, in a sensible, civilised manner?' Rinaldo observed.

'Where's the fun in that? Actually, I didn't mean to be so late, but I had to pick up the car I've bought on the way and that delayed me.

'I didn't mean to awaken you, so I arrived as quietly as I could. I didn't slam the door when I got out, and I climbed in by that window over there, the one that doesn't close properly.

'So here I am. This is my home too now. Get used to me, gentlemen, because I've come to stay.'

CHAPTER NINE

SOME women would have splashed out on a new wardrobe. Alex had splashed out on a car that reduced both brothers to awed silence. It managed to be stylish, glossily expensive and 'heavy-duty' at the same time.

'How much?' Rinaldo murmured.

'More than I could afford,' Alex said happily.

'I take my hat off to you.'

The car declared that she had come to stay, big time. She'd already said so in words, but this affirmed it.

'I'm going to drive a lot over the next week or so,' she said. 'I want to see every single part of Belluna. You don't mind, do you?'

'I have no right to mind.'

His tone was impeccably polite, but she would have preferred the knockabout that she had become used to. Since her return both men seemed to be treating her with kid gloves. Gino's manner was gentle, Rinaldo's was wary.

She began to study Belluna at close quarters. The year was moving on and it would soon be time for harvest. Wherever she went she found people who knew about her through the grapevine, and who treated her with cautious respect until they discovered that she knew a little Tuscan. Then there were smiles, laughter at her mistakes, eagerness to teach her.

One of her most enjoyable moments came when she returned from a trip to find Rinaldo standing by the side of the road next to his broken-down car.

It was rare for him to dress 'for best'. Old shirt and shabby jeans were his normal attire around the farm. But now he wore a charcoal suit that was both elegant and fashionable, plus a tie.

His hair was brushed and tidy, and he looked almost like a different man. A handsome man, with and 'air', an extra something that most men did not have. Combined with the authority that was natural to him, it made him startlingly attractive. Alex felt a soft thud in the pit of her stomach.

She drew up and sat waiting at the wheel as he approached.

'If you dare laugh—' he growled.

'Nothing was further from my thoughts,' she said untruthfully. 'Is the break-down truck on its way?'

'No, because I came out without my phone today. I'm warning you—' Her lips had twitched.

'Don't get stroppy with me,' she advised him, 'or I'll drive off and leave you here.'

'No, you won't,' he said unexpectedly. 'You'd never sink that low.'

'I could try and force myself,' she said, getting out of the car and heading for the boot. 'But I have towing gear, and it seems a shame to waste it.'

They recovered the equipment from the boot of her car.

'You'd better keep back and let me do the work,' she told him. 'Or you might spoil your suit.'

His answer was to strip off his jacket and shirt.

He shouldn't have done that, she thought, not when she was trying to concentrate on what she was doing. How was she supposed to keep her mind on work when he was standing there, the sun burnishing his torso?

She guessed he must work like this a good deal, for

the tan was even all over his broad back, shoulders and chest. With his tall figure and powerful neck, he looked exactly what he was, a forceful, virile male. And she was supposed to think about towing gear. There was no justice in the world.

She forced her attention back to the work, managing to do her full share, moving deftly and skilfully.

'I see you know what you're doing,' he said.

'If you'd experienced as much prejudice about women drivers as I have, you'd make sure you could do things for yourself, as well,' she informed him. 'The garages are the worst. They assume you're an idiot. One manager told me to bring my husband in and he'd explain it. In this day and age! Oh, heck!'

The exclamation was drawn from her by her hair flopping over her forehead. It was years since she'd needed to brush back her hair, but these days it seemed to happen all the time.

How long had it been since she'd visited a hair salon? Instead of being immaculately styled and coiffed, her hair had grown, becoming almost shaggy. When she finished work and stood up, the slight breeze made it blow about her face.

He replaced his clothes and got into the passenger seat.

'Where shall I take you?' she asked when they were on the road.

'There's a garage halfway to Florence that will repair the car. When we've dropped it there I need to go into the city to keep an appointment. I'll get a taxi home.'

'I don't mind waiting for you. I can do some shopping.'

'There's no need,' he said briefly.

'Oh, I see. Like that.'

'What do you mean, like that?'

'You know what I mean. You don't want me to know where you're going. I expect it's a secret assignation with a mystery woman—'

'Why would it have to be a secret? I'm a free agent. I do as I please.'

'Well, perhaps she isn't the only one,' she said, wishing he would deny it.

'You could have a whole harem dotted around Florence,' she persisted when he stayed silent. 'Or maybe—'

'I'm visiting the accountant.'

It took a moment to subdue the flicker of pleasure that he wasn't visiting a woman. When she was sure she could speak steadily she said,

'Ah! Yes, I understand. You're afraid I'll want to come too.'

'And I'm sure you will,' he said with a sigh of resignation.

'Well, I might drop in, just to do you a favour.'

He ground his teeth. 'Turn off here for the garage.'

He could be as grumpy as he liked, she thought. Nothing could quell the feeling that surged over her. She didn't analyse it, but it felt alarmingly like joy simply because he was here. She tried to file it away to be examined later, but it wouldn't be sidelined so easily.

When they'd delivered the car to the garage she swung back onto the road to Florence.

'Where am I heading?' she asked, as they entered the city.

'The Via Bonifacio Lupi. His name is Enrico Varsi.'

'Is it all right if I come in with you?'

'You're *asking* me?'

'I'm asking you.'

'And if I say no?'

'Then I'll wait meekly outside. But I'll put arsenic in your soup.'

He didn't reply, and she couldn't take her eyes off the road, but she knew, with total certainty, that he was grinning.

It was the area of Florence where lawyers and accountants congregated, a place of sedate streets and decorum. Alex had to park a little way up the road and walk back, studying the plaques by the doors. One, in particular, caught her attention, causing her to stop and study it for so long that Rinaldo had to call out,

'If you don't come now I shall go in without you.'

She scurried to catch up. 'You gave in,' she teased.

She could have sworn he ground his teeth. 'I did not give in, I merely recognise that you have certain financial rights, and I wish to behave properly.'

'Same thing,' she jeered.

'Get in there before I strangle you.'

Signor Varsi's offices were luxurious, the surroundings of a very successful man. He spoke well, covering complex matters without needing to refer to notes, and was clearly master of his material.

He behaved perfectly to her, showing the professional courtesy of one accountant to another. He did not talk down to her, and several times invited her opinion. She said as little as possible but her ears were pricked for anything she could learn.

Afterwards she and Rinaldo went for a coffee near the Duomo.

'You're very thoughtful,' he said, glancing at her face.

'I'm fascinated by the discovery that the Italian financial year runs from January the first to December the thirty-first.'

'But of course it does,' he said, puzzled. 'What else could it be?'

'In my country it's April to April.'

'And the British have the nerve to call Italians an illogical race?'

'I know.' She gave a brief laugh and went back to staring into her coffee.

'Alex, are you all right?'

His unusually gentle tone made her look up. His was looking at her with grave concern that had no hint of irony or suspicion.

'How do you mean—all right?'

'You've lost the man you loved. You don't let anyone see that you mind. You smile at Gino and me, you make jokes, and anyone who didn't know you would think everything was fine in your world.'

'Do you think you know me?'

'As much as you'll let me. And I know that you can't really be as bright and cheerful as you seem. You've given me a shoulder to cry on in the past.'

Looking into his eyes she saw kindness, something she had never found there before. The sight was almost her undoing.

'I'm not crying,' she said huskily.

'Most women would be after their fiancé dumped them for another woman.'

'There's no need to make me sound like a weeping wallflower,' she protested with a shaky laugh.

'No, you're no weeping wallflower. In fact, I can't imagine you ever weeping. You're too strong.'

'Strong? Are you sure you don't mean hard?'

'I might have thought so once. But not now. You have a deep-feeling heart, but you guard it carefully.'

'As you do yourself.'

'Yes,' he said after a moment. 'As I do myself. I think we've both learned to be cautious. But feelings have to be expressed one way, if not another. I still remember that dent in the wall.'

'Dent—? Oh, you mean when I threw the ornament?'

'That was why you did it, wasn't it?'

'Yes,' she said ruefully.

'So you are an Italian deep inside, after all? The woman who arrived here wouldn't have chucked things, merely uttered a few well-chosen words.'

'I wasn't quite as cool and collected as I seemed in those days,' she admitted, 'but I did feel that things could usually be sorted out with reason.'

She gave a brief inner smile, aimed at herself and the person she had been. How little reason seemed to matter, sitting here with the man who brought her to life as she had never thought to be.

'And now?' he asked.

'Let's just say that I'm having a re-think. There are times when a rush of blood to the head can be very satisfying.'

He grinned. 'Your mother would be proud of you.'

'Yes, she would,' Alex said, realising that it was true. She gave a crack of laughter. 'She'd have done exactly what I did. Oh, Mamma, I wish you could see me now.'

'What did she think of your fiancé?'

'She didn't like him. She said he was too organised.'

'A virtue, surely, in his profession? And yours.'

'Yes, but it's not just in his profession,' Alex mused. 'Everything in his life was organised, I see that now.'

She wasn't looking at Rinaldo, but at the tablecloth as she moved spoons back and forth into patterns.

'We had it all planned,' she said thoughtfully. 'Our home, our marriage, the way our professional lives would entwine. Married to each other, we'd have dominated the firm. Of course, that was what he didn't want. He wants to dominate it alone. I thought we loved each other, but all that time he was secretly planning to ease me out in any way he could. I guess he couldn't believe his luck when I came out here.'

She shook her head over her own naïvety. 'Lord, but I made it easy for him!'

'Because you trusted him,' Rinaldo suggested.

'Oh, yes. Conspicuous trustworthiness is David's big asset. It's worth at least thirty per cent on the bill.'

She knew she sounded bitter, but she couldn't help it. Fool! she thought. Fool to have been so deluded for so long!

'How long did you know him?' Rinaldo asked.

'Years. He was there the day I joined the firm, when I was little more than a kid. I supposed I hero-worshipped him, chiefly because he was so good-looking. It took a long time for us to come together.'

'You're very focused.'

'Decide what you want and go for it. That's me.'

'And what do you want now?' he asked, watching her.

'I don't know. For the first time in my life I don't know what I want. I feel cast adrift.'

'Yet you seem as sure of yourself as ever, Circe.'

'That's really unfair,' she said, smiling wistfully. 'Did it ever occur to you that Circe was a very confused person?'

'She wasn't a person, she was a goddess, an enchantress.'

'A witch,' she reminded him.

'A witch,' he agreed. 'But a witch who sows confusion all around her.'

'I never meant to. But you and I had such preconceived

ideas about each other. There was bound to be confusion.'

He nodded. 'No more preconceived ideas, I swear. I'll never again see you as an automaton who thinks only cold reason matters.'

'Can I have that in writing?' she asked sceptically.

'No, I'll just have to prove it to you.'

'For that, I'll let you drive the car home,' she said, handing him the keys.

He pocketed them. 'Is this you being sweetly feminine?'

'Nope. I'm just tired. You can do the work.'

Laughing they made their way through the streets in the direction of the car.

'I haven't abandoned reason altogether,' she hastened to say. 'But I've come to see that it can sometimes be overrated.'

'Only sometimes?'

'It has its place, even for you. You were very reasonable in Varsi's office.'

A noisy vehicle rumbled by as he answered, and Alex couldn't make out his reply distinctly. She gave herself a little shake, trying to believe that he had really said, *But I don't want to kiss Enrico Varsi.'*

'What did you say?' she asked, dazed.

'I said we turn here,' he said quickly.

Strangely his denial convinced her. He might pretend what he liked. He'd said it. Suddenly she wanted this afternoon to last for ever.

He was silent on the journey home, and Alex was also content to say nothing. Something was happening that words would only spoil.

*   *   *

Later that evening, in the quiet of her room, Alex called Jenny, her one-time secretary.

'I'm afraid I'm useless as a source of info,' Jenny told her. 'I've walked out of the firm. If I'd had to look at David's smug face any longer I'd have done something to it. But I'll always be glad I was there when you told him "what for" in front of everyone.'

'Yes, I enjoyed it too,' Alex mused. 'But I'm sorry you're out of a job.'

'I'm not. I've gone to—' she named another firm, equally prestigious, just across the street. 'I think they'd quite like to have you as well.'

'I'm glad you're suited, but I have a job to do here. Jenny, does the name Andansio mean anything to you?'

'I remember it from about five years ago, before I became your secretary. My then boss had some dealings with them.'

'What can you tell me about them?'

'A lot. Some of it's quite sensational.'

Alex listened for half an hour, making notes. When she hung up she was thoughtful.

A few days later, Varsi's secretary called to say that the books were ready to be returned, and should they be mailed? It was Alex who took the call, and volunteered to collect them. On her way out she met Rinaldo and told him her errand.

'And of course you'll deliver them to me without looking at them?' he said ironically.

'Did I say that?' she asked, wide-eyed with innocence.

'Well at least you play fair,' he said appreciatively.

Having got the books, Alex shut herself up with them for several hours.

'I notice that most of the pages were printed then put in ring-binders later,' she said to Rinaldo.

'My father used a computer for the accounts,' he said. 'He was very proud of the fact that he'd mastered it.'

'Can I see his files?'

Rinaldo showed her into the study, switched on the computer and showed her what she needed. Then he left her.

Alex's first impression was that Poppa's pride had been well-founded. Comparing his files to the receipts she came to the conclusion that he'd kept his records perfectly. They were detailed, informative and easy to check.

Next she managed to access files for previous years, and, after a search, located the books that matched them. She spent a long night checking and cross-checking.

It was early morning by the time she'd finished and switched off the computer. Instead of going to bed she put on her work-out clothes and went running. Then she showered, ate a swift breakfast, and drove into Florence.

She began spending lengthy periods in the city, sometimes driving back late at night, sometimes staying in a hotel. Without saying very much she gave the brothers the impression that she was enjoying a pleasure trip, shopping and going to the theatre. Rinaldo occasionally gave her puzzled glances, but he held his peace.

Soon there was no time for questions, for the harvest was due to begin. Wheat, olives, lemons, now ripe under the burning sun, had to be brought in, stored and sold to the waiting markets.

'And after them, the wine,' Gino told her. 'Maybe October.'

'Maybe? You don't know?'

'Judging the right moment for picking grapes can be

very tricky. You have to wait until they're sweet enough, or you can end up with vinegar. Try this.'

They were sitting on the veranda enjoying the last of the sun. On the low table between them was a bunch of deep purple grapes that he had picked that afternoon. He took one, peeled it carefully with a tiny knife, and offered it to her.

'Sweet?' he asked.

'It tastes very sweet.'

'But not quite sweet enough. It needs more than this before it's ready.'

'And you can tell the moment by the taste.'

'Rinaldo can, he's the real expert. He says he's never wrong. Mind you, he thinks that about everything.'

'Talking about me?' came Rinaldo's voice from just inside the house.

He came out and pulled up another chair, acknowledging Alex with only a brief nod, but sitting close to her. It was the first time she had seen him all day.

'I was just explaining to Alex how you value your taste buds above the achievements of science.'

'What has science got to do with it?' Alex wanted to know.

'Nothing,' Rinaldo said. 'Judging grapes is an art. You either have it or you haven't. And my little brother hasn't, so he tries to pretend that science is the next best thing.'

'No, it's the very *best* thing,' Gino said stubbornly.

'But what science?' Alex asked, baffled.

From his pocket Gino pulled a narrow metal tube, about six inches long. It reminded Alex of a small telescope, except that at one end was a piece of yellow glass that lifted, revealing a small box beneath.

Into this Gino inserted a grape and closed the lid, squashing the grape so that the juice flowed.

'Now look,' he said, holding it up.

Alex squinted from the other end and saw a tiny dial. The needle was hovering back and forth, almost near the red area, but not quite settling there.

'It tells you the sugar content,' Gino explained. 'When that's right, you know it's time to pick.'

Rinaldo gave a snort of contempt.

'I've known you use it,' Gino protested. 'When it suited you.'

'I've occasionally demonstrated that it backs me up,' Rinaldo agreed.

'And when it doesn't, you ignore it.'

'Yes, because I know grapes better than any machine. That's enough talk. I'm going to bed. If you're wise, you will too. We have a long, hard haul ahead of us.'

Just how hard a haul Alex was to discover. Both Rinaldo and Gino played their full part in the harvest, often picking with their own hands. Alex plunged in, determined to earn her place here by hard work as well as money.

Even she, inexperienced, knew that this would be a good harvest. The long, hot summer had brought the crops to perfection at exactly the right moment, until at last only the grapes were left.

'And we start on those tomorrow,' Rinaldo said.

The three of them were sitting on the veranda, in various stages of exhaustion. Gino was sprawled in his chair, his head right back. But he lifted it when he heard this.

'Tomorrow?' he echoed. 'You can't mean that.'

'I do mean it. The grapes are ready.'

'Not according to this.' Gino lifted the instrument that was used for testing the grapes, which was lying on the low table.

'I don't need a machine to tell me the grapes are ready,' Rinaldo said stubbornly.

'Rinaldo be sensible.'

'Machines don't drink wine. People do. The grapes are ready.'

'But nobody else is harvesting now. They're all waiting another week.'

'Great. We'll be ahead of the market and our grapes will be the best. We'll get the highest price. I'm going to bed.'

Gino's shocked eyes followed him until he was out of sight.

'He's taken leave of his senses,' he said. 'I've never known him like this before.'

'But you said he's the real expert,' Alex reminded him. 'Has this never happened in the past?'

'Only by the odd day or two. But a week? He's never been out on that much of a limb before. What's got into him to take such a risk?'

'Is it really a great risk?'

'Being wrong by a day can take the edge of perfection off the harvest. He's risking everything.'

Risking everything. Yes, Alex thought, Rinaldo had had the air of a man leaping into the unknown, ready to chance all he had on one reckless throw of the dice.

Next day, as he'd said, the grape harvest began. The work was long and laborious, for grape picking was another task Rinaldo wouldn't entrust to machines, saying they damaged the plants.

Alex piled in, picking until her hands were sore. If she tried to talk to Rinaldo he replied automatically. Sometimes she wondered if he really knew that she was there. She had the odd sensation that he was looking beyond her.

'Pick,' he said fiercely. 'Just pick.'

She never knew how she got through that week. Somehow she'd been swept up by his own intensity, driving herself on to some unknown goal. When the last grape was in she felt drained and futile, as though the purpose of her whole life had been taken away.

The Farneses were not wine makers, but sold their grapes to a company. When Signor Valli, the company representative who always dealt with them, received their summons, he gave a yell of pleasure.

'That's great. I know we can always trust Rinaldo's palate. I'll be right over.'

Alex had meant to be there for his visit, but at the last moment she had to make one of her trips to Florence for a long talk with the accountant, Andansio. What she heard from him was absorbing, but it was still hard to concentrate when her mind was with Rinaldo, learning the result of his life or death gamble.

She wasn't sure how she knew that it was life and death. But she had no doubt of it.

It was dark when she drove home, and hurried into the house. She found the two brothers standing in silence and her heart sank.

'What is it?' she asked, looking from one to the other.

'I got it wrong,' Rinaldo said bluntly. 'The wine was harvested too soon. It needed another week. I got it wrong.'

Her heart almost stopped. His face was ravaged, as though he were dying inside. And she could feel it with him, the pain of failure and defeat, almost beyond bearing.

'But how—?' she whispered.

'Because I believed what I wanted to believe,' he said

heavily. 'People do that every day, but I've cost us the best of the wine harvest.'

'You mean it's all unusable?' Alex asked, shocked.

'Oh, no, it's not unusable,' Rinaldo said with ironic self-condemnation. 'Valli will buy the grapes, not at top prices for Chianti, but as second grade to bulk out some inferior wine.'

'That's never happened to us before,' Gino said.

He spoke softly, but Rinaldo's lacerated sensibilities made every word pierce him.

'No, it's never happened before, and it wouldn't have happened this time if I hadn't been such a blind fool. Say it.'

'You made one mistake,' Gino said kindly. 'It's not the end of the world.'

Rinaldo walked to the tall window that opened onto the veranda, and looked back. Suddenly his voice was almost that of an old man.

'You're being generous my brother, as always,' he said. 'But it *is* the end of the world. I can't explain that, but take my word for it. I need time to think. Don't follow me either of you.'

He walked out into the darkness.

CHAPTER TEN

IT WAS warn for October and Alex slept with the window open to catch any hint of breeze. Even so her sleep was restless, and at last she awoke.

Climbing out of bed she went to the open window, not troubling to cover her nakedness as there would be nobody out there to see her.

She recalled how she had looked out of this window once before and seen Rinaldo burying Brutus. That was when she had known that he had a heart. It was awkward and prickly, and would never be given easily. But it felt deeply, powerfully. Perhaps it was then she'd begun to suspect that she wanted it.

She knew it now with total certainty. It would have been an understatement to say that she loved Rinaldo. Falling in love did not begin to express the way he'd taken possession of her heart, her mind, her hopes, dreams, instincts.

The only thing he hadn't possessed was her body, and now more than ever she felt the need to lie with him, taking him into herself so that they could be one in the complete surrender of love. Then perhaps she might find the means to comfort him for the wretched failure he had brought upon himself, for reasons that she still did not understand.

She'd longed to follow him as he'd walked away into the night, but his prohibition blocked her way.

When she saw the man moving between the trees she thought her imagination was reliving that first occasion.

Then she realised that Rinaldo was really there, and in the moonlight she could just see him well enough to know that he was crushed.

She couldn't bear it. Whatever he said, she must be with him. Hurriedly she pulled on a short nightgown and a light linen robe, thrust some slippers on her feet, and was out of the door, running down the stairs.

As she reached the trees she lost sight of him, and for a moment she was afraid he might have moved on. But then she saw him, sitting on a log, his hands clasped between his knees, his head sunk in an attitude of despair.

He didn't hear her approach until she dropped down on her knees beside him.

'Rinaldo— Rinaldo—' There was so much she wanted to say, but she could speak only his name.

She put her hands on either side of his face. 'Don't turn away from me,' she begged.

He didn't try to turn away, but he sat looking at her with the saddest face she thought she had ever seen. It made Alex abandon words and pull his head down until his lips were on hers.

He almost resisted, but he had no power to hold out against her for long. The next moment his arms went about her, drawing her tightly against him in a long, fierce kiss.

She could feel his desperation and it made her wind her arms about his neck, pressing herself against him, giving to him with everything she had.

'Alex—' he tried to say.

'No,' she told him fiercely. 'Not yet.'

'Not yet,' he agreed, the words almost smothered against her mouth.

Before this he had touched her face with his lips, but he had never laid them over hers. Now he did so and the feeling was as fiercely wonderful as her dreams had promised her. He kissed her with a hard, driving urgency, as though afraid that she would be snatched away.

She responded in kind, caressing his mouth feverishly, trying to draw him on to give her what she most urgently wanted from him at this moment.

But then she felt his shoulders turn to iron beneath her hands, his whole body tensed to put a distance between them.

'Stop!' he said hoarsely. 'I must tell you something.'

'Let it wait.' She was gasping. She wanted him and words were an irrelevance that got in the way.

'No, you must hear me out first.'

She forced herself to calm down, sensing that this was vital to him. When his hands fell from her she seized them, holding them between her own.

'Tell me what it is that's making you like this,' she said. 'It can't be just the grapes.'

'You don't understand,' he said so fiercely that she was startled. 'If I'd been right, I'd have got top price and been ahead of the market. And that was what I wanted more than anything in life.

'I wanted it so much that I blinded myself to the truth. I told myself I had to be right. When I tasted those grapes I found what I wanted to find. *Idiot! Stupid, conceited clown!*'

She was shocked by the agony of self-condemnation in his voice.

'I thought I could order things to be as I wanted.' He gave a crack of mirthless laughter. 'You'd think I'd have learned better than that by now, wouldn't you?'

'Please, don't be so hard on yourself,' she begged. 'So you let your pride get in the way—'

'Not pride, arrogance. I wouldn't listen, would I? And

now I've brought down my best hopes, and damaged the farm.'

'But the rest of the harvest was good—'

'Oh, yes, we won't go under. We'll survive, but not as prosperously as we should have done, because I was blind and pig-headed—*because it mattered so much I couldn't see anything else.*'

'But what mattered that much?' she asked.

He stared. 'How can you ask? Isn't it obvious?'

'Not to me.'

'I might have wiped out my debt to you, or most of it. For weeks I've lived and breathed that. I've thought of nothing else but the moment when I could repay you.

'I told you I could have got the best price if I'd been right. And I blew it. All I can do now is pay you instalments, but I'll still be deep in your debt.'

'Oh, I see,' she said. His words had raised a hideous possibility. She had been deceiving herself. He wanted her sexually, but he'd never lost the hope of getting rid of her in the end.

'You don't see at all,' he said with soft vehemence.

'You wanted to pay me off. Then everything would have been all right, wouldn't it?'

'Yes, because then I could have said things to you that I can't say while I'm your debtor. How can a man tell a woman what she means to him when he owes her money?'

She grew still, trying to see his face in the shafts of moonlight that slanted between the trees.

'I suppose—that depends on what she means to him,' she whispered.

He touched her face. 'More than I can find words for. I've dreamed of the moment when I had no *monetary* reason for marrying you, because then you could believe that I loved you. All this time I've wanted to say something, but I told myself it must wait until I had money.'

'To hell with your money!' she said vehemently. 'I don't want it, I want *you*, and if you weren't blinded with pride you'd have known that long ago.'

'Would I?' he asked with a touch of wistfulness that sounded strange from him. 'Then perhaps I'm not a very perceptive man.'

'There's no perhaps about it,' she breathed. 'Why must the mortgage be so important?'

'It's important to me to come to you with my head high.'

'You'll always have your head high. Do you think I'd suspect you of being mercenary? How could I after you fought so hard to drive me off?' She tried to lighten his mood with a mild joke. 'Nobody could ever accuse you of sweet-talking me.'

He gave a brief smile, but she could tell he was only half ready to hear her.

'I know you're stubborn and hard and awkward,' she said, 'but would you really turn your back on me because of this?'

Sombrely he shook his head. 'I could never turn my back on you,' he said in a low voice. 'I told myself I could, but it isn't true. I *must* love you. I cannot help myself. But I wanted it to be right between us.'

Tenderly she touched his face. 'You fool,' she said softly. 'You dear fool, don't you know that it will be right between us if we love each other? Not because of money. Rinaldo, listen to me. What has money to do with us? From the first moment it got in the way, blinding us to what should have been obvious.'

'I know you're right. But it hurts me here—' he

pointed to his heart '—that I can't approach you as an equal.'

'Do you love me as much as I love you? Because if you do, we're equals in the only way that matters.'

'A thousand times more. I thought I was so complete in myself before you came. You showed me that I wasn't. That's why I fought you so hard. I've never fought anyone as hard as I've fought you.'

'That's how I know you love me,' she whispered.

'Ah, you understand—'

He had said he would not approach her with love while he was still her debtor, but now he knew that he had no choice. She had carried him over the barrier by the strength of her faith. He had nothing to do now but surrender.

To this fiercely self-sufficient man surrender was hard, all but impossible. But she could make it easy by turning it into a triumph.

He drew her to him again, exploring with hands and lips, and now she was free to yield to him utterly. Her fingers caressed the back of his neck, rejoicing in a freedom long desired and now achieved.

Gradually she could feel the tension drain out of him. She parted her lips invitingly, letting him in to explore her. The feel of his tongue against the inside of her mouth stimulated her to fever pitch and she seized him with a hand on each side of his head, falling back against the earth and drawing him with her.

The light robe slipped away easily, then her thin nightgown. Beneath it she was naked and, as though the sight inspired him, Rinaldo began to strip off his clothes. She helped him eagerly. This was no time for false modesty. She wanted him and she wasn't ashamed to let him know it. Her arms were wide open to receive him as he lay beside her, running his hands over her body.

'I've wanted to do this for so long,' he said hoarsely.

How could any man's touch be so gentle yet so demanding in the same moment? There was fire in every caress. She turned her body this way and that, letting him know silently what she wanted from him.

The earth beneath was full of the scent of ripeness. The springtime and the long ripening of summer was over. It was harvest now, for them as for the land.

He kissed her everywhere, meaning to inflame her passion until she was ready for him, but she was already there, impatient of delay. When he moved over her she parted her legs in willing acceptance. Then he was inside her, his weight pressing her into the soft earth.

Her love possessed her completely, driving out all else except the feeling that this man was hers to cherish, to fulfil, and even to protect. Protecting him must be done in secret, for it was something he would not understand. But her passion need be a secret no longer, and she claimed him totally, with a full heart that was all his.

Afterward they lay together, shaking, clasping each other as if for safety. It took time to come down from the heights. The view had been lovely, opening prospects that would last all their lives.

Rinaldo kissed her tenderly. 'Let's go inside,' he said softly. 'We have only begun.'

He took her hand, drawing her to her feet and helping her on with her clothes. Quietly they slipped through the trees and across to the house, where they climbed the stairs to her room, and closed the door.

Alex awoke to find herself tightly clasped in Rinaldo's arms. After keeping her at a wary distance he had finally abandoned his defences totally, drawing her in and making her a part of himself, as though he would never release her.

The night that had just passed was a fevered blur in her memory. They had possessed each other again and again, slaking a passion too long denied. After each loving they would sleep for a little and awaken with renewed desire. Their final sleep was one of exhaustion.

They awoke reluctantly, not wanting to let each other go.

'I suppose we have to get up,' he whispered.

'Yes, it's a new day.'

'A new day for us. I shall never let you go. You do know that, don't you. If you wanted to leave me, it's too late now.'

She smiled blissfully. 'That's all right then.'

He kissed her. 'It's not going to be easy. I love you, but it isn't going to turn me into sweetness and light.'

She gave a soft chuckle. 'Good. I wouldn't recognise you.'

'It's been so long since I loved,' he said in a low voice. 'I thought I'd forgotten how.'

'I'll always be there to remind you.'

Slowly they disentangled themselves and rose. Rinaldo pulled on his jeans.

'Before I leave,' he said, 'you'd better check the corridor, to see if the coast's clear. I don't want Gino to see me creeping out of your room.'

'No, he mustn't find out about us like that,' Alex agreed.

After a moment's hesitation he asked awkwardly, 'Will there be a problem about telling him?'

'No, there was never anything really between us. Just him flirting with me, at your command.'

'I didn't exactly—' he began uneasily.

Alex gave a burst of laughter. 'Oh, my love, my love! You should see your face! Be careful what you say. Gino told me everything.'

'Everything?' he asked, even more uneasily.

'Everything.'

His face was a delight. Alex could see that he wasn't used to bantering, and he was all at sea.

'Just what does ''everything'' include?' he asked cautiously.

'Well, if I say ''two-headed coin'' does that convey anything?'

He groaned and dropped his head in his hands.

'I'll kill him,' he muttered.

To Alex it was joyously funny, but she reminded herself that this was a man with too little experience of humour. In the years to come she would have to teach him to laugh and be happy. That would be her pleasure and her privilege. So she hopped beside him on the bed and put her arms about him, telling him without words that it wasn't the end of the world.

'Look—' he said desperately.

'Darling, it's all right. I think it's hilarious. That'll teach you to reject a lady before you've even met her. One part of me wants to say that you should simply have ''taken your winnings''. But the other part says it's better as it is. All that fighting we did—we needed it. We could never have got to know each other so well otherwise.'

'I could never have ''taken my winnings'',' he said. 'To approach you like that—' he shuddered. 'On the other hand I was angry enough for anything. Perhaps I—'

'Stop this.' She put her fingertips over his mouth. 'You don't have to explain yourself to me. I *know* you.'

'Yes, you do, don't you?' he said slowly. 'You've

known me all through right from the beginning. That night you said I was lonely, and like a fool I shut you out because you'd seen to the heart of me. I'd kept my heart locked away for so long that I couldn't take the risk of revealing it to you. So I rejected you, then I turned on you, accusing you of deviousness, to protect myself. And it was all useless, because there's no protection from love.'

'That's true,' she said, leaning her head against him. 'There's no protection for either of us, except each other.'

'Except each other,' he repeated. 'I was so alarmed by my own feelings that I left the house that night, running like a coward. When I heard you'd gone I thought it was safe to come home, but that just made everything worse. I couldn't bear the thought of never seeing you again. If you hadn't returned I'd have given in and come seeking you in England. The night you broke in and we struggled—do you remember?'

'Yes,' she said with a reminiscent smile. 'I remember everything.'

'Feeling you against me, beneath me—I swear you weren't safe. If Gino hadn't been there I'd have—well, I wanted to, anyway.'

'Mm! Me too.'

'But I didn't know what to say to you. You came back with flags flying, full of confidence. I knew you were free from that man, but I didn't know how you felt about it. So many times I've wanted to take you in my arms and say that nothing else mattered. But it did matter, so I started counting on the harvest. And I got it wrong because I could only hear my heart, not my head. I wanted to pay you, and then face you with pride.'

He saw her looking at him with gentle understanding,

and sighed. 'I got that wrong too, didn't I?' he said ruefully.

'You think all the wrong things matter. Love matters. Not pride.'

'Is it really that simple, *amor mio*?'

'Yes, *amor mio*,' she said softly. 'It's really that simple.'

They kissed tenderly, but she could see that he was still troubled by one thought.

'Are you sure it will be that simple for Gino?' he asked. 'I thought once he was in love with you. Now I don't know.'

'He isn't. Oh, he made a big theatrical comedy of it, but I think that's just his way.'

Rinaldo nodded. 'You're right. All his life, everything had to be a production number.'

'But since I came back he's been a quieter, very polite, very respectful. Haven't you noticed?'

'Yes. And it's not like him.'

'He's probably just a bit embarrassed about backing off after all that theatrical "passion",' Alex mused. 'Especially after my engagement broke up.' She laughed suddenly. 'Oh, now I understand. Poor Gino. He was afraid I'd expect him to marry me, and he was trying to let me know, very kindly, that it's not on.'

Rinaldo's brow cleared.

'That would be it. But to be fair, he was probably madly in love with you at one time—for about two days.'

Alex raised an eyebrow at him. 'That's all you think I'm worth, eh?'

'No, but it's his record.'

They laughed together.

'Trust me, he'll be glad to have the problem solved,' she said.

She glanced into the corridor, saw that it was clear and signalled to Rinaldo. A brief kiss, and he was gone.

She followed him down a few minutes later and found him alone in the kitchen. Gino was just entering the house.

'Now?' Rinaldo asked her softly.

But Alex shook her head. 'No, I have something to tell you both first.'

He looked puzzled.

'Wait and see,' she said in a voice of teasing anticipation.

Gino came in, smiling when he saw Rinaldo.

'You look more cheerful than you did last night,' he said.

'And you're both going to look more cheerful when you've heard what I have to say,' Alex told them.

They looked at her expectantly.

'Enrico Varsi owes you money,' she said. 'Quite a lot of money if I've got my figures right.'

'But how?' Rinaldo asked.

Alex took a deep breath. 'Because he's been cheating you for years,' she announced.

'What?'

The exclamation was Gino's. Rinaldo was more wary.

'Alex, I really think that's very unlikely. Varsi is an eminent man—'

'Which makes it easier for him to get away with it.'

'He was also an old friend of our father, who trusted him completely.'

'Someone who trusts you is the easiest to deceive. I don't suppose it ever occurred to your father that his friend was stealing from him. It occurred to me as soon as I got a long look at your books.'

'I know you mean well,' Rinaldo said, 'And you're an

expert in British accounting practices, but this is Italy. We have a different financial year, remember?'

'I know, and all sorts of other things are different. That's why I've been taking a crash course in Italian accountancy.'

'Where? How?'

'From a man called Tomaso Andansio. His offices are just up the street from Varsi's.'

'Is that what I saw you looking at that day?'

'That's right. I knew I'd heard the name somewhere, then I remembered we had some dealing with him in London. Signor Andansio is brilliant and totally honest.

'I called him, and he let me spend a week in his office, learning all I needed. When I showed him my evidence he agreed there was a case, and gave me a whole lot of reading to do. There's no doubt of it. Varsi's stolen a fortune from you.'

She added wryly, 'But for that, your father might never have needed a mortgage.'

Gino flung his arms about Alex in a fierce hug that turned into an exuberant waltz about the room.

'You're a genius,' he yodelled. 'A genius, our good angel, our glorious, shining star—'

'Yes, that's very nice,' Rinaldo interrupted him, 'and I admit it opens interesting possibilities, but—'

'Interesting possibilities, you soulless man!' Gino protested, releasing Alex. 'Is that all you've got to say for what Alex has done for us? You've never appreciated her properly and I think it's time you—'

'I'm trying to be realistic,' Rinaldo cut him short quickly.

'Rinaldo means he doesn't trust me to get it right,' Alex said cheerfully. 'I anticipated that, so I'm arranging for us all to go and see Signor Andansio. I dare say you'll believe him, seeing that he's a man.'

'Seeing that he's an Italian,' Rinaldo said, smiling at her and refusing to be provoked. 'I think visiting him is a very good idea, Alex.'

She went straight to the phone, followed by Gino who whispered in her ear, 'You're having a really civilising effect on Rinaldo. Keep up the good work.'

They drove into Florence later that day and in a few brief words the accountant confirmed everything Alex had said.

'It's a matter of how you define things,' he explained. 'Transfer certain things from one column to another and the whole picture changes. In between the two "pictures" there is a gap. A lot of money can fall into that gap, and an unscrupulous accountant can help himself. For years your tax liability has been less than the amount you paid, and since the cheques were routed through him—' He finished with an eloquent shrug.

'And Poppa never checked because he trusted him,' Gino sighed.

'It would have made no difference if he had checked,' Andansio said kindly. 'It's been very cleverly disguised, and you need to know what to look for. This lady—' he indicated Alex '—was particularly sharp-eyed to notice it in an unfamiliar environment. I've already told her that if she chooses to take the exams in this country there'll always be a position for her in my office.'

'I may just do that,' Alex said.

'I told you she was a genius,' Gino said.

'Can we get back to the point?' Rinaldo asked. 'We now know that Varsi has been robbing us all these years. What's the next step? The police? Can it be proved?'

'Oh, yes, but I think there may be another way of

dealing with him,' Andansio said. 'We show him our evidence and demand restitution, not only to yourselves but to all the other clients from whom he has undoubtedly been stealing. That will do them far more good than prosecution, and believe me, he can afford it. In return we'll have to promise to keep quiet.'

'Which leaves him free to prey on others,' Rinaldo pointed out.

'Oh, I don't think so,' Andansio said smoothly. 'I shall make it very clear to him that he's under my eye.'

'How much can he be forced to return to us?' Rinaldo asked.

Andansio named a sum. The three facing him stared in shock.

Gino gasped, 'But that's—'

'Almost as much as the mortgage,' Rinaldo murmured.

Alex said nothing. She merely smiled.

'I assume you will be wishing to move your affairs out of his hands,' Signor Andansio said.

'And into yours,' Rinaldo agreed.

'In that case, may I suggest that you leave matters to me? I believe I'll have good news for you quite soon.'

In a daze they went out into the light, and stood looking at each other for a few moments. Gino recovered first.

'A celebration!' he declared. 'Because we really have something to celebrate.'

It was almost evening. Gino grabbed both their hands and led them into the best restaurant he could find.

'Because we can afford it now,' he said. 'Waiter, what's the best champagne you have?'

He seemed carried away by exhilaration. It was as much as the others could do to calm him down, and then only for a short while.

Later that evening, after an excellent meal, they piled him into the back seat of the car, where he fell asleep with a smile on his face.

CHAPTER ELEVEN

THE whole area around Florence seemed to be one great harvest festival. Every night there was a party somewhere or other.

On the evening when the neighbours gathered at Belluna the air was brilliant with good cheer. Coloured lights hung from the trees, heavily laden trestle-tables were spread out in the open. All day Teresa, Celia and Franca had worked to lay on the best party in the district.

'You're beautiful,' Rinaldo told Alex as she emerged from her room in a floaty blue and white dress and white sandals. 'I want to tell everyone that you're mine. I wish we could do it tonight.'

'So do I, but we must tell Gino first, and I can't seem to catch him.'

Rinaldo nodded. 'Ever since Varsi agreed to repay the money, and we found that it covers our debt to you, he's been on a high. What is it?'

He spoke anxiously because a shadow had crossed Alex's face.

'What am I going to do with all that money?' she asked. 'I don't want cash, I want to be part of Belluna.'

'But as my wife, you will be a part of it.'

'I know, it's just that—'

But Rinaldo was growing in understanding.

'If that's not enough,' he said, 'you can pay for next year's fertiliser, and the repairs to the machinery, and the new barns. That will save us having to borrow from the bank as we normally have to. Then you'll have the financial stake that you want.'

'That's better,' she said.

'Don't look so cheerful. Do you know what fertiliser costs?'

'After all the accounts I've read? Of course I do. It's a wonderful idea.'

'And when we can pin Gino down we'll clear it with him,' Rinaldo said. 'After all, it's his farm too, and I shouldn't be making financial decisions without consulting him.'

'I'll bet he's not used to being consulted about anything,' Alex teased.

'You're making fun of me, aren't you?'

'Yes, and you'd better get used to it.'

'You must teach me. Now I suppose we should go downstairs and be ready for our guests. Where the devil is Gino?'

'These last few days he's always passing through, and I haven't even seen him today.'

'Yes, he told me he had some important business in Florence but he won't say what. It's been taking him to town on and off for days.'

'He must have a girlfriend,' Alex said triumphantly. 'And maybe he's going to bring her to the party tonight. Perhaps he's collecting her now, that's why he's late.'

The first cars were arriving as they went down and they were immediately engulfed in festivities. Within half an hour there were a hundred people, laughing, eating, sipping the best Chianti.

Alex looked around, feeling joyously at home at last. Just one more hurdle to go. If only Gino were here.

And then, suddenly, he was. They saw the lights of his car approaching, and the next moment he'd parked, leapt out and was being greeted with riotous enthusiasm by every guest. Gino was deservedly popular.

He went right round the party, kissing every woman there, even the oldest, leaving smiles behind him, until at last he presented himself to his brother and Alex.

'I'm sorry,' he said penitently.

'So you should be,' Rinaldo growled. 'This is Alex's first party here, and she's put a lot of work into it.'

'Alex will forgive me when she hears what I have to say,' Gino said, looking at her with a light in his eyes.

Seeing that light, Alex knew a sudden sense of alarm.

'Gino, dear, why don't you have a drink?'

'Let that wait. There's something I must say to you that's far more important. I've waited until now, but oh, *carissima* I can't wait any longer. I love you. I want to marry you.'

'Gino—'

'Hush, don't say anything. Let me show you this.'

He pulled a little box from his pocket and opened it. Inside glittered a ring that she could see was antique. It was exquisite, studded with diamonds and sapphires.

'I saw this in the shop window ages ago,' Gino said. 'And I thought then how I should like to give it to you on the day I asked you to be my wife. But when I went back for it they'd sold it to someone else, and it's taken me a long time to track him down and buy it. But it's mine now, which means it's yours.'

'Gino—' she whispered, devastated by what was happening, yet unable to stop it.

'Don't look so surprised, *carissima*. You've always known how I felt about you. Even when I was playing the fool, my heart was all yours. Or perhaps you didn't suspect how deep my love is. Maybe this will convince you.'

Before the whole party Gino went down on one knee, took Alex's hand in his and said, 'Alex, my love, will you please marry me? Will you be my wife?'

Alex felt as though she were moving through a nightmare. She should have silenced him but shock had held her transfixed.

In the silence, Gino took her hand and slipped the ring onto it.

Alex stared at the ring, her eyes full of tears as she thought how she must hurt him. How had she let this take her by surprise? she thought wretchedly.

But she knew the answer. Rinaldo had filled her thoughts to the exclusion of all else. Gino had existed only on the periphery.

Gino was still smiling up at her, not yet understanding her silence. Behind him she could see Rinaldo, his face pale and shocked. Imperceptibly she shook her head at him. What had to be done, she must do alone.

'Gino,' she said hesitantly. 'Please get up. Don't let's talk about this now.'

'What is there to talk about, darling?' he asked softly, rising to his feet and looking at her with eyes full of love.

'No,' she said, removing the ring and putting it back into his hand. 'Gino, I'm sorry—I can't—'

She saw the joy and certainty drain out of his face, leaving behind not disillusion but bafflement. He'd convinced himself of her feelings, and now couldn't believe otherwise.

Alex pulled herself together. 'Come with me,' she said, seizing his hand and drawing him away from the crowd.

Cheers followed them. Only a few heard had heard their exchange. The others saw them as lovers who wanted to be alone.

Gino thought so too, for as soon as they were through the trees he tried to take her into his arms.

'I'm sorry *carissima*, I shouldn't have done that in public.'

'Gino—'

'I know you'll forgive me when I tell you how much I love you. But surely you already know that?'

'No—no, I didn't. At first you seemed to be playing at flirtation, and since I came back from England you've stayed away from me.'

'I've hardly done that, but I've tried to show respect for your feelings. I knew how the breakup with your fiancé must have hurt you, and that you'd need time to get over him. I'm not an insensitive oaf, darling.'

'No, you're not,' she said. 'You're a sweet, kind boy—'

'I'm not a boy,' Gino said firmly. 'I may look like one sometimes next to Rinaldo, because I think he was born old. But I'm man enough to know that I love you with my whole heart and soul, enough to wait for you to be ready. Darling, must I wait longer? You know now how much I love you? Can't you love me now?'

'Oh, no,' she said softly, already in pain for him. 'Gino, I didn't understand, you always made such a joke of it.'

'Yes, I did in the beginning. I don't think I fully realised what my feelings were until you went away. It was unbearable without you, and I began to understand how deep it went with me. If you hadn't come back when you did, I would have followed you to England.'

She gave a gasp as she heard those words, so similar to the ones Rinaldo had spoken.

'I'd have followed you because I knew you were the one,' Gino said, 'the only one, different from every other woman I've fooled around with and loved for five minutes. It's not five minutes this time, but all my life and beyond—'

'No!' she cried, distraught. 'Don't say that. It mustn't be true. It can't be.'

A shadow crossed his face. 'Why can't it be true?'

'Because I'm not in love with you.'

He looked at her, almost as though the words conveyed no meaning to him.

'You're still in love with that man in England,' he said at last. 'I spoke too soon.'

'No, no, it's not him, it's—'

But she checked herself. This was no time to tell him about Rinaldo. Not here and now, in the middle of a party.

'Please don't say any more,' she begged. 'We'll talk about it later.'

'Yes,' he said. 'Later. I did it the wrong way, didn't I? I rushed you. I can wait.'

He gave her a brief smile and walked away back to the party.

She watched him, bitterly blaming herself for not seeing this coming. It was as Gino had said. He was no longer a boy but a man, with a sensitivity to her feelings that she had not suspected. It had misled her into thinking he didn't care.

As if to prove his new-found maturity Gino did not storm off alone, or sulk, but became the life and soul of the party. He danced every dance, flirted without end, and generally exerted himself to make things go with a swing.

The general opinion among the guests was that he must have attained his heart's desire, because he presented the picture of a supremely happy man. Only a few people noticed that he and Alex never went near each other for the rest of the evening.

At last the guests began to drift away. There were crowing goodbyes, songs yodelled up to the moon, and an air of happy satiety.

'Where's Gino?' Rinaldo asked Alex when they were alone.

'I last saw him half an hour ago. Oh, Rinaldo—'

'I know. It's terrible. He'll understand in the end, but he's bound to be sore after he declared himself so openly, in front of all those people.'

'He's been marvellous since then,' Alex observed. 'It must have been very difficult for him to be so bright and cheerful after what I said to him.'

'How much did you say?'

'Only that I didn't love him. It wasn't the right time to tell him the rest.'

She approached Teresa who was clearing away with the girls, and gave them some help. Later she found Rinaldo.

'Teresa says she saw Gino driving away,' she said.

'I guess he wants to think for a while. He'll feel better afterward.'

But despite his confident words he stood on the porch for half an hour, staring into the darkness.

'Don't let him come back and find you watching out for him,' Alex suggested gently. 'He's not a kid any more.'

'You're right. I can't get out of the habit of thinking of myself as a kind of second father. I'll have to now, won't I? But it's going to be hard, telling him.'

'Do you think perhaps—we shouldn't?' she asked unhappily.

But he shook his head.

'I can't give you up for any reason. Not just because I love you, but because you're necessary to me, as air and water are necessary. I love my brother, but even for him I can't do without you. Come inside with me now, for I need, very much, to be alone with you.'

In the darkness they climbed the stairs. Almost before they reached the top she was in his arms, kissing and being kissed with a determined purpose that thrilled her.

Rinaldo put out his hand and opened the first door he came to, which was his own room.

'I can't wait to get to yours,' he murmured, drawing her inside and shutting the door. He was already removing her clothes with urgent hands.

She helped him, stripping him even as he stripped her until they lay on the bed together and he took her into his arms for a long kiss that was part affirmation, part exploration. She loved this moment, when his tongue teased the inside of her mouth, rousing her gently and expertly to the pitch of desire that only he could create.

When he withdrew his mouth she could see that his face held the brooding expression that excited her so much. His great hand drifted over her breasts, enclosed one, caressing it with subtlety so that she was flooded with warmth.

For this above all she loved him, for revealing her own sensuality to her, showing her that the woman of desks and good order was only one facet, and not the truest one. The real Alex was a woman who lived for the primitive force that united them, and could relinquish herself totally to the man she loved.

For so harsh a man Rinaldo was an unexpectedly gentle and skilful lover. He waited for her to be ready, but he didn't have to wait long. She wanted him, wanted more of the shattering sensation that pervaded her, wanted everything.

When her moment came Alex drove back against him, urging him on with all her strength until they reached fulfilment together. She saw his face in that instant, and wondered at its mixture of awe and surrender.

He fell asleep first, and she propped herself up on her elbow, watching him with eyes that were passionately protective, but also curious. The chance to study him unaware did not come often.

His face was scarcely softer in sleep than in waking. The chin was still stubborn, the nose too strong for comfort. They would still fight. He'd warned her of that, and the starkness of his face told her that it was true. But that was all right. Fighting wouldn't suit everyone, but to them it would merely be an aspect of their love. And she could give as good as she got.

But she would be careful, because deep instinct warned her that he was more vulnerable than she, more easily hurt, less able to show it, and therefore more at risk.

His mouth intrigued her the most. It was not, at first glance, a sensual mouth; too firm, too wary, even in repose.

But she was no longer fooled by the look. She had kissed that mouth and felt it soften against hers. She had shared passion with that big, lanky body with its longs legs, powerful arms and skilful hands. No woman who had experienced that sensation could mistake his essential nature. He was a man who could love with every part of him, mind, soul and body.

After a long while she lay down, gazing into the darkness, looking back along the road that had brought her here.

Since coming to Italy she had discovered that the country had two faces. There was Italy of the smile and the song, of the rich colours, flowing wine and bright laughter. This was romantic Italy. This was Gino.

And there was another country whose past had been steeped in blood and vengeance, a dark, sombre place, full of sullen shadows, deadly feuds, anger, bitterness, danger. This was Rinaldo.

If a woman had once been delighted by the smile and the vibrant youth, why should she turn away from that to the other land, where a man with a face like granite and a soul to match offered only his darkness, and his need?

Why? Because she could not help herself. That was why.

She raised herself again and touched his face with her fingertips. Then she kissed him so softly that he did not awaken. He was hers, to have and to hold, to love and cherish. Because he needed her. And that was all there was to be said.

Rinaldo was in a mysterious place, one where he'd been before, but which had no name. He knew that he was waiting for something, but he did not know what.

His father was there again, looking at him with troubled eyes. But this was the moment when he always awoke, and the message was never delivered.

With a shudder he sat up in bed, his eyes open and staring. His whole body was shaking.

'What is it?' Alex said from beside him. 'Rinaldo, *wake up*.'

She shook him gently. At first she thought he was too far lost in his unquiet dream for her to reach him, but at last, to her relief, she felt him relax.

Still she could not be certain that he was awake, although his eyes were open. She touched his face gently.

'Rinaldo,' she whispered, 'talk to me.'

At last he seemed to focus on her. He looked drained, and when she put her arms about him he clung to her.

'Was it a bad dream?' she asked.

'No. Something came back to me at last. It's been there all this time, hovering just out of sight. I've tried so often to remember—'

'And now you have?'

'Yes. It was the day my father died. I got to the hospital before Gino and I had a few moments alone with him.

'When he saw me, he tried to say something. His face was swollen and he couldn't get the words out—just the words, "Sorry". He said that over and over. I can still see his eyes—they were desperate. He wanted so much to tell me something, but he couldn't manage it.

'I kept waiting for him to tell me, but then I realised that it wasn't possible. So I took his hand between mine and told him everything was going to be all right. He seemed quieter. And then he died.'

'What do you think he wanted to say?'

'I think it was the mortgage. He knew what was going to happen, and he was trying to tell me that he was sorry.'

Rinaldo shook his head as though trying to clear it.

'I don't know how I could have forgotten that,' he said. 'It was as though my mind just blanked it out.'

Alex took him in her arms, speaking gently.

'With all that happened that day, and the state you must have been in, it's not surprising. You needed to be ready to remember.'

'And I'm ready now, here in your arms. All this time— I blamed him—but he did try to warn me.'

'He never meant you to find out the way you did,' she said.

'That's right. He didn't just abandon us without a word, the way I felt he had. That might have been unreasonable, but it was how I felt. Now it's different. It's as though I'd got my father back again. You did that.'

Her heart sang at his praise, but she said, 'It would have happened anyway.'

'No, it happened because I found peace with you. That peace had to come first, before I could be reconciled with him. Now I am. He's in my heart once more, and I'll never lose him again—because of you.'

Suddenly he clung to her. 'Don't leave me,' he said desperately.

'Never in life. As long as you need me, I'll be here.'

'I'll always need you. There was no warmth or light before you came.' He rested his head against her. 'Suppose you'd never come here, and we'd never met?'

'But we did,' she murmured. 'Maybe we were always bound to meet. Do you remember that first day?'

'At Poppa's funeral? Yes.'

'I think I knew then that you were going to be something important in my life. I didn't know what, but I knew it wasn't going to be indifference.'

'No, we could never have been indifferent to each other,' he murmured.

'And in those days it looked like we'd be enemies.'

'Is that what we were?' he whispered.

'Oh, yes.' She smiled tenderly. 'We had to be enemies first before we could be anything else. It's not a bad way of getting acquainted.'

'Yes, we did that,' he agreed with a faint smile. 'Now we have to get to know each other in another way.'

'You think we don't know each other?' she asked softly.

He didn't answer at once, but he raised his head and their eyes held, full of deep, shared knowledge. They knew each other.

'I'm looking forward to the rest,' he said. 'Being with you every day, learning all about you, the things you like, dislike. Growing old with you, becoming part of you, making you part of me.'

'I *am* part of you,' she said. 'I always will be.'

'I feel as though I've spent the last years wandering in a desert. And you've brought me home.'

She kissed him repeatedly, not in passion but in tenderness. There had been passion and there would be passion again, but for now their embrace was an assertion of profound peace and trust between them. At last they slept again, still holding each other.

When Alex found herself drifting back to the surface she wasn't sure whether it was happening naturally or because of some other reason. Despite her feeling of fulfilment she was pervaded by an uneasy awareness of something wrong.

Slowly she opened her eyes.

Gino was standing at the end of the bed, staring at them both with a face full of shock and disillusion.

CHAPTER TWELVE

FOR a long moment Alex couldn't move. Inwardly she was weeping. Dear Gino, so generous and affectionate, the last man she would ever want to hurt! But his face was telling her that he was stricken to the heart.

Rinaldo was sleeping with his head against her, his whole attitude that of a man who had come home to the place where he belonged. Her arms were about him in a way that would have told Gino how things were between them, even if nothing else did.

'Gino!' Her lips formed his name without sound.

Still he neither moved nor spoke, while his face seemed to grow paler every moment. Alex reached out a hand to him.

Then he moved, backing away to the door, his eyes, filled with bitter betrayal, fixed on his brother and the woman he loved.

Despairingly she gave Rinaldo a little shake, awaking him. When he saw his brother he tensed and gave a soft groan.

Gino had reached the door, shaking his head as though trying to deny what his eyes saw. Then he vanished.

'*Gino!*' Rinaldo shouted.

He hurled himself out of bed, pulling on his jeans and racing to the door almost in one movement. Alex sat with her head in her hands, devastated by the sudden catastrophe, torn with anguish for Gino, who didn't deserve to be hurt like this.

'No,' she whispered. 'Please, no! Oh, Gino, Gino!'

Huddling on her clothes she went down to where Rinaldo had caught up with Gino in the room that led to the veranda. The tall windows had been thrown open, showing the low table, and the chairs where the three of them had spent happy evenings.

Gino was striding about the room, as though his pain was something he could leave behind. He turned when he heard Alex and she was shocked by his face.

It was as though all the youth had drained out of it, leaving it haggard and joyless. He looked from one to the other.

'Why didn't you tell me?' he asked. 'It wouldn't have been difficult, would it? Hell—the way you pulled the wool over my eyes, pretending to be enemies, letting me believe what I wanted. The only thing I don't understand is why?'

His eyes were cold and hard as he faced Alex. 'Did it give you some sort of pleasure to lead me by the nose?'

'I didn't—truly I didn't—'

'Don't insult my intelligence, Alex. All this time—'

'But it isn't all this time. You talk about Rinaldo and me pretending to be enemies, but it wasn't a pretence. When you've seen us quarrelling it's been real.'

'So what changed?'

'Nothing changed,' Rinaldo said quietly. 'What we felt for each other was there all the time, but we didn't know it. Or maybe we suspected, and were fighting it. I resented her at first, you know I did. I didn't want to fall in love with her, but I couldn't help myself because she's a wonderful—'

'*All right,*' Gino said harshly.

'I'm sorry,' Rinaldo said. He seemed cast down in a way Alex had never seen before, and she realised that in his own way he too was devastated. He loved his brother, and it was tearing him apart to quarrel with him.

'I'm sorry,' he repeated. 'I just hoped you'd understand—'

'I understand all I need to,' Gino said.

'Gino, listen,' Alex begged, 'Rinaldo hasn't taken anything that was yours. It was always going to be him. It took us both too long to realise it, but it's as he says. There was something there between us right from the start. All the time we were quarrelling, we were falling in love as well.'

As she spoke she'd moved forward so that she was standing directly before Gino.

'Please,' she said softly, 'please believe me, I'd do anything rather than hurt you.'

'Would you? You could have warned me.'

'But I didn't know how you felt. You treat love as a game, and you play it so well that that's all it seems.'

'It started that way,' he agreed, 'but then I found I was really in love with you.'

'I didn't know,' she said. 'If I had—I could have told you earlier that I could never love you.' He closed his eyes. 'Not as you want, anyway,' she said desperately.

He nodded. 'Not as I want,' he repeated softly.

'What happened at the party—I would have prevented that if I could.'

Gino made a despairing gesture. 'So I made a fool of myself in front of our neighbours. That's not important.'

He looked at Rinaldo. 'I came back here tonight to find you. I wanted to speak to you, ask your advice—there's a laugh. And I'll tell you another thing that's funny. The one thing I never thought of was that I'd find her in your bed.'

'I wish that had never happened,' Rinaldo said gravely.

'But Alex and I love each other, and we're going to be married. I didn't take her from you. The choice was hers.'

Alex hadn't thought it possible for Gino to grow paler, but suddenly his face seemed to become grey, the grey of death.

'Be damned to the pair of you,' he said with soft violence, and strode out.

'*Gino—!*' Alex cried, reaching for him.

'No,' Rinaldo stopped her following. 'He can't bear the sight of either of us right now. When he calms down he'll forgive us. But right now he needs to be alone, and we should respect that.'

Bleakly she nodded and let him lead her away. Together they climbed the stairs but at the top they paused, looking at each other. Then, as if by a signal, they went their separate ways. They couldn't be together again tonight, not in the face of Gino's anguished condemnation.

Alex went alone in her room and after a moment she heard Rinaldo's door close.

It seemed strange to come down in the early morning and not find Gino there. His handsome, smiling face, his clowning and his kind heart had always been part of her pleasure in Belluna.

She did love him. Not as she loved Rinaldo, with a dark, burning passion, but with the tender affection of a sister. But he wanted so much more from her that the chasm was unbridgeable.

She went out onto the veranda, hoping against hope that she would see him. But the morning was quiet.

Then her eyes fell on the chair where he always sat. The jacket he'd worn the night before was tossed down there. Alex ran her fingers over it, thinking of him putting it on before the party, slipping the ring into the pocket, planning how he would propose to her. He'd been full of young, eager love, sure of being loved in return. And it had turned to heartbreak.

There was a clatter as something fell to the floor. It was the ring he'd tried to give her. She sat down heavily and leaned her head on her hands.

After a moment she heard Rinaldo, felt his hand on her shoulder.

'That's how I feel too,' he said.

They sat together for a while, just taking comfort from each other's presence.

'Gino's gone away,' he said at last. 'His car isn't there, and some of his clothes are missing.'

'But he'll come back?' she said quickly.

'Of course he will. We just have to be patient. Everything will work out.'

Meeting his eyes, Alex saw that he didn't believe it any more than she.

'All these years,' he sighed, 'watching him grow up, being a second father to him, and now—dear God, what have I done to him?'

'What have *we* done to him?' Alex said.

'He's changed. Grown up. Last night it was like talking to an old man.' He sighed. 'Whatever happens now, we'll never see the Gino we knew.'

Alex forced herself to say the words that terrified her.

'How can I stay here if it's going to do this to him? If I go away—'

'No,' he said quickly. 'I can't live without you. I won't let you go.'

'I don't want to leave you,' she whispered, 'but—'

'No buts. We have the right to our love. Besides, your leaving wouldn't solve anything. Gino and I can't turn time back to before you came, and even if I could do that, I wouldn't.' His voice deepened, became tender. 'Never to have known you, loved you, to return to the half-life where you didn't exist—I couldn't do it.

'Thank heavens!' she said huskily. 'I was so afraid you'd want me to go.'

'Then you don't know me very well. I can't live without you now. The only reconciliation my brother and I can have is when he discovers the woman who will really be his love.'

He took her face between his hands.

'I told him we were to be married, although I hadn't asked you.'

'You know you didn't need to ask me. All I want is to stay here with you.'

'That's all I want too. Please God, we'll have many years together.'

They set the date of their wedding for three weeks ahead, and chose a small village church, on the edge of the farm. Many of the guests would be the farm-hands who, more than any others, had cause to rejoice at this marriage.

Wedding presents poured in, but the only gift they wanted was news of Gino, who had not returned.

He arrived unexpectedly one day while they were both out, and they reached home to find his car standing outside while he loaded luggage onto it.

His appearance shocked them. He had actually aged. His face, once so full of smiles, looked as though it would never smile again.

'I came for the rest of my things,' he said. 'But I waited for you. I couldn't leave without saying goodbye.'

'You're going for good?' Rinaldo asked. 'But this is your home.'

He did smile then, wanly and with irony.

'What do you suggest?' he asked. 'That we all three live together? You know we can't.'

They were silenced, knowing he was right.

'Where have you been?' Rinaldo demanded at last.

'I'm staying with friends while I sort myself out. I think I'll go abroad.'

'But you own part of this farm,' Rinaldo reminded him.

'I know. We'll have to make some kind of arrangement about that.'

'We've got time,' Rinaldo argued. 'At least stay here until the wedding—'

Gino stopped him. 'No,' he said with finality.

'But you will be there?' Alex implored.

'I don't know. Don't count on me.'

'There's something I've been wanting to tell you,' Rinaldo said heavily. 'I never thought it would be like this, but you must know. It's about Poppa. You've often asked me what happened at the hospital, when I was alone with him, and I could never tell you, because I couldn't remember. It was as though a curtain had been drawn across it, blotting it out from me. But that night— the night you came home—'

'Go on,' Gino said.

'It came back, while I was asleep. He spoke to me, and he tried to tell me about the money. He couldn't finish the words, but he tried. He didn't want to leave us to discover it the way we did.'

Gino nodded. 'Thank you,' he said at last. 'I'm glad you told me. It seems to give him back to us somehow.'

'Yes,' Rinaldo said at once. 'That's exactly what I felt.'

For a moment they were brothers again.

'I'd better go now,' Gino said. He hesitated before asking in a low voice, 'May I speak to Alex alone?'

'Of course,' she said at once.

Rinaldo nodded, and turned away to go into the house.

'It's all right,' Gino said. 'I'm not going to embarrass you. I just wanted to say—I don't know. I'd planned to say so much, and now it's all gone out of my head.'

'Forgive me,' she pleaded.

'There's nothing to forgive. You had the right to make your own choice. You'll never know how much I love you, because now I'm not free to tell you.'

'I think you just have told me,' she whispered.

He shook his head.

'That doesn't begin to say it. It was like a miracle to me to discover that such feeling could exist.'

'You'll feel it again, when you meet the right person for you.'

'Perhaps,' he said, and she knew he didn't believe her. 'But if that shouldn't happen—thank you.'

It was a moment before she could speak.

'You have nothing to thank me for,' she said at last.

'Oh, yes, I have everything to thank you for. And I do.'

She put out a hand to him but he flinched away, softening the gesture with a smile that it hurt her to see.

'The truth was staring me in the face all the time, wasn't it?' he said. 'That night when we had dinner, and I said you always brought the conversation back to Rinaldo. There was the clue, if only I had the wit to see it. It's nobody's fault but mine.'

'Come in and stay for a while,' she begged. 'Don't go like this.'

'I think I'd better leave.'

'At least come in and get your ring. You left it behind.'

'You fetch it for me. I'll wait here.'

She went into the house, turning in the doorway to see him standing beside the car, looking at her.

Upstairs she found Rinaldo and explained her errand. He followed her into her room and waited while she found the ring.

'When I give this to him,' she said, 'perhaps we—'

She was stopped by the sound of a car engine.

'Oh, no!' she gasped.

From the window they saw Gino's car vanishing in the distance.

She couldn't help herself then. She hid her face against Rinaldo and wept.

The wedding was both sad and happy. If things had been different Alex and Rinaldo would have bickered lovingly about which of them would claim Gino's services—she wanted him to give her away, and he wanted him as best man.

As it was, she was given away by Isidoro, her lawyer, and Rinaldo's best man was his foreman.

But all other thoughts faded as they stood together before the altar. This was her moment of glorious fulfilment, the moment that would inspire the rest of her life. Looking at Rinaldo she knew that it was the same with him.

Suddenly she heard a faint whisper in the church. Turning her head a little she managed to look over her shoulder enough to see the door.

A young man was standing there, silhouetted against the light. Alex couldn't see his face, but the sun just touched his hair, giving him almost a halo. He stood very still.

Then she thought she saw him move, coming forward to sit in a pew.

Of course he had come, she thought, happy and relieved. Whatever his pain, Gino's warm heart wouldn't let him stay away.

The priest was asking Rinaldo if he took her to be his wife. In a firm voice he declared his intention of doing so. Then it was her turn.

She forgot Gino. All her attention now was for the man she loved, making her his, as he was hers, for life.

But as the service ended and he kissed her, Alex murmured, 'Gino's here.'

'I know. I saw him by the door.'

It was all they needed to be happy. As they turned and walked back down the aisle together their eyes were searching row after row of faces, looking for the one face that mattered.

But he wasn't there. If he had ever been there, he had gone again.

The reception was held in the largest barn, hung with flowers and ribbons. The bride and groom laughed, drank toasts, and danced, but each was secretly longing for the moment when everyone would be gone, and they could begin their true life together. There was no sign of Gino.

When the last guest had gone they made their way across to the house, and there found an unexpected face.

'Bruno!' Rinaldo exclaimed with pleasure. 'We hoped to see you earlier.'

'I came with Gino, but he left at once and I felt I should stay with him.'

'I wish he'd talked to me,' Rinaldo said heavily. 'I've been trying to arrange things so that he'll have some money to live on, but he writes to say he won't take anything. He should accept something. Part of this place is his.'

'I know, but he feels he can't draw an income from the farm when he won't be here to do any work. With the money he won't accept you can hire more workers.'

Bruno's manner suddenly became uneasy and he couldn't meet Alex's eye. '*Signora*, he apologises for the way he ran away before. I believe his feelings overcame him that day. The only thing he wants—'

'Is the ring,' she said. 'I'll get it.'

Recently she had locked the valuable object in Rinaldo's office for safe keeping. It took only a moment to bring it out.

'Thank you,' Bruno said, slipping it into his pocket. 'And finally, there is this.' He proffered a letter. 'He wrote it after he left the church, and asked me to give it to you. And now, goodnight.'

He slipped away, leaving Alex staring at the letter in her hand. From the kitchen came the sound of Teresa calling the maids.

'Come,' Rinaldo said, taking her arm and drawing her towards the stairs. 'Let us read it where we can be certain of not being disturbed.'

The house was quiet as they closed the door of her bedroom behind them.

Standing by the window, still in her bridal gown, Alex took out the letter and read the words on the envelope. Her heart leapt as she saw,

To my brother and sister.

'Read it to me,' Rinaldo said quietly.

Alex opened the sheet within, and began to read.

I thought I couldn't bear to witness your wedding, but in the end I had to come, just for a few minutes. You looked so right together. Forgive me for not staying longer.

Forget my cruel words. I was half crazy and didn't know what I was saying.

I can't come back. We three cannot live under the same roof. But there's no hatred or anger.

Alex, I thought you were the woman for me, but you can't be, and I think perhaps Rinaldo needs you more. Take care of him. He needs to be cared for. But you already know that.

Perhaps, as you said, there's someone else, waiting for me to find her. Then she and I can share what the two of you share. I hope so.

God bless you both!

Your brother, Gino.

The letter ended with a typical Gino joke.

PS: You might name your first baby after me.
PPS: Only if it's a boy, of course.

'How like him to say that,' Alex said between tears and laughter.

'Yes,' Rinaldo said, and his voice too was husky.

He switched off the light. Outside the open window the countryside lay quiet under the moon.

'I wonder where he is now,' she said.

Instead of answering Rinaldo drew her away from the window.

'He is where he will find his own destiny,' he said, 'as

we have. Don't fear for him. He is a far stronger man than we thought, and his time will come.'

He drew her possessively into his arms.

'But now, *amor mio*, the time is ours. Let us waste it no longer.'

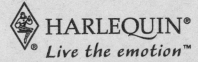

The world's bestselling romance series.

HARLEQUIN®
Presents

Seduction and Passion Guaranteed!

OUTBACK KNIGHTS
Marriage is their mission!

From bad boys—to powerful,
passionate protectors!

Three tycoons from the Outback
rescue their brides-to-be....

**Coming soon in Harlequin Presents:
Emma Darcy's exciting new trilogy**

Meet Ric, Mitch and Johnny—once three Outback bad
boys, now rich and powerful men. But these sexy city
tycoons must return to the Outback to face a new
challenge: claiming their women as their brides!

**MAY 2004: THE OUTBACK MARRIAGE RANSOM #2391
JULY 2004: THE OUTBACK WEDDING TAKEOVER #2403
NOVEMBER 2004: THE OUTBACK BRIDAL RESCUE #2427**

*"Emma Darcy delivers a spicy love story...
a fiery conflict and a hot sensuality."*
—Romantic Times

Available wherever Harlequin books are sold.

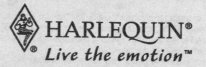

HARLEQUIN®
Live the emotion™

Visit us at www.eHarlequin.com

HPEDARCY

If you enjoyed what you just read,
then we've got an offer you can't resist!

Take 2 bestselling love stories FREE!

Plus get a FREE surprise gift!

Clip this page and mail it to Harlequin Reader Service®

IN U.S.A.
3010 Walden Ave.
P.O. Box 1867
Buffalo, N.Y. 14240-1867

IN CANADA
P.O. Box 609
Fort Erie, Ontario
L2A 5X3

YES! Please send me 2 free Harlequin Romance® novels and my free surprise gift. After receiving them, if I don't wish to receive anymore, I can return the shipping statement marked cancel. If I don't cancel, I will receive 6 brand-new novels every month, before they're available in stores! In the U.S.A., bill me at the bargain price of $3.34 plus 25¢ shipping & handling per book and applicable sales tax, if any*. In Canada, bill me at the bargain price of $3.80 plus 25¢ shipping & handling per book and applicable taxes**. That's the complete price and a savings of 10% off the cover prices—what a great deal! I understand that accepting the 2 free books and gift places me under no obligation ever to buy any books. I can always return a shipment and cancel at any time. Even if I never buy another book from Harlequin, the 2 free books and gift are mine to keep forever.

186 HDN DNTX
386 HDN DNTY

Name	(PLEASE PRINT)	
Address	Apt.#	
City	State/Prov.	Zip/Postal Code

* Terms and prices subject to change without notice. Sales tax applicable in N.Y.
** Canadian residents will be charged applicable provincial taxes and GST.
All orders subject to approval. Offer limited to one per household and not valid to current Harlequin Romance® subscribers.
® are registered trademarks of Harlequin Enterprises Limited.

HROM02   ©2001 Harlequin Enterprises Limited

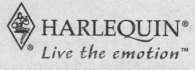

"Joanna Wayne weaves together a romance and suspense
with pulse-pounding results!"
—*New York Times* bestselling author Tess Gerritsen

National bestselling author

JOANNA WAYNE

Alligator Moon

Determined to find his brother's killer, John Robicheaux finds
himself entangled with investigative reporter Callie Havelin.
Together they must shadow the sinister killer slithering in the
murky waters—before they are consumed by the darkness....

A riveting tale that shouldn't be missed!

Coming in June 2004.

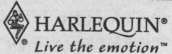

HARLEQUIN®
Live the emotion™

Visit us at www.eHarlequin.com

PHAM

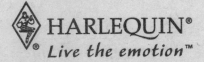